$\mathcal{U}$NFORGETTABLE

UNFORGETTABLE

The Life and Mystique
of Nat King Cole

LESLIE GOURSE

Cooper Square Press

Quoted material from *Down Beat* is used with permission—Copyright © Down Beat Magazine, 1946 and 1952.
Quoted material from *The New York Times* used with permission—Copyright © 1947/51/56/57/60/75 by The New York Times Company. Reprinted by permission.

First Cooper Square Press edition 2000

This Cooper Square Press paperback edition of *Unforgettable: The Life and Mystique of Nat King Cole* is an unabridged republication of the edition first published in New York in 1991, with the addition of two textual emendations. It is reprinted by arrangement with the author.

Designed by Judith Dannecker

Published by Cooper Square Press
An Imprint of the Rowman & Littlefield Publishing Group
150 Fifth Avenue, Suite 911
New York, New York 10011

Distributed by National Book Network

Library of Congress Cataloging-in-Publication Data
Gourse, Leslie.
   Unforgettable : the life and mystique of Nat King Cole / Leslie Gourse.— 1st Cooper Square Press ed.
      p. cm.
   Originally published: New York : St. Martin's Press, 1991.
   Includes biographical references, discography, and index.
   ISBN 0-8154-1082-4 (pbk. : alk. paper)
      1. Cole, Nat King, 1917–1965. 2. Singers—United States—Biography. I. Title.
ML420.C63 G7 2000
782.42164'092—dc21
[B]   00-057000

♾™ The paper used in this publication meets the minimum requirements of American National Standard for Information Sciences—Permanence of Paper for Printed Library Materials, ANSI/NISO Z39.48–1992.
Manufactured in the United States of America.

In memory of guitarist Emily Remler

$\mathcal{C}$ontents

AUTHOR'S NOTE

I would like to thank scores of people for their attempts to help reconstruct the events of Nat Cole's life and the landscapes in which the singer rose to eminence. First, I would like to thank James Haskins, author of *Nat Cole: The Man and His Music,* for his generosity with his interview tapes, especially those with the late guitarist Irving Ashby and the late bassist Joe Comfort, who played in Cole's trio in the 1940s and 1950s, and who died before I began my book. A few other tapes, which Mr. Haskins provided, of Nat Kelly Cole, Carol Claudia (Cookie) Cole, Nadine Robinson Coles, and Carl Carruthers also helped me gain insight as I developed my book. And thank you to the wonderful jazz pianist John Hicks, who tipped me off to the existence of Haskins's book to begin with.

Lee Young, the drummer who played with Cole, was invaluable, even for his memories of clubs in which Nat Cole played and socialized during the late 1930s and 1940s in Los Angeles. Pat Willard, the writer, also could recall clubs where she sometimes met Nat.

And Lee Young's insights into Cole's personality and musical development were crucial. Without them, the story would have been the less. Bassist Johnny Miller and bongo player Jack Costanzo also contributed their valuable information.

Sparky Tavares, Cole's longtime valet, contributed poignant memories of a man who inspired Sparky's immense loyalty. Val Molineaux, who regarded guitarist Oscar Moore as a friend and role model, was suggested as a source of information by Moore's widow; Molineaux proved generous and helpful. Joe Sherman, Marvin Fisher, Marvin Cane, Duke Niles, press agent Mike Hall, publicist and writer Gary Stevens, even Muse Records owner Joe Fields, who put me in touch with Oscar Moore's widow—all music- and entertainment-world insiders in New York—contributed their memories.

Cole's sister Evelyn, brother Ike, daughter Natalie, nephew Eddie (Ike's son), and Betty, the widow of Nat's elder brother, Eddie, gave depth and warmth by sharing some memories.

Milt Hinton, Scoville Browne, Les Paul, Buddy Collette, Buddy Banks, Benny Carter, Red Callender, Billy May, Paul Weston, Pete Rugolo, Neal Hefti, Frank DeVol, Harry "Sweets" Edison—musicians all—and comedian Timmie Rogers, for whom songwriting was an avocation, shed light on Cole's life. Robert Medina, the Cuban-born director of *The New York Times* morgue, provided research material and shared memories of Cole's performances in Havana. Carl Carruthers, a Cole valet and road management assistant, and Los Angeles restauranteur Maurice Prince, owner of the Snack 'n Chat, also contributed tasty tidbits to the story of Cole's life. The late Milton Karle, whom I interviewed in 1982, provided an invaluable initial guideline. Louis Victor Mialy, whom Nat befriended in the late 1950s, contributed his insights.

Capitol Records' former executives Alan Livingston, Tom Morgan, and Dave Dexter contributed evocative, pungent memories. Dorothy Wayne, Mrs. Stan (Audrey) Kenton, Mrs. Dave (Mildred) Cavanaugh, and John and Jean Kraus gave lively accounts of their relations with Nat Cole. Thanks, too, to Nellie Lutcher for her small but gemlike contributions. Former drummer John Tegler told an amusing and illuminating story. And guitarist John Collins helped to straighten out a few details. Singer Barbara McNair gave a cordial, helpful interview.

In addition to the memories of Cole's friends, relatives, and associates, many documents—magazine and newspaper articles, television scripts, memorabilia, and official discographies, whole or partial—have rounded out the facts and supplied the years for events. Particularly helpful have been the files of *The New York Times,* the University of Southern California's Doheny Library, and the Institute of Jazz Studies at Rutgers University. Dan Morgenstern of Rutgers is an endlessly selfless resource.

And my friend, John "Tasty" Parker, trumpeter and jazz lover, deserves special thanks for his advice and research assistance; he supplied me with videos of the King Cole Trio's early work, including a 1944 "shortie" done with Ida James. His kind support was precious.

There are still some unanswered questions, which only Nat could have answered. Jazz-oriented discographies omit work considered to be part of Cole's pop repertoire; a full published discography doesn't exist. Exact dates for some events in Cole's life are also in question.

For example, Nat's birth date has been written about as 1917 and 1919 most often; all sources agree on March 17, St. Patrick's Day. However, the Selective Service lists the year of his birth as 1916; since he filed that date with the government, I've used his information. The year 1915 is suggested by his marriage certificate to his first wife, whom he married in January 1937, when he listed his age as twenty-one. His sister Evelyn Coles believes that he had to say he was twenty-one so he could marry without his parents' consent; furthermore, his sister says definitely he was born in 1919. In 1948, when he married his second wife in New York City, his birth date was listed as 1919. John S. Wilson, jazz critic of *The New York Times,* has used the year 1916 consistently. Veteran biographer James Haskins uses 1919.

Friends of guitarist Oscar Moore, plus some documents in Europe, say he was born in 1916. *The New Grove Dictionary of Jazz* says 1912. However, because of other information, I've used 1916, which Val Molineaux and Moore's widow believe was the correct date. In addition, Johnny Miller, the bassist in the trio when it became popular, is under the distinct impression that Cole and Moore were the same age. Miller, Moore, and Cole played together in the King Cole Trio for about five years.

There are even varied dates cited for the formation of his original trio. The *Los Angeles Times* jazz critic, Leonard Feather, has said 1937; many other people say it was 1938 when Nat formed a trio and went into the Sewanee Inn, where the group first attracted a following. In 1937, he certainly did try to organize a few groups of various sizes in Los Angeles. I'm using the late 1937 date for the trio's start, because it was definitely going by then, even if Cole was often sighted after that date playing without his trio. Johnny Miller corroborates the late 1937 to early 1938 date for the trio's start. Miller joined the group in 1942.

Other details are in question. Some people remember Nat was driving a Studebaker—others recall a 1941 Buick—in his early days in Los Angeles, but which car he owned first has faded as a memory. And nobody—not even Paul Weston, one of the pillars of Capitol Records in its earliest days—recalls who arranged Nat's first recording of "The Christmas Song" done with strings in New York. If I've made mistakes or omitted small details of that nature, or even larger details in Cole's busy, detail-riddled life on the road, I'm sorry. I've tried to track down and deduce the truth and render an accurate impression of the quality of his mind, his music, and his career management. Historic Capitol files are not available for corroboration of dates, figures, and other memorabilia in connection with Cole's recording career. Some people who might have been able to confirm such information have died.

To cope with the varying dates in discographies for certain recordings, I simply have called attention to the possibilities. The discographies are listed at the end of the book in the Bibliography. Only the jazz world has provided two real, if partial discographies for Cole's work; they focus on him solely as a pianist accompanying his own vocals or playing instrumentals. One of the discographies was still unpublished by mid-1990. A third is being prepared in England.

Some people believe that the style of an artist's work is, in effect, the man, and that only an important man's work matters and endures. The great events of Nat's life were the songs he sang, played, and recorded in his unique style; he seems to have culled and concentrated the best, most empathetic instincts for his poignant performances. But his life, too, can be fascinating; his laid-back performing style sometimes masked his true feelings, and despite myriad pressures, he was so supportive of people connected to the music business that he inspired in them both love and loyalty. Furthermore, he was one of the few Negro superstars of his era; often under fire, he carried the outrageous burden of discrimination with grace. His civility and ease with people of all backgrounds were astonishing, especially in retrospect.

During Cole's lifetime, writers criticized him when he became famous for his pop singing and kept his piano playing to a bare minimum. This book has been written by a jazz fan; I don't find any style of music as consistently fulfilling or interesting as jazz. So the emphasis here is, at times, on Nat's jazz work as a pianist and singer. However, his soft, intimate jazz sound and rhythmic genius infused his singing in his popular stylings, too. He was an affecting singer no matter what material he used. So I have taken a mellow point of view about his choice to become identified as a popular singer. When he was a young man, it was his character, nurtured by his associates, to choose what seemed the most politically and commercially shrewd and feasible course. The road he took made him a millionaire by his thirties—certainly an enviable and distinguished position for any man. Had he lived long enough, his reputation might have opened the doors for him to succeed in several enterprises that he had set his heart on. He wanted to have a TV show; he also wished to star on Broadway. Performing as a jazz pianist was, in truth, only one of his many interests as an entertainer. Yet I do agree with jazz critics that the public was deprived of many valuable jazz piano performances and albums because of his decision to concentrate on popular trends.

He sometimes waxed nostalgic about his jazz roots. In a long, heartfelt interview backstage at the Apollo Theatre in 1948, he said, ". . . if I had a band, I'd be doing just what I wanted. I wanted to be a bandleader once . . ." Had he lived to a riper age, he might once again have identified himself closely with the jazz world. That, of course, is mere speculation, based on his gifts and on jazz's increased popularity in the United States since the late 1970s.

⨏N OVERVIEW

L ate in the 1980s, an American jazz musician on vacation in Canada was delighted to find a station that broadcast jazz consistently and kept him in touch with his overriding passion. One morning, he was alerted by "Prelude in C Sharp Minor" inserted into the show. The pianist played Rachmaninoff with the articulation and delicacy of touch expected of a classics player; then a lyrical guitarist joined him. The two began to swing the piece with clarity. A soft, barely audible bass followed suit. The tempo transformed the feeling of the piece into jazz, that ineffable, rhythmically based musical creation of the Afro-American culture.

At first, the American musician thought, "That's Art Tatum"—one of the most distinctive jazz musicians who ever lived—with a decidedly pianistic approach. A minute later, however, he remembered, "No, it's Nat King Cole." Even Tatum had admired Cole.

Perhaps only the jazz cognoscenti could identify the spare piano style of Nat Cole interpreting Rachmaninoff or remember that Cole had recorded that classical piece, because most people think of Cole strictly as a singer. The most important thing, though, is that everyone seems to remember him. Early in the 1980s, in my book *Louis' Children* about this country's best jazz singers and their artistry, I wrote about how a young beautician recognized a familiar singer's voice on the radio. The beautician had been born around the time when Nat Cole had died on February 15, 1965. Yet she recognized the whisper of a seducer extraordinaire, a man with the subtlety and warmth to let you know that any falling tear was merely part of the great American pastime, the romance game.

He had less than a two-octave range. But his slight voice had depth. His breathiness made his low-key delivery of a lyric sound heady; the older he got and the more he smoked, the deeper, hoarser, muskier and more hypnotic he sounded. There was a haunting intimacy to his style, in part the legacy of his jazz background. No matter how far afield he ventured into other musical genres—even into country and western—he almost always improvised, if ever so slightly, on the written song's melody and tempo, with a storyteller's sense of phrasing and timing. On "I'm Going to Sit Right Down and Write Myself a Letter," in his later years, when he was called a "pop" singer, he kept taking the song up by half steps, improvising on the melody and increasing the excitement. His rhythmic ideas made the song swing. It was jazz, backed by an orchestra with strings. At the other end of the spectrum, his whimsical humming at the end of "Paradise" is emblematic of jazz, too. An authoritative persuader, he sang exactly in tune with exceptional ease. By the late 1940s, he had polished his enunciation to the point where audiences listened to every syllable. His touch with a song was so light that his music had an aura of defying gravity. That was especially so when he served as his own accompanist, with his spare, dashing, improvised phrases. He played exactly the right notes and no more. And his presentation enchanted audiences visually; even his sidemen liked to see him sit catty-corner to the piano.

In his first career as a jazz pianist, many musicians wanted him to play with them, because his subtle swing could propel a group of any size. Nat's piano pushed the rhythms of the songs he sang so articulately that his piano-bass-guitar trio never seemed to need a drummer. Nat chose guitarists and bassists who could follow and embellish his lead. In the first trio, Oscar Moore had a genius for soloing, too, and Wesley Prince and Johnny Miller, the early bassists, were strong, engaging rhythm players. Other trios and quartets imitating the King Cole Trio's instrumentation with its deceptively soft sound never achieved the same excitement, because the drive, lift and imagination of Nat's inspired piano and the sensitivity of his tightly knit group were missing. His singing style grew directly out of his lyrical piano style, which was based on his ability to sing a song before he played it, whether he learned it by ear or from the written composition. He could tell by reading a composition what it would sound like. "Unforgettable," one of his smooth, popular recordings, came to be as much about the sound of his voice and musical instincts as it was a love song for fans of his ballads. There was a humming quality to his sound that suggested the murmur of a bee flitting around a rose garden. "Sweet Lorraine" was a tour de force, with the sweetness of the subject, Nat's affection for her, and the music's cool swing made palpable in a perfect marriage of his jazz piano and vocal styles. "Tea for Two" could be hot or effervescent, as he chose.

People who were about forty-five or older by 1990 could remember the evenings when they went to their television sets in the 1950s to turn on Nat's show on NBC. He sometimes sat sideways to the piano, playing deftly, singing softly, and looking straight at his living-room audience with his slanted, wickedly knowing eyes, often smiling broadly. His accompanists stayed in the background for the most part. The setting was simple. Yet Nat seemed to broadcast the message that he knew all about life; his musical interpretations emanated from the soul of a keenly perceptive, experienced sophisticate in a society that was becoming increasingly, if subliminally, complex and intense during the somber Eisenhower years. Some people focused on the seeming artlessness of his casual demeanor; it relaxed them. Others were touched by the kindness, tenderness, and patience in his voice; while others heard above all the stylized romanticism of the balladeer. Perhaps the best cues about Cole's inspiration—his secret, private thoughts—came from the sparkling intensity of his straightforward gaze. While performing, he was in command, but offstage he was often at the mercy of events.

Few fans knew anything about the man's personal life, except when headlines reminded them that he was a Negro—for instance, when he was attacked in a frightening racial clash in Alabama. He was a man who became famous before the civil rights legislation of the 1950s and 1960s set the country roiling. A man from a perenially persecuted minority, he cultivated an international following before the word *black* came into vogue and formal use during the civil rights movement. When he divorced his first wife to marry his second, the crisis was relatively glossed over in the news stories. It was just another entertainment-world imbroglio involving a star always on the road, and the story never attained the status of a scandal. His relations with his friends and associates were always handled discreetly by all concerned. Quite a few people amassed small fortunes and more because of his fame, influence, and positive image.

Above all, people were drawn to his sweetness; his closest associates guided him, cheered for him, loved him but sometimes used him. His life followed one of the most intricate paths taken by any black entertainer of his era. The eerie, gray, smog-besotted atmosphere some days in Los Angeles provides an appropriate backdrop for anyone delving into the man's private life twenty-five years after his death. He had become a public legend because of his creativity; that was irrevocable. Along with Bing Crosby, he was one of those stars whose private lives were left out of the columns.

A wide-ranging investigation reveals an episodic existence lived primarily on the road, in many climates and clubs, castles and concert halls. His life was inseparable from his career. His relatives, friends, and associates, who saw him for the most part as he was on the move, talked about Nat Cole as a sweet, enormously talented, and creative man. Each memory embellished a consistent portrait, from Nat's simple but character-building childhood in a devoutly religious family to his musical flowering brought about by his exceptional gifts, dogged persistence, and adaptability. The ambition and resourcefulness in his personality were softened by his shyness, laid-back charm, wit, warmth, and reasonableness. Four years after his first recording hit, he was able to say with easy, exquisite persuasiveness to a critic, "Stay for the next set. I think you'll like it."

A feeling of the gossipy, sometimes quirky milieu in which Nat Cole's career flourished also emerged from his associates' reminiscences. His white friends, who truly took him and his family into their hearts, often stood up for his civil rights, insisting on such civilities as making sure he was welcomed into famous restaurants for lunch. He lived at a time when that cordiality was not automatically offered. As puzzled and angered as his white friends were by racial prejudice, some of them were also often unaware of the traditions of the black culture in America. Nat's two resilient wives sprang from that culture, which provided him with the strong, conventional foundation on which he built his kingdom assertively and intelligently. Had he lived longer, he might have embarked on more daring enterprises than he had ever tried before, as some of his closest friends believed. He might have overcome racial prejudices, as Bill Cosby and his generation would eventually do, on television, in film and on Broadway. After he failed to find sponsors for his TV show because of racial bigotry, Nat longed for the status of a Broadway star most of all. How many changes he would have attempted in his personal and professional lives, no one will ever know, but as a result of what he did accomplish, he attained a level of fame as a singer to which few contemporaries could aspire. Even now, twenty-five years after his death, his records are still played on the radio and broadcast in public places almost as frequently as those of Frank Sinatra and Louis Armstrong.

Nat's method was simple; he struggled valiantly and good-naturedly, listened to practical advice about the important decisions he had to make about tricky questions, constantly helped others and let others help—and even co-opt—him, and took advantage of every opportunity he could find to play the piano—any piano anyplace. He believed in himself and stood up for his decisions.

After he became a star, though not yet a superstar, he was beguiled by a young woman whose judgment he trusted absolutely, and he turned to her to enjoy a new and better life than he had ever known before. Maria Ellington, née Marie Hawkins, was a vibrant-looking singer, "a frequent guest at the elite black parties in town," recalled Marvin Fisher, a young New York music publisher, who wrote "When Sunny Gets Blue" for Nat. Fisher noticed Maria at those parties, "because she was gorgeous," he said.

Though Nat was married at the time to Nadine Robinson, a pretty dancer, he found Maria irresistible, protective, and intelligent, and he decided to get a divorce so he could marry her. Many of his closest associates, including some of his trio members, were dismayed by Nat's decision, because they felt Maria was an unabashed snob. Nevertheless, she became renowned for her shrewdness about Nat's career management and for her stylishness and taste. People admired her for those attributes and strengths. There was a hint of the Helen of Troy mystique to her appearance. Men's heads turned to look at this striking woman. She wore tiaras to Nat's openings, emphasizing the image of her playing the queen to Nat's status as "King." Abandoning her own fledgling career as a band singer when she married Nat, she put the polish on his image, her admirers say, and influenced the direction of his career by insisting that he leave the piano bench and become a stand-up, starring singer. She reorganized his financial arrangement with his trio. And when he found himself in a whirl of trouble about his careless financial management, which began before he met Maria, she helped him take control of his personal spending. The jazz world rued his meta-morphosis under Maria's guidance from a stunning jazz pianist in a cooperative trio to a stand-up singer backed by strings supplying sweet backgrounds of whole notes in full orchestras. It was not sim-ply Maria's wish that Nat become popular. Capitol Records, for ex-ample, guided him by passing him the song "Mona Lisa," with its mysterious, intriguing lyrics, which would establish his fortune for-ever. And Nat's manager, Carlos Castel, who had a magic touch, nurtured Nat's career.

Nat's manners and innate classiness made the stylish facade natu-ral for him. His brother Ike Cole felt due credit for Nat's classiness should be awarded to his start in life as the son of "a successful Baptist minister," even if the Cole family had lived on a minister's meager earnings. Maria was in the habit of calling attention to her background, with her schooling in the social graces, her sophistica-tion and business sense, as the important leavening effect on Nat. Nat's friends and family were aware of the emphasis his proud wife put on these assets.

These images of Nat, beginning with the self-assurance inspired by his love of his work in music and his expanding horizons, lin-gered in the minds of his friends forever. The sweetness of their nostalgia impressed anyone seeking to discover the story of Nat King Cole's public rise and private complexities.

There were also striking images—which almost all of his associ-ates reminisced about or hinted at—of private tensions and suffer-ing. Some troubles had been sociologically caused; others could be traced to Cole's personality, family relationships, lifestyle and ex-traordinary fame. As a remarkable and professional musician, Cole could take any song and make it touching and believable. His zest for living could put across "Walking My Baby Back Home," "Those Lazy, Hazy, Crazy Days of Summer," "An Orange-Colored Sky," and "Rambling Rose," a seemingly out-of-character, country and western novelty tune—and make them fun. However many of his songs re-flect elements of his unique personal story as a stalwart and a ro-mantic soul. He could counsel his fans to "Pretend" that everything was marvelous when they were seriously upset. His sensitive bar-itone and rhythmic impulse could make "Sweet Lorraine" the ideal of every lover. He could question "Mona Lisa" about whether she felt lonesome on her pedestal. When Cole felt blue, he retreated into his music. "Music was his therapy," explained his valet. Or Cole enjoyed the finer things of life in his Los Angeles home, or his New

York apartment, at the ball games he frequented, or on the road, surrounded by glamorous, exciting women in the entertainment business and, perhaps above all, by male buddies and comrades in music, sports and politics. And he lit up a cigarette every place. "That's what gave him a fast death," reminisced Milton Karle, who handled Nat's record publicity on the East Coast for several years. It seems that Cole, above all anchored by music, hard work and success, and secondarily by old-fashioned standards for civility and love, believed that loving and being loved, as a musician and a man, were the most important values in the world in which he lived at a breakneck pace. But his celebrity and the relentless pressures in his life—from his anxiety about flying, which he did so much of, to the tensions in his marriages, against the background of the hydra-headed race discrimination in the country and the customs it engendered, and his depressing final illness and untimely death from lung cancer—relegated his formula for long-lived romantic happiness to the status of an impossible dream. Yet in his songs he is always reanimated.

UNFORGETTABLE

Chapter One

NATHANIEL ADAMS COLES IN CHICAGO

A round the time of his fourth birthday, Nathaniel Adams Coles* was dimly aware of a great undertaking; his mother clutched his hand and guided him onto a train in the station in Montgomery, Alabama. Nathaniel, as his mother always called him, was too young to understand what all the commotion was about. He was too small to help lift and load all the family's possessions. His sister Evelyn, about four years older than Nat, and his elder brother Edward James, two years older than Evelyn, and the eldest child, Eddie Mae, about a year older than Eddie, helped their father carry the family's scanty belongings in suitcases and boxes onto the dreary coach reserved for Negroes.

Everyone in the family of the Reverend Edward James Coles, Sr., was very dark-skinned, and the parents were well rounded and well

---

*Nat didn't use the name Adams on his marriage licenses or in his will, but it is believed to have been his middle name.

groomed, dressed in their sedate, best clothes. The family looked exactly like what it was—a quiet, closely knit Negro family, parents and well-behaved, helpful children migrating from a strictly segregated, meager existence in the South to a freer way of life, they hoped, in Chicago, where segregation wasn't legislated. The Coleses were swept along in the crowd of Negroes—some traveling alone, some in family groups—into a segregated railway car. All of them were heading to an unknown world, driven by intangible hopes, carrying all the possessions they could manage. As the adults hurried around, the Coles children were fascinated by an aromatic box of fried chicken, which their mother was carrying. She had packed the lunch for her family to eat during the journey. The scent of the food made the odor of the neglected coach more bearable for the family.

"Can I have a piece, Mama?" one of the children asked.

"Not right this minute, child! Didn't you just eat? Don't you remember?" she said in her soft voice.

It would have been unthinkable for Perlina Adams Coles to have left home without food for her brood to eat on the way to Chicago. For one thing, only white people could eat freely in the dining car, if there was one. Despite this and other discomforts of the trip, Negroes crowded into the train and traveled north. In Chicago, men found jobs in the stockyards and the hotels; women cooked, cleaned, and sewed for the wealthier white families, or they went to work in the post office, restaurants, and department stores. Many people worked hard and eventually invested in their own businesses—soul-food restaurants, shoe-repair shops, boardinghouses, beauty parlors, barbershops, real estate and all types of services for the migrants following them. Some became doctors, lawyers and other professionals within the black community.

Mrs. Coles knew that her children would go to public schools with facilities rarely enjoyed by Negroes in the South. She also might have been hoping for a change in her family's luck. She was not the sort of woman to complain about her fate with her husband in the South. He had been a respected deacon of the Beulah Baptist Church in Montgomery before he became a minister; he was a devoted, morally scrupulous husband who loved his children and ruled them vigilantly.* But Perlina Coles already had given birth to far more children than were alive to travel with her that day; she

* Reverend Coles was a deacon of the Beulah Baptist Church, became a minister, and went to Chicago to head his own church. He returned as a guest, or interim minister, to the Beulah Baptist Church once.

was happy for the chance to turn her back on the city where she had placed too many infants in their tiny graves. At the time she boarded the train, she had no idea she would face the funeral of another child; altogether, only five of her thirteen children would live to adulthood. She was as oblivous to that coming sorrow as she was to the indescribable joy her surviving children would bring her.

To pass the time and ease any apprehensions she might have on the train, she softly hummed the slow gospel hymns that she had known ever since she had been a child, one of several daughters of the Reverend Dan Adams, a preacher in a Baptist church in Montgomery.* He died in 1905. By the time she left for Chicago, she had buried her mother, too. Now she was a minister's wife and would lead the gospel choir in his church in Chicago; she would sing the old prayers in the old ways in a new church with other migrants from Montgomery, accompanying herself on the organ. She would teach the songs to her children, who would pass the faith to their children. She was not very homesick because some of her sisters, brothers, cousins and even a few of her husband's relatives were planning to visit or migrate to the North one day soon. She did not have time to dwell on the past, with four growing children to be fed every day.

Most of the Coleses and Adamses lived either in Montgomery or Birmingham. Perlina had taken Nathaniel and Evelyn with her to Birmingham to say goodbye to their cousins, Hattie Goines Thomas and her three daughters, and other relatives. Hattie was a daughter of Comfort Adams Goines, a sister of Dan Adams. Comfort and Dan had two sisters, Patience and Mercy, named for unabbreviated virtues, and three brothers with full and righteous Biblical names—Ruben, Benjamin, and Joseph. Dan and his brothers and sisters lived their entire lives in Alabama. Hattie and her children were among the relatives who migrated, as the Coleses did. By 1929, Cousin Hattie Thomas also took the journey in search of better opportunities in life, trading off the sunshine of the South for the rugged northern winters.

The Reverend Edward James Coles left his family behind, with the exception of one brother, Henry, who later migrated to Cleveland. Another relative, a blind preacher named Dulcie, visited the Coleses in Chicago. Reverend Coles returned to Montgomery at

---

* Either the Beulah Baptist or the Union Chapel Church, according to Deacon Charlie Hopson of the Beulah Baptist Church, who had been two years old when the Coles family left Montgomery. Hopson's father and Nat Coles's father were deacons together at the Beulah Baptist Church, where Nat's father and mother probably met.

least once, but his children rarely saw any of their Coles relatives again.

Although Evelyn resembled her mother, a large-featured, robust little woman, something about Evelyn's demeanor made her father nostalgic for Alabama.

"You remind me of my mother," Evelyn's father told her.

She had no idea of what memories she stirred in him, however, because her paternal grandparents had died, as her mother's parents had, (perhaps even before she was born in Birmingham). She had no memory of meeting any of them, but she knew that she was the only child in her own family to have been born in Birmingham. Her mother had been visiting relatives there. Eddie Mae, Eddie, and Nathaniel all were born in Montgomery.*

Evelyn had been just old enough to be very excited when she saw her tiny little brother, who had the family's characteristically dark skin and expressive, slanty eyes. Hardy and healthy, he had survived infancy. She felt very protective toward him, as if he were in some way her own child.

Nat sat in his mother's lap during most of the train trip. Occasionally, Perlina let Eddie Mae hold Nat for a while. Evelyn sometimes hugged him and sang to him; she liked it when he smiled as he listened to her sing. He was rather like a little doll, and she could tell him about whatever fascinated or annoyed her on the trip, even though he was too young to understand. While their brother Eddie, who was full of restless energy, started conversations with other travelers, Nathaniel sat still, smiling sweetly.

---

* Nat was born on St. Patrick's Day, March 17. That date was never disputed. Evelyn Coles said the year was 1919, and the family migrated in 1923. Various experts used several other years for Nat's birthdate. Nat himself used at least three dates on official documents. On his first marriage license, he wrote that he was twenty-one in January 1937. Registering for the draft in Los Angeles in 1940, he wrote that he had been born on March 17, 1916. When he signed his second marriage license in 1948, and for his will, he used the date March 17, 1919.

"This Is Your Life," a popular TV program, which did a show on Nat's life, with Nat as the surprise guest, said Nat had been born on March 17, 1919, and had been four when he migrated. Several other dates cited in that show seemed to be approximate, not exact. Since we presume that the show didn't consult the surprise guest for research purposes, Nat probably did not supply the information for the script. However, neither did he make any corrections in it, as the show progressed. Perhaps he was simply being polite. This biography uses the information Nat gave to the Selective Service regarding his date of birth, but it also takes note that Evelyn Coles believes his birthdate was 1919, no matter what date he may have used at various times—possibly to suit his immediate need. Experts such as John S. Wilson, jazz critic of *The New York Times,* used 1916 as the birthdate.

For Eddie Coles's birthdate, the authority is Betty Coles, his widow, who was eighty-two in 1990; she was two years older than her husband. He died at age fifty-nine in 1970. Eddie used the name "Cole" professionally but never changed his family name "Coles" legally.

Nat's first clear memory of a home was a ground-floor flat in a four-flat apartment house at Forty-first Street and 4036 Prairie Avenue, on the South Side of Chicago in a Negro ghetto. In the booming economy of Chicago, other kids' parents took the elevated train every day out of the neighborhood to their jobs in the white sections of town. The migrants from the South could earn countless times more money in Chicago than they had at home. Nat's family, however, was special; it had not traveled for two days and a night in a run-down old coach simply to seek out high-paying jobs in Chicago. The Reverend Coles quickly assumed the duties of minister of the Second Progressive Baptist Church, a tiny place of the store-front-church variety, though it was not a storefront. Perlina played the organ and led two choirs in the church, preferring the slow anthems. All the members, including the minister, spoke and sang with the familiar cadences of the Deep South. Many people who attended the church had come from Montgomery or Birmingham and kept their community going for a sense of continuity and comfort. Nat's vigilant parents remained close to home in the North.

Nat had a soft voice and a quiet manner of speaking, in contrast to his effervescent elder brother, Eddie, and the bright, friendly Evelyn. Even as Nat grew older, he never lost his low-key, shy style, though it developed into a down-to-earth, natural and direct sociability. An ease and pithiness in conversation made his language arresting and musical. As a child, he was in awe of Eddie, who had a gravelly voice and an outgoing, assertive personality. Though Eddie played the piano in his father's church, he preferred the little upright piano in the family's living room. Perlina had managed to make it a priority for the children to practice on. Reverend Coles didn't like to hear Eddie play popular music—that syncopated jazz, boogie-woogie, or the blues, or novelty songs, or emotional, trendy songs of the day. Eddie played it anyway. The minister could have lived happily without a piano, because the kind of music Eddie liked was an indication to him of the devil's undying, infectious sinfulness. But Perlina wanted the children to have a piano for their cultural development.

To counteract the presence of popular music in his house, as well as in so many halls, theaters, clubs, and bars in the neighborhood, which was close to Forty-seventh Street, an entertainment center of the city, the Reverend Coles preached to his children constantly about the righteous way to live. Every meal began with grace, as he reminded them of the great bounty of the Lord, who allowed them to enjoy their food and their dining room set. He exhorted them to love the Lord above all, to go to church every Sunday, to love and trust the Lord in their hearts every minute of every day. The Lord was relentless. So for the children, the blues and the sophisticated jazz in the neighborhood sprinkled spice on the bland, slow-paced rectitude of daily life in the Coleses flat.

Evelyn and Eddie Mae had their own bedroom; the boys shared another; the parents had theirs. The flat also consisted of a living room, a bathroom, and a dining room. And something—even if it were only red beans and rice and other soul-food staples—was always cooking in the kitchen. The family's small income came from their tiny church, which Milt Hinton, another child and a budding musician in the neighborhood, recalled as humble.

The Reverend Coles kept a collection of leather straps with which to punish the children if they didn't conform to his notions of fine, straitlaced Christian behavior. In that strict atmosphere, the children never dared to become intimate with any of the "rowdies," as the family called them, in the streets; instead, the Coles kids had branded onto their souls and outlined on their buttocks respect for their parents, their Lord, and the Protestant ethic of hard, honest work. Yet there was an ease and politeness to the Coleses' attitudes and manners with each other and everyone else. Evelyn and Eddie were never discouraged from talking and joking; they became as gregarious and chatty as Momma and especially Daddy were restrained. And perhaps the children developed joke-appreciating, tolerant attitudes instinctively as a counterbalance to the dutiful religiosity of their parents. At the same time, the high standards of the elder Coleses made a deep impression on all the children.

Nathaniel chose to pattern himself after Eddie, who was easy to know, quick to understand others, and outspoken about those things he believed in. Though Eddie was boisterous compared with his shy little brother, Nat could emulate Eddie's courage. In his early teens, Eddie began working secretly as a professional entertainer and musician. Rather than openly defy his father and lose the battle and the war, Eddie waited for the family to go to sleep. Then he sneaked out a window, into a wide back alley typical of Chicago's landscape. Nat watched Eddie go and learned his lesson well.

Eddie went to his gigs primarily on the South Side and downtown. He became adept on the bass in addition to the piano, and he learned to play the tuba, too, and a few other instruments during his nighttime excursions. The tuba, which had a louder, slower-moving sound than the bass, was being abandoned by jazz players, but most of the rhythm players learned both instruments. When Eddie, who could fit into any type of group, also sang his own amusing songs in his gravelly voice, he stood out as an entertainer.

Nat followed Eddie's lead to the piano and also listened to the radio and waved his arms at it, as if he were conducting. Learning to play by ear, struggling to use both hands at the piano, Nat taught himself to play "Yes, We Have No Bananas." He was about four years old at the time. And in his first year in public school, he played that song for the other children to march to. Evelyn thought Nathaniel was adorable. "He doesn't say much, but he keeps at that music," she remarked.

Perlina sat down at the piano with Nathaniel to teach him everything she knew how to do. From Eddie and the radio, he learned a preference for up-tempo, swinging music. Then Perlina sent Nat to Milt Hinton's mother, a piano teacher and an organist. Milt later remembered that his mother was disappointed when she couldn't convince her own son to play the piano, and she "farmed" him out to somebody else in the neighborhood for violin lessons. As Mrs. Coles did, Mrs. Hinton deeply believed a child should learn to play some kind of instrument and have a working knowledge and love of music.

The family routine ran along without major crisis until Nat was about ten and mature enough to understand grief. During a very cold winter in Chicago, his sister Eddie Mae became sick. Her condition worsened quickly; her temperature soared. Suddenly, Eddie Mae was dead from pneumonia. There was a somber funeral at the church. Evelyn, who may have seen a few of her mother's infants die in Alabama, undoubtedly made a special effort to comfort Nat, who was shocked and upset. Nat always thought of Evelyn as a sentimental and nurturing person; she grew up to be that way as a woman. She cried unabashedly and easily when great feeling welled up in her about her family. She kissed friendly visitors to her home on their cheeks to make them feel welcome and close. Happy to have her affection, Nat could hug her and trust her.

Nat noted that the family remained resilient after Eddie Mae's death. His father never doubted the will of the Lord for a moment. Eddie kept going out the window at night to play his usual gigs with great spirit. It's possible that, as often happens in a family where a child dies, the remaining children resolved to live not just for themselves but for the one who died, too. None of the Coleses lost heart.

About this time, the Reverend Coles moved his church to Forty-fifth Street and Dearborn, where it was called the True Light Baptist

Church. He was a success as a minister. His new church had room for two hundred people to pray on Sunday mornings. Although Milt Hinton's mother belonged to the Ebenezer Baptist Church, she played the organ in the Coleses church and took charge of the Baptist Young People's Union, too. When Milt accompanied her to church and heard Nathaniel play the organ for a gospel choir, Milt's mother didn't miss the chance to lean over and say to him, "Why can't you be nice and obedient like Nathaniel?" The force with which Milt gritted his teeth began in his chest, he resented Nathaniel so much.

Nat, as his friends began to call him, was having his own problems because of a different sort of disobedience. Though he stayed with the piano as his instrument, he began to embellish the gospel melodies and rhythms. In early adolescence, he, too, started sneaking out the window to sit in wide alleys and on fire escapes and listen to the music in the clubs and theaters. A trumpeter he heard at the Indiana Theatre was probably Jabbo Smith, who had a poignant style as a singer and an instrumentalist. A fine clarinetist, Jimmie Noone, led his own big band at the Apex Club. Many musicians played in the dance bands at the Savoy Ballroom and other places on the South Side. On Monday mornings, the clubs had Blue Monday parties, with music until noon to entertain the musicians and nightclub workers who had worked all night during the weekend.

Nat could hear Jimmie Noone on the radio, too, and most important for Nat as a pianist was Earl "Fatha" Hines. He led his own band at the Grand Terrace Ballroom at Thirty-ninth Street and South Parkway; his nightly performances were often broadcast on the radio. Budding musicians around the country, pretending to do their homework at night, actually stayed up late with their radios on, taking lessons from the inventive pianist. Nat never forgot: "Our house was near the old Grand Terrace, and I spent many a night in the alley listening to Earl Hines for ideas."

All the pianists before Hines had been rooted in the stride style, in which the left hand played a rocking, rhythmic accompaniment to the right hand. The fulsome, pianistic technique was imaginative and effective for soloists. Pianists had been left out of the marching bands for the obvious reason that a piano couldn't move through the streets. The pianists, playing alone, made up for the lack of all the other instruments. At Harlem rent parties thrown to raise the month's rent, the pianists developed their art by playing solo, supplying the melody and the rhythm by themselves. They did it at

Chicago rent parties, too. The stride style was the pinnacle of the instrumentalists' development in the northern Negro neighborhoods in the 1920s and 1930s. The pianists were paid a little of the money raised from donations to the rent-party coffers.

Hines, however, led an orchestra with a full rhythm section; he could rely upon his bassist and drummer to provide the rhythmic foundation for his band's arrangements. Both his hands were free to embellish the harmonies with a modern-sounding spareness, in comparison with the stride pianists or with the revered Art Tatum, who played with an unimpeachable but highly decorated style. Because Hines wanted to be heard along with the orchestra, he also invented a "locked hand" style of playing, with both hands playing the same thing—an innovation for dynamics; altogether his style was an excellent way to help strip the music of flourishes and develop the harmonies and the melodic flow. Hines's contemporary, smooth approach as a pianist within a rhythm section and a band appealed to Nat Coles so much that he couldn't keep the complicated jazz lessons out of his gospel stylings in his father's church. His father kept admonishing his artistic son:

"Tone it down, son," as Nat later recalled his father saying, "or take the consequences."

Perlina Coles intervened for Nat and reached a compromise with her husband. Nat could walk out the front door to work as a jazz pianist in the clubs on weeknights; in return for that privilege, he would continue to play the organ obediently, as he had been doing since he was about eleven, for his father in church on Sundays. He would even sing a little during the Sunday services. The Reverend Coles agreed reluctantly to watch his second son walk out the door into Chicago's exciting nightlife.

The minister didn't, however, permit Evelyn to go dancing to the music of the big bands at the Savoy Ballroom, to which everyone flocked on weekend nights. So Evelyn had to invent excuses to leave the house. Devoutly religious, she loved to play the organ in the church. But irrepressibly sociable, she saw no harm in relaxing a little. Even while she was dancing, she could love the Lord good-humoredly.

Eddie and Milt Hinton went to Wendell Phillips High School at the same time. Milt thought that Eddie was one of the most talented and vivacious boys in the crowd. Eddie sang a song about a fierce old bear with a loud bark, which Milt liked so well that he learned it.

In those days, Eddie was playing the bass with "big chops,"

Milt noted wistfully. He thought that he, too, would like to play the bass, but he was getting violin lessons. Furthermore, Eddie was protective of his territory and told Milt bossily, "Stay away from the bass!"

Eddie was serious and happy about his status as the crowd's accomplished bass player. He liked being older than Nat, too, and having the superior knowledge to advise his little brother: Learn to read music. If you want to make a living from music, you have to be able to read very well and quickly, because the big bands which come through town will choose only the musicians who can read music for their groups. If you can't read their arrangements, you'll be out of luck and money.

At age twelve, Nat began to study classical piano techniques and composers from Bach to Rachmaninoff for several years with a teacher named Professor Thomas. Nat made sure that he could read and write music well. Not only did he depend upon Eddie to give him useful advice about the ways of the world, Nat also leaned on Eddie for protection in the Coles house. As the brothers grew up, they became disgruntled with their father's collection of disciplinary straps. One day they stole them and discarded them behind a laundry house.

"Who took those straps?" the Reverend Coles asked Nat.

"Eddie did," Nat said.

Reminiscing years later, Nat also recalled: "For a long time after that, I didn't go out of the house until I found out where Eddie was."

Eddie, mixing gregariously with musicians on the jazz scene, impressed Noble Sissle, the bandleader and writer, who was passing through town. Sissle had already had notable hits on Broadway in New York, in collaboration with the pianist Eubie Blake. And when Sissle offered Eddie a job, Eddie jumped at the opportunity; his father protested, but Eddie went on the road.

The job took him around the country and even to Europe, where he managed to study music for a while at the University of Heidelberg, his wife, Betty, later recalled. He also learned to speak German fluently, Spanish adequately and two other languages well enough so that he could brag about speaking five languages, including English.

Milt Hinton remembered that, although he was about six years older than Nat, the two youngsters also went to Wendell Phillips high school at the same time. Nat was a few grades behind Milt, because Milt had lost three grades when he made the transition from Vicksburg, Mississippi, his hometown, to Chicago. The school's bandmaster organized a youth band to play at a party sponsored by an editor of the local black newspaper, the *Chicago Defender.* The editor conceived of the party to encourage black kids to improve the quality of their lives and to give them cultural goals and wider horizons. The bandmaster felt inspired to perpetuate the idea and keep the kids working in a brass band. A black woman from St. Louis, who had made a considerable amount of money from her cosmetics business, bought some houses in Chicago and invited the band to rehearse in her house at Forty-fourth Street and South Parkway. (It was renamed Martin Luther King Boulevard decades later.)

Milt Hinton wanted to get into the band so much that he started to play the bass horn; he was also playing the tuba and other low-voiced horns in his school days, but the band already had a tuba player. Lionel Hampton, who was attending a Catholic school in town, played the drums. At first Milt thought Hampton was annoyed that Milt was allowed to play alongside him, because Milt was younger. Ray Nance, also from Wendell Phillips High School, played trumpet in that band. Nat Coles wanted to play with the group so much that he took up another instrument; it may have been tuned bells, or a drum, or even a lyre. Milt noticed that Nat played all of those instruments at one time or another during their school days. Milt was irritated that the bandmaster allowed someone as young as Nat to perform with the older fellows. It wasn't until the 1950s, when Milt and Nat recorded together—and Milt was no longer living with his mother, who liked to compare him to "sweet" and "obedient" Nathaniel—that Milt and Nat became friendly colleagues. The differences in their ages no longer seemed important to Milt by then.

In high school, Nat had a second love: baseball. In that, too, he followed Eddie's lead. The brothers also loved football, but not as much as they adored baseball. Nat excelled as a first baseman and even entertained the notion of becoming a professional ball player. He received two feelers by mail from minor-league clubs—undoubtedly in the Negro leagues. Several talented black athletes from Chicago's South Side overcame racial bias to become national sports figures. However, Nat's sense of realism in those pre-Jackie Robinson days in baseball plus his love of show business kept him playing the piano. (His father would nevertheless recall those two invita-

tions proudly as an item in Nat's history, on January 6, 1960,* the
day Nat's life story was broadcast to the country on the popular
NBC TV show "This Is Your Life." By then, Nat was saying that he
never regretted following his love for music and his intention to
make a living as a musician. He joked about his sports mania as a
fan: "The only sport I'm not interested in is horse racing, and that's
because I don't know the horses personally." He really had few
other options, if he had any dream of an illustrious, exciting life in
those days, because the prejudice against Negroes in any field except for music was usually overwhelming. There was a hint, however, that after Nat went to struggle along in music in Los Angeles,
he still liked the idea of a future connected to sports. Registering for
the draft there in 1940, he listed his place of employment as the
Hollywood Recreation Center, then at 1539 N. Vine Street at Hollywood; it was under the administration of the Los Angeles City Parks
and Recreation Department, which always offered kids a chance to
play baseball and football. Though Nat was working as a pianist at
night, he apparently derived steady income from the sports center
during the days.)

As a ten-year-old boy, he had entered a musical contest at the
Regal Theater one Thanksgiving and brought home the first-prize
turkey for the family dinner. His mother had been so happy that he
promised to bring her a turkey every year for Thanksgiving from
the proceeds of his piano playing. He was so attached to his mother
that, if he didn't see her in church on Sundays, he ran home to find
her and be with her.

When he was about sixteen, he organized two musical groups—
a big band, variously estimated to have from ten to fourteen pieces,
which he called the Rogues of Rhythm, and a quintet, Nat Coles and
His Royal Dukes. He was still using his real name professionally. He
led whichever one of them he could find a job for. In the smaller
group, Nat hired Andrew Gardner as saxophonist, Charles Grey as
trumpeter, Russell Shores as drummer, and Henry Fort as bassist.
They played for twenty-five cents each or for hot dogs, hamburgers,
and soda.

In a story that may be apocryphal, Nat tried to sing, but his band
members wouldn't let him because they thought he sounded horri-
ble. That was a joke told on "This Is Your Life." Nat actually never

*The year 1957 is given in a documentary: *The Unforgettable Nat "King" Cole*, produced by
Jo Lustig. The 1960 date is provided in the NBC script in the Nat Cole papers in the Cin-
ema/Television Library at the University of Southern California. The show was taped on Dec.
17, 1959, and released on Jan. 6, 1960, from 10:00 to 10:30 P.M. EST.

had any idea of singing as a teenager. Joe Williams recalled that Nat had a "boy" singer working with his group. Nat disliked singing in church and did it only to please his parents. He was so painfully shy that he didn't even like to play the piano in front of audiences but forced himself to do it for the money. He begged his sister to go along to his gigs with him. Six feet tall in his teens, he knew that he appeared glamorous to the girls who saw him in the spotlight, but he had no idea of what to say to them. After his jobs, when the girls approached him, he told them, "I have to walk my sister home. I can't go along with you." Evelyn felt so sorry for the tongue-tied, awkward "child" that she let him use her as an excuse. Sometimes, she passed messages to him for the girls. He never responded to them.

Probably in gratitude for his comradely sister's cooperation, he told Evelyn, "I'm going to call you 'Bay'."

She didn't know what the nickname meant; it may have come from the word *baby*, she later thought. Without bothering to ask him about it, she countered, "I'm going to call you 'Bay', too," but she never did. He called her "Bay" so regularly that the rest of the family did, too, forever.

Free of any inhibitions in music, Nat was able to write arrangements for his groups. Though he listened to every musician critically, he especially adored Duke Ellington and wanted to play with the élan of Duke leading his orchestra. Nat developed undying admiration for Art Tatum and later was delighted and shocked to learn that Tatum liked to listen to him play, too. Nat's style seemed radically different from the elaborate Tatum's, however, because Nat pared his work down to the essential notes. Above all, he preferred the style of Earl Hines.

"It was his driving force that appealed to me," Nat reflected in an interview with John Tynan of *Down Beat* magazine on May 2, 1957. "I first heard Hines in Chicago when I was a kid. He was regarded as the Louis Armstrong of piano players. His was a new, revolutionary kind of playing, because he broke away from the Eastern style. He broke the barrier of what we called stride piano where the left hand kept up in a steady, striding pattern. I latched onto that new Hines style. Guess I still show that influence to this day."

All the fine instrumentalists and blues and popular singers in Chicago impressed him. He heard singer Savannah Churchill, with whom he would later tour. Among her hit songs was "I Want to Be Loved by Only You." Joe Liggins, a pianist and singer, who had a big

hit with "The Honeydripper," and Roosevelt Sykes, who called himself the Original Honeydripper and led his own group, were well
known on the Chicago jazz scene during Nat's early Chicago career.
Nat and Eddie brought records into the Coles house and played
them over and over—music by Erskine Hawkins, Jay McShann, Illinois Jacquet, Coleman Hawkins, and Wardell Gray. Fats Waller and
his girlfriend, Una Mae Carlisle, impressed Nat, too. Una Mae was an
exotic-looking, slight woman with a sparkle in her slanty eyes, who
could accompany herself on the piano while she sang sophisticated
songs with engaging style. Studying a wide variety of music, from
classical to jazz to the blues and gospel, Nat began to develop his
own distinctive style, with an incredibly light touch, clarity, fleet-
ness and effervescence. All of these qualites were guided by
his unerring sense for playing the right notes and not playing too
many of them. His economical style was combined with a driving
rhythmic sense and a whimsical imagination for melodies and bits
of melodies—phrases, or licks or riffs, as musicians call them. There
was an exceptional control and ease in his playing, which infused
his creations with elegance and sophistication; though muted in
tone, his music was a stimulant. He seemed psychologically sly, because he was so deft that he could lift and control his audiences'
moods.

And he was humble and clever enough to take advantage of
any opportunities that came his way without quibbling about such
details as the amount of pay. When one group booked to play
for a dance at Warwick Hall at Forty-seventh and Vincennes asked
for more money than the show's producer wanted to pay, Nat allowed his group to be hired for the lesser fee. His group played so
well that word of mouth boosted its reputation and led to more
jobs.

Detroit-born comedian Timmie Rogers, who was working with
Earl Hines and others—the Four Blazers and Earl "Snakehips"
Tucker among them—at the Grand Terrace Ballroom, recalled how
Nat, who was three years older than Timmie, led his own band at
Warwick Hall on weekends and went to the Grand Terrace Ballroom to listen to Earl Hines rehearse in the afternoons. Timmie
opened a side door for Nat to come in. He and Nat became so
friendly that Timme went to Nat's family's house sometimes. The
young comedian, a vaudeville veteran by his teen years, found Nat's
mother very "compassionate." Everyone called her by her nickname, "Nancy," he noticed; she had "a cherubic, very mobile face
and exceptionally expressive eyes," which were as slanty and bright

as Nat's. "She spoke a lot with her eyes, and she had respect for others and always treated them like human beings," he recalled. She had the generosity to put a meal on the table for him when he visited. Her kitchen was an oasis for the hardworking child, who traveled without parents and relied upon backstage tutors for his education. Eventually Nat would sing songs written by his multi-talented young friend.

Somehow Nat came to possess arrangements that Earl "Fatha" Hines rehearsed in the afternoons. Some people have speculated that arrangements may have been passed to Nat by one of the musicians in Hines's band. As shy as Nat was, he was so amiable that he made friends easily. The Hines arrangements improved Nat's groups' abilities and fortunes. Nat was a quiet but tireless, good-natured worker, an instinctive buddy, and therefore a fine self-promoter without ever appearing to be pushy.

One Sunday at the Savoy Ballroom, where the dancers competed and big bands had "cutting contests" to see which one could play the best, Nat's big band went up against Earl Hines's. Hines's personnel list included Bud Johnson on tenor, Trummy Young on trombone, and a few other talented men. Nat borrowed money from the gig so that he could pay a tailor for the light green suits the band members wore. They looked so classy that Dempsey Travis, who later became a millionaire and wrote a book about the jazz scene in Chicago, saw the band that day and remembered the color of the suits for decades. Scotty Piper, who was the entertainment community's popular tailor, probably made the suits. Nat's band was a hit with the audience at the Savoy that day and, despite all the fine professional musicians in Hines's band, won the contest. Nat later told Barry Ulanov of *Metronome* magazine that the Savoy's management was so impressed, Nat's group of high schoolers was hired to play for dances at the Savoy. The group went up against Ray Nance's in another cutting contest; Nat hinted that the trumpeter-violinist led such a fine group that nobody won unless it were Nance.

With Eddie out of town, Nat explored the vibrant music scene and found his way around alone very well. In 1934, Les Paul, then nineteen years old, arrived from Wisconsin to seek his fortune in Chicago. Making his way to the South Side, where the black musicians congregated, he soon met Nat. A bright-eyed, outgoing, red-headed guitarist, Les shared Nat's passion for music, and they went jamming together at night on the club scene. "We jammed in every joint on the South Side," Les Paul remembered.

The youngsters sometimes saw Earl Hines on the scene; Les, too, idolized Hines. They met pianist Teddy Wilson in the clubs. John Collins, becoming a professional, progressive guitarist, was around Chicago in those days. He would eventually work in one of Nat's trios. The famed Club DeLisa on the South Side had Blue Monday parties, with music for the entertainers and clubworkers who had worked all weekend; Les went to that club to jam with Nat Coles on Monday mornings.

Les thought that Nat already had his fanciful, intricate style then, and it didn't change very much over the years—and certainly not through deliberation on Nat's part. Even in those early years, Nat smoked a lot, Les noticed. The habit was simply part of Nat's personality—and almost everyone else's.

Les had to go to the South Side to play with the black musicians, because they didn't come to him in the white neighborhoods. Though some black musicans did work in the white neighborhoods, most did not, and they stayed in the ghetto to jam. Les made a point of going to them, because "they had it all together," he summed it up for himself. He had great times working with Eddie South, a noted violinist, right away.

In a story that could have taken place during the summer of 1935, Les recounted that he and Nat became friendly with Louis Armstrong, then just back from Europe and hanging out around Chicago's jazz scene for a little while. Les did work as a disc jockey on WJJD, under the name of Rhubarb Red for his hillybilly show, and then under his own name for his jazz show. A woman baked a cake for Armstrong. He and Nat took it to Les's radio studio. Then Armstrong and the two teenagers ordered coffee and milk "and sat around eating the damn cake," Les recalled.

Also in 1935, the legendary pianist Art Tatum was playing at the Three Deuces in Chicago; it was known as an after-hours place for musicians who went there to jam. Les, who was addicted to the late-night jamming scene, recalls being around as usual with Nat while Tatum was in town. Nat later recalled that he was pretty young when Tatum went to Chicago. "He was considered a virtuoso of jazz. He impressed us all tremendously, but I wouldn't say his influence [on me] was a major one," Nat told an interviewer. Nat had heard a Chicago bandleader, Cass Simpson, who played in Tatum's ornate style before the commanding Tatum appeared in Chicago.

At night, Les and Nat would jam until 5:30 A.M., when Les had to slip away to his early morning job at WJJD. Finally, one morning,

Art Tatum asked, "Where does that kid go at this hour?" And Nat took Tatum to the radio station, where Tatum was very amused. "That kid is a cowboy!" he said.

Such stories underscore the spirit of the scene, where Nat and Les drew in a great deal of their musical education. The one time they worked together on a recording date in Los Angeles, it became instantly plain that they had played together often and knew each other's styles, abilities, and strengths very well.

In 1936, Eddie Coles, then in his mid-twenties, came off the road from working with Noble Sissle. Eddie brought home with him the glamour of speaking foreign languages and playing several instruments—he had seen the world.

"In our little black community at that time," Milt Hinton recalled sixty years later, "that was a miraculous thing, to be able to speak foreign languages."

Eddie announced that he was going to stay in Chicago for a while and get his music degree from a university in the area. Around the same time, the Coles family moved into a gray frame house at 1412 Greenfield in North Chicago, which they had all to themselves. Reverend Coles became head of the First Baptist Church on the Waukegan—North Chicago border, about forty miles from the family's former home and church on Chicago's South Side.

There were other major changes in the Coles family by then. Two new babies had been born to the Coles, Isaac, whom everyone except his parents called Ike, had been born on July 13, 1927, just after Eddie had left home. Ike was followed four years later on October 15, 1931, by Lionel. Almost everyone called him by his nickname, Freddy, for the rest of his life; Freddy would be his professional name as a pianist and singer. Eddie had the wit to invent his own pet names for the babies, who were young enough to be his own. The Coles children used the names forever, interchanging Eddie's pet names for the nicknames. Though Ike grew to be six feet two and towered over Eddie, who was only five feet nine, Ike wad dubbed "Fats," he recalled in his sixties because he had been a chubby, bowlegged kid.

Both Ike and Freddy were already showing signs of following in their brothers' footsteps; the kids had fallen in love with jazz and blues records that Nat and Eddie brought into the house. The Reverend Coles was baffled as he watched every son head to the piano and grow up to become a professional musician. He never understood why it happened, when, on both sides of their family, they had grandparents, uncles, granduncles, and cousins who were preachers, deacons, church people. The Reverend Coles marveled to a friend that he couldn't understand why none of his sons wanted to become a preacher.

The Coles family remained close-knit, however, with all the surviving children living with their parents under one roof again for a while in North Chicago.

Sometimes on Sundays and always on holidays, the Coles and the Adams relatives had a big dinner party. Usually, about forty people showed up. Alberta Thomas, who migrated north with her mother and sisters in 1929, after Eddie Mae had died, loved the blended aromas of fried chicken, ham, barbecue, neck bones, collard greens, yams, and chittlins, with potato salad, steaming rolls, and sweet-potato pie. "All handmade stuff," she recalled, musing with the soft Southern cadences that infused the speech of all the relatives. On Mother's Day, after the Reverend Coles and Perlina had moved to North Chicago, the family still on the South Side took the elevated train to the Coleses' Sunday church services and the traditional dinner. Eddie was the entertainer and joker, weaving his way among the relatives. Nat remained so quiet in company that his cousins "didn't pay him any mind," Alberta Thomas reminisced. Sometimes he went out into the street and played ball with his friends.

The lively Coles brood had their own way of taking stock of themselves and valuing their gifts and spirit. Though money was scarce, the children tried to emphasize encouragement for each other. At one time or another, each brother would say that one of the others was the best or most versatile musician. Evelyn heard Nat say eventually, "Ike plays more piano than I do." Everyone agreed that Ike was the best piano player in the family apart from Nat. After Nat died, Ike was often hired to play his brother's repertoire for commercials and film projects. Freddy's singing was nearly indistinguishable from Nat's; it was almost impossible for the casual listener to tell them apart, until, as Freddy neared sixty, his voice lowered a little, as all singers' voices do with age. Friends recalled how much Nat admired Freddy's singing. Ike thought with pride that all the brothers sounded as alike in the expressive qualities of their voices as the Kennedy brothers, even though Eddie had a gravelly tone to his singing voice, and Ike's voice was deeper and huskier than Nat's. The Coleses had a bond of pride in their talented family, admiration for each other as a group. Each one valued his own work, too, and knew that he was a good musician. Though

Nat's genius stood out from the crowd, the brothers' gifts and affection allowed them to override and resolve any potentially hurtful competition between them. They were never alienated from one another and maintained warm relations. It would not have been Christian of them, they may have believed, to let jealousy divide and conquer them in a world that had constantly rewarded one brother above all the others. Musicians who met all the Cole brothers on the road thought they came from a basically happy, talented family, without chips on their shoulders and without pretentions.

Chapter Two

HANGING ONTO THE BUZZARD FOR DEAR LIFE IN CALIFORNIA

*F*or a while, Nat's parents expected him to go to school every morning, even though he was playing at night. In about 1935, however, Nat simply decided to give up school for music, and he never got his high school diploma. By the time Eddie returned home to Chicago, Nat's piano playing had developed so much that it inspired Eddie. He merged some of the musicians in Nat's big group into a new quintet (or some say sextet), the Solid Swingers, with Nat at the piano. Eddie booked the new group to play for six months in the Club Panama on the South Side.

Nat earned about eighteen dollars a week there. Eddie also managed to get the Solid Swingers a recording date with Decca's Sepia Series, or race records division, which produced records for sale in black communities. (Nat recalled later in a May 2, 1957 article by John Tynan in *Down Beat* magazine that he was nineteen when he made the records.) Barry Ulanov of *Metronome* magazine was one of the few critics to hear them. "The ensemble is fairly rough," he wrote. "The arrangements are not especially interesting, but Nat plays some good Hines-style piano."

The Solid Swingers recorded four tunes in mid-1936—"Honey Hush," "Thunder," "Bedtime," and "Stomping at the Panama." Though they didn't have more than a regional distribution, for the most part, the Coles brothers' records boosted their reputations and their egos.

Then Eddie booked the group, which he expanded, to tour in the South for a few weeks. Traveling groups normally earned enough money in one city to continue to the next. The Solid Swingers became stranded without money because a club owner— probably a dance promoter—didn't pay them after a job. Milt Hinton heard that the Cole's group was stranded in Texas.* Somebody else heard that it was in Jackson, Mississippi. A long way from home, on unfamiliar terrain, the musicians put up their instruments as collateral to persuade their bus driver to deliver them to Chicago, this time without Perlina's chicken to see them through. Nat had the pluck to survive the incident in good spirits.

He arrived to find that a new production of *Shuffle Along*—the show that had been the successful Noble Sissle-Eubie Blake collaboration on Broadway in the 1920s—was going into rehearsal in Chicago. Eddie, Nat and Nadine Robinson, an attractive, petite, chorusline dancer from the Club Panama found jobs in the show. Born on June 10, 1909, Nadine, with light brown eyes and beautiful legs, was in her late twenties when she met Nat. She had traveled from her native East St. Louis, Illinois, to Chicago, because she wanted to be in show business; Chicago was the big time compared with St. Louis. Nadine had enough experience and taste by the time she worked in the Club Panama to encourage and believe in the tall, appealing, quiet man's talent. She told James Haskins, author of a biography of Cole, that she and Nat fell in love over a period of eight months in Chicago, after Eddie and Nat went to work in the club.

Shuffle Along finished a six-week run; the promoters announced they were taking it on the road. Eddie, who, with characteristic Coles family resourcefulness, had found the jobs for himself, Nat and Nadine, quit the show because he didn't want to go on the road. He preferred to keep his Solid Swingers active, with Nat included. Very protective, Eddie may also have been worried about the fragility of the show's finances. But Nadine wanted to go on the

---

*The brothers used the professional name Cole in this group.

road. The idea appealed to Nat, too. He later told Barry Ulanov that Eddie said, "The only reason you're sticking in the show is for Nadine." Nat agreed that Nadine's "dancing on the show," as he said, influenced him. The brothers fought very hard; Nat said they nearly hit each other. Their parents managed to keep them apart. Nat left town, though he felt terrible about the fight and rued it for quite a while.

Life on the road was arduous. In one town, Henry Fort, the bassist in the band, recalled on "This Is Your Life," Nat became too sick to work one night. There was no place for him to stay, except in the theater, because the local hotel didn't accept black guests. Everyone slept in the theater.

Nevertheless, the adventure of the road stepped up the tempo of Nat's love affair with Nadine. The couple decided to get married. They were so eager to get through the ceremony that they didn't wait for the luxury of a private house, which they had arranged in advance for their wedding. They were married in Ypsilanti, Michigan, by a judge. Two days later, they went through a ceremony again in the house of temporary hosts. "Married her twice, ha ha. Not too many people know that," said comedian Timmie Rogers, who remained friends with the Coles for many years.

Two months after they left Chicago, the couple arrived in Long Beach, California, and moved into the New Strand Theater there. Then, according to legend, about eight hundred dollars in receipts from the show evaporated, perhaps stolen by someone connected with the production or the theater. Saxophonist Buddy Banks, who was working in a small restaurant in the amusement park district near the beach, called "the fun zone," remembered it differently. *Shuffle Along,* which was playing in the theater across the street, didn't attract audiences; he had the impression that it closed because of a lack of receipts.

Banks, working in a pianoless quartet led by trumpeter Claude Kennedy, invited Nat to sit in with the group. "We split our tips with Nat," Banks recalled, because the group admired Nat's playing, and the Coles had no money at all. Buddy and his wife, who lived on Fifty-first Street in East Los Angeles then, invited Nat and Nadine for dinner several times. Buddy liked Nadine's soft, drawling voice. He had the impression that she was very supportive and uncritical of Nat. "She loved him very much," Banks remarked about the older woman. "She was with him, right or wrong." He knew for certain that the couple had a very difficult time financially, as they struggled to find work. The people in Nat's *Shuffle Along* band went home to Chicago.

"It was a tough workout," Nat later reminisced. He took a small band, possibly a septet, into the Ubangi Club in Maywood, but the gig was short-lived. But Nat and Nadine seemed determined to stay in California after *Shuffle Along* came to a standstill. They decided to stay "mostly on account of the climate," Nat recalled a few years later, "and a little because I didn't want my dad to see me busted. . . . Pop was always preaching at us. It was mother who finally convinced him that playing music was an honest day's work."

Tall, slender, mustachioed Johnny Miller, a sensitive bassist with a soft voice, excellent rhythm and strong fingers, had become experienced enough in his twenty-three years to play fleet tempos on his cumbersome instrument. He was working in a club in Long Beach when he saw the cast of *Shuffle Along* on the RKO circuit move into the New Strand Theater—and move out and scatter, virtually penniless. Miller heard a rumor about the theft of the show's profits. A veteran, professional bassist on the Los Angeles scene, he was in touch with all the happenings there; he had been born and brought up in nearby Pasadena and already had played with Lionel Hampton in the Paradise Club on Main Street near Seventh Street in Los Angeles.

Even the bassist Red Callender, who had arrived in Los Angeles on New Year's Day, 1936, with the *Brown Skin Models* show and had decided to stay in the balmy climate, knew about the closing of Nat's show. King Kolax, a well-known bandleader based in Chicago, had brought the show's orchestra from Chicago.* When it closed, Kolax, about ten years older than Nat, went home.

Nat might have returned with him, though he wasn't eager to do so, without any money and with a wife in tow, and ask for his job back in his brother's group. Why go backward? Nat considered. He already had stood up to his elder brother for the right to go out on his own. Nadine, with her easygoing, accepting outlook, liked the prettiness of Los Angeles, too. Somehow the disaster of having no money didn't seem as pressing to Nat when he looked at the emerald green palm trees; the warm, sunny weather was seductive. He had Nadine by his side to keep his spirits up after all. The Coles

---

*Some sources say it was Nat's band; some say Kolax led. Kolax was too ill by 1989 to be consulted.

encouraged each other to try to get through the lean times. Maybe their luck would change for the better. So both of them went looking for jobs. If nothing worked out, they could always go back to Chicago later. Nadine eventually told interviewers that she always had believed in her husband's talents. They lived in a house that may have belonged to Nadine's aunt. It was in the Forties near Avalon Avenue, a Negro neighborhood not far from Central Avenue, with an avocado tree in the backyard. Nat loved to eat the soft yellow fruit. It's unlikely that he had ever seen an avocado before he arrived in California. By 1940, the couple had moved to 2910 South St. Andrew Place off Adams Boulevard, a neighborhood with many Negroes a few miles west of Central Avenue. That was Nat's official address when he registered for the draft under the name of Coles. In at least one and perhaps all of their houses, the Coles had a small upright piano, probably a spinet, on which Nat could practice.

He found jobs playing for about five dollars a night, sometimes less, and afterward explored the jazz scene, going to the clubs downtown. He "sat in"* and introduced himself to the other musicians. Right away, the locals and the émigrés heard the arresting style of the newcomer. A soft-spoken, unassuming, particularly dark-skinned young man, he clearly had the rhythmic drive, imagination and lightness in his spare, bright contemporary style. He saw some old friends from Chicago on the scene, too.

Nat tried to keep his septet working, but club owners wanted to book only the well-known dance bands. A septet led by an unknown was still too risky for club owners to gamble on. Booking agents told Nat that his groups were too small in view of the popularity of big bands. The agents teased him about playing "chamber jazz." Though he was accustomed to big bands and had never really thought about leading anything else, he liked the intimate sound of a small group. He knew that the booking agents didn't know what they were talking about from a musical standpoint, but he couldn't argue with failure on an empty stomach. So he turned to playing solo jobs for income and later told interviewers, "I played every beer joint from San Diego to Bakersfield." He also wrote many arrangements for the shows popular in restaurants in that era.

Nadine worked as a chorus girl and a hostess in little clubs in and around Los Angeles. A charming, friendly woman, who was easy to talk to, she found a string of jobs easily. Clubs in those days

---

* Played the piano for no salary.

eagerly hired ten or twelve pretty girls—always an even number—
in the chorus lines; this precedent had been set by New York's
Cotton Club. She and Nat put together enough money to buy a used
car. He drove Nadine to work and then went to his own jobs in
joints with out-of-tune pianos, keys that didn't work, and audiences
that didn't listen. Some people have speculated that his unusual
chord voicings and harmonies may have come from techniques he
devised to deal with keys that didn't work. Actually, he was experimenting with the more complicated harmonies that would distin-
guish bebop in the 1940s and 1950s, though he would never forgo
his soft, intimate sound rooted in the Swing era in favor of the more
aggressive bebop feeling.

In his earliest days in Los Angeles, Nat was virtually anonymous—except to his new friends on the scene and old pals from
Chicago. Anyone who heard Nat play before 1938 in Los Angeles
wasn't clear about which joint he was working in, but assuredly it
was a small place. Nat sought work relentlessly. In 1938, songwriter
Johnny Mercer saw Cole, who looked underfed (and about eighteen
years old) in a steak house called Jimmy Otto's on Lacienega. Trumpeter Harry "Sweets" Edison, who arrived in town with the Basie
band that year, also heard Cole playing in a small place, possibly the
Century Club on Santa Monica Boulevard. A legendary tale arose
about a musician who saw Nat walking around alone one night in
the rain and told him, "Come inside." Nat replied, "I don't have
enough sense to." His clothes were threadbare; Nadine kept them
clean and pressed, but the dimmer the lighting in a restaurant, the
better Nat's frayed collars and cuffs were hidden from view.

To relieve his own homesickness and draw encouragement from
his memories of an assured roof over his head, Nat wrote at least
one song based on a lesson he had learned at home. In his repertoire of sermons, to exhort people to become believers, his father
had sometimes used the memorable metaphor of a monkey and a
buzzard. A monkey took a ride on a buzzard and refused to let go
and fall to his death. Don't give up, was the message, even though
it's a cold, cruel world and the buzzard doesn't care whether you
survive. Nat always regarded his strict, devoutly religious father
with awe. "Whatever sincerity I have," he told an interviewer, "I get
from him." "Straighten up and fly right," his father used to call out
in a rich voice in his sermon, urging people to cling to their Christian beliefs no matter how precarious their lives were.* Nat turned

---

*This is the most-quoted version of Nat's inspiration.

the metaphor into a whimsical lyric, in somewhat the same vein as his brother Eddie's song about a threatening old bear, which had charmed Milt Hinton. Frustrated by poverty, Nat took his song to Irving Mills, a songwriter, musician, and arranger, who made a deal for his brother, Jack Mills, a music publisher sitting a continent away in the Brill Building on Broadway in New York City. Jack Mills bought the song for fifty dollars. Irving Mills Music took credit for the composition. The fifty dollars, which Nat used for rent, gave Nadine and him temporary relief. It must have seemed like a good deal to Nat on the day he received his cash.

Some nights, he and Nadine got together with other struggling young musicians in Los Angeles. Before she became a well-known recording artist with her hit record "He's a Real Gone Guy," Nellie Lutcher was singing in little clubs in town. Through her brother, who knew musicians on the scene, she met Nat and Nadine and spent several evenings with them. Nat rehearsed at Nellie's house a block east of Central Avenue; Nadine went along sometimes. The personable couple dined on red beans and rice with Nellie, her husband, and son. Their admiration for each other's talents fed their souls with hope for their future successes.

Leonard Feather has said that Cole put together his first trio in 1937, while other accounts place the trio playing professionally together for the first time in 1938. In any case, Bob Lewis, who owned a fairly popular musicians' hangout called the Sewanee Inn, stopped in the Century Club one night and heard Nat Cole playing solo. Since Lewis liked the young man's style, he approached and asked if Nat would assemble a small group and bring it to play at the Sewanee Inn for a few weeks. Nat said sure, he could do that. According to some versions of the story of the trio's genesis, Nat then went to clubs where he knew he would find musicians. In the Paradise Club, Nat found Lionel Hampton, the vibraphonist and drummer, who was disbanding his own group to play vibes in clarinetist Benny Goodman's historic group, with Teddy Wilson as the pianist and Gene Krupa as drummer. Hampton's bassist, Wesley Prince, was therefore out of a job. Hampton thought Wesley would play well with Nat. So Hampton either introduced Nat to the Pasadena-born Prince or sent Nat to the musicians' union to find him. Born on April 8, 1907, Prince, also a minister's son, came from a musical family, too; his brother Henry played piano with Les Hite's big band, which was then popular on the West Coast. And Wesley's cousin, Peppy, played drums.*

*Lee Young calls Peppy a cousin. An authoritative discography of Nat's records by Klaus Teubig says Peppy was a brother.

Prince had a friend, Oscar Moore, who played guitar with lyricism and imagination. Nat may have found Oscar Moore through the union or directly from Prince—or Nat may have found Oscar first and then Prince. The chronology remains unclear. Certainly all the young musicians on the scene knew each other or else had heard about each other from friends, since they traveled in the same circles and had such a lively grapevine and highly developed critical sense about each other's musical abilities and tastes.

Summing it up, Nat himself said succinctly, "The way we got together was the most natural thing in the world. When I was playing around town, I ran into Oscar Moore and then Wesley Prince. Seemed like a good idea to get a group together." Nat discovered that Oscar Moore was a guitarist with everything—great rhythmic and melodic feeling, improvisatory genius, soloing charisma, and sensitivity to the musicians whom he played with.

Oscar had been working on first call at MGM, among other studios, before Nat asked him to join the new group. Behind the scenes, Oscar played the guitar that Mickey Rooney mimed strumming in the film *Girl Crazy*. Although not a singer with a mellow voice—he was strictly an instrumentalist—Oscar had the spirit to try to sing a little in a style attuned to Nat's playing and singing. Moore also came from a musical family. Both he and his guitar-playing elder brother Johnny had been born in Austin, Texas—Oscar on Christmas Day in 1916.* The Moore family moved to Phoenix, where Oscar grew up. Other musicians passing through Phoenix in the early 1930s began to hear about Oscar's immense talent even before he went to Los Angeles in 1936.

Oscar had learned to play the guitar by listening to his brother Johnny. Quickly he became a much better player than Johnny. According to Val Molineaux, Oscar may have taken lessons from more accomplished musicians. Molineaux, just a youngster polishing shoes backstage at the Apollo Theatre in 1944, was trying to play guitar himself; he would eventually teach drums, bass, and guitar in his own workshop and store in Portland, Maine. Val became enamored of Oscar's playing and followed the trio around to learn from Oscar's bell-clear, flowing, adventurous style. Oscar confided to his admirer that he had idolized Eddie Lang, Bing Crosby's guitarist, who worked very often with violinist Joe Venuti, and who died of

---

* *The New Grove Dictionary of Jazz* says 1912, but 1916 is the date given by Val Molineaux, one of his very good friends, whose memory Moore's widow trusts. Bassist Johnny Miller, who played with Moore and Cole for years, had the distinct impression that Nat and Oscar were the same age.

tonsillitis in 1933. Moore also loved the French gypsy guitarist Django Reinhardt.

Between Nat and Oscar, there was so much melody, propulsion, and imagination in their music, with Prince's strong foundation as the perfect foil, that the trio sounded larger and stronger than it was. The men played together with perfect communication, emanating from each other's lines with magical effect. Although a drummer could supply special accents, the swinging group didn't absolutely need them. "Nat was not a muscular man," Jack Costanzo, who played bongos with Cole's group later, reminisced. "He was a delicate person in his playing, singing, and talking. The only time he was not delicate was when he laid down a beat." Sometimes Nat played in groups with his friend Lee Young, the drummer and younger brother of the legendary tenor saxophonist Lester Young. A slender, athletic, physical-fitness buff, Lee became a close friend of Nat's; the two of them played ball together in a park near the musicians' union headquarters. Lee was an organized, loyal friend of Nat's. Nat didn't use a drummer for the trio at the Sewanee Inn, however, where the group earned seventy-five dollars a week, split it evenly three ways, and developed a following for its very soft sound—an intimate, eccentric sound in the Big Band era, with its great brass and reeds players and dynamic drummers.

"We called ourselves King Cole and his Swingsters, and I guess we went over all right," Nat said later for a *Down Beat* interview.

If Nat's group was supposed to have a drummer, Lee Young, who would have been the only drummer to work with Cole regularly in those days, didn't know about it. A practical, reliable man, he was surprised to find out later that a legend arose about his failing to show up for the gig the first night. Nat had never invited him to the job. And with good reason, Lee thought.

"The Sewanee Inn was such a little place," Lee said, defending himself against the amusing rumor. "You couldn't get fifty people into it. Once the bass and guitar joined the piano, there was even less space for customers. And if a drummer showed up, the group would displace another ten customers."

If Lee had worked at the Sewanee Inn, he could have used only the snare drum, the high hat, the top or ride cymbal and brushes, without a bass drum or a tom-tom. Around that time, Lee had bought a new drum set, giving himself the luxuries of tom-toms, temple blocks, and different cymbal stands. When he got a call in the early 1940s to play with Les Hite's band, Young went along happily. "Playing with a trio was enough already," Lee said, excited by the opportunity to play with a big band, though he had enjoyed playing with Nat often enough by then and would always love to play with him. Nat was one of the greatest jazz pianists who ever lived, Lee always thought; in addition to being an intimate friend, Lee would become Nat's musical director in the 1950s. The legend about Lee endured, however, despite his self-defense and reasonable analysis of the situation.

Nat's drummerless trio pleased Bob Lewis and the customers. Its dynamics were, apparently, just right for the small club, where Nat had a steady gig that lasted six months—according to a *Metronome* article—while his friendship with Lee remained unrippled. So one gets the notion that either Nat asked another drummer to show up—an unlikely possibility—or else the resourceful Cole analyzed the musical situation as Lee did and was able to provide each man in the trio with twenty-five dollars a week. With that little wage, Nat had to take other jobs on the side to survive.

Both Nadine and Lee's wife worked for a while together at the Bal Tabarin in Gardena, California, about fifteen miles from Los Angeles. After Nat and Lee finished work, they went in Nat's car to pick up their wives and made the rounds of the clubs and joints and jammed. Another friend, the bassist Jimmy Blanton, sometimes joined them. He eventually went into Duke Ellington's band and assumed the mantle of the first modern bassist during his short life, eschewing slap bass and other techniques strictly for entertainment, and exploring the solo possibilities of the bass. Blanton brought along his bass to jam. Lee transferred his drums from his own car trunk to Nat's, unless they used Lee's big Oldsmobile with its capacious trunk to make the rounds. They had their choice of quite a few night spots in Los Angeles in those days. Ivie Anderson, an elegant singer who worked for ten years with Duke Ellington's band until 1942, had retired nearly completely that year, because of her severe asthma. By 1941, she and one of her husbands had opened Ivie's Chicken Shack, a popular soul-food restaurant on Vernon Avenue just off of Central Avenue in Los Angeles. Stuff Crouch, a friend of musicians, ran the place for her. Though Ivie never hired musicians, she put a piano in the simple place for musicians who stopped for food and conversation; the pianists entertained everyone without charge. Even Art Tatum went to play there. Nat, Lee and Blanton used to go to Ivie's Chicken Shack and jam together.

Another club they visited was Brothers, either on Central Avenue or Adams Boulevard. Everyone had a feeling of being safe in the places and neighborhoods where the musicians went to jam around

Central Avenue, Lee Young thought. The clientele of the clubs was about 60 percent white and 40 percent black, Lee estimated, though other musicians didn't see a great deal of mixing of the races in those days in Los Angeles clubs. A law barred nightclubs with white customers from admitting Negroes. Cole said he was the first Negro to entertain in some of the rooms where he played. Several club owners paid no attention to the law—Bob Lewis, for one. Billy Berg ignored it altogether, too, by the time he got to his fourth and last club in the 1300 block on Vine Street in about 1943. Before that, he ran the Trouville on Beverly Boulevard near Fairfax Street, starting at the very end of 1941 or the first days of 1942; that's where Norman Granz, beginning his career as a jazz impressario, ran jam sessions, with integrated musical groups and audiences, too.

Pianist Jimmy Rowles, who played at the Trouville during the week, thought it was Berg's best club. He played there with Lee and Lester Young and Lady Day; Big Joe Turner, dancer Marie Bryant, who also had a lovely singing style, and guitarist Teddy Bunn, Slim and Slam, and the inventive scat singer and triple player Leo Watson and the Spirits of Rhythm starred there. Pianist Eddie Beale, very active in the Los Angeles music scene, with his own music publishing firm, and even Barney Bigard, the clarinetist, played in the club. Their audiences were segregated on weekdays, but on Sundays, Granz and Berg attracted crowds to their integrated jam sessions, for which Nat Cole worked as the house pianist.

In Los Angeles around this time, whites always could go to the Negro clubs without any problem. Les Paul, for one, and Norman Granz, for another, went to them. Musicians thought that the races mixed in the clubs around Central Avenue with less tension than would exist in town in general fifty years later. Central Avenue was, in effect, an integrated neighborhood in the late 1930s, although the white people owned the businesses. They hired no Negro clerks, until one Negro man led an effective picket action. Without violence, Negroes started to get jobs as employees in the stores. In the 1940s, other restaurants besides Ivie's and Brothers attracted musicians searching for places to jam.

In those days, Nat's marriage to Nadine seemed fresh and workable to the couple's friends. One woman had no idea that Nadine was so much older than Nat, because the petite dancer had a youthful look. There was also a mature air about her, however, Nadine's friends noticed. That was the only hint of anything unusual in the Coles' relationship. Everybody liked her soft-voiced, friendly manner. Nobody overheard any quarrels between the Coles; if there were tensions, they didn't surface in public.

Nadine, who had simple tastes, was apparently eminently suited to be the wife of a struggling musician, who needed her encouragement and the freedom to use all his resourcefulness. At least seven and perhaps ten years older than Nat, she could nurture him instinctively. She liked to cook soul food, and she and Nat invited friends to dinners. If the menus were humble—"rice and beans," as one musician recollects—the talk was fancy; it was about the music they loved. Nat venerated Earl Hines, Duke Ellington, and Count Basie, whose spare style had evolved with his bandleading in Kansas City from an earlier, more elaborate one he had used as a stride piano player and a sideman in New York. Nat also loved the tenor saxophonists Herschel Evans, who played with Count Basie, and Coleman Hawkins. Nat made a point to hear Hawkins playing in the 1930s, when he came back from Europe for a while and led his own group.

Nellie Lutcher liked the way that Nadine talked to Nat's friends; when she worked for a while as a hostess at the Club Alabam on Adams, a popular place with musicians, Nadine knew how to make people feel welcome. She was so adept at the job that "she made the place," Nellie thought. After Nadine left, the club didn't fare as well, in Nellie's opinion.

Nadine also danced at the Club Alabam, when Lee Young had a band there. He, too, admired her friendliness; she was a fine-looking little woman, he thought, with fascinating legs and light brown eyes that contrasted prettily with her dark complexion—though it was not as dark as Nat's, Lee noticed. Nobody was as dark as Nat Cole, Lee joked to himself. Nat's complexion made Lee think of the song lyric "What did I do to be so black and blue?" The more serious side to the humor was the premise endemic within the African American culture that the lighter a person's skin was, the more important the person seemed, and the easier and better life was. One of Nat's close associates thought that Nat was quite sensitive to this prejudice.

How happy the Coles' marriage was, not even their closest friends in those days could say for sure. "No one knows what goes on behind closed doors," commented one musician who saw them frequently throughout their marriage. Nadine recalled their time together, when Nat was working in near anonymity on the West Coast, as romantic and happy. "It was Nat's nature to get along with

most people; he was an easygoing man," Lee Young observed. Nat
kept himself constantly busy with music in one way or another in
those days and seems never to have confided in anyone, not even in
Nadine, about his ambitions. She was not aware that he had dreams
of becoming famous as he struggled along, she told James Haskins
when he was writing a book about Cole in the early 1980s. She also
was oblivious to Nat's drawling and accented speech, though invari-
ably other people noticed it.

Sometimes Lee and Jimmy Blanton sat outside Nat's house, waiting in Lee's car for an hour until Nat finished his daily practice
routine of two hours. Without their wives, the men would drive
away to jam someplace. The musicians' union—the black local 767,
before the union was integrated—prohibited jamming. The union
didn't want musicians giving music away for free at places such as
Alex Lovejoy's upstairs at Vernon and Central avenues, another
place that musicians liked. Lovejoy's had a piano and invited trios to
jam with the hired pianist; only the pianist was paid. Art Tatum
liked to play there, too.

Musicians loved to jam, because it meant more practice in en-
sembles for them. They also enjoyed several side benefits from jamming in public. Club owners heard them and hired them to work
for pay. No matter how poor the musicians were, women crowded
around them, lining up for attention. That was the musicians' lot in
life. Every night could hold excitement, with the attention of
women, the camaraderie of men, and the beauty of pretty music.
Since Nat spent his entire adult life as a married man, the phenomenon of musicians' attractiveness to women posed problems for him,
sometimes beyond his wildest dreams. Les Paul later joked about
the many times he told Nat, "Wipe off the lipstick." Oscar Moore,
who was a handsome man with a dashing Latin-lover-style appearance, found that women flocked around him. Wesley Prince, very
mild-mannered in appearance, and the clean-cut Johnny Miller, who
would follow Prince, had their female followings, too. Oscar
Moore's early marriage did not survive his years with the trio. As
Lee Young put it, "If you know anything about musicians, you know
that there are always women around."

Lee found himself getting fined every week at fifty dollars a fine
for jamming, in the days when he was earning twenty-five to thirty
dollars a week at the most. Nat wasn't caught jamming as often, it
seems, because he could slide off the piano bench if a union official
or informer walked into a joint. Lee got caught red-handed with his
drums; it would take him some time, even at top speed, to pack and

stow the drum set in a car. At Alex Lovejoy's, where the pianist was actually hired, Nat could claim that he was working, whether that was the truth or not. But drummers, bassists, and horn players worked illicitly.

Lee's fine was always suspended, since he couldn't pay it. Nevertheless, he and many other musicians decided to invent a ploy to make the union change its mind about their jamming for free in clubs. Lee, who lived next door to the union, convinced the officials to let the musicians jam in a rehearsal hall upstairs at the union, just above the offices, Monday through Friday, beginning at 1 P.M. The sessions became well attended. Charlie Christian, the consummate guitarist, and Ben Webster, a tenor player with a haunting breathiness, came by. The people who worked in the offices downstairs were so disrupted by the music that they couldn't concentrate. They wanted the musicians to leave; so they did. After that, the union relented and didn't bother them very much about jamming wherever they went.

Often, after Nat became famous, his rise was written about glibly. The storyteller in him must have liked the magical tale of how he was given the title of "King."

The drummerless trio with a soft, intriguing sound entertained at first with strictly instrumental music at the Sewanee Inn on La Brea. Nat reminisced later for John Tynan's May 2, 1957 *Down Beat* article. "I really didn't think about singing. Oh, I had a conception of it, but my main interest was in playing piano. I was a jazz piano player. Who thought of singing?" In the tale which arose, there is probably a grain of truth someplace: A tipsy customer asked Nat to sing a song. The customer may have asked for "Sweet Lorraine," or he may not have specified the tune. Nat demurred; he didn't like to sing, because he didn't "sound good," he said. The customer insisted. And Bob Lewis, the club owner, suggested that Nat sing or he would find himself out of favor. So Nat sang "Sweet Lorraine," Jimmie Noone's theme song, which Nat had always liked in Chicago. It was part of Nat's repertoire with his trio, anyway. The customer tipped Nat fifteen cents—five cents for each musician in the group. When the customer asked for another song, Nat said he didn't know it. "The customer asked for his fifteen cents back," quick-witted Wesley Prince said, putting the finishing touch on the sweet tale when it was related on "This Is Your Life."

Nat said that he began singing occasionally, sometimes in unison with his trio to vary the pace of the gig, and customers liked the singing and kept asking for it. The men worked out vocal arrangements. Bob Lewis was so happy with the singing that he placed a tinsel crown on Nat's head one night and said that the pianist was Nat "King" Cole—a sobriquet, Lewis added, that could come to mind easily about a man named Cole. (By that time Nat had permanently dropped the *s* from his professional name, following his brother Eddie's lead.*) Nat wore the crown uneasily for several weeks, until it disappeared mysteriously from the club, to his relief.

Nat never totally disowned the legend of the tipsy customer, "Sweet Lorraine," and a coronation. He knew a good story when he heard one. Wesley Prince probably gave the group its first name, the King Cole Swingsters; it evolved into the King Cole Trio. When Cole began singing—if not all the time—with the trio in the Sewanee Inn, it was clear that his was the special voice. His baritone had a mesmerizing, masculine edge that stood out when he took a solo vocal part. Because of his shyness, he liked to share the limelight, however.

One of their vocal routines, which showcased his voice, demonstrated how entertainingly the men could sing together: "There's No Anesthetic for Love." It began with an odd falsetto voice—probably Wesley Prince's—singing "Who's that knocking on the doctor's door?" Prince knocked on his bass for the accent.

"It's me, nurse, old Oscar Moore," sang the guitarist in a timberless baritone without embellishment.

"What do you want to see the doctor 'King' Cole for?" "nursie" continued in a parody of a woman's voice.

"It's about love, because it's got me on the floor," Oscar talked-sang.

And in came Nat's deeper, more authoritative voice with properly jive inflections: "I *am* the doctor! What can I *do* you for?"

". . . The doctors look at the chart and end up right where they start," Moore explained.

"I'm sorry, son, there's no anesthetic for love," sang Nat.

There was such fun in the trio's attitude toward the song that it is hard to believe Cole resented singing. According to a discography of Cole's work compiled by Klaus Teubig, the song was done for Davis and Schwegler label, essentially Decca, and was used primarily for disc jockey shows on radio in Los Angeles. In 1989, Savoy Jazz released it on the LP, *Birth of the Cole,* 1938–1939.

---

*Nat did not change his name to Cole legally until after 1948, when he married his second wife. Eddie Cole never changed his last name legally. Evelyn Cole was called Coles as her legal name in Nat's will. Nat's younger brothers and their families used Cole as their legal name. Though, Evelyn used Cole as her name for convenience, legally she remained Coles.

In any case, when the trio began singing, it was not exactly off and running anyplace. It kept working at the Sewanee Inn, attracting enough regular customers so that the musicians enjoyed the stability of a six-month run. In 1938, their salary went up to $110 a week, and they kept building their reputation as a fine Los-Angeles–based group.

By 1940, Nat toyed with the idea of taking his rhythm section into the Lionel Hampton band, as Lionel invited him to do. But Lee Young had just returned from New York City, where he had heard the fine Clarence Profit trio. It had the reputation for being the "baddest" trio in existence. Lee didn't think it was as good as Nat's and told Nat to stay free of Hampton's band. Nat recorded with Lionel at that time, anyway—for Decca, at the C. P. MacGregor studios on Melrose Avenue. Among the seven tunes that Nat played on were "Jivin' with Jarvis," with a vocal by the trio with Hampton and the drummer Al Spieldock. The record naturally attracted the attention of Al Jarvis, a disc jockey on a local radio station.*

Jarvis played the song, which displayed Oscar Moore's ringing, lyrical guitar and Nat's imaginative, pulsing piano. Riding the crest of a small wave of popularity in town because of the exposure, Nat's trio went back into the Decca studio on Melrose Avenue in May and July of 1940, and recorded four songs, including "Sweet Lorraine," "Gone with the Draft," written by Wesley Prince—a prophetic tune that Cole sang, and two instrumentals—"Honeysuckle Rose" and "This Side Up". The songs received considerable airplay in Los Angeles, because of Al Jarvis, who was still flattered by Nat's participation in the song "Jivin' with Jarvis."

As soon as Nat began singing, people marveled at how he seemed to have sprung as a fully developed and charismatic singer out of an instrumentalist's background. He had a mellow, easily identifiable voice with a sexy, masculine hoarseness and wonderful phrasing, even in tight rhythm with the trio or with Lee Young, whom he still played with at times. Ordinarily, it took even the most gifted singer years to develop such an assured, distinctive style.

In those days before he achieved a wide following, Cole was recognized primarily as a superb pianist by people on the music scene in Los Angeles. A handful of singers hired him for rehearsals

---

*Some sources say it was KLAC. Bing Crosby said he first heard Cole at 11:45 A.M. Saturday on a program on KFWB, but that was probably in the late 1930s.

and practice time, as Lena Horne and Dorothy Dandridge would later do with pianist-arranger Phil Moore, a friend of Cole's. When singers hired Nat for small fees, he coached them about their phrasing. His phrasing on the piano was polished and expressive; he clearly had a special respect for lyrics. By teaching singers, he developed a storytelling style of his own, before he knew he would become one of them, as Lee Young noticed.

Nat's life in those days centered around the musicians' community in Los Angeles, while his career inched slowly along. He eked out a living in myriad ways. Learning that he could arrange, his friends asked him to write for them. Lee Young, for one, had a band for which he used several arrangers, one of them Nat.

Lee noticed a curious habit which to his knowledge only Nat had. All the arrangers did their work for fees ranging from five to seven dollars for an arrangement. Then a copyist redid the pencil-written arrangement in ink for a dollar or two. But Nat copied his arrangements in pencil himself and handed them in that way, because he was happy to have the whole fee for himself. He wasn't a professional copyist. If he had made a mistake in copying his own work in pen, he would have ruined his entire arrangement. "There was no 'whiteout' in those days," Lee Young reminisced with a laugh. So Nat redid his work in pencil. If a leader kept an arrangement by Nat in the band book for a while, the pencil would smudge and wear out. Lee never liked to use his arrangements for long; after a while he simply threw them out. And sometimes he wondered how other leaders coped with Nat's pencil.

At Christmas and Eastertime, Nat sent seven dollars to Chicago with the instructions that Evelyn should buy something pretty to wear. He wanted his family to think that he had a little money to spare.

The saxophonist Buddy Collette, a native of Los Angeles, was playing in the group of the leader C.P. Johnson, "the only black band working in Hollywood clubs," Collette reminisced. Nat wrote wonderful arrangements for the group. Johnson's band played in many places, including the Rhum Boogie at 300 N. Highland Avenue at Melrose Avenue. The chorus-line dancers included Marie Bryant, Lovey Lane, and Millie Monroe. "Dancers were very particular about having a little kick to their arrangements," Collette noticed. "Not everybody could write for dancers. But Nat could do it; they loved his arrangements."

Nat used to stop at the clubs and pass out his arrangements to the Johnson band. Johnny Miller, the bassist, who would later join Nat's trio, may have been working with Johnson at this time. Not only Nat's but most arrangements, in Collette's experience, were written in pencil in those days; Nat wasn't the only one trying to conserve his meager earnings.

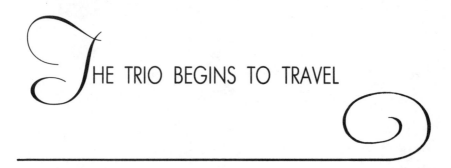

Chapter Three

THE TRIO BEGINS TO TRAVEL

A betted by his growing local celebrity, Nat found a good booking agent to arrange a tour for the trio. In the late winter of 1941, the men set out in Nat's well-worn car, to play at the 2800 Club in Dayton, Ohio, the Panther Room of the Sherman Hotel as the relief group for Bob Crosby's band in Chicago, and also in Chicago's Capitol Lounge, where the trio alternated with the saxophonist and singer Louis Jordan. Nat's men may also have played in the Blue Note in Chicago at this time; they definitely played there later in the 1940s. Then they went to the Rendezvous in Philadelphia and Hotel Senator in Washington, D.C. The jobs were a prelude to a long stay in New York.

Along the way, the trio recorded in Chicago on March 14, 1941, for Decca, with Nat singing on "Babo," "Scotchin' with the Soda," and "Slow Down"; only "Early Morning Blues" was an instrumental.

Nat joked, in his soft-voiced way, that nobody knew he was back in Chicago except for his family, but the truth was that he appeared in good showcases for performers, such as the Blue Note, where Count Basie's world tour would regularly stop over the years. It was the first time that anyone in his family, except for Eddie, had seen Nat and Nadine since 1937. Eddie—who had visited Nat, stayed with him in Los Angeles, and gone to Nellie Lutcher's house in 1938 to play with him—may have explored the possibilities of working with him again. Eddie was working in town at that time, touring with his new group, Three Loose Nuts and a Bolt. But he didn't stay in Los Angeles. He kept touring and soon settled in Philadelphia. In Los Angeles, he and Nat recovered from the fight they had had before Nat left Chicago.

Nat's family was very happy to see the couple. Even though his father had the reputation of being very straitlaced, he sat down for friendly chats with Nadine at the dining room table. Nat's cousin, Alberta Thomas, remembered how friendly and warm Nadine was with his family. At least once, Nat left Nadine for a few weeks' visit in Chicago while he continued a tour. Nadine fit in very well with the Coleses' lifestyle, customs and values. At least one of her uncles was a Baptist minister. Alberta, who was much larger than the shapely little dancer, thought that Nadine was an attractive woman, actually a beautiful woman, in part because of her down-to-earth personality. Though the Coleses were quiet, strict churchgoers, they were informal hosts and bent the rules in the interest of letting reason prevail. (Eddie's wife, Betty, whom he met in Philadelphia, remembered a time when she and Eddie were traveling by car, with their clothes packed in the trunk. When they arrived at Reverend Coles's door in Chicago, Betty was wearing slacks. "And Daddy didn't allow women wearing pants in his house. When he saw me wearing pants, he said something that let me know. It wasn't anything derogatory, but he let me know." Then he invited her into the house dressed that way, because her dresses were in the trunk.)

In New York City, Nat's trio played for four weeks, probably for a total of $105 a week—union scale at that time—at a popular club for Dixieland and New Orleans-rooted music, Nick's on Seventh Avenue in Greenwich Village. From there, Nat moved the trio for eight months on and off into Kelly's Stable on West Fifty-second Street—Swing Street—in midtown. The street had not yet felt the force of bebop: Dizzy Gillespie, Charlie Parker, and others were still developing the new style of jazz uptown in Harlem, primarily at Minton's Playhouse. Among the stars on West Fifty-second Street were Art Tatum and Billie Holiday.

Billie was singing as the headliner at Kelly's Stable when Nat took his group in as the intermission entertainment. He made enough of an impression on the *Down Beat* piano columnist, Sharon A. Pease, to warrant an excellent review in *Down Beat* that year. The trio tacked in and out of New York to Dayton, Ohio, and Chicago. The exposure that the trio received made the trip across the country worthwhile. Especially praised by Pease were the trio's "evergreens," as critics call the familiar standards; Pease advised everyone to ask Nat to play "I Can't Get Started." He recorded the song, possibly as soon as the following year.

The people who frequented the Fifty-second Street scene became familiar with Cole, though his records weren't played on the radio in New York City. "None of his records was a hit," observed Dave Dexter, then the New York editor for *Down Beat*. Dexter later rose to an influential position in the artists and repertoire department of Capitol Records. He was as impressed as his good friend and colleague Pease by Nat's piano playing.

Gary Stevens, a highly respected public-relations man, who also became a television producer and wrote a column for newspapers, met Cole at Kelly's, too, when both of them were still struggling to get established. Stevens, however, didn't hear Nat sing in performance at the club.

Kelly's was owned by Ralph Watkins, a former bandleader, George Lynch, a former sandwich cutter in a Broadway cafeteria, and a third partner. As far as Stevens could tell, the trio was strictly an instrumental group.

Stevens heard Nat sing only in the afternoons, when Stevens went to the club to pick up his fifty-dollar paycheck for his press-agentry work. The check was never ready for him, so he would have to go back the next day and even sometimes a third day. Each time, he saw Nat come in, carrying sheet music, and head for the piano. Nat sat down in the empty club with a bulb on a unshaded floor lamp shedding the only light, the tables turned upside down, and the floor smelling of disinfectant. On these afternoons, the place had a desolate air. Nat toyed with the tunes, then played and sang them.

Gary liked the singing and finally spoke up. "You should sing at night."

Nat seemed shy about the idea and said, "No, it's not for this room. Maybe sometime."

At night, Nat walked onto the bandstand with Moore and Prince and never introduced them to the audience. He smiled a lot but never spoke. An offstage voice announced, "And now, the King Cole

Trio." They played for about twenty minutes at a time. Nat wore a beige-colored sports jacket with a darker-toned beige-colored shirt and black or dark gray slacks, as Stevens recalled, while the bassist and guitarist wore sports shirts and slacks, without jackets, in the opposite color scheme from Nat's. Eventually, the trio would dress in exactly matching outfits in the early days of their national success.

As the weeks went by, Stevens spoke more often with the shy, friendly pianist. Nat's schedule seemed to be to wake up, have lunch, and go to the music publishers for songs, since they weren't approaching him. If he had any airtime in New York, it was negligible that year. He explained to Stevens that he was trying out the new songs to see whether he liked them for the trio. "I'm going to add new material," he always said.

Stevens liked Nat's singing and thought it was virtually his secret. Other sources say that Kelly's owners had heard "Jivin' with Jarvis" and wanted the King Cole Trio because it sang, too. In still another version of the story of Nat's early engagement in New York, the owners didn't know that Nat sang until someone telephoned them and told them that Nat was doing a great job of singing one night. After that, he was obliged to sing in Kelly's Stable rather regularly, and he may have filled in for Billie Holiday one night when she was too ill to go to work.

Nat spent a good deal of time jamming in clubs where he wasn't working, becoming familiar with the New York scene. Some New Yorkers recall hearing him at the Apollo Theatre in 1941. The trio recorded for Decca on July 16 and again on October 23, 1941. Nat decided to do "I Like to Riff" on the first date and "That Ain't Right" on the second. The *Down Beat* review was the best publicity he received during his stay in New York.

Then he returned to the West Coast before the cold weather began. Later on, Gary Stevens was astounded to discover that Nat was singing all the time. After becoming friendly during Nat's first trip to New York, they kept up the friendship for the rest of Nat's life. Nat had a special rapport with press agents; he liked to hang out with them because their tastes, interests, down-to-earth observations, savvy analyses, and humor relaxed him. Many were sports buffs, as he was. He loved to watch the games and somehow find his way into the locker rooms, too. Famous football and baseball players became his good friends and casually called out "Hi, Nat," when he went to the games. So Nat kept his warm relations with Stevens active.

In the late 1950s, Stevens was asked to do a favor for a film producer on a tight budget and find a cast for the movie *Blue Gardenia*. Stevens tapped his friends to play for peanuts: Raymond Burr as the villain; and in assorted other roles, Anne Baxter, Ann Sothern, and Richard Conte, with Nat King Cole for $1,500 or possibly $2,000—*much* less than he was usually earning by then. Out of that glorified B picture, only the title song which Nat sang became popular and endured.

It was the type of situation Nat often found himself in—doing favors for friends. Most often, he would record their songs, if he liked them, or sometimes even if he were dubious about them.

Often he didn't even realize that he was doing favors or influencing people. In Kelly's Stable, a young trumpeter named Neal Hefti heard Nat for the first time. Hefti became a lauded arranger and wrote several songs for Nat to record, at the request of Capitol Records. In 1941, Hefti knew only how charmed he was by the soft sound of the drummerless trio. He had never heard one before, and he was especially touched because it reflected his own artistic instinct to play in a soft-toned style on trumpet. He dreamed of having that trio to back him up for his gigs. It was exactly the way he wanted music to sound, and it influenced him as he began teaching himself to arrange. Even the types of songs which Nat chose for his repertoire excited Hefti; later on, when Nat added strings, he kept the same ethic for his sound, based on the foundation he had established with his trio. "I was a mellow spectator," Hefti recalled of Nat's performances throughout his career. "And you could always go backstage and say hello."

By the end of 1941, Cole, Moore and Prince were playing in Los Angeles again. Music world insiders heard Cole's trio in different places between 1937 and 1943. In a mid-1944 *Metronome* magazine article, which was based on an interview with Cole, Barry Ulanov stated that the trio went into the 331 Club in 1941 and stayed there for eight months, took a ten-week trip to Omaha, Nebraska's Beachcomber Club, then went back to the 331 Club in Los Angeles for forty-eight weeks through the 1943–1944 winter. According to Ulanov, Cole's trail in Los Angeles, beginning in 1937, led from many small "joints," as Cole called them, in Southern California, to a short stint with a large group in the Ubangi Club, then to the Century Club. From there, Bob Lewis took him to the Sewanee Inn for six months. Then Cole's trio went from spot to spot—Jimmy Otto's Steak House, Fox Hills Club, or Lounge, opposite the Twentieth Century–Fox lot, Shep Kelley's in Hollywood, the Club Circle in

Beverly Hills, and the 331 Club, until Bob Lewis again came into the picture and brought the trio into the Radio Room on Vine Street across from NBC studios and at the hub of musical activity in Hollywood. The trio stayed there for two months and "made lots of friends," Nat said.

Among them was Johnny Mercer, the great songwriter; Mercer, who was among the summer replacement artists for "The Bob Hope Show," used to leave the NBC broadcast studio and cross the street to hear Cole singing in the Radio Room. Mercer took Paul Weston along to hear Cole. When Mercer helped to start Capitol Records, he remembered Cole and brought him into the fledgling company as one of its first artists.

In any case, Cole's trio was earning more money in 1941 than in the Sewanee Inn earlier. Nat had the prestige of the glowing review in *Down Beat* to present himself with. When the trio recorded again for Decca in the Melrose Avenue studio, one of the town's small but popular studios, Lee Young joined them. All of them sang together with breathtaking synchronization, barely discernible from one another. "On the Sunny Side of the Street" was a spectacular showcase for Nat and Oscar as the soloists. Prince and Young supplied exceptionally exciting, tasteful accents. Young recalled for the rest of his life exactly what he had played.*

But it was "That Ain't Right" from Nat's recording session in New York City in 1941 that began to circulate, in his hometown, Chicago, for one place, by the next spring. Some people recall hearing it in a variety of Negro neighborhoods at about the time that Nat stopped in Chicago again in the spring of 1942, to play with the trio in the Sherman Hotel on his way back to New York City. Though his 1942 tour to New York City was omitted from the Ulanov account of Nat's trail, the trio definitely returned to the Big Apple that year; Nat recorded there. He was driving a 1941 Buick by that time. Among the presents he bought for the family in Chicago were some sweaters for Ike and Freddy. By then Nat was providing a little unaccustomed luxury for the Coles family, even though he was still not a highly paid musician. He was still doing arrangements for small fees whenever a request came his way; he still may have worked at the sports center in Los Angeles or had another daytime job instead.

Freddy was very proud of his brother, as he would say in many

---

* The *Jazz Discographies Unlimited* date is 1941; a Klaus Teubig discography to be published by the Scarecrow Press/Institute of Jazz Studies, Rutgers University, says 1938–1939.

public interviews and performances. Ike was always glad to see Nat, regarding him first and foremost as a brother and second as a star. Eddie wasn't living at home. By 1939, he had already changed his base to Philadelphia, where he had married a Philadelphia woman named Elizabeth "Betty" Coles, a professional pianist. They had bought a house, and Eddie had become the adoptive father of her five children by an earlier marriage.

When Nat passed through Philadelphia, playing in the Sheraton Hotel in 1942, Eddie and Betty played host to the trio and Nadine; Nat and his wife later did the same several times for Eddie and Betty in Los Angeles.

In Manhattan, the trio usually stayed in a YMCA or a hotel in Harlem. Those were their only choices, because the midtown hotels were segregated de facto and would remain that way for a number of years. The trio's professional schedule in 1942 was similar to the previous year's. The men performed at Kelly's Stable, where Billie Holiday was singing again. Billy Daniels, another well-known singer, came in during Nat's engagement, too. The trio was still the intermission group, playing opposite "Hot Lips" Page's headlining group for a while. Nat's old friend Scoville Browne, a saxophonist who had been raised in Chicago, was playing with Page. Ralph Watkins, the club owner, told Browne how proud he was of himself because he was paying decent salaries; the King Cole Trio was earning $165 a week, which actually was neither good nor bad pay; it was all right. Nat's trio was charming the audiences, who loved the style of singing—"a whispery thing," Scoville Browne called it. He loved it, too.

Essentially Nat and the trio were still struggling. Few people except for the club audiences where he played had heard of him. He also recorded without his trio for wartime V-Disk records; Shad Collins played trumpet, Illinois Jacquet tenor sax, Gene Englund bass, and J. C. Heard drums, with Nat singing on "Heads," "Pro Sky," "It Had to Be You," and "I Can't Give You Anything but Love."*

When Nat returned to Los Angeles, he made a record with tenor saxophonist Lester Young, an exceptionally smooth stylist with a mellow, subtle tone, in comparison with Jacquet's fiery, sometimes screaming, and completely uninhibited Southwestern approach. Though both were brilliant, no two styles could have been less alike. Young's concept would have the greater influence on the playing of generations to come. Red Callender played bass in the Cole-Young trio, which chose "Indiana," "Tea for Two," "Body and

---

*Teubig says the recording date was later in the 1940s.

Soul" and "I Can't Get Started" in July 1942. Nat did not sing. Jazz aficionados regarded the record as a classic, probably Nat's most spectacular performance as a jazz pianist on any recording. It was done on a very small label and produced by Norman Granz, then a fledgling jazz impressario. The group's songs were among the best of their era, and the records were produced about two weeks be-fore the Petrillo ban on instrumentalists' recording began. James C. Petrillo, head of the musicians union, called for an instrumentalists' strike against the record companies, because they were underpaying musicians for recording. The strike lasted until late 1943, when the companies began to sign agreements with the union on behalf of musicians.

Staying in Los Angeles, Nat's trio accepted another offer from Herb Rose—the owner of the 331 Club between Normandy and Irola on Eighth Street in West Los Angeles—to play as the house group, entertaining musicians, actors, song pluggers, press agents, songwriters, record and film company employees, and executives in town. Judy Garland, Lena Horne, and Cab Calloway sometimes went to the intimate club and sat in, doing a number or two with the Cole trio, for the pleasure of the music.

"The 331 Club became the place to go," Cole reminisced years later. "We used to get quite a lot of movie stars down there. It was just a small room, and the place was always jammed."

By that time, Les Paul had found Nat again. Les had noticed that all his friends in Chicago seemed to start leaving town in 1936. With his usual humorous way of sizing up events, he thought that everybody in Chicago who played jazz had gotten on the same bus that year and headed for New York. So he went that way himself for a while and took his own trio, with Chet Atkins's brother, Jimmy, also a guitarist, and bassist Ernie Newton, into Fred Waring's or-chestra in 1937. His trio was "happening" in the Waring band until 1941, he saw with joy. Then he headed for Los Angeles and, as usual, immediately started jamming again, sometimes with Nat. Les thought Nat's piano style remained essentially unchanged from his Chicago days. Nat's touch became lighter, and his playing gained clarity, however, as he matured. In Los Angeles, as he had done in Chicago and Harlem, Les headed for the black neighborhoods to jam. Les never understood segregation, and he knew that Nat didn't, either.

More people were becoming aware that Nat Cole and the trio were in town. The 331 Club was another step up the ladder for the painstaking, dogged Cole group, whose magical and highly stylized yet easeful sound dispelled any hint of the persistence it had taken for the musicians to arrive in the club. In the anxious days of the war, the King Cole Trio's sound had a soothing effect, without losing the rhythmic impulses of the big bands. As the Big Band era began to fade, nobody was laughing at the small group anymore. For one thing, musicians in the big bands were being drafted for World War II. Nat's trio was affected, also. Oscar Moore was called briefly by the army, but he returned to the group quickly. Then in 1942, Wesley Prince, who was married but had no children, was drafted. Red Callender replaced him for a little while. At the end of 1942, Callender recorded as part of the trio for the small Excelsior Label, on two instrumentals—"All for You" and "Vom Vim Veedle"—which received excellent reviews. (The rights to this record and others that Nat recorded before signing a Capitol contract in 1943, eventually were bought by Capitol Records, Inc. They were released for wide distribution and began to receive critical praise for the first time in 1943. "All for You" became Nat's first record to rank on the popularity charts.)

Callender, however, had his own strong ideas for his career; he would become a successful studio and broadcast musician and composer. Eventually Nat found a bassist who was happy to work as a sideman in the King Cole Trio and make it a priority. Pasadena-born Johnny Miller, who had witnessed Cole's ill-starred entry into Long Beach as a part of *Shuffle Along,* had the attitude needed for the long haul of touring. Miller, who had already met Nat on the scene, was working with Eddie Beal's group in San Diego when he received a telephone call. Nat said, "Would you like to come and try out with the group for a while?" Johnny said, "That will be all right."

Miller was married and had two daughters, and so he had no fear of being drafted unless there was a general call-up that included fathers. Oscar Moore, who had a wife and son, was in the same position as Miller. Nat himself had been classified for health reasons as 4-F. One version said that he had "nervous hypertension." Another story claimed that he was disqualified for having flat feet. That seemed correct to Johnny Miller, who noticed Nat's feet always troubled him. He was always pruning and scraping his calluses and corns; he even walked as if he had flat feet, despite his athleticism and elegant posture. In New York City a few years later, a new friend, music publisher Ivan Mogull, introduced Nat to a podiatrist, Ivan's father, whom Nat visited for treatments.

Miller joined Nat and Oscar at the 331 Club. In a brief time, it became clear that Johnny Miller fitted in. He never discussed his technique of playing with Nat, but if Johnny were playing in the lower register for a long time, Nat might suggest to him, "Try playing a little higher for a while." Johnny would do that, and it would work. He would also take some fleet, brief solos. Every now and then, one of the group would try something a little different, based on his instinct about what would suit the song, make it brighter, lighter, more ineffable, swinging, interesting and expressive. Oscar, who worked on the music with Nat in detail at times to determine exactly what they would play, felt especially free and creative in live performances. There was a well-analyzed design to the distinctive interpretations of the Cole trio.

Both Nat and Oscar were so contemporary that they defied labels. Rooted in the Swing era, they nevertheless heralded the more progressive jazz style emerging in Harlem—bebop—and their harmonies and improvisations were new and surprising to their audiences. Furthermore, they played so clearly and articulately, with all their notes ringing and communicating, that they set a standard that never really was surpassed for quality and fluidity or made to sound outdated by later trios. Nat's work also had some adeptly integrated boogie-woogie inflections, a hallmark of his Chicago background. What really fascinated critics, however, were his elaborations on the chords he played, "adding major and minor sevenths" to create "five-note chords," explained Will Friedwald succinctly in his liner notes for an album, *Birth of the Cole.* The technique expanded the jazz idiom and led to the bebop style. Soon Ahmad Jamal, the pianist, and then trumpeter Miles Davis would take lessons from the spare style and dynamics of the Cole trio's cohesive work, Miles learning from Ahmad. Later, pianist Bill Evans, who worked in Miles's group, displayed Nat's influence in his own innovative, modern trio work.

Johnny Miller could sing in tight harmony with the group, too. In March 1943, Miller did his first recordings with the trio for the Excelsior label. The songs were later released, along with the two tunes on which Red Callender had played, by Capitol Records. Johnny's first songs on record with the trio were "I'm Lost," "Beautiful Moons Ago," which was written by Oscar Moore and sung as a haunting bittersweet ballad by Cole, and "Let's Spring One." Then in November 1943, for Premier, the trio recorded. "F.S.T.," an instrumental, "Got a Penny, Benny," "Let's Pretend," with exhilarating work by Oscar and Nat, and "My Lips Remember Your Kisses."

What the group needed most of all by the end of 1943 was even more exposure from a hit tune, a record that would make the racial crossover and become popular with white Americans, as well as a record contract with a major label.

Red Callender recalled that neither he nor Nat had any idea of their futures. Callender knew that in the 331 Club, Nat was playing in a spot that offered high visibility to a regionally well-known musician.

Both he and Nat felt fortunate when they got any lucky break. For example, "Pops" Foster, a forerunner of Jimmy Blanton on bass, was supposed to play for a Decca Sepia Series date at the recording studio on Melrose Avenue. But "Pops" became sick. A tough-minded business agent in the black musicians' union recommended Red Callender as the replacement. Callender's reputation was building on the scene, as Nat's was. So Callender recorded "On the Sunny Side of the Street." In retrospect, he would feel that he had been in the right place at the right time. He had played with Lee and Lester Young as "a student," when he hadn't been ready for anything as prestigious and demanding as the bass chair in Duke Ellington's band. Later he was recommended for that, as the replacement for Jimmy Blanton. Red was establishing himself by then on the West Coast; his head was "someplace else," as he put it, as a performer and composer, leader and teacher, so he decided not to go into the Ellington band, though Duke remained an idol.

In the late 1930s and early 1940s, however, neither Red nor Nat knew how far they would go. They saw each other often; their paths ran parallel, crossed and doubled back on each other's. Red observed Nat's characteristic persistence and willingness to deal with whatever happened. One Sunday in town, a storm with strong winds knocked a tree across Nat's Studebaker. He was supposed to pick Red up and drive to a jam session at Billy Berg's Trouville, where musicians earned seven to ten dollars each for playing. Nat showed up with his car so dented that Red was surprised the car could run in that shape. However, Nat shrugged it off as unimportant and drove them to the club. He doesn't let anything stop him, Red thought.

Nat, too, was in the right city at the right time, making friends with the right people—a brilliant manager and the people who would found a brave new recording company.

Chapter Four

ENTER CARLOS GASTEL

G len Wallichs was a businessman who owned a store called Music City at Sunset Boulevard and Vine Street. He was a music fan as well as a businessman, a record-store owner who loved to encourage and mingle with musicians. It excited him to hear a good song and sell it. He liked jazz and admired the imaginative musicians who invented and interpreted it. Not a very stylish or artistic man, he was a salesman. His haircuts were so unattractive that people joked about finding out who his barber was so they could avoid him.

Glen Wallichs had the insight, however, to open a record store and invite some of his favorite musicians to record there. In Music City, which he ran with his brother, the records were 78 rpm wax acetates. If the recording sessions didn't go well, the acetates had to be melted down, so the musicians could try again. The store had one microphone; a musician had to step forward to the microphone each time he was supposed to play a solo.

One day, Wallichs invited Nat, Harry "Sweets" Edison, a drummer named Clifford "Juicy" Owens (whose nickname suggested the reason why he would die young), and George "Red" Callender to come to the store and record. Dexter Gordon, the tenor saxophonist, then developing as an imaginative, forceful bebop stylist and a masterful ballad player, worked with the group of older musicians that day. Stan Britt's biography, *Dexter Gordon,* suggests the young, enormously tall, tenor saxophonist with a driving, plaintive, fluid style got the chance to play this date because of Nat Cole's encouragement. Nat did introduce Dexter to Glen Wallichs. Harry "Sweets" Edison thought the songs they played—"I've Found a New Baby," "Rosetta," "Sweet Lorraine," and "I've Blowed and Gone"— sounded wonderful, despite the unorthodox setting. The date was most likely in 1943, though it could have been before then, even in 1940. In 1940, Dexter left Los Angeles with the Lionel Hampton band for three years. After November 1943, Nat was supposed to record exclusively for Capitol Records, Inc. Once Wallichs started that company, he dissociated himself from the retail business, leaving it to his brother, Clyde, to run. The record, billed as the Dexter Gordon Quintet, was later released on the Mercury label in the 1940s. Nat didn't use any of the pseudonyms he would have had to use after signing an exclusive contract with Capitol in late 1943. Still without a hit after he recorded in Wallich's store, Nat kept plugging, playing at the 331 Club.

Nat wanted Carlos Gastel, a well-known, gregarious, worldly, and effective manager, who was then in charge of the Stan Kenton band, to start booking the King Cole Trio. So Nat approached Carlos, but the big, burly fellow didn't think he could do anything for a small group. Carlos had worked with dance bands, Sonny Dunham's, for one, before Kenton's. However, he had been aware of Nat for several years and liked Nat's music. In 1941, Nat's first tour to the East had been booked by Tom Rockwell of the General Amusement Corporation.* Rockwell was Carlos's "guru," as Lee Young referred to him.

Eventually, Carlos's sister Chickie, a quick-witted woman with good taste in music and an intuitive sense of the business, urged Carlos to manage Nat. So in 1943 Carlos Gastel stopped by to see Nat and told him he would like to manage him and the trio. It was then earning about $225 a week, according to some versions.

---

*It would become General Artists Corporation, under whose aegis Carlos would work as Nat's personal manager.

Carlos added that he wouldn't take any money from the King Cole Trio until it was earning eight hundred dollars a week. Nat was unsettled by that; he thought it was a farfetched, high figure, and he wanted Carlos to take a percentage right away so that he would promote the trio with seriousness. "You'll never make anything if you wait for that much," Nat told Carlos. Carlos said he didn't need the impetus. The men didn't sign a contract, either. They simply shook hands on their agreement. Carlos then booked the King Cole Trio into the Orpheum Theatre in Los Angeles for one thousand dollars a week. Nat was overjoyed. Carlos took his percentage. His tally showed that the theater earned over thirty thousand dollars in gross receipts during the first week of the King Cole Trio's engagement.

Soon the trio became a wildly successful and consistently high-paid group. After expenses were deducted from the trio's gross, Carlos took his percentage—probably 10 percent. From James Haskins's book *Nat King Cole: The Man and His Music* come the following figures: Twenty percent of the gross, after Carlos took his percentage, went for overhead—booking, management, travel expenses. Sidemen paid for their own hotel rooms but not for transportation. Cole took half of the remainder of the money. Then, according to Maria Cole, who would become Nat's second wife, Oscar took 60 percent of the rest, while Johnny got 40 percent. Nat also paid the men bonuses stemming from royalties from his records. As the 1940s progressed, Oscar sometimes earned $1,500 or more a week, and Johnny's pay averaged $600 a week. Technically, sidemen never earn royalties from records, but Nat wanted to pay his men, because their records were excellent money-earners.

Carlos managed Nat for the rest of Nat's life, except for the last year, when new people entered the picture and took over. However, throughout the 1940s, Carlos and Nat never signed a contract, working together with mutual trust. Eventually Carlos devoted most, if not all, of his attention to managing Cole. Several of Cole's intimates were under the impression that Carlos was given the choice of making Nat his priority or else dropping the singer. Carlos chose to stay with Nat as his primary client. That was lucky for Cole, his friends thought, because Gastel had always known exactly what to do for Cole's career. They believed Nat would not have become a star in the first place without Carlos.

Nat said the same thing about the "happy walrus," as Carlos's friends called him. "Carlos and I thought generally the same way," Nat told John Tynan for a *Down Beat* article. "This is really unusual in an artist-manager relationship. Generally an artist signs with a manager because he thinks the manager can do him some good and leaves it at that. Often the manager has ideas very different from those of the artist . . . basically different, I mean. This wasn't the case here, though. I knew the direction I wanted to travel in and realized Carlos could help me. Actually he was thinking on something very different from his past associations. He'd managed the Stan Kenton band and other groups and acts that were nowhere near our trio format. It was a gamble for him, but he was willing to give it a try. I can honestly say that much of the success I enjoy today I owe to Carlos. Our association was—and is—a good one, and it worked out the way I wanted it to."

The free-wheeling, high-living Carlos, who had grown up in Mexico, the hard-drinking son of a hard-drinking German father and a Honduran mother, loved nurturing Nat's career.* Carlos may have played the the trumpet himself as a discerning, music-loving amateur. He fell in love with the world of entertainers while he was a student at UCLA. Not only did he value Nat's musical gifts but, in Nat, Carlos found a warm, undemanding companion with a professional temperament. Though Nat was never a very heavy drinker, he, too, loved to sit and talk with his friends until dawn, as Carlos did. For Nat, the nightlife style of drinking fitted in well with his sociability. As a drinker, Carlos went overboard, however.

Carlos didn't believe that he would live a very long time, he confided in his friend, Alan Livingston, an artists and repertoire man who later became president of Capitol Records. Gastel said his father had died of a heart attack in his fifties, and he was convinced that the same thing would happen to him. In the meantime, he wanted to get the most enjoyment that he could out of life. For relaxation, he liked to get on his forty-foot Twin-Screw cruiser and sail down the coast to Mexico. On working days in New York, one man recalled, Carlos drank a couple of Bloody Marys at the Plaza Hotel at about 11 A.M. He was always looking for someone to join him, because he hated being alone. Music publisher and songwriter Marvin Fisher, who later became an intimate friend of Nat Cole, spent several years running the West Coast branch of his family's firm in Los Angeles, and he sometimes used to join Carlos for a drink between 11 A.M. and noon at the Cock and Bull on Sunset Boulevard near Beverly Hills. Marvin knew he could find Carlos at

*One source says his father was Honduran and his mother Austrian while all his other friends surviving in 1990 say the opposite.

that restaurant. Fisher described him as "a big lovable drunk and a brilliant manager." Sparky Tavares, who became Nat's valet and constant companion in 1949, saw Carlos drink only at night, beginning at 5 P.M. and going into the wee hours. It was fashionable for people to do so, as Sparky delicately put it. Sparky never saw Carlos take a drink during the day. Along with most other people, he also never saw Carlos's drinking interfere with his highly professional work, even though a couple of Cole's friends cast aspersions on Carlos's performance in the long run. Gossip was a normal part of the competitive milieu around Cole, according to Carlos's friends, who were numerous. Marvin Fisher, for one, never saw Carlos's powers diminish an iota over the years. Carlos's clients became thriving stars. At one time, he managed Peggy Lee, Nellie Lutcher, Mel Torme, and the majority of Capitol's premier recording stars. He concentrated on Nat's career, however.

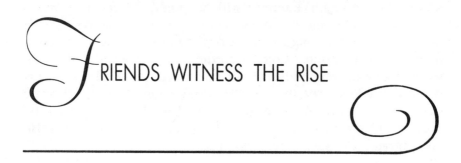

Chapter Five

FRIENDS WITNESS THE RISE

John Kraus had a job in a research laboratory in a defense plant, where he was assigned to take air checks on Saturday mornings in Los Angeles. During the course of his job, he discovered that Al Jarvis, the host of the "Make Believe Ballroom," featured Nat King Cole every Saturday morning at 11:45 A.M. Except for its copycat name, the show—most likely on KLAC—had nothing to do with Martin Block's "Make Believe Ballroom" popular in New York City. Jarvis introduced Nat; they chatted for a while. Then Nat played three or four songs live on a studio piano. John Kraus loved Nat's style. So every Saturday morning, he tuned into the show.

Though he had no connection to the music industry at that time, Kraus began going to the 331 Club to hear Nat, for the sheer joy of listening to the music and relaxing in the offbeat, sophisticated atmosphere. John took his fiancée, Jean, to the club, too, because he wanted her to hear the King Cole Trio. Nat never announced Oscar or Johnny Miller to the audience. When John gave some discs to Nat, Cole was very grateful and introduced John and Jean to the sidemen. Each time John went to the club after that, he said hello to the trio and bantered with them about how life was treating all of them. Nat asked John and Jean what song they would like to hear. Since they had begun dating in April, they asked for "I'll Remember April." Jean told Nat, "That's our song." After that, Cole often played it for the couple.

Oscar was having trouble with one of his guitar strings. He told John, "It's so worn out that I'm afraid I'll turn on an amp and I'll pick up the World Series game."

Wartime rationing was so strict that Oscar couldn't buy electrical cord. Because John worked in a defense plant, he could get some. On the other hand, John needed gas. So Oscar traded his gas stamps for John's cord.

The news then circulated that Nat would be leaving the 331 Club, about eight months after John and Jean had begun to frequent the place. Nat was taking the trio to play at the Orpheum Theatre in Los Angeles, then to tour the Northwest. The owner of the 331 Club was throwing a farewell party. Because they were Nat's friends, John and Jean were invited to stay for the party after the club closed on the trio's last night there. Many of Nat's other friends showed up. They were drinking at the bar, eating the food piled high on platters on a buffet table, and chatting with Nat. Someone called out, "Nat, play something for us."

Without hesitation, Nat went to the piano and began playing solo. Everyone stayed at the bar, talking and laughing so noisily that they couldn't hear Nat. However, Jean, who had fallen in love with the trio's music and the ambience of the room, went to sit quietly with John near the piano. For Jean, the night was bittersweet. She always treasured her romantic memories. Even then, she knew what an incredible talent she was sitting close to. Nat played "I'll Remember April" for the couple, who seemed to be the only people in the room listening attentively to him. A woman called out, "Nat, play the mashed-potato song."

Jean was a bit annoyed at the way the woman shouted for a song by its wrong name, but Nat seemed happy. He smiled, knowing what she meant. So did John Kraus, because he had taken an air check of the song—"Solid Potato Salad"—on his glass-based discs coated with lacquer. Nat didn't record that song, which he had written, until May 1945, with Capitol's approval. He had played the up-tempo tune often enough at the 331 Club, however, to give it a cult following among the habitués there. He sang about a wonderful potato salad, "solid potato salad," and urged a fellow named Jack, who often popped up in Cole's songs, to heap potato salad on his plate and come back fast for a second helping.

It was one of several songs about food that Nat liked to sing in his early days, when food money wasn't plentiful, and it had just begun to come in. The song had an engaging pulse and a zany lyric that amused Jean, and it annoyed her that the hubbub at the bar continued, with no one paying attention to Nat singing at his own farewell party. Nat didn't seem bothered in the least. He never did, she thought.

Soon afterward, she and John went to see the trio at the Orpheum Theatre, "the big time," in Jean's mind. At intermission, she and John went backstage, because they had been invited to visit Nat there. She and John were wearing new beige-colored garbardine zoot suits with big shoulders and long jackets, which they had bought at Sy Devore's for the event. Everyone with some fashion sense, including Nat Cole, liked to shop at Devore's, a popular tailor in downtown Los Angeles near Music City, the record store. The idea of their friend Nat appearing at the Orpheum thrilled the couple enough to send them to Devore's.

About twenty-one years old then, Jean became aware that she and John, in his late twenties, were the only white people in the dressing room. Everybody seemed so cool to her. She felt so hip to be there, dressed well, and careful not to say "hep"—a square's word—lest she be pegged as square. A big, round, heavy tumbler of gleaming cut glass with a liquid in it was passed around. She had never had a drink of whiskey before, but she took a hefty slug. It was straight bourbon. She tried to act as if it were usual for her. She hoped that she was holding her face steady, not wincing or grimacing; Nat smiled and didn't bat an eyelash as he observed her. She went back into the audience and, warm and flushed, watched the rest of the show in a daze.

For the booking in the Orpheum, the King Cole Trio shared the bill with Freddie Slack and his orchestra as the headliners. Nat told Barry Ulanov that the prospect of their first legitimate theater booking had filled the trio with trepidation: "We didn't know what to do, how to do, or anything." The trio got all the applause in the theater, singing "Do Nothing 'Til You Hear from Me," a boogie-woogie medley including "All for You," "That Ain't Right," "Straighten Up and Fly Right." And fans yelled for "F.S.T." A critic wrote that "it was Freddie Slack's show when it started but Nat Cole's when it ended."

Cole's trio played in the Orpheum again four weeks later on a bill with Benny Carter, though it was unusual for a group to have a return engagement in the same year.

The men headed south to play in San Diego, then set out on a tour of the Pacific Northwest, including Seattle, the Golden Gate in San Francisco with Jimmie Lunceford's band, the Orpheum in Oakland, where the trio was the sole attraction, and then back to Hollywood, east to Washington, D.C., and home to Los Angeles again. John Kraus didn't make any more recordings. Nat suspended his regular personal appearances on the "Make Believe Ballroom." By the time Cole went into the Orpheum, John Kraus had a big cardboard carton filled with recordings taken from the radio show. When John and Jean were married in 1945, they kept the air checks with them in their house, though they didn't really have space for them.

John went to work for Capitol Records as a recording engineer on April 18, 1949. He would work on several of Nat's great hits: "Those Lazy, Hazy, Crazy Days of Summer," the "Wild is Love" album completed in two days, and a jazz album recorded in the mid-1950s, "After Midnight," on which Nat played piano and sang. In the meantime, John Kraus stored the air checks from the Jarvis show in Capitol's library. By then, John felt, nobody would want them, because Nat had made so many records of better technical quality. For some reason, John stored the air checks later at the Pantages theater and never went to reclaim them. For all he knew, on the twenty-fifth anniversary of Nat's death, the records might still be in the Pantages. John regretted having put them there, because they were rarities on which Nat played the piano live as a soloist. "Solid Potato Salad" was on one of the discs. So was "I'll Remember April"; "Straighten Up and Fly Right" was on another.

Chapter Six

A RECORD CONTRACT, AND THE HITS BEGIN

The trio had been playing in the 331 Club in 1943, when Carlos Gastel arrived one night, shaking hands with everyone he knew in the audience. Introduced to someone new, he immediately impressed that person by saying "I know you, aren't you the person who wrote . . ." or "Didn't you sing at. . . ?" and "Hello, trouper." His friends thought his interest in other people and his informal, ebullient personality made him such an effective manager. With a drink in one hand, the square-faced, overweight man, with his little upturned nose contrasting with his big physique, made his way to Nat at the piano and told him the good news. Nat and the trio had an exclusive seven-year recording contract with Capitol Records. Nat would not be permitted to record for anyone else, but he would receive a 5 percent royalty, the maximum allowed by the recording industry until the 1960s. The seven-year term was the longest period for which contracts were signed.

Capitol had been founded in 1942 by three partners: Glen Wallichs, Buddy DeSylva, a producer at Paramount Pictures, and the prolific and great songwriter Johnny Mercer, who saw the company as a chance to record the best musicians doing the best music, including his own. Musicians had the highest respect for Mercer and the small company. Wallichs's friend Buddy DeSylva put up ten thousand dollars to start, then fifteen thousand more, and found himself too busy to get involved in running the company actively from day to day. Wallichs gave the figures to Richard Hubler for a *Saturday Evening Post* article—"$12,000 a Week Preacher's Boy"—published on July 17, 1954. Wallichs was the firm's administrator, while Mercer divided his time between his own songwriting career and building the artists' stable for Capitol. Among its early artists was Margaret Whiting. Ella Mae Morse had a hit quickly with "Cow Cow Boogie," with Freddie Slack and his orchestra. Jo Stafford and the Pied Pipers signed up right away. Mercer recorded many of his own songs. His first very successful record—a "click," in the publicity slang of the day—was "On the Atchison, Topeka and Sante Fe"; it won an Academy Award in 1946. The bandleader Paul Weston, Jo Stafford's husband, and Mercer were the people operating in the recording studio when the company began as a very small fish in a very large pond.

The big successful companies then were RCA Victor, Columbia and Decca; Capitol would be among the first of the small companies to gain recognition as an important label. Its recordings for children became leaders of the genre in the early years of the company. Right away, Capitol bought the rights to some of Cole's records done earlier for other companies. The 1942 record of "All for You" with "Vom Vim Veedle" on the other side, done on the Excelsior label with Oscar and Red Callender, was released in late 1943 by Capitol. It became the first trio record to show up on the charts; "All for You" ranked in eighteenth place by November 20, 1943, according to *Billboard* magazine.* "Vom Vim Veedle" also pleased the critics, who called it a delightful bit of nonsense.

It's likely that Nat's recording of "All for You" as the trio's first tune to become a hit actually led to the recording contract arranged by Carlos. In the fall of 1942, Dave Dexter, who had forsaken New York City and *Down Beat,* began a job as a full-time artists and repertoire producer at Capitol Records. It then had only a tiny office below Sunset and Vine—"below Drugstore corner," as

---

*According to *Top Pop Singles, 1940–1955* by Joel Whitburn, based on *Billboard* supplemented by *Variety.*

it was called by insiders, near Music City. At the time, Capitol wasn't putting out many records because of the recording ban.

As Dave Dexter recalled, a young white man—"a kid in his early twenties; we were all kids in our early twenties"—came to Capitol with four little trio masters and asked Dexter whether the company wanted to buy them. "I listened to them, thought they were good, and went to tell Wallichs. So we bought them for twenty-five dollars a master. The kid thought that he was doing well at that price per song in those days. He was the guy who had produced the records." One of them was "All for You", which was released with "Vom Vim Veedle" on the flip side. The records had been previously released in a tiny pressing by Excelsior Records, a very small company in Los Angeles, which may have put out a total of one hundred different records during its existence. Otis and Leon René, who were black, owned the firm and used very clever techniques to produce the records in the face of wartime shortages of materials. The few people who had heard the Cole records on the radio in the area had liked them. When "All for You" was released on the Capitol label and climbed onto the charts, Capitol asked Carlos to sign Nat to a contract in late 1943.

Paul Weston, who alternated all the time with Johnny Mercer in the recording booth for Capitol in its earliest days, knew that Johnny had the final word on whether to buy the masters from Excelsior. At Capitol, Mercer made the decision about whom to record, while Wallichs tended the business side. Mercer had already become a staunch fan of Nat's when the trio played in the Radio Room across from an NBC studio.

In a *Down Beat* interview, Nat confirmed the story of how the trio went to Capitol. "One night at the 331 Club, in late '43 it was, Johnny Mercer and Glen Wallichs came in . . . and asked if I'd be interested in recording for them. Well that sounded groovy to me. Of course we had been with Decca, but I wasn't too happy there— so I decided to go in with Mercer and Wallichs and just see what happened." Carlos negotiated the contract.

Nat walked into a company that had begun with an office measuring twelve by fourteen feet, with all the masters kept in the drawer of one desk. The founders functioned on top of one another. One day, as Wallichs was trying to arrange a business deal for distribution in Pittsburgh, Johnny Mercer and Paul Weston were listening to a record a few feet away. Wallichs called out, "Do you have to play that so *loud*?" Mercer didn't care anything about distribution, Weston recalled. "He got really bugged when he found out you had to have regular releases," Weston added.

Eventually the company took over two floors in the building, with future president of Capitol, Alan Livingston, future vice president Jim Conkling, and artists and repertoire man Dave Dexter on the staff; soon they went to offices above Music City. There Weston had his own office for the first time. Dexter, too, regarded his tiny private office near the front door with affection.

The little company grew throughout the 1940s because of the collective enterprise of many talented instrumentalists, singers, orchestra leaders and arrangers as well as the gifted men behind the scenes. Nat and the trio recorded for the first time at the usual Melrose studio of C. P. MacGregor, on November 30, 1943. As he always did in those days, Nat selected the tunes which the trio played for its first session, and again for sessions on December 15, 1943, and January 17 and March 6, 1944. Mercer usually discussed the repertoire with Cole.

"Nobody told Nat what to record," Weston recalled. "We knew what he liked to sing. 'Sweet Lorraine' was one of his first songs. And he knew what he liked. And it was usually the best choice for him. There was very little pressure at Capitol in those days. We loved music, and we could hardly wait to get to the studio. Nat was a remarkably gracious person to work with. He made recordings with a spark. And when you were in the recording booth for Nat, it was as if you were sitting in a rocking chair. All we had to do was get the balance with the guitar and bass at the beginning."

"Straighten Up and Fly Right" went on a record during the first session. His sidemen thought that Nat had a genius for selecting songs. He tried them out, honed and polished them with the trio, working on some passages especially with Oscar. If he felt the songs were successful and due for long weathering, he put them into the repertoire for good.

During his first seven years in Los Angeles, he had had plenty of time to choose and polish the songs away from the spotlight. Nat told interviewers that one of the reasons for his trio's success was its repertoire, which had been carefully chosen and practiced. He didn't pick up a song one day because it was trendy; he stayed with what he knew was good for him and the trio as a tightly knit, swinging, virtuosic and emotionally affecting unit. If he played a trendy song, he did it only because a radio-show host had made a special request for Nat to play something popularized by someone else. The audience wanted to hear it.

The trio played six instrumentals for its first Capitol dates, among them "Jumpin' at Capitol," "The Man I Love," "Body and Soul," "What Is This Thing Called Love?" and "Easy Listening Blues." "Prelude in C Sharp Minor," the sixth instrumental, began with Cole playing the Rachmaninoff composition straight; then it became transmuted by the trio into a swinging jazz creation with intimate, fun-loving style. Among the songs that Nat sang and made into Cole classics were "Gee, Baby, Ain't I Good to You," "If You Can't Smile and Say Yes (Please Don't Cry and Say No)," which Timmie Rogers wrote especially for Nat, "Sweet Lorraine," "Embraceable You," "It's Only a Paper Moon," "Look What You've Done to Me," "I Realize Now," and "I Can't See for Lookin'." Cole's connection with Capitol made it easy for his old friend Timmie to work with Johnny Mercer, who encouraged Timmie to try lyric writing. Timmie wrote several songs that Nat, Sarah Vaughan, and other well-known jazz musicians recorded. "I'm Crazy" was one of Timmie's tunes that Nat sang. Of all the songs that Nat chose for his Capitol debut, his own novelty song, "Straighten Up and Fly Right," with "I Can't See for Lookin'" on the other side, became the hit he was looking for. It showed up as number nine in the charts beginning on April 9, 1944, and remained there for seven weeks.

Without any education in long-range business planning, except for his own tenacity and resourcefulness (and without a crystal ball), Nat had sold the copyright for "Straighten Up and Fly Right" to Mills Music, Inc. Nat was crestfallen, when he learned that the royalties for the music and lyrics were going to Mills Music, which had its name on the song as the composer. Nat sued Mills and lost. However, as the performer, Nat had a very respectable financial success with his royalties from the record sales. So he had to accept the situation—and he lit up a cigarette. That was his way of dealing with stress; cigarettes took the edge off calamities and gave him a lift. Pretty women, who flocked around him during his entire career, never dominated or affected his life to the extent that cigarettes did. Philip Morris was his brand, morning, noon, and night— and shaped his destiny.

Years later, Nat met Jack Mills of the music publishing firm that had bought the rights to "Straighten Up and Fly Right." Irving Mills had been the middleman. Jack had never offered to share any of the profits with Nat, though Jack had been approached several times through the years. Nat and Jack happened to be at the same party in

New York. Nat chatted with the man in a seemingly amiable way, others noticed, and never gave Mills any hint of the great unhappiness that he had caused.

By the time his path crossed Mills's at the party, Nat no longer needed any of the money from his first hit; he also enjoyed more than enough prestige. Eventually, the song credits began to read, "By Nat King Cole and Mills Music."

While Nat was becoming a national star, his friend Lee Young, the drummer, was playing regularly in the studios in Los Angeles. In one of those racial quirks that has sometimes favored black drummers, he was chosen over white drummers for studio work because he was black. Whites regarded black drummers as the best, most authentic players. Lee was a good connection for his friends: bandleader Jimmie Lunceford, trombonist Trummy Young, Red Callender, and other black musicians sometimes found work in the studios through Lee. Even Lester, Lee's brother, played for some MGM films because of Lee's recommendation. Lee was a reliable musician with good taste in music and good business sense.

One day, a white musician named Scott approached Lee in a club where he was playing and asked for help in teaching Mickey Rooney to play drums. Rooney was starring in a film called "Strike Up the Band" with Judy Garland; he was supposed to play drums for a big band in the film. An MGM fellow had been unable to teach Mickey to play drums. Then a Twentieth Century–Fox man had been called in, but he failed, too. So MGM had gone to Scott, who hit upon the bright idea to ask Lee Young to teach Mickey.

Lee said, "I'll know in a few minutes if I can teach him."

Knowing that Mickey was a dancer, as Lee had also been, Lee said, "Do you know the time step?"

Mickey said, "Yes."

"And the break?" Lee asked.

"Yes," Mickey replied.

So Lee said, "Do them with your hands, then hit the cymbal last."

Mickey could do it. That success gave Lee even greater prestige in the studios. Eventually, he was asked to bring his friend Nat Cole to MGM to perform for Lucille Ball. MGM was thinking of having Nat and his trio play their new hit, "Straighten Up and Fly Right," in a film starring Lucille Ball. Lucille listened to Nat demonstrate the song as a soloist. When he finished, she delivered her opinion.

"That's the filthiest song I ever heard in my life," she said.

She was dead serious, Lee and Nat noticed right away; she wasn't kidding a bit. Something about a monkey urging an old buzzard to straighten up and fly right had touched her imagination. In her mind, the monkey was urging the buzzard, whom Nat called "Jack" in the song, to have an erection. Lee understood that a brilliant comedienne might get that message from the lyrics. So the song could not make the transition from the True Light Baptist Church to Lucille Ball's movie.

As they drove home after the audition, Lee and Nat joked with each other. "She could have been right, if you listen carefully," one of them said, and the other laughed.

By May 1944, it was clear that the King Cole Trio and Capitol Records had reason to celebrate. "Straighten Up and Fly Right" would sell half a million records; Capitol's men and industry insiders thought it would have sold more if wartime shortages of materials hadn't prevented the requisite printings to satisfy the demand. However, 500,000 constituted a major hit in those days, when 200,000 was considered a hit. Nat, Oscar, and Johnny were so happy that they had to caution themselves not to be disappointed if the brush with fame didn't last. "All For You" had done well enough, just after the Petrillo ban on instrumentals ended. People were glad to have instrumentals back. During the musicians' strike, singers had made records without instrumental accompaniment for the most part; choral groups provided the backup usually. "Straighten Up and Fly Right" had been a novelty, and even its flip side, "I Can't See for Lookin'," was seducing people to put their nickels in jukeboxes. The trio knew that it was somewhere on the map at least for the moment.

Chapter Seven

MERGING JAZZ AND POP AND CLIMBING ON THE ROLLER COASTER

*N*at's commercial success didn't suddenly lift him out of the world of jazz instrumentalists, nor did he want it to. He continued to travel and play in their circles happily, even though jazz musicians were usually lesser known than the pop stars. Nat still considered himself part of the jazz scene, and regularly performed in jam sessions. In the early 1940s, Norman Granz, then a young film editor, started running the Trouville's Sunday sessions, with Nat as the pianist. Granz had fallen in love with jazz during his days as a college student in Los Angeles. The legend is that he consulted Nat, who was playing with his trio in local jazz clubs, for lessons in jazz appreciation.

Billy Berg may have run jam sessions in his earlier club, the Capri on Pekoe and Lacicnaga, which closed in late 1941. A week later, he had the Trouville underway, where Granz took over the sessions. Eventually, Granz's sights rose higher. He began to dream of producing a major jazz concert. He planned it to take place at the

Philharmonic Auditorium in downtown Los Angeles at Pershing Square. The concert would pave the way for Granz's Jazz at the Philharmonic tours—in essence, traveling mini-jazz festivals.

Nat's trio was scheduled to perform in the concert, along with several other musicians on July 2, 1944. He had no inkling that he would ever be considered anything but an obscure, excellent jazz pianist who sang for diversion and to satisfy public demand. So, when he knew that he was going to be recorded in the Philharmonic auditorium concert, he dreamed up the pseudonym Shorty Nadine; he didn't want to run afoul of his exclusive recording contract with Capitol Records. Also scheduled for the concert were the trombonist J. J. Johnson, tenor saxophonists Illinois Jacquet and Jack McVea, trumpeter Shorty Sherock, with bassists Red Callender and Johnny Miller, drummer Lee Young, and Oscar Moore on guitar.

Les Paul was not recording for anyone in those days because he was in the army, stationed with the Armed Forces Radio Service in Los Angeles. He was not supposed to play as a civilian, as he understood his instructions. However, on July 2, the day of the concert at the Philharmonic, Les received a call from Nat, who said, as Les recalled, "Les, can you come to the Philharmonic and play with us today? We need you to sit in for Oscar. He's been shacking up in a room with a chick for three days, and we can't get him out. We're shoving pizzas under the door. So come and play."

Les stripped himself of all identification except for his uniform, he recalled. He reversed his name from Les Paul to Paul Leslie enroute to the Philharmonic. And he arrived to play without having rehearsed for a single moment.

"The first number we beat off. I threw my amp under the piano," he recalled, "and we took off. Nat and I had been playing together so much for so long. I had jammed every place he ever played. And we tore it apart. Nat and I chased each other; he played a run; I played a run. The pitch got so high, people were standing in their seats, *screaming*! Everyone was wearing a hat. I played a run. Nat slapped the piano keys with his hat. And everyone threw a hat into the air, in the audience, everyplace. It was so exciting to see that! The concert made Norman Granz's career!"

Apparently nobody from Capitol Records paid any attention to that jazz concert, or someone would have recognized Nat's piano style and seen through his transparent name inspired by his short wife, Nadine. The incident bespoke the marked division between the jazz and pop-music fields. However, Capitol's Dave Dexter, for one, became aware that Nat occasionally made records for other companies. So the incident also bespoke Capitol's unpressured attitude toward Nat's occasional moonlighting as an instrumentalist. Nat never moonlighted as a vocalist; his recorded work at the Philharmonic appealed to jazz audiences and didn't divert fans of his trio work on records and in public appearances. Those fans rarely knew about his virtuosity as a jazz pianist.

Other pseudonyms that Nat would use for his piano recordings were Aye Guy, Eddie Laguna, Sam Schmaltz and "Nature Boy." Eddie Laguna, was the real name of the president and owner of Sunset Records, for which Nat would make a bootleg jazz recording in 1945, showing off his whimsical imagination, swing and articulate touch. Laguna's name would be used, too, as the composer of every song. Except for "I'll Never Be the Same," all the songs were head arrangements—riffs and embellishments—of existing songs—"Honeysuckle Rose," for one. The date would be notable for Charlie Shavers's spectacular trumpet work and Nat's piano playing.

The record that Nat made at the Philharmonic with a handful of youthful pioneers became a jazz classic. In the company of the formidable Louisianan, Illinois Jacquet, then only twenty-two and already swinging and screaming with a brazen, standard-setting "Texas tenor" style characteristic of southwestern tenor players, Nat pulled out all the stops and played vibrantly and forcefully. He was daring; he was fleet. On "Tea for Two" and "Lester Leaps In," on "Body and Soul" and "Blues" and the Earl Hines composition "Rosetta," without compromising or sacrificing an iota of his articulation, light touch, or taste, he gave a driving performance, with ebullience and imagination that matched Jacquet's. Les Paul was fiery; so was Sherock. The group transcended itself and became a liberating force; its music—and its style of music in its era—persuaded many imaginative people to fall in love with jazz.

In Nat's other world, the pop-music world, Capitol released "Gee Baby, Ain't I Good to You?"—a jazz vocal record in his trio's soft, appealing style; the song rose to number nine on the charts by October 21 and stayed there for two weeks. When Nat played piano for his own vocals, he gave himself a gossamer tracery of chord signals and rhythmic impulses. The success made the men feel more secure. Their good luck hadn't ended. In Nat's adopted hometown, the Trocadero's manager, Georgie Goldie, named a small room the Troc's King Cole Room for Nat. The trio attracted more people to the room than any other entertainers, *Newsweek* reported on August 12, 1946. Nat's small group became the number-one poll winner in its category in *Metronome* that year, while Nat and Oscar took honors on their instruments. Victories in music-magazine polls became an annual tradition for Cole throughout most of the 1940s.

All the while, Cole disparaged his own voice, saying that a doctor had once advised him to go home and take care of his sore throat. Summing up the public reaction to his hoarse, breathy sound, Cole told his friends, "People are just crazy." Yet he could see that people liked his singing. There must be something to it. He thought it must be his stylistic talents. He was a persuasive story-teller, he knew. His tone set a mood, which people adored. He had perfect pitch; so he astounded other musicians by being able to finish one song and, without any prompting, start another one exactly on the right note. All his other assets—his choice of material, intimate delivery, ease, and warmth—distracted people from the shortcomings of his small range and southern drawl. The word *penny* came out as *pinny* (in "Got a Penny, Benny") in 1943. But people loved the naturalness. He even maintained an easygoing facade when he talked about his piano style: ". . . a lot of notes lying around on that old piano. I just pick at the ones I like," he told Richard Hubler for *The Saturday Evening Post.*

The trio branched out to films, appearing in musical vignettes in films as soon as "All For You" and "Vom Vim Veedle" became popular—*Here Comes Elmer* released on October 1943 and *Pistol Packing Mama* released in December 1943. Cole's trio appeared in vignettes that censors could easily cut for the southern audiences. Among the people who saw the trio on film, the critics praised the tasteful, story-enhancing music. The trio also made Hollywood shorts in November and December, 1943. In one, Ida James sang "Is You Is Or Is You Ain't My Baby?" with the trio accompaniment. Nat was a very slender young man at the time, and his laid-back musical style, though he didn't smile once, provided an interesting foil for the attractive Miss James with her attention-getting, piping voice. The trio featured itself singing "I'm A Shy Guy," "I'm an Errand Boy for Rhythm," and "Whose Been Eatin' My Porridge?" with her in "shorties," too. The little films were either aimed at theaters in black neighborhoods or used as "soundies," or Scopotone, in jukeboxes, which featured videos with music in bars and taverns. Customers put a nickel in a slot to see their selection as well as to listen to the music.

On January 12, 1945, the trio appeared in the film, *Under Western Skies,* and by then had also appeared in a Columbia picture featuring many entertainers, "Calling All Stars." In England in 1946, a film called *The Mad Hatter* opened, including a vignette of the

Cole trio; the film may have been one of the American releases renamed for the British audience. The trio also appeared in a film with an all-black cast definitely intended for black neighborhoods in 1948; with Johnny Miller on bass, Cole kept his customary sideways approach to his keyboard and played bravura passages on "Breezy and the Bass" in the film *Killer Diller.*

Riding the crest of their new eminence in 1944, the trio played on the radio show "The Hollywood Showcase." By the fall, Carlos Gastel organized a show starring Benny Carter leading his orchestra, the popular singer Savannah Churchill and comedian Timmie Rogers, with the King Cole Trio to tour the country. Opening in Washington, D.C., at the Howard Theater, the show had a few awkward moments with its timing, which the *Metronome* writer Barry Ulanov spotted. He also gave an intimation of a hue and cry to come when he wondered in print why Cole sang so much and played so few piano solos. The question would dog Cole for the rest of his life, as he became exceedingly rich and famous for his singing, while his piano virtuosity remained a secret reserved for jazz aficionados. (Critics waxed irate at times, while many musicians, who admired the financial security Cole achieved by his singing and understood his liking for the luxury, tended to feel less cheated, more philosophical. Artistically, however, Nat's choice would prove to be of dubious wisdom; he would have been well advised to maintain a regular schedule of jazz piano performances and recordings, too. Since the mission of critics is to alert the world to the best works and standards in any field, it was understandable that in the music world, writers kept urging Nat to play the piano more. In most performances, as time went on, he obliged audiences with one piano number.)

The show moved to Baltimore's Royal Theatre, Detroit's Paradise Theater, the Plantation Club in St. Louis, Cleveland's Palace Theater, and the Apollo in Harlem. Barry Ulanov was intrigued enough to show up in Harlem for another performance; he reported that the production had been polished; women screamed for Cole's singing. The show broke attendance records there and in several other theaters. The trio sometimes received two thousand dollars from theater receipts. In late 1944 or early 1945, possibly still touring with the Benny Carter orchestra, the trio played Loews Theatre on Broadway. Nat had already attracted the attention of writer Buster Sherwood for an article published in the April 1945 issue of *The Orchestra World.* Even if Sherwood allowed himself a little po-

etic license, his unbridled article revealed the backstage camaraderie of the high-spirited, informal trio.

Sherwood was trying to interview the "king," while his "jesters,"
as Sherwood called Oscar and Miller, kept popping in and out of the
dressing room. Cole was reminiscing about his busy Sundays at two
church services and a tea dance in his father's Chicago church.

Sherwood eventually wrote:

> "When did you ever get your homework done?" I asked. Before his
> Majesty had a chance to answer, the door flew open and several of
> the jesters entered. There was a lot of horseplay and kidding around,
> which amused the king greatly, and then the jesters disappeared.
>
> "Where were we?" he asked. "Oh, yes, the homework. Well, I
> guess it didn't get done."

Nat added that his mother had to cajole his father into letting
Nat work as a musician. Sherwood continued:

> I opened my mouth to ask another question, but before it came out
> the door opened again, and one of the courtiers came in. He walked
> to the king's dressing table and helped himself to some lotion which
> he applied generously to his face and hands. "I like this stuff, it stinks
> swell," he remarked and without a bow to the king, he walked out.
>
> His majesty looked at me and smiled. "It's like this all the time,"
> he explained.

The interviewer asked:

> "What happens after you leave here?"
>
> "We're going to the Trocadero in Hollywood on March 22,
> [1945] and we'll make a picture called 'Stork Club' in which many
> stars have guest appearances, such as Bing Crosby and Bob Hope,
> and incidentally we're going to be on Bing's program soon, also
> Frank Sinatra's."
>
> The door opened again, and one of the "fiddler's three" entered
> with a paper bag. "Have a cookie," he said, proferring the bag.
> "They're very delicious." It turned out to be my favorite kind. . . .

So Nat Cole was a star in the constellation of his trio.

For two days of work in the United Artists film *Breakfast in
Hollywood* released in 1946, the trio earned about $13,500, the
newspapers reported. For *Stork Club,* done by Paramount, for
which Capitol's co-owner Buddy DeSylva was a producer, the King

Cole Trio earned a twelve-thousand-dollar fee. Nat and Nadine bought a new car. Nat indulged himself in a wardrobe filled with wide-lapelled suits and bold-patterned ties. The trio needed an elaborate wardrobe, since it had to change clothes several times a day for all the shows it put on at such theaters as the Paramount in New York City. In Los Angeles, Nadine began taking golf lessons, which the Coles could easily afford.

The song pluggers and writers gathered as usual, day and night, in Lindy's restaurant on Broadway in New York, near the Brill Building, where so many famous music publishers had their offices. As the habitués watched the door to see which stars might walk in and gossiped about the business, the name of Nat Cole's trio slipped into the conversations often. The group had recorded a series of hits. The critics were praising Nat and Oscar in particular, and the whole group worked excitingly well together. The hawkers had their hunches and their dreams that some of their songs would be right for the group.

In Hollywood, Nat and his wife were invited to parties, where they met some famous people. Nadine found herself thrust into an unfamiliar milieu, with glamorous people who had a witty, gossipy way of making idle conversation. Nat had his self-confidence shored up and his naiveté minimized by his music, so he could bring himself to face down any shyness he felt in his new circles. If he felt self-conscious or uncomfortable with his new fame, he never really showed it. There was happiness and gratitude in his easeful demeanor. The only hint of his awe at the change in his life was his persistent self-effacing style. He never walked into a room and tried to make himself the center of attraction; he looked for a corner and kept quiet. If there were two things that everyone gossiped about behind his back, they were how shy and gracious he was. People speculated on the causes of his shyness. To be shy and famous at the same time did unnerve him, as his daughter Natalie would one day perceive; he lived in a world with pressures he had never been prepared for. Yet he had a streak of instinctive authority in his personality that allowed him to delight in the spotlight; his years of experience as a leader helped him, too. Carlos was always there to guide him.

Nat kept straddling the line between his "pop" and jazz worlds, and it never occurred to him either to stop playing the piano or singing popular songs. Bing Crosby kept inviting the trio to be his guests on "The Kraft Music Hall," a radio show on which the King Cole Trio substituted for Crosby during the summer of 1946.

Staying in touch with his jazz milieu, Cole did an album on which he didn't sing a note; he played piano with the Capitol International Jazzmen, with trumpeter Bill Coleman, clarinetist Buster Bailey, alto saxophonist Benny Carter, tenor saxophonist Coleman Hawkins, guitarist Oscar Moore, bassist John Kirby, and drummer Max Roach. Kay Starr sang one tune on the album: "If I Could Be with You One Hour Tonight." The whole thing was Dave Dexter's idea.

Nat was offered a forty-one-dollar fee for the session and no royalties for the record, which was done at Radio Recorder. By that time, MacGregor's had been painted; the sound was altered and "ruined," as Dexter discovered with dismay. Every musician on the date got forty-one-dollars, except for Coleman Hawkins. Dexter had to pay him double scale because he was so eminent, Dexter reminisced years later. The group played "You Can Depend on Me," "Stormy Weather," and "Riffamarole" as instrumentals and backed up Kay Starr for her vocal. She was paralyzed with fright when she saw the great musicians with whom she would perform. Even though she had sung with Charlie Barnet's band briefly and then violinist Joe Venuti, she couldn't bring herself to sing right away with the Capitol International Jazzmen, as Dexter dubbed the group.

Dexter loved the music and didn't care whether it sold. And the bosses let him do the record. If it sold ten thousand copies, they would pay for all the studio costs in those days. The men were happy to have forty-one dollars for an afternoon's work—tantamount to two hundred dollars in 1990. Dexter knew that although jazz didn't mean anything to the bosses of record companies, the musicians were delighted to get together and work, playing the music they loved. Nat was no exception, amiable and happy to be there. Dexter also once paid Benny Goodman and Stan Kenton forty-one dollars each for a recording session on which they did a vocal duet.

If Nat had a very laid-back attitude toward his paychecks for playing jazz piano at that time, he was soon going to be tutored to take a more practical position. The teacher/coach/director was an extraordinarily good-looking, dramatic woman with executive brilliance named Marie—or Maria, as she preferred to call herself during her brief stage career and thereafter.

By the time Nat had undertaken a second tour with Benny Carter, who had trombonist J. J. Johnson and drummer Max Roach in his band, Savannah Churchill and Timmie Rogers in 1945, Nat and

Nadine's marriage was in trouble. Their intimacy may have been diminished in part because of all the time he spent away from her, since he was working constantly. However, there was nothing new about that. He had always spent a great deal of his time working or jamming.

By 1945, Nat was earning more money in a few days than he had been accustomed to seeing in a year from music or anything else. He was having the time of his life. In Kansas City, the show with Benny Carter broke records, grossing nine thousand dollars for one night, according to newspaper reports. That meant that the Carter-Cole share was four thousand dollars, with Nat taking two thousand. In one midwestern city, however, the show was nearly stopped dead in its tracks behind the scenes—in the kitchen of a popular club, Johnny Miller recalled. A man in town wanted Savannah Churchill's loving attention, but she wasn't at all interested. Benny Carter, whose courage was legendary among musicians, stepped in to help her. Ordinarily a gallant, very polite man, Benny Carter showed no fear of Savannah's would-be suitor, who had a gun. "He slapped the gun down," Johnny Miller recalled about Carter. Afterward the musicians left town without finishing their engagement.

In Chicago, Nat took his trio away from the madding crowd downtown and went to his father's church in North Chicago where the men played the background music as a benefit for a fashion show produced by women members of the church. As Nat's stardom grew, he attracted hordes of autograph seekers to his father's rectory. Nat's father got him to sing a song for the kids there and then told them, "Nat can send you with his songs. You come to church, I'll send you with my sermons." Newspapers wrote about the fashion-show incident as proof that Nat hadn't lost touch with the folks at home because of his stardom. "He never forgets his church work," his mother told the press. A few years later, Nat played a benefit for a local boys club, which went unnoted by the press in Chicago. His group had a bongo player by then, Jack Costanzo, who had been helped to follow a straight and narrow path in life by that little club. Nat also sometimes volunteered to play extra shows in nightclubs.

By the mid-1940s, Nat's public life was blooming, but his private life was wilting. As he neared his thirtieth birthday, and Nadine her fortieth, their marriage was surviving as a legal contract on which the emotions were running out.

Chapter Eight

ENTER THE STRINGS

A fter making the rounds of the theaters, including Loews State on
Broadway in New York, with Benny Carter in 1945, Nat re-
turned to New York in 1946 to take his trio into the Club Zanzibar
on Broadway at Forty-ninth Street. Intended to repeat the success of
Harlem's Cotton Club, the Zanzibar, near the Royal Roost and later
Birdland, was a fine club. The trio, whose record *The Frim Fram
Sauce* went to number nineteen on the charts on January 5, 1946,
was hired to substitute for the Mills Brothers, who couldn't keep
their planned engagement at the Zanzibar. Nadine didn't travel to
New York with Nat for that job or for the extended engagements
that kept him on the road before the Zanzibar booking.

Soon after arriving at the Zanzibar, Nat saw a tall, attractive
young singer. She may have been standing on the Zanzibar stage; he
may have been watching her from the wings. Something about
Maria Ellington's posture and movements attracted Nat right away.
She had palpable style. As a man passionately in love with music,

Nat probably was intrigued by Maria's low, lovely singing voice, too. Maria, had a striking face, a sophisticated manner, polished speech with a trace of the broad *a* of a Massachusetts accent, and bright ideas. He later told a friend, "I've never heard a Negro woman speak so well before." Cole's valet at the time, Johnny Hopkins, introduced the two to each other, as Nat's next valet, Sparky Tavares, learned the story of the start of the romance.

If Nadine had traveled to New York with Nat, she probably couldn't have done anything to prevent Nat's sudden, overwhelming infatuation with the young, exciting Maria Ellington, who hobnobbed with such people as pianist Hazel Scott. Maria's elder sister Charlotte was a Cole fan, but Maria wasn't—and seemed to be unaware that CBS had banned his song "The Frim Fram Sauce" from the air for a while, considering it too suggestive; at the same time, a food-products company toyed with the idea of using a photo of the trio placed on the product's label. Maria was equally oblivious to the influence Cole had exerted on jazz and popular music.

Other small groups patterning themselves after the King Cole Trio had gained in popularity. In the postwar year, it had become too expensive for leaders to move big dance bands around the country, because dance halls had to pay a tax to feature the bands, as well as pay the salaries. Though Cole's wasn't the only piano, bass, guitar trio in the late 1930s, Cole paved the way for the public's acceptance of the small group with a soft sound. His beat was so strong that he could play for dances with ease. Trios and quartets led by Vivien Garry, Red Callender, Page Cavanaugh, Lucky Thompson, Art Tatum, Herman Chitteson, Joe Mooney, and the singer-pianist-vibraphonist Dardanelle Hadley (whom Cole particularly liked) all had their followings.

In the 1950s, Ahmad Jamal's trio, which would become famous for its interpretation of "Poinciana" and other songs, would clearly show the lessons the leader had learned from the dynamics, if not the instrumentation, of the King Cole Trio. Using a drummer instead of a guitarist for a harder sound, Jamal made space for every instrument to take a solo and build and enhance the entire performance. It was Cole—not the great pianist Art Tatum, the exceptionally dominating force of his own trio's sound—who intrigued Jamal. Miles Davis would look to Jamal for lessons in dynamics for the great Davis-led groups beginning in the late 1950s. Bill Evans, the influential modern pianist, who played with Miles, would take the Cole influence to his own trio. The pianist Oscar Peterson, who would become the world's most acclaimed jazz pianist, said his much-praised trio originally took its cues from Cole, though Peterson was absorbed by instrumental work. When he did sing, however, he had an uncanny vocal resemblance to Cole. Nat even mistook Oscar's playing on a record for a Cole performance in a *Down Beat* "blindfold test" administered in the late 1940s by Leonard Feather. In several such tests, in which musicians were asked to guess who was playing on a record, Nat usually recognized the players by a single tune. Only a few of the younger players began to baffle Nat as his attention wandered away from the jazz world. When he didn't like someone's work, he just skimmed over it.

"You have no idea how much satisfaction I get from the acceptance of the trio," Cole told John Tynan of *Down Beat,* "because we opened the way for countless other small groups. Units before that were strictly for cocktail lounges."

Guitarist Oscar Moore's elder brother Johnny, also a guitarist, was leading a group called The Three Blazers, patterned on Cole's group in the 1940s. Neither Johnny Moore nor anyone else had the phenomenal success that Cole enjoyed. But Oscar Moore began to yearn to play with his brother's group, because the family tie had its allure. Furthermore, Oscar knew he could feature himself as a soloist with his brother. Several times, Oscar mentioned that he was thinking of joining his brother's group; each time, Cole nipped the dream in the bud by raising Oscar's salary, according to legend. In any case, Nat had the influence to do it.

Soon after he began his engagement at the Zanzibar, Nat Cole began to draw Maria Ellington into his orbit. He invited her to a boxing match, giving her his fifty-dollar ticket to a Joe Louis–Billy Conn fight on June 19, 1946. Maria was very impressed by the glamour and generosity of Cole's gift. She went to the fight with Eddie "Rochester" Anderson's wife, she told a reporter years later, adding, "We had a great time, dressed like real ladies." Cole escorted Maria to the horse races. The flirtation escalated into a love affair.

Maria was born Marie Hawkins in Massachusetts on August 1, 1922.* Her father, Mingo Hawkins, worked for the post office. Maria's mother died while giving birth to the third and youngest child, Carol. Mingo Hawkins had such difficulty in working fulltime and running a household with three little girls that his sister, Dr. Charlotte Hawkins Brown, a highly respected Negro educator with

---

*The date comes from Cole's longtime valet, Sparky Tavares, with the year confirmed by Maria's marriage license when she married Nat.

honorary degrees from Wellesley College and Brown University, took the children with her.

Dr. Brown directed her own private school, the Palmer Memorial Institute, in Sedalia, North Carolina. Among her visitors were Eleanor Roosevelt, W. E. B. Du Bois, Langston Hughes, and Mary McLeod Bethune, according to Maria Cole's recollections of her childhood. Although the Hawkins girls were subjected to the indignities of segregation in theaters, restaurants, hotels—any public place in Sedalia—they lived in the protected atmosphere of their aunt's school filled with educational advantages and instructions in the social graces. Maria was proud of her privileged childhood. The lifestyle was a far cry from the survival school of the Chicago joints where Nat Cole had clung to his elder brother's example and to his own musical talent for guidance. Although Maria was raised as an Episcopalian, with the social prestige of that denomination adding to her self-esteem, and without the soulful music of the Baptist church in her daily life, she and Nat Cole shared in common the background of families with vision, broad horizons, and strict standards for behavior. Nat's father was a respected Baptist minister in his community.

After high school, Maria studied at Boston Clerical College to please her aunt, who disdained show business. Maria, however, had an irrepressible inclination toward performing. She began singing professionally. By the time she met Nat Cole, she already had sung with three of the best bands—Benny Carter's, Fletcher Henderson's, and Duke Ellington's.

With Carter, she used the stage name Marie Winter. Carter thought she was very good. "She could sing any kind of song," he said. She later married a serviceman, whose last name was Ellington and who died in an accident at the end of 1945, as she related in her book. She began singing with Duke Ellington as one of three singers, including Joya Sherrill, all of whom the critics thought were talented and pretty. The job was extraordinarily prestigious. Maria, no longer calling herself Marie, was using the last name Ellington by then. Both she and Duke told people repeatedly, privately and in interviews, that they were not related. At least one critic, who liked her work with the band, calling her the most sophisticated of Duke's band singers, thought she was not featured enough in performances to show off and develop her talents. A few weeks before the King Cole Trio arrived at the Club Zanzibar, Maria left Ellington's band, which had starred at the club; she was now working there on her own.

In New York, Maria mingled in Negro society circles and with jazz musicians, too; she knew many people, some of whom would become important in the music business. Marvin Fisher, a songwriter and musician whose father had founded a music-publishing firm, sometimes saw Maria at elite parties in Harlem. She caught his eye because he thought she was "gorgeous." She was photographed around that time wearing a coat with a leopard-skin collar, on the cutting edge of fashion in the mid-1940s, with her hair pulled straight back and fastened at the nape of her neck. The style emphasized her aristocratic Roman nose.

Nat was now torn between his legal marriage to Nadine and his love for Maria. Easing the strain on him was the itinerary that Carlos Gastel scheduled for the trio. There is nothing more difficult than retracing the steps of the King Cole Trio after it became a hit in 1944, going from a salary of a few hundred dollars a week at the 331 Club to one thousand dollars a week at the Orpheum Theatre. Newspaper clippings from all over the United States and Canada reported appearances by the trio, because it moved ceaselessly.

In the summer of 1946, the itinerary included "The Kraft Music Hall," for which the trio was signed as the music replacement group for Bing Crosby; Crosby had invited the men on his show many times as guests by then. Crosby and Cole, with their mellow singing and speaking voices, charmed audiences with their amusing repartee. It was impossible to say who was the straight man in their exchanges, for Cole's lines garnered him a good share of the laughs. Stepping away from his piano, he poked fun in a deadpan way at Crosby's attempt at jive talk. When fellow-guest Lena Horne once complimented Cole, mentioning that he must have heard the praise countless times, Cole replied that she was very different from his other fans. "How?" she wanted to know. "Well, for one thing, you don't cool my fevered brow," he told her in his sinuous, honeyed baritone.

The trio also played in one-nighters in Gary, Indiana, and Chicago, Illinois, where they were guaranteed five thousand dollars for each show. In July 1946, the trio kept tacking in and out of New York City for "The Kraft Music Hall" broadcasts. The itinerary allowed Cole's romance with Maria to blossom on the East Coast, far from his wife on the West Coast. There were reports that Maria traveled with Cole at least some of the time. On July 31, 1946, the trio performed with Jo Stafford on "The Chesterfield Supper Club";

on August 1 the men played at Radio City Music Hall. On August 2, Nat flew to California to spend three days with Nadine—not a very long time but surely enough for Nat, who had a far more exciting emotional connection in New York City. The pace of life was grueling, even for a young man. Cole disliked flying; it made him nervous, but he had no choice. No longer did he have the leisure to drive in his old jalopy across the country. On the bright side, he no longer had an old jalopy. By August 19, Cole flew back to New York City to record a new song, which would become a milestone in his career.

Singer Mel Torme, whom Carlos Gastel managed around that time, and Bob Wells presented their new composition, "The Christmas Song," to Cole. It was filled with sentimental symbols of the season. They thought the heartwarming song would suit Nat's talents perfectly. Maria, Capitol executives, and Carlos agreed that Nat should record the song with strings and a studio orchestra, not just with his trio. The guitarist and bassist would meld into the sweet musical background. It would also be ideal, everyone thought, if Nat got up from the piano bench to sing the song. Nat decided to play the piano for himself on the record. He really didn't like the idea of standing up. However, as many musicians and others in the music business would come to notice, Nat trusted Maria's judgment absolutely. As Duke Niles, a New York song plugger with a straight-from-the-hip style put it, "Maria saw that Nat had a limited future as a jazz pianist. He couldn't just sit there and sing and become a big hit. He had to stand up and sing with strings." A host of others involved in the pop music world agreed that this was the bright side of Maria's influence and the deciding factor for Nat's career direction.

Strings were added later to "The Christmas Song," with Nat's agreement. He may have been curious himself to see how the experiment would turn out, as much as he was eager to please Maria, Capitol and Carlos. With his impeccable taste, Nat would never have agreed to the arrangement with strings, if he had felt that it were gauche, vulgar or impossible. It turned out to be charming.

On December 17, still being heralded as a jazz star, he was back in a New York recording studio to do his first "Metronome All-Stars Record," with Charlie Shavers on trumpet, Johnny Hodges, the great alto saxophonist in Duke Ellington's band, the immortal Coleman Hawkins on tenor saxophone, legendary drummer Buddy Rich, Duke Ellington's baritone saxophonist Harry Carney, bassist Eddie Safranski, guitarist Bob Ahern, and the vocalist who had been singing with Stan Kenton's band, June Christy, and the singer who became Nat's primary rival and only nemesis for the sobriquet of the most popular male singer in the country, Frank Sinatra. Nat played for Sinatra's vocal on "Sweet Lorraine." Eddie Sauter wrote an arrangement for the group, but it was too difficult for them to play on the spur of the moment, the session's producer, George Simon realized. So they did a head arrangement, with Nat playing and singing with June on "Nat Meets June."

There are photographs of a slender Nat, dressed in casual clothes, in deep thought on the piano bench for the *Metronome* recording session. Just at the moment when he was playing with the illustrious jazz group, his recording of "The Christmas Song" with strings was electrifying the country. By November 30, it rose to number three on the charts and remained near the top for seven weeks, well past the Christmas season. People didn't want to let go of the haunting voice and the sentimental feelings the record spawned. The National Academy of Recording Arts and Sciences, founded in 1957, would elect the song to its Hall of Fame as a holiday classic.

In the fall and winter of 1946, a bevy of other Cole songs, some done only with his trio, others with strings, became popular. "Route 66," which the trio recorded on March 15, went to number eleven on the charts by August 3 and stayed there for eight weeks. On September 9, his May 1 recording of "You Call It Madness" had a one-week reign as the number-ten song. And on November 11, "I Love You for Sentimental Reasons," which he had recorded on August 22, became the most popular song in the country. It was an appropriate time in his life, when he was newly in love with Maria, for Nat to sing that soft ballad so convincingly. Ordinarily, his up-tempo songs caused the most excitement, but this hit remained near the top, in the number-seven spot, into 1947. It was the first time Nat had a song at the very top of the charts. By then, he had just replaced pianist Teddy Wilson in the number-one position in the Critics Poll of *Metronome.*

At the end of 1946, Nat's trio signed a contract to do the radio show "The Wildroot Cream Oil Show," which lasted until the beginning of 1949. The mellowness of Nat's arresting tone refreshed his fans on that once-a-week show, which he broadcast from whatever city in which he was working in. When Nat Cole sang, life's experiences seemed to become clearer, more straightforward, less complicated, and often very lovely. So soothing and tender was his voice that he seduced people away from their concerns, at least for the duration of his songs. One publication said that Nat received $68,000 for the show, but Sparky Tavares, who began working for Cole at the end of the radio series, thought the figure represented Cole's share alone; the other musicians may have had their own contracts, because the fee for the show was more than $68,000.

 NONSCANDAL

Very little was written about Nat Cole's love triangle with his wife, Nadine, and his exciting girlfriend-fiancée, Maria. There was an unwritten code of ethics in show business that the personal lives of Cole and many other celebrities were off limits; the gossip columnists adhered to the rules of the game, lest they cease to be invited to the right parties or lose their information sources. Furthermore, Cole behaved discreetly for the most part in his romance with Maria. He was, in any case, a quiet fellow. Controversies of several sorts arose, anyway.

Despite her loveliness, Maria, with her forceful personality and lack of inhibitions about asserting her ideas and opinions concerning Nat's career, began to acquire a wide circle of critics in the music industry. Not everybody believed that she would have a bright and shining future based on her musical talent; it wasn't outstanding enough, not universally appealing, some musicians said. "She wasn't Ella, or Sarah, or Carmen, or Anita," as one eminent jazz musician put it. Certainly Maria wasn't polished by years of apprenticeship at the time she met Nat. Some of his friends thought that she might be more interested in his professional popularity than his personal happiness. They also felt that she prized the glamorous times and the good, beautiful, and artistic things that money could buy.

Maria, of course, had plenty of company in her aspirations for a life of luxury; she also had the rarer qualities of discernment and— the sine qua non—the spirit to pursue forcefully what she wanted. It was her luck—and Nat's—that they met each other when they were young and fiery. Some of Nat's friends also had their misgivings about Maria because she took particular pride in her background as the niece of an eminent Negro educator. The romantic view is that she loved Nat and the life he could give her enough to overcome her qualms about his lesser sophistication. She also felt an irresistible urge to take care of him.

A few years after he met Maria, Nat explained that the first things he noticed about a woman were her carriage and her taste; he could tell a lot about a woman's personality from them. So it was easy to understand why Maria first riveted his attention because of her attractiveness. He had always paid a great deal of attention to the visual, even in his teen years when he insisted on his band members wearing eye-catching suits; his attention to the visual impact of his performances was intense.

The sidemen in Nat's trio advised their shy leader to stop seeing Maria as she became more influential and, they thought, overbearing and snobbish in Nat's affairs. Nat's brother Ike many years later remembered the story passed to him by the sidemen: When Oscar Moore and Johnny Miller had told Nat to forget about Maria, Nat had replied, "If you don't like it, you can quit."

They decided to try to like it. Nat had so much prestige that kids in New York were wearing black-rimmed glasses in imitation of his. As a matter of course, he was photographed with celebrities in his daily routine—Eddie Duchin, Steve Allen, Leonard Feather, Orson Welles, Duke Ellington, and Woody Herman—an endless list. Maria herself, acknowledging her critics, said that everything she insisted upon strengthened Nat's popular career. In retrospect, her very loyal, fond admirers among the Coles' circle of friends stressed the alcrtness of her judgment. It tempered their view of her forceful bids to keep everything pertaining to Nat's career under her aegis. When they tried to assess the situation from Maria's perspective, they could understand that she wanted to be an influential part of

Nat's life. She had his financial welfare—and therefore of course her own—at heart. Also, it quickly became clear to most people who met the couple, before and after they married, that Nat loved Maria and deferred to her gladly, with respect.

When Nat began courting her, Carlos Gastel warned him that a divorce from Nadine would cost about sixty thousand dollars. Nat was undaunted. Eventually he told everybody, "I love Maria and I want to marry her."

For a while, Nadine was unaware of the passionate love affair between Nat and this younger woman. In 1946, Nadine may have been tipped off, and she decided to see for herself what was going on, though she told writer James Haskins that she traveled to New York by train simply to say hello to her husband. In New York City, she found out that Nat wanted a divorce. She didn't answer Haskins's question in 1984 about how she found out exactly what Nat Cole wanted. After a pause in her interview, she simply said that she felt she had handled the situation well, going to see friends and keeping herself busy.

However, when she returned to Los Angeles, she went to visit Buddy Banks, the saxophonist who had befriended the young couple when *Shuffle Along* folded. She began to cry, Banks recalled, as she told him that Nat had sent a valet to meet her instead of going to the train station himself. Exactly why Nat hadn't gone to the station, Nadine didn't say. His schedule was so crammed with work that he may have been recording, or rehearsing, or traveling out of town for a one-nighter. He may have been distressed at the thought of the confrontation. Nat never liked nerve-racking scenes, and he definitely had made up his mind. Once he made a decision, he usually treated situations matter-of-factly. "Nat doesn't want to be with me anymore," Buddy Banks remembered Nadine telling him.

Nat never ceased to like Nadine. He signed papers to give her their new house and to pay her one hundred dollars a week for ten years or until she remarried. One report said that the house cost the unlikely high figure of seventy thousand dollars. The settlement took a long time to negotiate. Even so, Nat and Nadine, who had once given the impression of being a gentle couple, didn't break relations entirely after the divorce.

At the time of the breakup, Nat employed two valets, Johnny Hopkins, a bear of a man who stood about six feet six and served as a bodyguard, and Otis Pollard. Another man, Mort Ruby, whom Nat had met when he had worked in the Radio Room, became the road manager, as Cole began to travel more. Carlos Gastel worked as

Nat's personal manager. Ruby stayed until the 1950s, when Sparky took over the road manager's chores in addition to his valet work. Nat never discussed Nadine with Sparky Tavares, who replaced Johnny Hopkins in 1949, but Sparky knew all about her.

One year on June 10, Sparky's birthday, he bumped into Nadine in a club where Nat was appearing. Friends had taken her to the performance because it was her birthday, too. Sparky went backstage and told Nat, "Your ex-wife is outside celebrating her birthday." Right after the performance, Sparky went looking for her, at Nat's request, but she was gone. Nat told Sparky to send her a birthday card. Sparky sent flowers instead.

"I love to send flowers," he explained. He signed the card, "Best wishes, have a happy holiday, Nat." Nadine knew that Sparky had done it; he did it every year after that. When he spoke to her on the phone from time to time, she said, "You sent flowers."

Sparky asked, "Did you see me sending flowers?"

Nadine said, "That was you, because Nathaniel don't send no flowers,"

Sparky replied, "He could learn, and don't you ever question that. We've been friends too long for you to do that to me."

When Sparky heard Nadine say "Nathaniel," the name Nat's mother always used, Sparky told himself, Uh uh, don't touch that with a ten-foot pole. Something's coming to the surface—a feeling—and you don't want to do nothing about it.

The affection implied by Nat's remembrance of her birthday was indisputable. He liked Nadine so well that he left her a life insurance policy. But once he had fallen in love with Maria, he hadn't hesitated for a moment to divorce Nadine and marry Maria, he confided to a friend a few years later. Nat had no regrets about the divorce.

Back in Los Angeles, while divorce negotiations were going on, Nadine found herself taking golf lessons in the company of Maurice Prince, a southern-born woman with a charming directness that invited people to talk freely with her. Nadine implied that she felt unhappy about the end of her marriage, but she never cried about it, as far as Maurice could see. Maurice, who had gone to Los Angeles to seek her fortune and who eventually, after ups and downs, became a successful restauranteur, hadn't met Nat Cole yet. She herself was a couple of years younger than Nat and considerably younger than Nadine. Even if Nadine did look somewhat mature— the thought crossed Maurice's mind for a moment—Nadine was very pleasant and attractive. Maurice didn't guess that Nadine was nearing forty at the time. Nadine never spoke about Nat with rancor. Sometimes she showed up for her golf lesson, saying that she had just spoken with Nat by telephone and she had told him how much she enjoyed his records. Maurice surmised that the phone calls were about the financial settlement for the divorce. Nevertheless Nadine seemed unresentful and uncritical of Nat and Maria.

An interlocutory divorce decree was awarded to Nadine in 1947; the divorce became final in 1948, freeing Nat to marry Maria. During their long engagement, Nat frequently took pains not to exacerbate the situation with a public display of his new love, though the press carried reports that he had announced his engagement to Maria as early as 1946. When he took Maria to a highly publicized boxing match in New York, he bought three tickets—one for himself, one for Maria, and one for Marvin Fisher, who went along as "the cover," as Marvin described with amusement the way he viewed his function.

Some of Nat's friends felt that part of his reason for divorcing Nadine, who had nurtured him as he struggled to build a career, was to start a family. He very much wanted children; he could support them well at last. By then, he and Nadine had been married for nearly a decade and they had no children. Overridingly, Nat wanted Maria and no one else. Some people thought that he made a very canny decision, for Maria not only could fit into his new lifestyle; she could also guide him to take advantage of every opportunity and create a glamorous image for himself in the lucrative pop music field.

Nadine used the last name Coles for the rest of her life, spending some years in Los Angeles, then selling her house and moving to another Southern California community, Lake Elsinore, where many retired people lived. Arranger and bandleader Billy May heard a rumor that Nadine had worked for a while with handicapped people—perhaps blind people, he thought. Nobody else in her coterie of old friends was sure. She lost touch with them, whether by accident or design. Eventually, she moved back to St. Louis, where into her late seventies she listed herself in the phone book as Nadine Coles. She wasn't listed anymore by the late 1980s. Nat's sister, Evelyn Coles, who had always stayed in touch with Nadine, couldn't reach her by telephone in 1990 and heard that she had died.

If anyone had known more than the obvious situation—that love, which is always mysterious, had led Nat to a younger, more worldly woman's arms—nobody ever discussed it.

The King Cole Trio continued to inspire one another; the performances reflected the musicians' joyousness. Fans followed them from city to city. New Yorkers who loved the group at the Apollo trailed it to Philadelphia. Val Molineaux, the budding guitarist who shined shoes backstage at the Apollo Theatre, was so enamored of Oscar Moore's lyrical guitar that he went to Philadelphia to hear the trio perform live again. Press agents and songwriters did the same for Nat, entertained by the poignancy and liveliness of all the musicians' work. For many guitarists, Oscar became a standard against whom they measured themselves.

Early in life, Moore had outstripped his brother Johnny's tutoring. Bassist Johnny Miller, who was born on February 24, 1915 in Pasadena, was essentially the chordal and rhythmic foundation of the trio. Sometimes he managed to garner his just rewards from reviewers who heard the vitality of his playing. "Johnny Miller gives a fluid drive and solid background," wrote a Boston reviewer in late 1947. And a *Down Beat* reviewer that same year praised the "impeccable" Miller; "his selection of notes is unerring. His tone and technique are the best among the best. The least sung member of the trio is not the least one musically."

Miller and Oscar reveled in the public recognition, as Nat did. When they had time, between all the traveling and the costume changes, to take walks in the streets, some people recognized them. Their salaries helped to console them about the changes in the behind-the-scenes relationships of the men. Johnny Miller had always felt at ease with Nadine, while he disliked the way that Maria kept him at a distance; she regarded him as an employee with the status of a servant, he felt. Sparky Tavares who admired Maria, too, and found the entire Cole family endearing, noticed that Maria would treat him as a confidant in private but in the company of others would shift her attitude and require him to defer to her as the boss. Sparky spoke up and teased "Lady C"—one of his nicknames for her—about her "snobbishness." She said, "Oh, Sparky," and shrugged it off with an affectionate laugh. Moore and Miller were not as sanguine about taking a virtual rumble seat to Nat while Maria steered through traffic. The sidemen suffered in silence for a while, because, in so many ways, their professional lives had never been so glorious before and would never be so remunerative again. Their old affection for Nat sustained them, too. They were understanding about Nat's marital woes; they had been through their own romantic turmoils.

Even so, it was not an era when husbands left their wives for "other women" with the tolerant blessings of the divorce courts. It helped Nat and Maria from spring 1946 to spring 1948, that there was never a garishly exploited news story about the couple. Except for Nat and Maria not being married while they lived and traveled together in that period, there was nothing scandalous about their life together. Most of Nat's ordinary fans didn't even know that he was going through a divorce. Nat lavished attention and luxuries on Maria; she loved the feeling of being able to go out and buy whatever she wanted without worrying about the cost.

The couple's friends always noticed how much she loved shopping. When people found them in their hotel suites throughout their marriage, Maria was either just about to go shopping, or had gone shopping, or had just returned from shopping. Les Paul remembered that he and his wife, Mary Ford, had enjoyed shopping with Nat and Maria when she guided them to one of her favorite stores in Brooklyn. As much as Maria obviously loved shopping, Nat appreciated learning about style from her. His drawling speech became polished, with none of the softness of his tone sacrificed. His wardrobe began to grow and change; photographs of his voluminous new tie collection appeared in a magazine, and the taste in every color and design was extraordinary. His lapels narrowed; the tailoring of his suits showed painstaking care. On his tall, slender, erect body, the drape of the material emphasized his natural grace. He tied and retied bow ties until he learned to get them exactly right. Maria showed him how. He was her brilliant pupil. Just as he encouraged fledgling songwriters, he accorded Maria's talents respect, and the couple's fortunes flourished. Nat and Maria took care of each other. When he walked down Fifty-second Street in the 1940s, with his fluid gait, his erect posture, and his fastidiously tailored clothes, young, ambitious musicians watched him admiringly.

Back in Los Angeles, Jo Stafford, the singer, with her husband, orchestra leader Paul Weston, Capitol's music director, made a record with Nat as pianist for Capitol in March 1946. As usual, Nat was a spark in the music, Paul Weston thought. Soon after that, the Westons began to see Nat with Maria in the Radio Recorder studios on Santa Monica Boulevard at the corner of Orange Drive. That was where Stafford and Nat recorded in the evenings after dinner. Jo Stafford noticed that Maria was a stylish, reserved, attractive woman, with nothing of the high-spirited, casual, or ebullient youngster in her mannerisms. Even in her early twenties, Maria had an air of sophistication and pride in her own apperance, whether she were in the studios or around the corner in a place on Sycamore Street, where the musicians sometimes went for a drink after work.

With familial feeling, Capitol's group of talented artists, founders, and executives went to office parties, played softball, and got together in various ways. Occasionally, the Coles or the Westons and others spent a weekend at the Palm Springs house of Glen Wallichs. By that time, Capitol had moved to larger offices above Music City and was on its way up the Vine Street hill to the Tower offices. All of them in the Capitol crowd were young and high-spirited, bonded by the adventure of their successful, creative careers in an unpredictable, glamorous field. Everyone was at ease and comfortable. If some people found Maria's forceful personality overdone, or overwhelming, others were attracted to her for her mind—and even for her idiosyncratic sharpness. A few men felt protective toward her, exactly as Nat's old friends had felt about his first wife. The divorce didn't hamper Nat's personal likableness or professional success. In some ways, the best was yet to come.

Chapter Ten

TYING THE KNOT

*M*any of Cole's friends believed that Nat, a down-to-earth fellow, tended to follow Maria's directions to an extraordinary degree even before she became his wife. He had a kindly, soft voice emblematic of his charm and friendliness, even if he seemed aloof at first with new acquaintances. He was eager to please people usually, and when he wasn't eager, he could often be persuaded. However, it would be farfetched to say that he stopped thinking for himself once he began listening to Maria. With all his valued associates, he kept an open mind about the steps they thought he should take, but he followed his own instincts about his interests. He spoke rapidly and forcefully for himself if he thought that anyone was usurping his prerogatives or stepping on his toes.

Dave Dexter recalled how, in 1948 or 1949, as Capitol Records was preparing Nat's album *Nat Cole for Kids* for release in 1949, Nat became adamantly opposed to a planned advertising design. Glen Wallichs was in the habit of hiring an old woman who lived in the Hollywood Hills to create advertising designs. For Nat's record, at a time when Capitol's children's records were bolstering the company's financial viability, the woman drew something that included a bunch of small black children. Dexter couldn't recall years later exactly what the design was.

"But when Cole saw it, he was incensed," Dexter recalled. "And he jumped on me, probably because my office was closest to the door."

"Dammit," Cole objected, "you're making fun of the race!"

"Dammit, that's not true!" Dexter answered.

Dexter reminisced, "Cole explained his objection. And we agreed it was a stupid drawing. So we tore it up. We were wrong. It wasn't intentional. That's the only time I saw Nat truly angry."

His friendships with Wallichs, Dexter, and scores of other Capitol executives deepened with time. When Capitol moved to the Tower—which employees thought looked like a gigantic stack of records—on the Vine Street hill, Nat still visited Dave Dexter's office regularly, even though it was no longer near the door. As the company grew, Lee Gillette was hired and produced the majority of Nat's records. Often, after visiting Gillette, Nat would stop to talk about baseball with his fellow fan Dexter. Cole loved the Dodgers and, along with Capitol's country singer Tex Ritter, had season tickets to the Dodgers games every year. Though Dexter didn't share Cole's passion for the Dodgers, the men played softball together enthusiastically on the Capitol team. "Cole was very tall and slender and remarkably well coordinated," Dexter recalled. "Cole could move so gracefully. Every time I think of him, I think of him playing baseball. Then I think of his music second."

It was also true that Nat often followed Maria's lead in many practical matters. Nat's music afforded him an outlet into which to put his deepest emotions, while Maria could steer a course in the practical politics of the world, and she didn't flinch from trying to orchestrate her way to her goals. Once Stan Kenton was shocked and amazed during a rehearsal when he saw Maria approach Nat and demand that he do something. Nat remained quiet, showing no emotion. He forgave her for the little ruckus that she caused that day.

"Nat was a Pisces," Sparky Tavares, the valet, later explained about Nat's behavior. Citing a person's astrological sign was always a common practice among musicians and their retinues to help them explain life's mysteries, for musicians always felt that their gifts came to them from a divine source, which used musicians as vessels. "He didn't like any arguing or unrest. He didn't like to get upset about things and, when necessary, he knew how to make you listen to him." Sparky also thought that it was perfectly natural for Maria to wield enormous power over her husband. In Sparky's experience, the arrangement usually came with the territory of being married. "A good man [was] hard to find," Sparky said, while "a good woman [was] a miracle."

Baldwin "Sparky" Tavares had latched onto his nickname early in life, because it described his energy and alertness. Both his parents had emigrated from Cape Verde, Africa, a Portuguese colony at the time, to New Bedford, Massachusetts, where America's largest Portuguese and African-Portuguese community thrived. The Portuguese also lived in nearby Fall River and on the offshore islands. Sparky retained his ties to southeastern Massachusetts forever; he took his vacations at his sister's house on Martha's Vineyard but after a few days wished he was back in the hurly-burly of show business.

Right away, Sparky noticed the farsighted intelligence of his boss's forceful wife; Maria attended to details ranging from Nat's personal hygiene to his business arrangements. Sparky did not always agree with Maria's tactics or mannerisms, he said, but he also often thought that her stated objectives were excellent.

She was a boon to Nat's professional image, Sparky thought. She observed that Nat's complexion needed special care, because he had large pores and an infection under the skin from grease that had built up from his stage makeup and the pork in his diet. She took him to a dermatologist for treatment. After he came offstage every night, Nat had to clean off the makeup and splash his face twenty times with cold water as an astringent. The treatment worked; Cole's complexion improved. Then, after about ten splashes, he tired of the regimen and said to Sparky, "Is that enough?"

Sparky would say, "Mmmm, mmmm, no, we're cheating."

"Look at my skin," Nat would say.

"Hey, you need it. Do you want it to go back to what it used to be? You heard Maria; keep going."

That's where Maria was helpful, Sparky knew.

Arranger Neal Hefti had always thought Nat and his trio were well dressed. When Hefti learned that Sy Devore was the trio's tailor, Hefti started going to Devore for his clothes, too. Nat had always wanted to dress with flair and elegance. He had a penchant for the flashier styles until Maria took charge of his wardrobe.

She designed the first lace tuxedo shirt that Sparky had ever heard of. "She derived her idea for Nat's shirt from a woman's blouse. She took it to Lou Magram, who had a telephone booth—sized shop then, and she had him make three dozen dress shirts for Nat. He wore Italian lace added to where the ruffle had been on the woman's blouse. His tuxedo was of mohair without the satin stripe on the side. That was Maria's idea, too. And he wore file-top shoes—Maria's idea. His stage attire was very different from anyone else's."

Sparky saw how much Nat learned to like to sit down in the evening before he was going on stage and put on his shirt first, tie his tie for ten minutes, then put on high socks with garters. Just before showtime, he put on his pants. There was never a wrinkle because of the way he had Sparky handle them. "No one dressed better than Cole. Maria suggested things, and Nat said, 'Okay, let's try it.' The Slim Jim necktie was his idea," Sparky remembered.

Nat also adopted the Rex Harrison-style narrow-brimmed tweed hat for his trademark. An old friend in music publishing, Marvin Cane, thought that he prompted Nat to start wearing the style, because Nat admired a hat on Cane's head, and Cane gave the hat to Cole. Sparky believed that it was Tony Martin's hat in that style which had first caught Nat's eye.

"Where did you get that hat?" Nat asked Martin, who was visiting backstage one night. It was a Scotch plaid, Thomas Begg hat. After that, Nat wore the style all the time. Cane sent him several hats a year. And Cole's wealth allowed him to indulge himself in all the fashions he had always admired. He built a big collection of hats.

Buddy Banks traveled home to Los Angeles from a gig in Portland, Oregon, in 1946 or 1947, delighted at the prospect of seeing Nat and his trio again. Buddy could recall the lean days when Nat first hired bassist Wesley Prince. Now Nat had Johnny Miller along with Oscar Moore. Banks went backstage at the Lincoln Theater where the trio was starring. "I could hardly wait to congratulate Nat," Banks recalled. "He was putting on his tie between shows. Marie was there. He kept looking in the mirror and never turned around. He saw my reflection in the mirror and said, 'Hi Bud,' like he had just seen me the day before. Marie didn't say anything. Nat said, 'The guys are down the hall.'" So Bud went to talk with Johnny and Oscar, while Nat worked on perfecting the knot he had tied.

That, too, was part of the ambience that old friends and acquaintances noticed Maria establishing for Nat. He was exceptionally reserved when he was with her. His changed manner extended to his relations with his sidemen. Among the people who noticed Maria's possessiveness and protectiveness throughout the years, some would applaud her for asserting a wife's rights. Others, who missed their easy camaraderie with Nat and the attention they used to get from him, were irritated by Maria. Buddy Banks thought that Nat himself lacked enthusiasm at seeing his friend from earlier days. In any case, not only did Nat trust Maria with his best interests, she was his "Skeez"—his affectionate nickname for her; he had chosen it from a comic strip—"Gasoline Alley," as Sparky recalled. Nat didn't let her or anyone else irritate him usually, Sparky said. "Don't go to bed angry with anybody," Nat counseled Sparky, "because you won't sleep well."

Chapter Eleven

1948—A YEAR WITH NEARLY EVERYTHING

In 1948, Marvin Cane, a song plugger for Shapiro Bernstein, a music-publishing company in the RKO Building in Manhattan, was very impressed when Nat Cole told him, "Jesus Christ, I love Maria. I'm getting married." As soon as Nat's divorce became final, his wedding plans with Maria got under way.

Cane had known Nat for about a year by then. He had traveled with another song plugger, who had never met Cole before, to Washington to see Nat perform in a theater. Cane went backstage and introduced himself. As usual, Nat was friendly and hospitable. He took several new songs that the hopeful young song pluggers—contact men between the publishers and their customers—proffered.

Gradually, Cane's acquaintance with Nat deepened into friendship, so that Nat confided in him his intentions toward Maria. There was another man, Ivan Mogull, working as a song plugger for one firm and starting his own fledgling music-publishing company, who also became friendly with Nat. He was forever grateful to Nat for recording several of the little company's songs; Mogull also published several of Nat's original compositions—"Oh, Kickaroonie," cowritten with Billy May, to name one. ("We wrote it backstage someplace," May remembered when a $750 royalty check came to him by surprise in 1989.) Mogull had been an amateur trumpeter in a New York high school, where he had led a band and once had his idol, Louis Armstrong, sit in with him. Stationed in Europe during the war, Mogull had fallen in love with Cole's V-Disks. He had made a beeline for the Copacabana lounge, where Nat and his trio were working by 1947, or at the latest by early 1948. Mogull went with Eileen Barton, the pop singer, and Buddy Rich. Though Nat was hesitant to become friends with the outgoing Mogull at first, Nat extended himself to take several songs that Mogull offered— "Makin' Whoopee," for one. Mogull was earning his living as a song plugger for Benjamin Vocco and Conn in those days, before his own firm was established. That was done primarily through the encouragement of Cole and Vic Damone; eventually, songwriters would try to get their songs to Cole through the conduit of Mogull Music Publishing, Inc.

Mogull and Marvin Cane, who were close friends, were taken into Nat's confidence by the time the wedding was in the offing. Mogull wanted to hold a wedding reception for Cole at a fashionable midtown hotel, but, he recalled, the hotel didn't want to have a party for the Negro entertainer there. Mogull left the problem in Cane's hands. Cane thought he had an ideal opportunity to help Nat, who might in turn keep helping Cane with the songs he was plugging. Marvin really put his mind on throwing a splendid party for the engaged couple. He also was aware of the strong color line still in effect in New York City hotels. When Nat sang in New York, he still occasionally stayed in the Theresa Hotel in Harlem or at the Capitol Hotel at Fifty-first Street and Eighth Avenue. At one time, he had little choice except for the Harlem YMCA or a Harlem hotel. The Capitol was in the vanguard of downtown hotels when it came to accepting Negro guests. Cane recognized Nat's position as a black entertainer who was idolized by white audiences.

He even thought that they loved Nat's singing more than black audiences did, though there really was never any substantiation of that idea. Women of all races screamed and cheered for Nat's singing, as Barry Ulanov had noticed in the Apollo Theater in 1944. Nat insisted on emphasizing his role as an entertainer. Meanwhile, black activists saw the civil rights struggle as the preeminent issue in the country and became angry when Cole shied away from an aggressive stance. Nat had the platform but not the predilection. Virulent criticism of his quiet approach arose in the 1950s.

In the late 1940s, Cole attracted the unmitigated admiration of every black and white musician who heard him play the piano and sing. He was established as a starring singer in black and white popular-music circles. Cane thought that he would use Cole's fame, which crossed all lines of prejudice in the New York entertainment world, as the springboard for a transcendent wedding party, with a guest list of celebrities, socialities, and music-business people of all colors and religions.

The wedding ceremony took place at the Abyssinian Baptist Church in Harlem, where the prominent politician the Reverend Adam Clayton Powell, then married to the lovely, popular jazz pianist Hazel Scott, Maria's friend, performed the ceremony. Maria had decided to marry Nat in that Baptist church, which didn't require her to wait for special dispensation to marry a divorced man, as her own Episcopal church did. The wedding had already been postponed long enough, and Reverend Powell's pulpit was prestigious.

Maria later wrote her recollections of that festive Easter season marriage on March 28, 1948. She and Nat were not on speaking terms just before the wedding ceremony, because he had been so carried away at a bachelor party the previous night that he had failed to keep a wedding rehearsal date. Maria's aunt, the distinguished educator from Sedalia, North Carolina, took a dim view of her niece marrying a divorced musician. The teacher's opposition added to the tension. Maria's attraction to show business struck her aunt as peculiar, to say the least. Actually Maria's education had given her a limited familiarity with jazz. "I had sung with Duke Ellington's band," she reminisced in 1989, "but I considered him to be beyond jazz." She had also sung with arranger-alto saxophonist Benny Carter's orchestra and with Fletcher Henderson's, as well. Henderson's arrangements had served as role models for white jazz bands to copy. And Caster enjoyed an illustrious career. When Nat once told Maria he was taking her downtown in Manhattan to hear the pianist Art Tatum, Maria had asked, "Who?" Nat taught her about jazz, the swinging art of musical improvisation. It was unlikely that Maria was totally beguiled by jazz for jazz's sake, as Cole often was. But she went along.

On his side of the family, the bridegroom faced an irate brother. Ike Cole recalled that, with the Coles family assembled in

New York, Nat broke the news to his brother Eddie: Maria didn't want their sister Evelyn to take part as a bridesmaid in the wedding procession. When Eddie, who was not reluctant to speak his mind about anything, heard Maria's objection to Evelyn, "he raised hell," Ike recalled.

By then, Eddie had been married for about eight years to Betty, the Philadelphia-born pianist, who was extremely happy as his wife. All the emotional uncertainty of her life in the years before she had met Eddie was behind her. She had been looking for a man to help her raise her five children after her divorce. Eddie Coles had fallen in love with her and walked good-naturedly into the job of step-father and husband with a full-blown family. Betty would always have easy, dignified relations with Maria. So Betty stayed in the background, while her husband, who had a very close, affectionate relationship with Nat, effected a solution quickly with a firm, loud voice. Evelyn Coles took her place in the wedding procession. Pictures of Nat and Maria* cutting their wedding cake, as Nat's mother stood beside them peaceably, gave no hint of the turmoil before that happy moment. (Maria had warm relations with most of Nat's family for the rest of his life. Even so, Ike Cole went away from the wedding with the lingering impression that "Maria was just a little girl in gingham until Nat Cole came and took her along.") Once the family conflicts were subdued, about three thousand people attended the church ceremony. The photographers' flashbulbs going off all the time unnerved Nat. Although he didn't normally flinch before cameras, he told a reporter that on that day they made him shake.

By then, however, all the controversy was taking place in the mind of a manager of the new Belmont Plaza Hotel on Lexington Avenue in the East Forties, where the cake was being cut. The Belmont Plaza was a fashionable new ballroom facility. Marvin Cane had decided it would be the ideal setting for the reception. Several estimates of the wedding's cost, which Nat paid for, were passed to the press. They ranged from $13,500 to *The New York Times's* figure of $19,500—to even more. Whether the cost included the ballroom's rental, the food and drink, the gowns, hotel rooms, and all the expenses of everyone involved in the Coles' entourage was never published. The ballroom rental agreement was signed by Marvin Cane, the pivotal advance man.

---

*On her wedding license, Maria still used the name Marie—Marie Ellington. In Nat's will, she was referred to as Maria.

When he had tried to rent the ballroom, a manager had said, "That's going to be hard to arrange. There's a color line."

Cane recalled, "I took a deep breath and gave him a big spiel about how Harlem wouldn't invade New York City. There wouldn't be many blacks there. And I convinced him to let me run the reception." The contract was signed for the party. *Life* and *Look* magazines covered the wedding at the church. *The New York Times* mentioned it in a brief story. A tremendous number of celebrities, black and white, including Sarah Vaughan, Maxine Sullivan, Bill Robinson, and *Esquire* jazz writer at the time Leonard Feather, attended the wedding and the reception. There were more blacks than whites. And when the manager saw how many blacks were arriving in the wedding party, he was livid. "He wanted to come after me with a posse, because he was convinced the party would put him out of business," Cane reminisced.

Cane dodged the manager and felt delighted with his handiwork. "To me, Maria Cole seemed to be a tremendous, high-class lady, with a finishing-school background and a college degree," Cane recalled. "If she didn't have a college degree, she seemed educated and affluent. And Nat Cole was madly in love with her." Forever pleased with what he had done, Cane, who later became the president and chief executive officer of Famous Music Corporation, a division of Paramount Pictures, publishing such songs as "Mona Lisa," "Call Me Irresponsible," and "Love Song," sent the couple a painting as a present every year after that, asking Maria to pick it out, because Marvin revered her superior taste.

There was one oddity about the wedding party. Though Johnny Miller's wife took part in the bridal procession at the church, Oscar Moore's didn't. Oscar's tenure with the trio had ended by then. He was not the guitarist to play "Nature Boy," the melancholy melody with a spiritual message in its lyrics that Nat had recorded a few months before the wedding. The new guitarist was Irving Ashby, who had joined the trio at the end of 1947.

The change had no place in the published accounts of the splendid wedding. Nat and Maria set out on a honeymoon in Mexico City and Acapulco that they later would recall as idyllic. So famous was Cole by then that *Ebony,* which had already featured Maria in previous stories, sent along the photographer Griffith Davis to Mexico with the Coles.

Nat kept a diary as the accompanying narrative for the story published in August 1948. His economical, easeful way of talking was reflected in the picture captions. "Alone at last" was the caption

Nat supplied for a photo of himself kissing Maria on the terrace of their Acapulco suite—to which the photographer had followed them. *Ebony* reported it cost sixty dollars a night—indeed a luxury-class hotel in 1948. Nat said he was as moony as any newlywed, but he didn't omit some of the quirks of the trip—an earthquake, for one, which lasted more than a minute in Mexico City. He also noted the welcome at the Hotel Reforma there: "The bellboy quickly grabbed our six pieces of luggage, and Maria's two fur coats, which she never did have a chance to wear because of the warm climate."

The couple also saw bulls slaughtered and a horse gored at the bullfights. The goring upset Maria. The shopping bargains were soothing, however—Chanel No. 5 at thirty-one pesos an ounce, at an exchange rate of twenty-one cents to the peso. An airplane ride from Mexico City to Acapulco was rough. Nat watched brushfires from the window to keep himself occupied. The couple splashed a bit in the water, though neither of them was fond of swimming, he said. More relaxing for him was his Scotch and soda, while Maria tried a pineapple-grenadine drink. They watched the daredevils who dived off the cliffs into a narrow canyon and landed safely in an inlet of water below a nightclub on the Pacific Coast, and they shop-ped for white duck pants for Nat and a sunsuit for Maria. They were drenched in a motorboat ride in Acapulco Bay, and they signed autographs for people who thought that Maria was Sarah Vaughan. They made the rounds of several other tourist sites; at one of them, Nat rented a boat called *Maria* for a romantic cruise.

Their happiness was heightened by a telegram about "Nature Boy." Released around the time of the wedding, the record had become the number-one hit around the United States. By the fall of 1948, it would sell more than a million copies. Even before it had been released, Nat had been so tantalized by the haunting song that he had used the pseudonym "Nature Boy" on one of his non-Capitol bootleg recordings. It must have seemed to him that his star was rising—for himself and Maria—in the clearest of all possible skies.

They had only a week's idyll before Nat had to fly home to re-sume his touring, starting April 9 through April 15 at the Regal The-ater in Chicago. Then he went to the Orpheum Theatre in Omaha for April 16 through 22; to Minneapolis for April 23 through 29; on to the Lake Club in Springfield, Illinois, for April 30 through May 6. By June 2, he was in New York City's Paramount Theater for a three-week gig, and he went back there again in October. Aside from his nighttime performances, he stayed busy in the days, too; on June 7, he gave a benefit performance at Syndenham Hospital, which was written about as the only interracial hospital of its type in the United States. As usual, his schedule left him no time to alight in one place.

In an interview in late 1948, Cole analyzed the "Nature Boy" phenomenon, his most lucrative hit up to that time. "'Nature Boy' went over," he said, "because it had a lot of simplicity with a lyric that was a songwriter's dream." Ivan Mogull later made the observation, undoubtedly out of affection for the affable Nat's attention to him, that Nat was a "Nature Boy" himself, an enchanted, guileless fellow who bore a message of love and goodwill. Certainly the hypnotic power of his singing reached its zenith in this song. In July 1948, the *Chicago Defender,* Nat's hometown paper for the black community, awarded his group first place as the best small combo. Not only was he lionized in the small paper but he won first place alone as a pianist and together with his trio as the best small combo in the national *Metronome* poll once again. He made his second "Metronome All-Stars Record" along with another young man destined for international fame, Dizzy Gillespie, then still struggling to find universal acceptance for his assertive, harmonically adventurous style called bebop—a style that Cole had intimated in his own playing for years. To a degree Nat watched the bebop development with interest—and even took it upon himself to try to explain to audiences at times what it was, though he was more occupied with his own popular singing. Someone ascribed to Nat a critical comment against bebop. "Bebop hasn't died. It was never alive," he reportedly said. But it's difficult to believe that he said it this way unless he was referring to its financial success at that time.

Nevertheless, the bebop revolution and the fiery, independent musicians who were bringing it about had nothing to do with Cole's daily life and the glamorous aeries in which he was playing. Jim Conkling, Capitol's vice president, used to go to the Trocadero Room in the late 1940s, where the audience kept requesting Nat to sing Billy Strayhorn's "Lush Life." The song had a virtual cult following; people kept telling Nat that they went to the club particularly to hear him sing that sophisticated, eerie composition by Duke Ellington's transcendently gifted colleague, who was technically a Swing era musician, arranger, and composer. Fans begged Nat to make a record; they would buy it, they promised. So Capitol's men said, "Why not?" They asked Pete Rugolo to arrange it and conduct the orchestra behind the trio. Then almost nobody bought it. The song never went into the charts. Nevertheless, it may have been the first vocal recording of the song by anyone. Nat loved it; he and

Rugolo were proud of the recording. That was Nat's kind of gentle adventure.

In October 1948, the newspapers also reflected another aspect of the King Cole Trio's development. It got a fine review in Canada for an appearance at the Palomar, with Irving Ashby on the guitar and Joe Comfort as the bassist. In the fall of 1948, Johnny Miller had left the trio. "Striking Mrs. Cole was also along," wrote a Canadian reviewer, apparently as taken with her appearance as with the new bassist's sound.

Essentially, the couple had been living out of suitcases in hotels for years. When he could, Cole had tried to protect Maria from direct confrontations with hotel managements that were reluctant to rent them rooms. Sometimes she stayed in New York City instead of traveling through the South with Cole. Nevertheless, Maria had often shared the stress and boredom as well as the exciting moments of life on the road, which didn't always lead to the finest neighborhoods in the key cities. Very often, however, in many cities, black families vied with each other for the right to have the Coles as houseguests. A network of black families around the country saved the Coles (and many other black entertainers) from the depressing conditions of segregation.

At some point, however, in mid-1948, as Cole kept all his promises to perform and Maria traveled with him, the couple set aside time to go househunting in Los Angeles, using a hotel as temporary headquarters.

Maria has said that Nat chose the enormous brick Tudor mansion in a section of Los Angeles called Hancock Park. Duke Niles, a New York press agent then working on the West Coast, recalled Cole inviting him to visit the house as it was being renovated and decorated. Cole said that Maria had decided upon that house. "At first I didn't think it was me," Cole said. "But I'm getting used to it," he added, pointing to a sweeping staircase, which reflected Maria's flair for living with the best of everything. Cole did seem very pleased with the mansion. Maria accumulated lovely articles; other women admired them enormously. Songwriter Dotty Wayne, visiting the house years later, never forgot the brilliance of an ornate chandelier. It created the atmosphere of a luminous universe in the Cole house.

It was in an exclusively white Christian enclave of old money; lawyers and other Establishment figures lived there. Several sources say that someone—perhaps Chickie, Carlos Gastel's sister—put a binder on the house and then signed it over to the Coles, or it may have been a light-skinned black woman—someone with a complexion, even fairer than Maria's—who did the service for the Coles. No matter who made the initial payment, the result was the same.

In green, grassy Hancock Park, with its subtle slopes and stately mansions, neighbors arose to fight the Coles' decision to live in their own house. Los Angeles Police Department records about the incident have been destroyed (the police consider anything that has had no repercussions after ten years as a dead issue). In 1990, however, Sergeant William Rhine, a watch commander in the police department's Records and Identification Division, could still recall the commotion over the Cole purchase of the house. Rhine had been a little boy in 1948, when Hancock Park had served as home—"the elite area," as he described it—for the business and professional community. He was not surprised to hear that a shot may have been fired through a window in the Cole house to convince the family to move.

William Lacey, a president of the Los Angeles Chamber of Commerce, had built the house at 401 South Muirfield Road. By the time the Coles bought it, a Colonel Henry Ganz owned it, according to several sources. Neighbors were so incensed when they learned of the Cole purchase, with a $6,000 binder on the house estimated to cost between $65,000 to $85,000 in those days (and a few million by 1990), that they quickly formed the Hancock Park Property Owners Association. A lawyer from the enclave spearheaded the neighborhood action. The house had such grandeur, and it became the focus of so much controversy, that a few of Nat's associates may have objected to his plan to live there. Some feelers from neighbors failed to budge the Coles from their resolve. Several of Nat's white friends tried to buttress him. Cole and his wife waited in a hotel for the closing date on the property. Both Colonel Ganz and a real-estate agent were threatened with professional and physical damage if the sale went through. They called the police for protection, and the police remained on duty through the closing.

Opponents tried to invoke restrictive covenants regarding California real estate as the legal basis for forcing the Coles out of their house. However, the U.S. Supreme Court had decided earlier in 1948, in a case known as *Shelley* v. *Kramer,* that federal and state courts could not enforce restrictive covenants. The essence of the decision meant that the covenants were legally unworkable. Some Los Angelenos tried to amend the U.S. Constitution to permit restrictive covenants to prevail. The movement never got off the ground, however; several organizations came forward to pledge a fight against the covenants.

At some point in the controversy, Cole offered to meet his new neighbors in an attempt to allay their fears and reach a rapprochement. One person had mentioned a fear of zoot suits. Nat appeared to remain calm, though more than one hundred lawsuits were threatened. He issued the following statement: "I would like to meet all my new neighbors and explain the situation to them. My bride and I like this house. We can afford it. And we would like to make it our home." The lawyer leading the property owners' group told Nat, "Mr. Cole, I want you to understand our position. We don't want any undesirable people coming into the neighborhood, you know."

"Neither do I," Nat said. "If I see anybody undesirable coming in, I'll be the first to complain."

The story reached the headlines in some southern newspapers, including the black press. "There was more sand raised in the newspapers there than there was here," Cole told writer, Richard G. Hubler in 1953. "Some people threw rocks on the lawn and someone shot through a window, but I think that was a mistake." No bullet was ever recovered, but something did crash through a window in the house—probably while Nat and Maria were traveling a little later in the year. Caretaker Chauncey Shaw and his wife, Wohona, were living in the Hancock Park house. Certainly signs were left at the house by anonymous rabble-rousers, undoubtedly from the neighborhood. One sign read "Get out"; another sign was more scurrilous.

Soon after Nat and Maria had married, Maria received the news that her younger sister, Carol, had died—possibly from tuberculosis resulting from another ailment. Carol's husband died a few months later. Nat and Maria adopted their little girl, also named Carol, who was born on October 17, 1944, in Medford, Massachusetts. Though Maria's aunt wanted to adopt the child so much that she and Maria went to court in a custody battle, Nat and Maria prevailed. "Cookie," as Nat and Maria nicknamed the beautiful child, had been their flower girl and was then four years old. Cookie may have been living in the house with the Shaws already when something crashed through the window. She later recalled, in a family-authorized documentary about Nat's life, that a racial slur had actually been burned into the lawn. Cookie passed it every day on her way to school, she related in one of the film's most poignant moments. It seemed to her that the shadow of that word had taken forever to disappear from the yard; it was etched into her memory forever.

Hancock Park eventually simmered down, but the Coles must have felt anxious at times in their outpost during the crisis. Nat and Maria lived there for a while without police protection. When they moved in during August 1948, Nat told the sentries to go away, apparently preferring to rely upon his luck. Luck was always an element in which he trusted. Maria maintained an image of fortitude and decisiveness, too. One bright note might have been the hot platters of soul food which Maurice Prince, who owned a small restaurant and catering service at that time, recalled delivering to the mansion. By the fall, the Coles were on the road for their livelihood.

Appearing calm before reporters, Cole said only, "We just happened to like it there, and we bought there. I figure if a man can pay, he is entitled to live there. I never did consider it a racial issue. I don't know what we were 'flaunting,'" he remarked, answering the charge of ostentation that had been leveled against him—but not against his neighbors in equally elegant houses. "They couldn't do anything but complain," he summed up, adding that it was too bad that he couldn't get a chance to spend more than three months of the year there, because he spent so much time on the road.

More than thirty years later, Nat Kelly Cole, another child whom the Coles adopted, told James Haskins that he had played with the white children in Hancock Park. Nobody discriminated against him at all, he said. Occasionally Maria objected to his spending time with a few neighborhood children who seemed too wild to her. They didn't measure up to her standards for civilized, cultured behavior, which she enforced at home and reinforced by sending the children to private schools. Kelly had been obedient and awestruck by his mother's aura and rules.

No one remembered any of the neighbors ever dropping in on the Coles or inviting Nat or Maria to their houses. The neighbors never displayed any curiosity about the gaiety next door, when the Coles decorated their house to the hilt, adding a three-car garage and a recreation room with a piano, and invited their famous, creative friends to elegant parties in the backyard near a lovely patio and pool.

Marvin Cane often dwelled on the dramatic changes that Nat went through. Cane had traveled to Florida and seen Cole staying in the segregated Sir John hotel in Miami. Cane also thought about how Nat stayed in the Capitol Hotel in New York, not a very elegant place, before he began to be welcomed at the Warwick. Cole would go to Harlem to get a haircut at a barbershop in a building owned by Sugar Ray Robinson. From there, Cole, with Cane along, went to eat spareribs at a simple restaurant. Cane contrasted all those scenes with the splendid house in Hancock Park.

By the end of 1948, the danger that the Coles might be physically attacked dissipated. The American Civil Liberties Union offered a reward to anyone supplying information about harassment of homeowners such as the Coles in Southern California. Yet about five years later, Richard Hubler's article mentioned that Cole didn't seem quite at ease in his Muirfield Road house. Hubler gave no explanation of his impression. How far Nat actually went in overcoming his nerve-racking baptism to the enclave, one can never know. His discomfort at the time of the interview may have stemmed primarily from being forced to stay at home for months because of an ulcer operation when he would have preferred to be traveling and performing. By then, he had lived nearly half his life as a musician on the road. Semi-invalidism shocked him.

By January 1954, he had survived several traumatic experiences. Perhaps the least of them was the litigation over "Nature Boy," which started in 1948. That year Oscar Moore, the guitarist, who had left the trio in 1947, sued Nat. Shortly after resigning from the trio in 1948, so did Johnny Miller. Nat had to weather two storms in Hancock Park. The second one left him so short of cash that he couldn't pay alimony to Nadine Robinson Coles. She went to court to try to collect the money. Eventually he paid it. Just before his interview with Hubler, Nat suffered life-threatening illnesses. Maria had helped to set a new direction for his intense career. His malaise was hardly mysterious.

 "Nature Boy"

Of all the disc jockeys in Los Angeles in the 1940s, Gene Norman played the most jazz; he was known as the one most involved in the jazz world. He broadcast at night on station KFWB, which was owned by Warner Brothers. In Pasadena, he often produced jazz concerts sponsored by the Los Angeles Beer Company. Dave Dexter wrote program notes for some of Norman's concerts.

According to *Jazz Discographies Unlimited,* Nat King Cole had played in Gene Norman's Just Jazz All-Stars concert in Pasadena on June 23, 1947. Bypassing his Capitol contract, the pianist billed himself as "Nature Boy," alongside trumpeter Charlie Shavers, alto saxophonist Willie Smith, guitarist Oscar Moore, bassist Johnny Miller, and drummer Louis Bellson. "Nature Boy" was on his mind at the time of that concert.

Earlier that month, according to one source, Nat had had his first contact with the song "Nature Boy." Right away, he was intrigued. Several versions exist about how Nat came to possess the song and how it possessed him. At the center of all the tales stands the song's lyricist, Eden Ahbez, a latter-day bohemian with a dash of early hippie in his outlook and appearance. Blond, bearded and very short, Eden Ahbez, perhaps about Cole's age, went to the stage door of a Los Angeles theater where Nat was appearing. Either Ahbez gave the sheet music of "Nature Boy" to a stage-door guard or a member of Cole's retinue or to Cole himself. Since Cole had an open-door policy in his dressing rooms toward aspiring songwriters, it's possible that Cole simply welcomed the odd-looking man. Johnny Mercer may have given him a calling card.* Ahbez showed Nat several songs that night, but Cole chose the one called "Nature Boy." Since Nat had the ability to look at sheet music and know how the song would sound—and he preferred to look at lead sheets rather than have a composer play a song for him—Cole thought he might like the haunting melody with its liturgical overtones. He took it home, played it, and decided that the music combined well with the preachy but ingenuous lyrics, which promised that love conquered all. He liked the device of the singer dramatizing that message by reporting its arrival with a magical child.

The offbeat song, without a trace of syncopation, was presented as a waltz. Nat wanted to dispense with that rhythm. "Nature Boy" became a song for plainspoken, down-to-earth folks in Nat's conception; even though he sang it, it had the feeling of parlando, a narrative half-talked, half-sung. Perhaps there has never been an era so simple in U.S. history that people didn't yearn for a less complex time. In the postwar years, "Nature Boy" was a natural vehicle for Nat's tender voice and straightforward storytelling talent, and its lyrics must have especially appealed to his imagination and spiritual values—and his instinct about what touched other people's hearts.

"He could sing any song and make it comfortable," jazz saxophonist Buddy Collette later recalled of the songs he played in Nat's recording sessions under Nelson Riddle's leadership of a Capitol studio orchestra.

Eden Ahbez was undeniably eccentric. Most song pluggers arrived dressed in their best clothes and hoped to make a wonderful impression. Ahbez had arrived at the theater barefoot, or in sandals at most, and dressed in rags, with his pale-colored beard untamed.

---

*There's speculation that Nat knew Ahbez earlier in the 1940s, according to Will Friedwald's liner notes for the Savoy Jazz release *Birth of the Cole, 1938–1939*. The unpublished Teubig discography of Cole's work gave Friedwald this idea, because in March, 1947, Cole had recorded another song, "Land of Love," written by Ahbez before doing "Nature Boy."

Then he had disappeared without leaving any phone number or address on his sheet music.

Cole decided to sing the beguiling song during his next engagement that summer. He followed his friend Nellie Lutcher into a small Sunset Strip club called the Beaucage. There, he introduced the song. Legend has it that Irving Berlin was sitting in the audience and wanted to buy the song. The story may be apocryphal, because the melody is so very different from any of the major mood songs that Berlin wrote. Yet "Nature Boy" did have a message which echoed Berlin's penchant for stirring philosophies. In any case, Cole wanted to record the song, and he sent scouts in search of Eden Ahbez.

They found him; either he was living in a double-sleeping bag with his pregnant young wife under an *L* in the Hollywood sign or the couple was camping out in someone's garden in town. They subsisted on fruit, vegetables, and nuts, Ahbez averred. Eventually, his tale would make a good promotional story for the newspapers. Ahbez signed the necessary paper for Cole to record the song—but not right away.

From August 1947 until the end of the year, Cole recorded over eighty songs, including ten instrumentals plus the *Metronome All-Stars Record* in New York. Before Thanksgiving 1947, Marvin Cane presented Nat with a pretty ballad, "Lost April," from the movie *The Bishop's Wife,* starring Cary Grant, Loretta Young, and David Niven. "Lost April" seemed to have star quality, reflecting the luster of the film's stars. With Irving Ashby replacing Oscar Moore as the trio's guitarist, the trio recorded "Lost April" in December 1947, done with Carlyle Hall conducting an orchestra for that one tune.

Another orchestra leader and arranger, Frank DeVol, had been building a bright career, beginning in 1943, in Los Angeles. He had a radio show called "California Melodies"; because of that, he was approached to put out an album called *California Melodies* for Capitol Records. His station refused permission. Nevertheless, DeVol became friendly with the talented young men at Capitol, and he was hired as Paul Weston's coworker, to ease everyone's fears that Jo Stafford, Weston's wife, would get all the best songs at Capitol. DeVol's assignment was to record ten to twelve different artists. Between Capitol, his own radio show, and his work with Rudy Vallee, Ginny Sims, and Jack Carson on their radio shows, and with Rosemary Clooney and "The Colgate Hour" starring, among other rotating hosts, Dean Martin and Jerry Lewis, DeVol became very busy. Eventually he earned five Academy Award nominations for background music for the motion pictures *Pillow Talk, Hush . . . Hush, Sweet Charlotte* (nominated in two categories, for writing and background scoring) *Cat Ballou,* which he wrote for Nat Cole, and *Guess Who's Coming to Dinner?*

But in 1947, all those nominations still lay ahead for him. He was very nervous about an odd song called "Nature Boy." First, vice president Jim Conkling at Capitol talked with Frank DeVol and Nat about the song. "Nat set the key," DeVol recalled. "And he as usual never told me how the arrangement should go. In the studio, Nat said he didn't like the song as a waltz. So we took the rhythm out and had to change the time value." The arrangement of "Nature Boy" ended up being "far out," in DeVol's opinion, "something all out of tempo, except when pianist Buddy Cole played some licks, and Harry Bluestone played violin, done as an acetate in December 1947."

Cole had been recording many songs in the last days of 1947 because of an impending musicians' strike, when no one would be able to record with an orchestra. DeVol hoped the song would never be released at all, because he thought it was so outré. DeVol actually worried that he might never record again. It wasn't supposed to come out as the A side, the important side that everyone thought would earn the money. "Lost April" was going to be the A side. Nat himself loved "Lost April" and thought it was the better song. However, DeVol had the instinct to play his record for a friend who was visiting his house. The friend liked "Nature Boy" a great deal. DeVol came to realize that it was special.

In spring 1948, when Capitol released "Nature Boy" and "Lost April," Cole himself was very happy. He really expected "Lost April" to become the popular side, but he kept including "Nature Boy" in his performances, even though he noticed that audiences merely gave it restrained applause. It turned out that "Lost April" was just another thirty-two-bar song to the public, "Nature Boy" went to everyone's heart. If Nat had given a second thought to the cost of the wedding to Maria, he didn't have to consider it again once he learned about the record's popularity. By April 17, it was the number-one song for sales and airplay; it remained in that position for eight weeks and would end up selling one and a half to two million copies. Altogether it stayed on the charts for eighteen weeks. "Lost April" ranked at best as number twenty and stayed on the charts for four weeks. By May, it was really lost. Beyond the sales figures, Nat's fame escalated to the point that comedians included him in their routines. "Nature Boy" and Cole himself became a part of the fabric of the country's folklore.

Eden Ahbez told reporters that he would continue to live on nuts and berries and stash the money he was earning someplace where it wouldn't corrupt his ideals. However, he was reported to have bought a car with his first royalty check. Nat Cole, asked about Eden Ahbez, told the press in his light, soft way, "He sure is a funny guy."

In the world of the Yiddish theater, or during the vestiges of its heyday, Ahbez wasn't regarded with much amusement. He was supposed to collect about ninety thousand dollars in royalties from his composition, as Frank DeVol recalled the composer's share. However, Ahbez may have first heard the song's melody when he had come into contact—perhaps as a chorus boy, or a singer, or in some small role—with a Yiddish play in New York, before he trekked in his sandals across the country. Ahbez had thought that the melody was an old Yiddish folk song in the public domain. He had used the tune for his lyrics. James Haskins and Richard Hubler reported that Herman Yablakoff claimed to be the real composer and sued Ahbez for plagiarism of a tune called "Schweig Mein Hertz" ("Hush, My Heart"), in a musical called *Pappirosen*, which had played in a Second Avenue theater. J and J Kammen, a publishing firm for Jewish songs, launched the lawsuit on Yablokoff's behalf, Haskins wrote.

Several sources confirmed the facts about the suit. A court decided and reported that Ahbez settled out of court for twenty-five thousand dollars.

"It didn't affect Nat's earnings or the arranger's fee," DeVol recalled. He received a $1,200 bonus for his work. At first he thought that the money had come from Capitol. Later on Jim Conkling said that Nat Cole had been responsible for the bonus. "Yes, he was a very nice man," DeVol mused.

Though Nat told reporters that he was going to look at other songs by Ahbez, Nat never recorded another one by him, perhaps made wary by the legal repercussions of "Nature Boy."

Duke Niles, a song plugger who had met Nat a few years earlier, recalled being in Carlos Gastel's small office in Los Angeles. By 1948, Niles had moved there to work for music publisher Gene Goodman—Benny's brother—in the Harmon Music Company. As Duke was sitting in Carlos's office, he overheard a conversation between Cole's manager and Eden Ahbez. Carlos said, "Are you trying to tell me that you were inspired to write this as you were walking barefoot on the beach?!"

The hypnotic song nevertheless burrowed deeply into the country's culture in a variety of ways and every now and then surfaced to make its spiritual point. In March 1949, as one example, Nat played the song on the piano and sang it for an audience of teenagers at the *New York Herald Tribune*'s Record Review Party. "Not a member of the audience moved throughout the performance," a *Tribune* reporter observed.

". . . It's always this way," Nat commented to the editor of the paper's "Today's Moderns" column. "People sit and listen and think. I don't expect to ever find another song like it—but I keep on looking and listening. Folks need songs that go to their hearts—like 'The Boy.'"

As Nat moved ceaselessly about the country, he kept singing "Nature Boy" for audiences, who never failed to request it. And Nat may have told friends behind the scenes that the song was coming out of his ears, even though he had a great reverence for its success. At least one publicist for an important jazz organization in Chicago made up a funny press release about Nat's new aversion to hills, fields, and streams. He was alarmed to learn that he might be slipped a song called "Nature Girl." And he was astounded at the innumberable jokes that the famous comedian Jack Benny told about Nat linked to "Nature Boy," which turned them into a show business legend.

Chapter Thirteen

NAT BEGINS FAMILY FEUDS WITH THE JAZZ CRITICS AND HIS OWN JAZZ TRIO

*B*efore "Nature Boy"'s success, Nat had several other vocals ranking among the top twenty-five songs for sales and airplay in the country—"Save the Bones for Henry Jones," "Harmony," done with Johnny Mercer, and "Those Things That Money Can't Buy." "The Christmas Song" came back for a second year. It would surface in the charts nearly every year for a long time, until it was redone with Nelson Riddle and his orchestra in 1954. "What'll I Do" also preceded "Nature Boy." Right after it, Nat's mystique put "A Boy from Texas," a recording which he did with his trio, on the charts. Anyone with a song to sell beseeched Cole to sing it.

A journalist trying to interview Nat in a New York hotel suite had an intimation of the blitz to which Cole was subjected daily. Every few seconds, the phone rang. Cole always answered it. He was obviously always speaking to someone with a song to sell. The ringing phone jangled the nerves of the journalist and gave him a telling detail around which to focus his story. Nat remained cheer-

ful and calm throughout the barrage—or so it seemed to the journalist.

In 1948 after "Nature Boy," Nat's "Put 'Em in a Box, Tie It with a
Ribbon," an up-tempo song with his soft, driving voice, arrived on
the charts. "Don't Blame Me" and "Little Girl" followed; "The
Christmas Song" came back for a third season.

Nat still liked to unwind in the company of press agents and
salesmen, people behind the scenes who talked straight from the
shoulder and had no ax to grind with Cole about the crucial decisions he was making about his work. There were musicians who
would never quibble about whether Nat was singing popular or jazz
music. Dizzy Gillespie, for one, many years later remarked that Cole
had always been a jazz singer, even if he were singing all sorts of
tunes in a straightforward way. For his popular song "I'm Going to
Sit Right Down and Write Myself a Letter," which he did late in his
career, he kept taking the melody up a half step, swinging it all the
way to an exciting ending. Such elements connoted the jazz roots of
Cole's musical garden. Critics never ceased to scold him because he
was singing popular songs instead of playing jazz piano, taking a
more certain path instead of experimenting with his adventurous
bebop peers. Frank Stacy, who interviewed Cole in 1946, two years
before the "Nature Boy" phenomenon, wrote a magazine article reflecting the controversy (which had an element of success bashing)
apropos Cole's seemingly mellow life in pop. The critic's position
also reflected the incontrovertible truth (which would become increasingly apparent even to Cole's pop-music fans if they had any
sophistication and taste) that Cole's best work, without excluding
many of his pop vocals done as a stand-up singer, encompassed his
jazz work—instrumentals and vocals with his trio and other jazz
musicians. His jazz work would endure.

Stacy wrote about how Barry Ulanov, *Metronome*'s editor, had
boosted Cole early in his career. "Nat has never forgotten this, and
he places a lot of stock in anything that Ulanov says by way of
advice or criticism," Stacy wrote. "What *Metronome*'s editor had to
say to Cole on his latest trip to the West Coast [when Ulanov visited
Nat at the Trocadero Room in 1946,] wasn't too pleasant." Bluntly
he wanted to know why Nat was playing so much pure pop music
and almost entirely ignoring the fine kind of jazz that first won him
critical applause. Nat saw Stacy at a noisy party in Westwood a few
days after the encounter with Ulanov and set up a brunch date at
which the musician could air his side of the story.

"I know that a lot of you critics think that I've been fluffing off jazz," Nat told Stacy, "but I don't think that you've been looking at the problem correctly. I'm even more interested in it now than I ever was. And the trio is going to play plenty of it. Don't you guys think I ever get sick of playing those dog tunes every night?" (And he named a few, which Stacy did not repeat.) "I'll tell you why [I keep on playing them]. Frank, you know how long it took the trio to reach a point where we started making a little prize money and found a little success. For years we did nothing but play for musicians and other hip people. And while we played that, we . . . practically starved to death. When we did click, it wasn't on the strength of the good jazz that we played, either. We clicked with pop songs, pretty ballads and novelty stuff. You know that. Wouldn't we have been crazy if we'd turned right around after getting a break and started playing pure jazz again? We would have lost the crowd right away."

Stacy admitted that Nat had a point.

"But . . . don't think we're fluffing off jazz," Nat continued, and he said that he and the trio were planning to make more jazz sides. He mentioned "Sweet Georgia Brown" (which he had recorded in his first sessions with Capitol, and which was released several years later) as a good example of the tunes he would sing more of. He was also putting together a tour of the country to play a jazz program and said he would include some original songs he was writing in 1946. "We'll play the regular good trio stuff, there'll be special numbers for each instrument and maybe I'll sing a couple of tunes . . . not pops but good jazz standards," he said with heartfelt sincerity.

The concert tour, however, consisted of his usual, growing pop repertoire; Cole said that he hadn't had enough time to do all the things that he had dreamed of including. The critics felt obliged to mention his omission. They were still watching him.

To be sure, their negative comments upset Nat. He countered them with the truthful comment that critics didn't buy his records. "They get them for free," he said. Fans bought his records, pop records, he said. He saw no point in suffering in poverty on purpose, especially because he loved to live in a world of songs; he loved to have them rain down upon him. Any which way he turned, he could find a lead sheet in front of him, and if it were a good song, oh kickarooncy.

By 1946, too, the trio had become rife with tensions, though its fame kept increasing. At some point during his ten years with the trio, Oscar had been approached to record as leader for a record producer who thought that the guitarist made a fine leader himself. At least one tape by a quartet led by Oscar with Joe Comfort on bass was still extant in big record stores in 1990; on the V.S.O.P label, it included "Up Tempo" and "Walkin' Home," two Moore originals among the Vernon Duke, Victor Young, Gomey-Harburg, Bergner-Nelson, Carr, and Blackburn-Suesort compositions. And the hornlike fluidity of Oscar's guitar playing and the contemporary arrangements of the songs was breathtaking.

Oscar won the *Down Beat* Readers Poll and the *Metronome* Poll for his guitar playing every year from 1945 through 1948. He also won the *Esquire* Silver Award in 1944 and 1945 and the *Esquire* Gold Award in 1946 and 1947. He was an ideal colleague for Nat, who won the *Esquire* Gold Award in 1946 and the *Esquire* Silver Award in 1947. In 1947, 1948 and 1949, Nat took first place in the *Metronome* polls. With his trio, he won the *Down Beat* poll from 1944 through 1947 and the *Metronome* poll from 1945 through 1948. Those were the most prestigious polls and awards in the jazz world.

Johnny Miller, the bassist, watched Oscar edge himself out of Cole's trio for about a year. Ten years after he left the group, Oscar, who was then playing in the Hollywood studios again, reflected on his trio tenure. The first time he had seen Nat, Oscar had found Nat's eyes arresting: "He looked like a real mean guy—his eyes almost closed, glintin' out at you, diggin' what was goin' on. After I met him, I found out how wrong I was." He was also wrong about. the direction Nat would go in. "I didn't even think of Nat as a singer. We just thought that the trio was going to be a good thing. We had faith in it. Then, after I left, I noticed that Nat was featurin' himself more, standin' up and singin'. We always did the vocal things, of course, but I never thought Nat would become really important as a singer. To me, the cat was always a crazy piano player," he told *Down Beat* magazine writer John Tynan for an article published on May 16, 1957.

Oscar said that he left the trio because "I got tired of the road. . . . Through the years, there's a lot of people want to make it that Nat and I were shootin' at each other. That's a lot of nonsense."

Without acrimony, Moore graciously welcomed his successor, Irving Ashby, in 1947. Ashby was less of a standard-setting virtuoso as a soloist and more of a boon as a versatile accompanist with a good feeling for popular music; he began traveling with the King Cole Trio while Moore was still playing in the group.

Not long before he died in the mid-1980s, Irving Ashby told

James Haskins that Cole's manager, Carlos Gastel, hired Ashby with a contract letter. During a period of weeks, Ashby traveled on the train with the Cole trio. Learning everything he could about Moore's part in the repertoire, Ashby earned $150 a week. When he assumed the guitar seat, he earned $350 a week for fifty-two weeks a year. Ashby agreed to work exclusively for Cole on radio, in films, in personal appearances and for any other event that came up, unless the American Federation of Musicians scale exceeded that price.

Ashby's reviews for his debut concert in late 1947 were excellent. The repertoire that night at Boston's Symphony Hall included a mixture of pop, jazz, and novelty songs: "Sunny Side of the Street," "Embraceable You," "Sweet Lorraine," a much-clamored-for "Christmas Song," and several originals that received thunderous applause, including Ashby's "Allegro Suite," Cole's "Laguna Mood," "Nature Boy," though he hadn't recorded it yet, and "That's What." The audience wouldn't leave after the first two-and-one-half-hour concert by the small combo in Symphony Hall. The Boston-raised Ashby's style was declared fast, clear-cut, and refined with tonal sensitivity.

On October 19, 1947, a very heartening review of the new trio in a Carnegie Hall concert appeared in *The New York Times*, too.

"The trio has perfected a style which blends sophisticated harmonies with a clean, agile solo technique and poignant ensemble variations. The bass leads support, the guitar color and the piano rhythm in as neat a manner as you will find. . . . The instrumental performances were beyond reproach. A word must be said for the able program planning . . . which might well be the envy of more serious recitalists." The review was signed C.H.

The reference to more serious recitalists might seem like a quaint notion years later, as jazz began to receive the respect its artistic stylists had so arduously worked for, but the critic's perception of the the trio's dynamics and arrangements hit the target exactly.

Ashby, who was born in December 1920 in Somerville, Massachusetts, had studied first with his brother, Julie, in Boston, where their father worked as a building superintendent. When Ashby moved to Los Angeles, where he lived with his first wife, Corinne Howe, a Boston schoolteacher, and their daughter, Ervelle, he played with Lionel Hampton and pianist Phil Moore, among others.

Though Ashby knew he would be receiving far less money than his predecessor in Cole's group, he was happy to accept the job. In 1947, $350 was a handsome salary for him.

Despite the seemingly easy transition, Johnny Miller thought
that Oscar had been provoked into making his final decision to
leave by a new financial arrangement which Nat handed him. Both
Oscar and Miller had been earning a great deal of money. It may
have been a modest living in comparison with Nat's riches, especially because Nat collected royalties from his records. (Tradi-
tionally sidemen take fees for recording; the leader earns royalties.)
Nat had made up for the disparity by paying bonuses to the sidemen.

Then, Johnny Miller recalled, Nat was prompted by Maria to put
the sidemen on lower salaries. Nat was the star, Maria reasoned, and
she convinced her husband to see the light. All the leadership and
push for the trio's business commitments and engagements had
been in Nat's hands from the beginning. So Nat offered Oscar a
salary tantamount to nearly a 50 percent pay cut; the new salary
was around five hundred dollars a week without bonuses averaged
in. Nat offered a similar arrangement to Miller. Naturally the sidemen didn't like that. According to Miller, Oscar's pride led him to
bolt, although his long affection for Nat kept him from leaving Nat
stranded about six months before his marriage to Maria. Though
Sparky Tavares wasn't hired until after Moore and then Miller left
the trio, Sparky became privy to the inside story of the trio's
breakup. The fatal blow to that trio's personnel lineup was the re-
structuring of the pay, he knew. According to him, it was done because of "outside interference! It wasn't Nat's idea; it wasn't
Carlos's. I don't know who else it could be except for Maria. It
couldn't be anyone else! And it was a bad scene."

Only Oscar's friend Val Molineaux discounted the rumor that
the salary cut convinced Oscar to go his own way. Molineaux was
even under the impression that tensions existed between Miller and
Moore by that time. The varied speculations paint a picture of the
lively but serious and sometimes volatile milieu, with its gossipy,
sensitive cast of characters, all with their own ambitions. It was
clear nevertheless that the salary cut symbolized a new status for
Moore, who had been a founding member and the partner responsible to an incalculable degree for the trio's success. Though Miller
knew that Moore had stirrings of interest in playing with his
brother's group, Miller also correctly assessed that Moore was really
far more unhappy with the changed relations of the trio members
and the pay cut than he would ever talk about for publication.
Moore may have held Maria responsible for at least part of his dis-
tress, as Miller did. Moore decided that he couldn't continue to

work with a full, inspired heart for the trio anymore. Molineaux also knew that, though he ascribed the cause to Moore's other activities. Moore felt sufficiently chagrined and angry about the financial loss to sue Nat King Cole in 1948. According to *The New York Times*, Moore sued Nat for eight thousand dollars, or a percentage of his former annual salary, plus a share of all future royalties to be made from the record sales of the Cole-Moore-Miller trio. Nat settled the case out of court, preferring not to face a lifetime of recurring complex suits as the fortunes of the trio's records fluctuated. Nat told Richard Hubler the cut-and-dried facts without sentimentality: "Oscar used to get $500 a week with me, and bonuses pushed that up to $57,000 the last year. He quit anyway, and I paid him off."

The mysterious chemistry that had made the trio stick together and brave the early hardships had obviously evaporated. Maria Cole repeatedly suggested that the trio's sidemen resented her influence over Cole's business affairs. In effect, she claimed responsibility for holding the reins. Some of Cole's former associates felt, as Maria also said, that Cole concurred with her suggestions and that she bore the brunt of the criticism for herself and her husband. According to Sparky Taveres, Carlos stood up for the sidemen but was overruled. It was clear that Maria, with Cole's acquiescence, organized the financial split in a rational way when the effective leader became the indisputable star of the trio. It was also likely that Cole was so mesmerized by Maria, so desirous of pleasing her and reliant upon her judgment as well as in awe of her, that her goals, which depended upon asserting his elevated status, became his goals.

Had Maria not come into his life, Cole would probably have left the trio's original financial arrangement intact, several of his old friends thought. Cole and Carlos, however, kept working together without a contract—on a handshake agreement—until about 1950. When "Mona Lisa" became a big hit, Carlos's lawyer told him to set up a contract.

Johnny Miller gave his notice later in 1948. Cole asked, "What's the matter, Miller?" Johnny recalled. "He called me 'Miller'."

"Nothing," Miller said. "My wife's sick. I have to get off the road and stay with her for a while."

Miller's wife at that time wasn't feeling well, so he wasn't lying. However that wasn't the reason why he left, Miller added: "Nadine and I got along. We were real tight. But Maria wanted to run the trio. That was the real reason the trio broke up."

As creative professional musicians, neither he nor Oscar was the sort of person to linger in place, come what may, until it was time to collect the gold watch. Anyway, for free-lancers, there is no gold watch, and so they are relieved from the duty of having to opt for it or not. Neither Johnny nor Oscar Moore went on to greater commercial heights, though both of them found a variety of jobs.

Furthermore, after the wedding, published reports of the cost caught the attention of the IRS. Soon after Johnny left the trio, with the idea that he would rest at home and plan a new direction for himself, he received a bill for thousands of dollars from the IRS. "In those days, it was a lot of money," he recalled. The trio's management hadn't taken care of the tax bills as Johnny Miller thought would be done. Nobody had paid the IRS enough.

So in 1948, Johnny Miller also sued Nat Cole for two weeks' pay and the annual bonus to which he had become accustomed and now needed so he could get himself out of hot water. Oscar may have needed the money for the IRS, too. Nat Cole made an out-of-court settlement with Johnny Miller, as well.

(By this time, Wesley Prince, the trio's first bassist, was no where around. There was an air of of mystery about his feelings concerning the trio's success after he left it. In the mid-1940s, he told friends that he didn't want to play in the trio again, but *Down Beat* reported in 1945 that Prince tried to get his job back. Failing to do so, he worked with New Orleans drummer Zutty Singleton's group and then with singer Charles Brown's trio instead. In 1979, at age seventy-one, he worked as a night watchman in Los Angeles. By the 1980s, he was believed to have died.*

Despite all the challenges Nat had met during 1948, he exuded an air of confidence. He had dreams and plans. In conversations about music, he could go on for hours, talking thoughtfully and articulately about his ideas, fueled by his underlying single mindedness.

Backstage at the Apollo one night, Nat waxed voluble about the state of popular music. He felt that entertainers were repeating themselves and would have to find new material. "For a while it was swooners; anybody who could stand up and sing a little was in. . . . Then it was trios, but now all trios sound the same. Back in the old days, every band had its own sound—Benny Goodman, Count Basie, Jimmie Lunceford, Duke Ellington. Now all bands sound practically the same except Dizzy and Kenton. So now the public sits back and says, 'We don't care what you're going to do, but you've got to do something.' And if it appeals to them, they'll buy it."

*This information about Prince comes from the Klaus Teubig discography of Nat King Cole.

Nat was restless and energetic, pacing, smoking, smiling his broad smile. "That's why everybody who has a creative mind should sit down and try to find something new. And that's why I give Stan Kenton credit; he's going his own way. He may not be playing the authentic jazz beat, but he has a new sound. That's something fascinating to me," Cole told Barbara Hodgkins interviewing him for *Metronome Magazine.*

He added that his own trio was stagnant, and he was planning to try to blend strings into his concerts in 1949. "Maybe if we try the strings, when we go back to the old way, (with just the trio), they'll appreciate it again," he said.

He went on to air his differences with critics. First of all, he thought that they didn't take enough time with one musician and judged too quickly. Musicians weren't as critical as critics, because musicians had a better grasp of each other's intentions. Furthermore, music was such an emotional art that it wasn't fair to judge a musician on the basis of one night when he might be in an unemotional mood—or even in the midst of an unemotional period. "A critic will often say a musician he used to like is slipping. People don't slip; time catches up with them," Cole said. His valet Johnny Hopkins and the bebop singer Babs Gonzalez joined the tête-a-tête and turned it into a free-for-all discussion. Nat remained in command of the session by his authoritative tone, but the others added their bits of information and heartfelt yelps, or they simply nodded assent. The air was thick with smoke around Nat. When he didn't have a cigarette, he went off in search of one to have a prop to wave.

The interview concluded with his private assessment of his own work. "When I first had a trio on Fifty-second Street, all the critics came around and said it was wonderful. I thought it stank. They raved about our first records. I thought they were awful. They liked my piano playing, but I think I'm playing much better today than I did then. They put down our 'commercial' records, but they don't listen carefully enough to what we play behind the vocals. They say we don't play jazz anymore, but they should come out on one-nighters with us. We can't play too much jazz in theaters, and we can't put too much of it on record, but we're still playing it."

He did add that he was rather wistful about a dream he had nurtured when he had been growing up during the Big Band era. "If I had a band, I'd be doing just what I wanted. I wanted to be a bandleader once . . ."

He knew deep down he would probably never lead another

band, and he said that soon afterward to a writer in Pennyslvania. By 1949, he dismissed the idea of violins for his group, telling John S. Wilson—who was writing about jazz in New York, though not yet for *The New York Times*—that a bongo and conga player had been added to the group to supply added scope. "As a trio, we'd gone as far as we could," Nat said; he picked bongos because they would be less intrusive than a horn player. Through arduous work and devotion, Nat had developed his group with its distinctive sound, featuring himself, and he didn't want to relinquish the spotlight to someone else. For the same reason, he had no intention of ceasing to sing, even though he considered himself a pianist. "I'm a musician at heart," he said. "I know I'm not really a singer. I couldn't compete with real singers. But I sing because the public buys it."

The dichotomy was still striking. Nat managed—or bothered—to conduct two careers at once, as Sarah Vaughan would begin to do a couple of years later, emerging as a pop star in the 1950s, while maintaining her jazz singing career begun in the early 1940s. In that way, she developed her career with intelligence and relevance to her gifts. In 1949, Nat traveled with Jazz at the Philharmonic, produced by Norman Granz, and still kept his jazz connection vital and his options open—and lucrative.

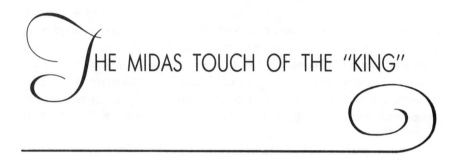

Chapter Fourteen

THE MIDAS TOUCH OF THE "KING"

*B*etween 1946 and 1950, Nat Cole was very important to Capitol Records. The company grew to become one of the big four record companies. In 1953, Capitol did nearly $17 million worth of business and expected to boost that by one-fifth by the next year. Glen Wallichs would look back from the vantage point of 1954 and reflect that Nat Cole had been one of the pillars of Capitol. With an average taken, Cole's gross annual record sales for Capitol came close to $2.5 million during his first decade there. Four of the company's ten best-sellers would be done by Cole through the early 1950s—"Nature Boy," "Mona Lisa," "Too Young," and "Pretend." "The Christmas Song" had become a classic, and "Answer Me, My Love" would join the list of Nat's major commercial achievements by the time 1954 was over. "Unforgettable" was another very popular song that Cole sang in the 1950s, and it would endure beyond the meteoric but briefer fireworks of "Mona Lisa." "Unforgettable" came to symbolize the sound of his voice as much as it served as a song title.

"He's our most consistent solo artist, among perhaps twenty that we have under contract," Wallichs told an interviewer. "All the publishers offer us a tune for him first, because they know if Cole sings it, they have an eighty-twenty chance of having a hit."

Cole's personal salary sometimes went as high as twelve thousand a week, and he also received as much as seventeen thousand a week for a series of one-night stands. He sometimes earned $400,000 a year, and never less than $250,000 a year beginning in 1947. About 19 million copies of his singles and 1.2 million copies of twelve albums released by that time sold. In those days, when the recording industry considered 200,000 sales a hit and 500,000 a smash hit, Cole sold over 1 million copies of two of his songs and about 2 million copies each of "Mona Lisa" and "Too Young."*

Capitol disclosed these figures to Richard Hubler, who was writing for *The Saturday Evening Post* in 1954, and, if they weren't exactly correct to the dollar, they accurately reflected the position which Nat held both at Capitol Records and in popular American music. Everyone who joined his camp in those years was delighted to revolve around him. Many had worked with him before and maintained their connection. Many came along to beseech him to pay attention to their talents; quite often, he encouraged them, or he actually helped them catch the brass ring. People were always vying with each other for the seat next to him.

Bassist Joe Comfort remembered meeting Nat in an after-hours club during Nat's first days in Los Angeles. Comfort heard Nat sing "Straighten Up and Fly Right" there. They weren't close friends, but they knew each other well enough to chat. Comfort, who had been born on July 19, 1919 in Watts, a black neighborhood in Los Angeles, played on a record led by Dexter Gordon, with Nat as the pianist, in the early 1940s. Like Wesley Prince and Johnny Miller, Comfort had played with Lionel Hampton. When Comfort played at Earl Carroll's, a showplace on Sunset Boulevard in the early 1940s, his job ended earlier in the night than Nat's did. Nat was performing at the Radio Room around the corner from Earl Carroll's then. So Comfort used to sit in with Nat. He eventually revealed that he had

---

*A Capitol Records executive in the 1940s, 1950s, and 1960s estimated "Mona Lisa" sold about 1.5 million copies. And a *Time* magazine story published on July 30, 1951, three years before Hubler's article appeared, said that 12 million copies of Nat's recordings had sold between 1944 and 1951. The figures appear congruent with the later figures.

actually been slated to replace Wesley Prince in Nat's group, when Prince was drafted. Then Comfort turned around to discover that he, too, was being drafted. So Miller stepped in. Nat called Comfort for the job when Miller left.

Comfort had always thought that Nat was a great pianist. After Art Tatum, then Teddy Wilson, Nat was Comfort's favorite pianist. "He could sit down at any old raggedy upright and get his sound out of it, with his touch. Oscar Peterson can do it, too," Comfort reminisced in 1984. Even when Nat was featured more as a singer, Comfort continued to love Nat's music. "I had every record he ever made. I'd turn the lights down low and listen to all those pretty songs. When I joined the group, I didn't mind 'Portrait of Jenny' and other such songs. I got mad when he stopped playing and stood up."

Dabbling as an amateur in photography, Comfort made films of the Cole group on the road, in Canada and in the southern United States. Comfort recalled that he started to play with the trio in 1949, with his first performance at the Million Dollar Theater in Los Angeles. At the time, the group was still called the King Cole Trio. After Comfort joined it, Nat made other changes in his entourage. Johnny Hopkins, one of his valets, was leaving the group. Nat had always felt very safe when crowds milled around him, because Hopkins stood six foot five or six inches tall and weighed about 250 pounds. Exactly why Hopkins left the trio isn't clear. He was more easygoing about details than his successor would be, some of his friends recalled. Cole's other early valet, Otis Pollard, also left the group in early 1949. Irving Ashby, the guitarist, was married to the sister of the small, energetic "Sparky" Tavares. Ashby suggested "Sparky," who had half a dozen baptismal names, didn't like anyone to call him by his real first name, Baldwin.

When Sparky met Nat in New York, Nat said, "He's too small." About a foot shorter than Johnny Hopkins, Sparky came as a shock to Nat, but he decided to audition Sparky as valet for a night. Sparky did a fine job. So Cole told him that he needed someone to go along for a ninety-one-night tour. Sparky was eager and willing. When Cole finished his next engagement in Chicago's Blue Note, he sent for Sparky to join the trio for the arduous haul; Hopkins left the group in Chicago.

In Chicago in 1949, Cole met a southern-born man with markedly countrified manners. Carl Carruthers from Chattanooga, Tennessee, was a dining car waiter with the Pennsylvania Railroad when he saw Nat in the audience at the Persian Room in Chicago.

Cole went to unwind there one night after he had finished his performance at the Blue Note. Recognizing Nat, Carruthers stepped up and complimented him on his beautiful hat and coat.

"And we took it from there," Carruthers told James Haskins. "Nat was getting ready to go on tour with Woody Herman. I did transportation, lights, sound, and he approved. I didn't do clothing. Irving Ashby's brother-in-law, Baldwin Tavares, did that," Carruthers said, using Sparky's formal name and mispronouncing his last name, emphasizing the first syllable instead of the second.

Though Carruthers worked closely with Cole, Sparky became even closer as the personal valet, a clear-headed confidant with no taste for self-aggrandizement and with a gift for front- and back-office responsibilities. Sparky worked consistently for Cole for the rest of his life. Carruthers, too, was an able staffer. He was so conscientious that he broke a foot once, tripping on a cable as he ran to correct a lighting error during a performance in Providence, Rhode Island. For a while, after several years in Nat's entourage, Carruthers went to work for other musicians, then returned to Nat for the singer's last years. Sparky and Carl were actually assistant managers and often functioned as deputy road managers, attending to all the details as the caravan made its way around the world. When Mort Ruby left his job as road manager, Sparky took over such duties as making reservations at hotels.

Sparky always stood in the wings when Cole performed. The last thing Cole did before he went on stage was to give Sparky a light punch on the arm or the shoulder. Sparky cued the lights during performances. "I was never bored, because his shows were always just right," Sparky reminisced. Soon after Cole hired him, Sparky moved into a house in a black community a few minutes away by car from the Hancock Park enclave where the Coles lived. Sparky didn't drive a car; he relied on taxis and friends with cars. And he assumed many duties for the Coles in their house.

Quickly Sparky learned the ropes there. Nat, an affectionate pet owner, held conversations with his boxers, Mr. Cole and Mr. Pep. The first December that Sparky worked as Nat's valet, he learned that Nat was supposed to put up the Christmas decorations at the house. It was Nat's first year with that assignment, and he commandeered Sparky to help right away. "We are going to put this up," he said to Sparky about a ten-foot tree for a room inside the house and a Santa Claus float with a sleigh and reindeers for the lawn. A mechanical device played a medley of Christmas carols with the lawn display. As soon as the men started working, Cole got a business call and had to leave Sparky working by himself.

It became an annual ritual. Sparky always constructed the lawn display on the first day of his decorating chores. The next day he went back and set the tree up in the house. "I didn't mind that he was gone," Sparky reminisced, "because I enjoyed it."

Sparky also became accustomed to Maria's habits and standards. One very hot day, he showed up at the house wearing shorts, and Maria scolded him: "Don't you ever come into this house on your job in shorts."

Though Sparky thought that he occupied a very different niche in the Cole family life than the butler, the cook, and the houseboy and should be allowed to dress as he pleased, he said, "Okay," and never wore shorts to the house again. It had actually taken Maria a while to acknowledge Sparky at all, he had noticed. That didn't bother him, either, but he noticed everything. However he instinctively didn't quibble with "Lady C" about what she expected of him, and he sometimes counseled her about how to handle delicate relations with Nat.

One day, Sparky showed up to pack the couple's bags for a road trip scheduled to start the next day; he always went to the house to pack the bags and put the music in order a day before a trip. This particular day, he asked Maria, "Shall I take your bags out, too?"

Maria said, "Nat didn't ask me to go with him."

"He didn't tell you to stay home, neither, did he?"

"Oh, Sparky, you're so goddamn brilliant," she said. She went on the trip.

She was traveling with Nat in the South in 1949 when she discovered she might be pregnant. She told Sparky of her suspicions first. He advised her to go to a doctor and make sure she was pregnant before she told Nat and got him terrifically excited about what might be a false signal. She took Sparky's advice and then told Nat she was indeed pregnant.

Sparky later reflected that he and Nat had one misunderstanding during Sparky's years as "aide-de-camp," one of the titles Sparky thought suited him. One night, he had done "one little thing wrong." Nat chewed him out for ten minutes, then went onstage; when he came off, he asked Sparky to have a cup of coffee with him. "The whole thing was forgotten," Sparky recalled. Nat didn't like things to interfere with the smooth running of his operation; he became fast-talking and forceful if wires were crossed. That didn't happen often.

Sparky also knew how to sidestep being overused. Nat would occasionally call him from an adjoining room on the road. And Sparky wouldn't answer. "I know he just wants to gossip about nothing in particular," Sparky told himself. One day Nat asked Sparky why he wasn't answering, and Sparky replied that he knew Nat just wanted to waste some time.

These were the sorts of stories that Sparky felt free to tell writers, while he kept Cole's confidences away from public scrutiny. Sparky talked about helping Cole change clothes after a performance; then Cole went out on the town to unwind or relax with friends. Sparky went his own way, too, often to play golf. The twain didn't meet or know what the other was doing until the performance or the next travel hour approached. Sparky managed to maintain a personal life, while he was on the road, too, and he was proud of fathering four children, who bore him myriad grandchildren by the time he was "sixty years old and change," as he put it.

It is quite likely that Cole actually did have secrets from Sparky, because Sparky wanted him to. Sparky did know about financial arrangements—even ballpark figures for each of Cole's engagements. For after a while, Sparky was put in charge of collecting the money on the road. Cole could rely on Sparky—and yet keep his distance to a point, too.

Sparky never felt moved to say more than one critical word about Nat King Cole. He was also extremely fond of Carlos Gastel— "the best thing that ever happened to the trio and to Nat King Cole," he remarked. In Sparky, Nat truly found "my man." Sparky even knew exactly how to deflect controversy instantly, humorously, and loquaciously. He recalled a tale that sounds apocryphal. It made a pungent point, however.

"One night," Sparky related, "a guy came up to Cole and said, 'You're my father.' Nat was thirty-six at the time. And so was the guy.'" Sparky explained his attitude. "We had been brought up in the school. Phil Braunstein [of Braunstein, Plant, and Chernin, the accounting firm that began to handle Nat's affairs in 1951] came to the Copacabana in New York, [where Nat worked every year from the late 1940s until 1964,] and gave Nat Cole advice. He said, 'You're a very wealthy man, and it's open season on you for anything that you do. *And you've got to watch your step.* You're going to be taken by a lot of people. Be careful.' And he said to me that it was my responsibility," Sparky added.

Stretching out for ninety-one days, the first trip, a Jazz at the Philharmonic tour, didn't seem arduous at all to Sparky. He didn't mind the road, and he loved the entertainment. Nat's group traveled with Woody Herman's Thundering Herd, an extraordinarily talented group that included a few black musicians—bassist Oscar Pettiford, vibist Milt Jackson, and a trumpeter, along with the white musicians trombonist Kai Winding, trumpeters Buddy Childers and Ed Badgley, drummer Shelly Manne, and saxophonist Serge Chaloff. Sparky experienced a bigotry-free three months when the group began playing in Champagne, Illinois, on February 14, 1949, and stopped in many key cities—Carnegie Hall in New York, Washington, D.C., Philadelphia, Pittsburgh, and Boston among them. The music had been superb.

By the end of the tour, when the Cole group finished their last performance in Texas and flew to Los Angeles on the Fourth of July, Sparky Tavares had a firm footing aboard the juggernaut. As an accessory to his regular business card, he eventually passed out a card that read: CRAFT: CHARTER MEMBER, CAN'T REMEMBER A FUCKING THING.

One man who noticed Sparky's particularly discreet character also joined Cole that year. Nat had the bright idea to hire the bongo and conga player Jack Costanzo, who had become well known with the wildly popular Stan Kenton orchestra. Though it had critics including Nat and Dizzy Gillespie in the jazz world, who thought it didn't swing, the Kenton band in its heyday in the 1940s had filled Carnegie Hall and the Civic Opera House in Chicago. By 1948, Kenton had dissolved the band. The Big Band era had been over for a while by then. Jack Costanzo, who had been showcased in the Kenton band, found himself at liberty.

Nat Cole put an ad in *Down Beat,* saying he was looking for the bongo player with the Kenton band. Nat may or may not have used Jack Costanzo's name. Cole's group had once played opposite Kenton's, and Nat had met Costonzo face-to-face and been impressed with the way Jack could play jazz as well as Latin rhythms. By that time, Chano Pozo, the fiery Cuban *conguero,* had joined Dizzy Gillespie's revolutionary bebop band. Kenton had been persuaded by the example of Machito, the Latin bandleader, to have a bongo player. Nat thought that Kenton and Dizzy were the pacesetters, as *Down Beat* reported when Nat took the blindfold test in 1948, trying to guess which musicians he was listening to on records. Nat liked new sounds and trends in music. A restless man, he had tired of his own sound by then.

Comfort admired Costanzo as a player, even though Comfort longed for the soft brushes of a jazz drummer or the hint of a snare drum. Ashby took a dim view of Costanzo, period. There was some confusion among the sidemen about how Costanzo came to be chosen for the group. Costanzo remembered that he headed to Florida to his brother's house for a vacation when Kenton's band broke up. After a while, Costanzo headed for his home in Los Angeles, without any idea that Nat had placed an ad in *Down Beat*.

Carlos Vidal, who had played bongos for Kenton before Costanzo did, called Nat and said, "I played bongos with Kenton." So Nat hired him sight unseen. Then another of Jack's brothers, who lived in Chicago, called Jack and asked whether he knew that Cole had hired another bongo player. Jack didn't even know about the *Down Beat* ad. So Jack's brother went to see Nat, who was playing in Chicago, and showed him a picture of Jack. "Is this the man you want?" the brother asked. "Yes," Nat said. When Nat found out that he had hired another man, whom he may never have heard play, he straightened out the situation. Jack Costanzo got on a train and joined Nat in Chicago.

"I took the train that time," Costanzo reminisced. "After I joined Nat, we took a plane even to go to the men's room."

Costanzo, too, was on the juggernaut to famous and obscure places, from Carnegie Hall, when Cole toured with Woody Herman's band, to the Blue Mirror Club in Washington, D.C., and the Casbah Club in Los Angeles, working ten and a half months a year, as Nat always did, on the road. Costanzo traveled as the only white musician in the group to the South and Las Vegas, as well as to London, sometimes watching helplessly as the black musicians suffered the indignities of segregation and bias.

Costanzo had begun his career in Chicago as a fifteen-year-old in a dance team with his wife, Marda, then twenty. Costanzo, who was the son of Sicilian immigrants, also played bongos. Later, he was playing in a Los Angeles club, the Masquerade, when Kenton heard him and asked him to join the band to replace Carlos Vidal. In Kenton's band at the time were bassist Eddie Safranski, drummer Shelly Manne, guitarist Laurindo Almeida, singer June Christy, and arranger Pete Rugolo. It was when Kenton's and Cole's paths crossed that Pete Rugolo became acquainted with Nat and rewrote a few endings for "The Christmas Song." "So I was in good company," Jack recalled of the fine jazzmen in Kenton's band. Jack's wife decided not to go on the road with him, but he was thrilled to be swept along as part of the "storm," which surrounded Kenton's appearances.

Carlos Gastel had been managing Kenton and Cole at the same time. Carlos may have had something to do with suggesting Jack Costanzo to Nat. It was Cole's idea, probably augmented by Capitol's artists and repertoire department, as well as by Maria and Carlos, to hire a bongo player in the first place and effect a change in the group's sound. "Nat was musically very adventurous," Costanzo recalled. "He wasn't reluctant to try something new." At first, the group was billed as the King Cole Trio Featuring Jack Costanzo. It was soon changed, however, to Nat King Cole and His Trio, so that the emphasis remained on Nat, while the trio concept was preserved. Costanzo could understand that, though he had been gleeful to have special billing for a while.

Irving Ashby and Joe Comfort didn't like the sound of the bongo drum, which they thought had a choppiness, intruding on the soft, fluid, subtly pulsating music of the trio. Actually Jack played with sensitivity to the trio's concept. Nat liked the bongo except on ballads, for which he told Jack to pretend to be playing. Then Jack would barely touch his drums. Nevertheless, to Ashby and Comfort, the bongo always sounded loud and clacking. Ashby and Costanzo had palpable tensions between them at times, though Comfort and Costanzo became friends and stayed in touch with each other long after they left the Cole trio.

These were just a handful of the people whose lives came to depend for a while upon the fortunes of Nat Cole and who remembered him as gracious, kind, generous, and likable years after he died. Costanzo for one, who became involved in a drum-shop business with a partner, was astounded and delighted when Cole volunteered to pose in a picture with the shop's owners to promote the business. The publicity was worth a great deal of money, but Cole didn't ask for any payment; Costanzo knew Nat didn't tell Maria about what he had done, either.

In key cities, Cole had record-promotion men whose livelihoods depended upon him. They worked for him full tilt in New York, Chicago and Los Angeles. One of these men was Milton Karle, who began working for Nat in 1945 as the East Coast manager for record publicity and stayed until 1953.

Karle regarded his relationship with Cole as the big boost to his own professional life: "I was in *Billboard*'s list of top record-promotion men because of Cole. I made a fortune because of him. I had

Peggy Lee, Tony Martin, Mel Tormé, Nellie Lutcher, Johnny Desmond, because of Cole's influence," he said in 1982.

In return, Karle gave Cole such fealty that Karle's friends made up little jokes. They saw that he was totally "Nat King Cole-ized," as press agent Mike Hall described Karle's state of mind. Hall eventually had Cole for a client for years, too. Somebody would say something such as "It's going to rain tomorrow," Hall observed, and Milton Karle would say, "What's that got to do with Nat King Cole?" Then he walked away from the conversation. Mike witnessed this himself. Why waste Karle's time with anything other than Cole? Karle sometimes fought battles for Nat. He would argue the merits of a Cole song, the Cole style, the voice. Cole was a god to him. Mike Hall knew that. Karle lionized him, adored him.

Karle himself recalled that once he sat with Nat in a hotel lobby until the management honored a reservation. Karle found it painful to sit there and know the room was being delayed because of Cole's race, yet Karle wouldn't leave Nat to wait alone.

In 1953, Karle received a telegram from Capitol, telling him that he was no longer to work on Cole's record publicity. Karle was terribly shaken up, Mike Hall recalled. Karle sent a telegram back, begging to be kept on the job. He wasn't. He never suggested in later years that he bore Cole or his advisers any grudge, and he continued to speak of Nat with affection and of Maria with respect. Karle knew how much Nat relied upon Maria's business judgment.

Karle had never been one of the Cole family's closest friends on the East Coast. Nat seemed to be completely sanguine about the charge in his publicity staff in New York, where his best friends were Marvin Fisher, the songwriter and publisher, and song publishers Ivan Mogull and Marvin Cane. Among Nat's good if less intimate buddies were songwriters Joe and Noel Sherman. Marvin Cane became head of Famous Music years after arranging the wedding reception for Nat and Maria. When the couple went to New York, they were likely to go out to dinner with their best friends. Nat favored two Italian restaurants, Patsy's and especially Amalfi in midtown; he also went to Sardi's and the Warwick Hotel's dining room, the latter two particularly if he were sitting for an interview with a reporter. Maria, Nat, and his buddies took their restaurants seriously. If one of them found a good new one, he might suggest the group try it.

Marvin Cane was always struck by Nat's manners. "If a woman left the table to go to the ladies' room, Nat stood up. When she came back; he would help seat her. He was just an elegant, lovely guy. When you were with him, you forgot he was Nat Cole. He was never temperamental; he was a man's man."

Karle wasn't usually a dinner buddy of the Coles; yet he kept in close touch with Nat. Because of Nat's influence, Karle obtained an apartment on Sutton Place, a very fashionable East Side enclave. Nat knew everybody, Karle bragged, and could arrange to have nearly anything happen. He could procure a Sutton Place apartment for Karle, even though Nat himself could never have rented an apartment there in those days. In effect, Nat had a Sutton Place apartment, because Karle always made the place available to Nat whenever Nat wanted to get away from it all. It was probably because of his memory of the personal goodwill that had existed between Nat and himself that Karle suffered without rancor or angry words the loss of this, his most important client.

Chapter Fifteen

NAT KING COLE AND HIS TRIO ON THE ROAD—AND ANOTHER TRANSITION

Nat and the trio traveled incessantly from 1949 into 1951, some-times with other performers, sometimes on their own, and finally with the Big Show of 1951. The Big Show would continue for at least five more years. It would stand out in Sparky's mind as a stellar affair, because Cole traveled with such fanfare himself and in such illustrious company. Newspapers writing about the Big Show coming to town called it "The Biggest Show of '51." "For it is just that, an extravaganza of singing, clowning, dancing and some of the best music ever heard," said one advance article.

The first year, Nat shared top billing with Duke Ellington, Sarah Vaughan, and Timmie Rogers, with prominent notice given to Peg Leg Bates, Stump and Stumpy, the Marie Bryant Dancers, and the Patterson and Jackson dance team, two agile men weighing at least 250 pounds or more each. Patterson and Jackson also had comedic flair; they could imitate the Ink Spots, parodying the high tenor and the bass singer. For their stage exit, each one hurried offstage in a routine suggesting that someone was chasing him, then ran back on stage, following each other. They kept up the flight parody until they collided. Their size made the slapstick hilarious.

The Big Show of 1951 started in Boston on September 11, 1951, and moved to Philadelphia, Washington, Baltimore, Montréal, Toronto, Buffalo, Cleveland, Cincinnati, Atlanta, Birmingham, Houston, New Orleans, Dallas, Fort Worth, Tulsa, Oklahoma City, and other places during the rest of the year. Nat and his trio sang their popular repertoire—"I'll Always Remember You," "Make Believe Land," "My Brother," "Early American," "Song of Delilah," "Because of Rain," and the more enduring "Too Young," "Unforgettable," and "My First and Last Love." Sarah Vaughan's road manager, Johnny Garry, who would become the manager of Birdland, thought the show had too much talent. Performances lasted two and a half hours. Sarah closed the first act; Nat's trio, the last act. The tour traveled for nearly three months.

Sparky loved the gala affair of the show, a self-contained entertainment universe. Johnny Garry was impressed by how firmly Sparky protected Nat from unwanted visitors in his dressing room. One day in a southern city—perhaps Shreveport, Louisiana— Johnny saw a local disc jockey try to bluster his way past Sparky and get to Nat. Sparky kept saying no. The disc jockey became so insulting that Johnny Garry stepped in and said, "You can't talk to my friend that way." Garry pushed the fellow off a loading platform on which they were standing. Then Garry and Sparky became alarmed because of how far the man fell.

Nat's trio members were more engrossed by other gigs and tours, with Woody Herman in 1949 for Jazz at the Philharmonic, and on their own to the southern United States in 1949, and then to England in 1950.

Jack Costanzo wasn't hardened to the problems that his black colleagues had to face on the road. One night, during a break in his performing, he decided to go upstairs into a section of a southern theater reserved for blacks only. A white guard told him to get out. Jack felt even worse than before he had gone to sit in the section. He told Nat this. Nat said, "I know you mean well, but you can't carry our cross for us."

"He straightened me out," Jack mused later. "He told me, in effect, 'Don't get yourself aggravated.' People don't realize how much he did for the black race, just by his innuendos and the way he carried himself. He was one of the most gentlemanly, kindest, most helpful persons I've ever known."

Ashby and Comfort, too, were so disgusted and disheartened by the segregation in the South that they couldn't remember the names of the hotels in which they stayed, nor the restaurants where they ate, nor the theaters in which they performed. They did the work because it was their living, and they got through it.

In 1950, they also played at the Thunderbird Hotel, which was strictly segregated. "We couldn't go out front and gamble at the tables," Comfort recalled about one of the restrictions. The bias cut Comfort, Ashby, and Cole off from white society in Las Vegas. The men weren't allowed to stay in the casinos or to eat there or swim in the pool or mingle with the guests in any way; the musicians, with the exception of Jack Costanzo, were only allowed to entertain. After the shows, they had to go across town to eat, live and relax in a black neighborhood called Dustville. The sting of segregation was as lacerating as a dust storm; the pretty mountains ringing the outpost and forming all of its horizons could have accentuated the musicians' feelings that they were being held in a pen.

Apparently oblivious to the effect of Las Vegas's racial policies on the musicians' spirits, a local newspaper wrote an elegiac review of Nat King Cole and his trio at the Thunderbird. The reviewer reminded readers of the group's wonderful reputation, said the show was sold out at the dinner and late shows at the Thunderbird, and went through the list of the songs that were done so well: "Route 66," "Make Believe," "I Love You for Sentimental Reasons," "I've Got a Way with Women," "Bring Me Another Drink." "Yes Sir, That's My Baby" was done "like we have never heard before," the reviewer said. She added that the Thunderbird's publicity man said to her, "Well, we rang the bell again." The reviewer said, "Yep."

Nat heard a different bell tolling for him in Las Vegas, and he told his musicians that racial discrimination had so bothered him there that he would never go back. (By the time Joe Comfort left the trio the next year, Nat still hadn't returned to that city. But he did go back in 1951 on his own terms about his treatment; he was one of the people responsible for breaking down racial barriers in Las Vegas.)

In 1950, when the group went to England for the first time, the sidemen noticed that Nat began to distance himself from the group more and more. The trend started rather abruptly when the group met its English manager, who insisted that Nat, Maria and their valets, Carruthers and Sparky, stay at a first-class hotel, while the trio stayed at another, plainer place. It had never occurred to Nat to lodge his trio in a separate hotel; he questioned the arrangement.

The manager explained that English people never stayed with their "help." Nat said, "What help?" He explained that the men were his trio, part of the lifeblood of his career. Sparky knew that if Carlos had been along on the trip, he would have stood up for the musicians, too—perhaps even more than anyone else did. That was Carlos's style.

The English manager's plan prevailed, for some reason. The trio stayed in a different hotel from the Coles. When they traveled north to do a string of one-nighters throughout the country, the trio went in one Rolls-Royce with all the clothes and equipment, while Maria, Nat, and the English manager used another Rolls-Royce. The convoy went all the way to Scotland in the Rolls-Royces. Nat became so aggravated by the slow pace of the trip that when the tour ended in Glasgow, he insisted on hiring a small plane to fly the group back to London in a hurry.

Furthermore, the trio was not a rousing success that year, as it would be on two later trips. A Manchester, England, critic wrote a small item: "Nat King Cole and the Trio . . . may not be to everybody's liking. But even those without a particular liking for the lazy drawling tunes and paroxysms of rhythm of these American entertainers must admit that their art has a peculiar fascination. There is a careless charm about Nat King Cole's singing and piano playing and, despite myself, my feet began tapping in time to the primitive rhythm of the bongo player who beat native-style drums with his hands."

There were other reports of the lukewarm, condescending reception in England. Older members of the audiences sometimes walked out during the trio's performances. The trio's records had not yet become commonplace in the country. British audiences were not familiar with Nat's voice or instrumental work. England was a bastion of Dixieland and dance-band-music fans—"trad" jazz, the British called it; they formed clubs in all sorts of communities to play or admire it. Nat felt belittled by some of the English reviews, which were disdainful not only of his work but even, Costanzo noticed, of his appearance; Costanzo discerned a trace of racial prejudice in the British attitude.

Irving Ashby, who apparently felt demeaned himself by the separation of the leader from the trio, and who paid close attention to the trio's relations with Nat, also noticed that Costanzo's inclusion in the group meant the trio needed a new wardrobe. Instead of simply adding clothes for Costanzo, Nat began to wear a gray suit if the trio wore blue suits. Nat therefore cast himself in relief against the background of the trio. Ashby thought the arrangement was Maria's idea; though it undoubtedly made the group more interesting to look at, it grated on his nerves to be used as a virtual bookend.

For his own amusement and to make up to himself for what he perceived as a slight, Ashby said he felt wonderful traveling back to the United States on the *Queen Mary* in cabin class, because he could do whatever he wanted; he could play in jam sessions all night with the ship's crew and entertain the women aboard. He saw Nat standing against the rail on the first-class deck, on which he traveled with Maria, and felt sorry for "poor Nat" having to dress with formality for dinner every night. However, Nat, who was free to go to the lower decks had he wanted to, never made the short descent once.

Costanzo noticed similar trends afoot in the trio. He saw that Nat was doing more singing, allowing less time for the instrumental work, in which the bass, guitar, bongos, and conga could stretch out. Costanzo felt sorry that he couldn't do more playing. At the same time, concluding that Maria was behind the drift, he thought that she was doing exactly the right thing for Nat's career. He believed that it was because of Maria's management of Nat's image that Cole sustained his career as a superstar for as long as he did.

Costanzo and Ashby did not often see eye to eye on many issues. Ashby, for example, came to take a dim view of his own salary, even though it was more than Costanzo's, while Costanzo took his $175 starting salary with goodwill. Costanzo's salary went up to $250 a week by 1951—still less than Ashby's. Ashby also disliked watching Costanzo discuss fashions with Maria while the rest of the men in the Cole group were playing cards and having a drink as they traveled. Costanzo never drank or smoked in his life; he enjoyed talking about current events, clothes, and people in the news with Maria.

Costanzo thought that Maria could be aggressive and abrasive at times, but he admired her. He concentrated on the good times, maintaining a sunny outlook. A bundle of energy and enthusiasm, he was delighted when the trio and the Coles visited a bicycle factory in England and picked out bikes to take back to the United States. He could also remember nearly coming to blows with Ashby over some tiny issue, which itself was quickly forgotten. With a bowler hat and a furled umbrella in his hand, Ashby stepped out of the Rolls-Royce. Within seconds, Ashby took a bottle of milk from Costanzo and threw it on the ground. Costanzo was going to punch

Ashby, but Sparky jumped in between the men and stopped the fight. "Don't do that, Jack!" Sparky said.

Costanzo knew that both he and Ashby had prickly tempers; they could lose control perhaps a little too quickly. He was glad that the fight didn't materialize. Another time, he narrowly escaped fighting with someone else in Nat's entourage in a nightclub. A musician had stopped that fight by slapping Costanzo and telling him it was beneath him to fight over a woman in a bar. Life wasn't dull on the tour.

Costanzo always retained his sense of depression over the reviews in England, which disparaged Cole's élan and appearance as well as his music. Nat was not, feature for feature, a handsome man; he sometimes joked with friends that he was not good-looking, with his wide mouth, broad nose, and exotically slanted eyes. On television—and everyplace else—because he became such a familiar face, his wardrobe was so elegant, his voice so charming, and his bearing so regal and natural, his fans—friends and strangers—perceived him as a very good-looking man. The impeccable singer with the teasing, sparkling eyes delighted people. Costanzo knew firsthand that women found Nat very attractive.

Often enough on the road, Carlos Gastel and others moved in when Nat was hanging out at a bar with friends, because women approached Nat and tried to fling themselves at him. Women called him "The Black Panther" and "Mr. Silk." If women became especially flirtatious when they were escorted by their dates or their husbands, Cole staffers moved in fast to extricate their star from potential trouble.

Sparky had even received a directive from Maria Cole forbidding women, even family friends, from visiting Cole's dressing rooms. So Nat always said hello to them as they stood in the doorway for a minute. Then Sparky sent them to the bar; Nat met them for a drink. Sparky helped enforce the rule to protect Maria's interests, his own job, and Nat's reputation. Without that rule, perhaps some tiny incident could have escalated into a bizarre headline.

Back in the United States, when the group went to the South with the Big Show of 1951, Joe Comfort became disheartened again; he had been stationed in Alabama during World War II, and he had encountered segregation to a degree he had never had to endure in his native Los Angeles. Returning to Alabama, including Birmingham, in 1951 with Nat, crossing several state borders in a red, white and blue bus, Comfort also crossed the color line several times, accidentally on purpose.

Once he simply went into a segregated luncheonette and sat down next to the group's Northern-born white bus driver, Comfort told James Haskins. When the waitress told Comfort that the restaurant didn't serve colored people, he said he didn't blame the management. He gave his food order. The bus driver laughed so hard that his big fat stomach made the counter jiggle. Comfort was able to get himself served. Nat and Ashby were so alarmed that, after Comfort came out of the restaurant, they shouted at him excitedly, "You're going to get us thrown in jail!"

Costanzo had many indelible memories. To begin with, Nat had stirred up some controversy by hiring a white bongo player. "Why did you do it?" he was asked several times. "I hired the man I thought would do the best job," he replied. In Birmingham, Shreveport, and perhaps one other city, policemen actually took Costanzo off the band bus at the city limits as part of the routine of civic government. Furthermore, Costanzo was forced to stay in a separate hotel from the Cole group. He also wasn't allowed to play with the trio in some places. Duke Ellington had brought along a white drummer, Louis Bellson, for the tour. Bellson was allowed to play because, essentially, nobody noticed him very much. He had not yet made the headlines because of his future interracial marriage to singer Pearl Bailey. Duke didn't advertise or feature Bellson, as Cole had done with Costanzo. So Bellson could keep a low profile. Perhaps because he sat in the back of the orchestra, he blended in with the crowd better than Costanzo did. Costanzo sat in front of Cole's piano, and usually in front of the bassist and the guitarist. Costanzo's previous publicity as Nat's bongo player also made him conspicuous. Nat told Costanzo that a telegram had arrived, warning him not to let that "white boy" on the stage. So Jack was kept off for safety reasons, even though he was allowed to go backstage.

Despite the tensions between Ashby and Costanzo, Ashby remarked to James Haskins years later that the separation of Jack from the group was very upsetting. "We would have given up our salaries to have him be with us, because he was part of us," said Ashby. Learning about that remark years later, Costanzo was surprised. Yet all in all, he had thought that the group got along well. He and Joe Comfort were friends. For as long as Costanzo traveled with Nat, he observed that Nat was devoted to his wife. She sometimes traveled with the group for a while, then left it to go home, and later returned to the tours. She went along for the glamorous, splashy trip to Europe, of course. When Maria was not with the party, Nat and Costanzo became "hanging-out buddies" at night after the performances.

Costanzo recalled one night in San Francisco when the group played at the Fairmount Hotel; then he and Nat went to the Edison Hotel, which was a black hotel. Downstairs that night, Slim Gaillard was playing; with him, he had a wonderful *conguero,* Armando Parasa, who later went with Santana. Lionel Hampton arrived that night, too, to "hang out." When the show was over at about two o'clock in the morning, Hampton, who not only played drums and vibes but piano deftly—"two fingered piano," as it's usually called—sat down to play the top part of the piano, while Nat took over the bass register. They played "Stomping at the Savoy" so excitingly and imaginatively that Costanzo was transfixed. It was the most thrilling jam session that he ever had heard, he said years later. "Lionel, who likes to sing when he plays, was virtually screaming. I had played in Carnegie Hall three times by then, but that jam session was one of the highlights of my life, better than playing in Carnegie Hall."

Other memories stayed with Costanzo. One time, the group did what he believed to be the first racially integrated print ad—for Calvert's, as he recalled—in a magazine. He also remembered the times when he worked especially closely with Nat. "Nat told me that we were going to play 'Calypso Blues.' He said, 'Make up a beat.' I used an Afro-Cuban beat, and that's how we did the song. He sang, and I played. We did it on the Perry Como and Ed Sullivan shows. We also did 'Rhumba Azul' on a three-minute film. You could put a quarter in a machine like a jukebox and see a short film in those days. And we did 'Go Bongo' together. It happened when I was doing some gibberish in tempo, and we got a beat going, and we started something terrific. Nat had a beat when he sang and played. That's why he played dances. We were able to swing so much. Irving Ashby had a great beat on the guitar. Joe Comfort had a strong, moving beat and great musical abilities. If he had practiced, he would have been a great bassist; as it was, he was a wonderful bassist. Nat made all the decisions about what Ashby, Comfort, and I would use in the arrangements, and it was a happy playing group. Ashby and Comfort didn't play like they didn't want the conga and bongos." Sometimes Nat decided to include Costanzo on a ballad, too—to wit, "Lush Life," though Costanzo's performance was subtle, almost muted, on such a tune.

Hanging out with Nat, who drank two or three glasses of Scotch while Costanzo drank no alcohol, Costanzo was able to share confidences with his boss. Nat said that he had felt very bad about the breakup with his first wife, because she had helped him so much when he had been young. She was a wonderful woman, Nat confided.

He had left her because he had fallen in love with Maria, not because he had become famous. Nat added that Nadine and Maria were opposite types. Maria was alert, aware, and protective of Nat as a musician and a star. Nat listened to her because she was very intelligent and educated, if opinionated, he said. She was so influential that, in general, if she told him to do something, he would do it, or if she told him not to do something, he would refrain, he told Jack.

Sparky had the same impression—and at the same time knew that Cole on his own had a very playful side. It helped keep him and his entourage amused. The men liked to rate good-looking women in the audiences, Sparky recalled; Nat, the trio, and the staff would survey a crowd and assign it a number from one to ten for the attractiveness of the women. The men also played a ribald courtroom game. Carl Carruthers may have started it by saying to Irving Ashby one day, "I saw that girl you were with last night."

Ashby countered, "What do you mean? The girl you were talking to was no great shakes."

"We knew who had gone with whom," Costanzo reminisced, "so we decided to hold court." It became a ritual in which Nat served as the judge. There was always a prosecuting attorney, a defending attorney, and a defendant who had to defend himself against the charge of having been seen with a homely woman.

One night, Jack passed several hours after a show by talking with a very unattractive but especially pleasant woman. He was prosecuted in "court."

"She had a great personality," he protested.

Nat charged, "But was she *ugly*?"

Jack wouldn't admit that she was ugly.

Irving Ashby charged, "She was a walking gorilla!"

Nat stroked the underside of his chin with the back of his hand thoughtfully; it was a mannerism he often used.

Costanzo sometimes had flings on the road. Maria, who knew about them, once asked Jack whether he didn't feel guilty about infidelity. Jack, whose wife had refused to travel, said that he didn't feel guilty; he was gone for long periods of time, and she had chosen to stay at home. The marriage eventually broke up. Jack didn't confide in Maria that the opportunities for a well-publicized white bongo player traveling and playing with Nat Cole were priceless and continuous; Jack would have been a fool to hide.

At times, the weather broke the monotony for the travelers, especially when they flew in airplanes. Joe Comfort feared flying so much that, even though he rarely drank alcohol, he always had a few shots of whiskey to prime himself to get on a plane. Costanzo became inured to flying. Nat never really liked it. He would often ask Costanzo, "What do you think? This guy knows how to fly this plane?" He would stroke the underside of his chin while he flew.

Once a flight from Los Angeles to Florida was so rough that even Costanzo felt terrified. The fog was thick; the men couldn't see the wing tips during the whole flight. Nat paid rapt attention to every minute of the airplane's progress, mumbling about the fog, the pilot, the turbulence.

"We had a ball," Costanzo reminisced. "There were some fun things."

By the end of 1951, Joe Comfort and Irving Ashby left Cole's group. Not until many years later did Costanzo learn that Comfort had wanted a raise and was unable to get it. Nat was going through a problem about back taxes by then. So Comfort headed back to Los Angeles to play with the studio bands including Nelson Riddle's for Frank Sinatra albums. Irving Ashby contended that he left the group of his own free will, with a feeling of dissatisfaction about his salary and Nat's priorities for money management.

Comfort held Maria responsible for the sidemen's unhappiness with their pay. He told James Haskins that he had heard her remark that Nat was paying the sidemen more than Kenton paid his men. Ashby objected to Nat living in high style and indulging in a bit of gambling at Lake Tahoe at a time when he had tax problems. Ashby would have preferred that Nat share some of the wealth with the sidemen. Sparky Tavares was under the impression that both Comfort and Ashby really wanted to get off the road. He thought that was why they left. Someone else connected with the Cole group thought that Nat wanted to change his guitarist, anyway. His first choice was the standard-setting Wes Montgomery, as contemporary, articulate, fluid, and imaginative a jazz player as Nat could possibly have dreamed of taking along, but the brilliant improviser Montgomery wanted to stay home with his family in Indianapolis. Ashby had financial problems after he left Nat; he drove a taxi for a while before he was hired by pianist Oscar Peterson to play in his group. Comfort and Ashby both went through marital difficulties and divorces in their years with Nat and right afterward.

No matter what was happening behind the scenes in his trio or personal life, Nat fulfilled all his promises and engagements. Even though an announcement was made in late 1951 that the trio was breaking up, the event never took place—at least the concept of the trio never ended. Nat hired a bassist from Baltimore, Charles

Harris, and the progressive guitarist John Collins, who had known Nat in their high school days in Chicago. By early 1952, the trio was working on its usual schedule.

Leonard Feather, writing for *Down Beat*'s February 1952 issue, gave a bright welcome to the new personnel when Cole took the trio to an intimate Los Angeles bar called the Tiffany. "Waves of nostalgia, visions of the old days at Kelly's Stable and Nick's . . . overcame us as Nat played and sang, softly and superbly, aided by Johnny Collins's great guitar and Charlie Harris's able bass.

"Whether it was a ballad or 'Route 66' or an instrumental, it still reminded you that Nat was the first man to make it with a group of this kind, and today, more than a decade later, he still has the greatest group of them all. . . ." Though Feather wasn't fond of the bongo sound in the group, he said that "Costanzo played well on the numbers where his rhythms were called for. . . ." He praised Nat; ". . . still one of the great pianists of jazz; this, too, has become overlooked since he began standing up to work at the tall . . . microphones. . . .

"Nat has reasons for making all his records nowadays with big bands. . . . He explained it succinctly in a recent interview in *Jet*—'I may be doing jazz a lot more good than some of these real hip, cool people. I play and sing for a lot of folks who you could call square. They have confidence in what we're doing, so we can sneak in some jazz— and they like it because it isn't being forced down their throats.'

"But what was nice about the Tiffany was that the people there had their throats and their ears wide open; and Nat was as happy as the probably hip, possibly cool customers he played to. Nat, please find yourself a New York Tiffany and a couple of other Tiffanys and spare them six or eight weeks out of each year."

Nat played often at the Tiffany Club in Los Angeles after that. Feather reminisced thirty-nine years later for *Memories* magazine that he had taken one of his own songs to the Tiffany—"Where Were You"—for Nat to consider recording. "We'll see what we can do," Nat said with what Feather described as Nat's usual courtesy and friendliness. Nat included the song in his 1955 album, *The Tenth Anniversary Album,* for Capitol. By then he had been with the company for twelve years; perhaps the record had been named in 1953. It was excluded from *Jazz Discographies Unlimited,* in the usual martialing of some of the jazz world's forces to signal its disapproval of Nat's posture as a stand-up singer.

Chapter Sixteen

"MONA LISA" ENSURES A LUXURIOUS LIFE-STYLE FOR THE COLES AND THEIR NEW BABY, "SWEETIE"

*I*n one of the most important events of his life—from a commercial point of view—Nat recorded a song, "Mona Lisa," in 1949. Most people agree that it became his biggest hit. Only "Ramblin' Rose" a decade later may have come close to matching it (and perhaps surpassing it in the long run) for income earned.

The song "Ke Mo Ky Mo" had been easy to associate with Nat. It had a whimsical lyric. He had sung about "The Frim Fram Sauce"; he had crooned "Oh Kickeroonie" with sensual effect in an up-tempo love song. From his *Nat Cole for Kids* album in 1949, "Ke Mo Ky Mo" emerged as a special hit; at a time when Capitol Records was building its fortunes as an important company with a strong children's section, the album went to the top of the charts. Nat himself liked singing "Ke Mo Ky Mo" to his kids. Natalie would

recall his singing it to her and Cookie as one of their favorite childhood memories.

Nat himself nearly missed his cue about whether to record
"Mona Lisa," which eventually won an Academy Award in 1950.
The previous year, Paramount Pictures, eager to publicize an otherwise forgettable film called *Captain Carey, U.S.A.,* asked Capitol
Records to persuade Nat to record a song from that film, but Nat
didn't like the song. When he heard it was called "Mona Lisa," he
asked, "What kind of title is that for a song?" Later on he would
reflect that he had thought the song was "too highbrow." Without
confidence in it at the outset, he passed up the chance to record it.
So Paramount's music chief, Louis Lipstone, approached Carlos Gastel.

"I've never done this before in my life," Lipstone told Carlos,
"but I want you to do something for me out of friendship. I want
Nat to record "Mona Lisa.'"

"But Nat doesn't like it," Carlos said.

Lipstone persisted. "Try it."

Nat often recorded songs simply because music-business friends
asked him to. Alan Livingston, the Capitol executive, who would
become the president of the company after Wallichs, hesitated to
approach Nat about the song, because his brother, Jay, a composer,
had cowritten it with Ray Evans. Alan didn't want to press Nat and
so left the matter in Carlos's hands.

Nat said sure to Carlos and agreed to record "Mona Lisa."

The talented young arranger Nelson Riddle, who had been living
in the shadow of Les Baxter at Capitol, stepped into the job of arranging the song, though Baxter led the orchestra for the recording
date. Nat requested Riddle as the arranger and orchestra leader for
later Cole dates. Two other important arrangers and orchestra leaders, Billy May and Frank DeVol, who were also aware of Riddle's
talents, were glad to see that he was moving ahead because of Nat's
support.

"Mona Lisa" was one of the last records Capitol made at the
Radio Recorder studios on Santa Monica Boulevard before moving
to the 5100 Melrose Avenue studios in 1949, then in 1956 to new
studios at the Tower at 1750 N. Vine St. John Palladino was the
recording engineer for "Mona Lisa," as he had been for "Nature
Boy." Both out-of-tempo ballads were long shots for Nat, Palladino
thought. Nobody had much confidence in them; they were experi-
ments. Lee Gillette, who produced most of Nat's recordings,
worked on "Mona Lisa"; he later oversaw the conversion of Nat's

monophonic records to stereo versions, then stereophonic cassettes, as the recording industry developed better techniques in the 1950s.

As usual, for the "Mona Lisa" sessions, Nat was businesslike, not joking around at all. There was a screen separating Nat from the orchestra in those days when there were few and flimsy barriers in recording studios. Isolation booths for recording artists would come much later.

Nat wore his little, narrow-brimmed, trademark hat; Palladino always thought it was a crazy little hat. A Capitol executive had a photo of Nat wearing that style of hat hanging on an office wall. Nat also showed up as usual with his cigarette holder, which Carlos had given to him. Nat smoked a lot while he worked, but he never coughed.

Palladino knew that Nat's range was limited from a recording engineer's point of view. The quality was just not there, but the expressiveness Nat could wrest from his phrasing and the real tenderness in his voice enchanted Palladino. Capitol was always trying new things with Nat, because he had the musicality and talent to do anything.

Palladino felt nostalgic about Nat's piano playing. He had loved the trio's work with Oscar Moore and Johnny Miller because of the superb piano playing. But by the time Nat recorded "Mona Lisa," he had to be coaxed into playing the piano every time Palladino was in the studio with him. Nevertheless, Nat remained "a super gentleman and always prepared," as Palladino put it. The only thing that bothered him was Nat's recording of such a song as "Ramblin' Rose" in 1962. Taking sides, as so many people did on the question of what style of music Nat should perform, Palladino opted for Nat's jazz feeling and piano playing.

Once Nat finished recording "Mona Lisa," Capitol's executives didn't want to release it, because they didn't think it was commercial. Nat told them he had grown fond of it. "When I play it at home, even the dogs like it," he said, referring to his pet boxers.

Eventually Capitol made space on the back of "The Greatest Inventor of Them All," a swinging spiritual that was supposed to become popular. Nat recorded that one with his trio, and the song was included in a jazz discography that ignored "Mona Lisa." Capitol executives advertised "The Greatest Inventor" until salesmen began to send back word from the field. The disc jockeys were playing "Mona Lisa" all the time. It rose to number one on the

Billboard charts on June 10, 1950 and retained a popular rating until 1951, becoming Nat's longest-lived hit.

Just before its release, Nat felt some misgivings about the public's acceptance of the song and asked Lionel Hampton and Jack Costanzo what they thought. Costanzo said the music was poignant, the song told a story, and Nat was a storyteller. Costanzo thought it would be a hit. Hampton heard it and thought so, too.

Years later, the impeccable arranger, bandleader, composer, alto saxophonist, and trumpeter Benny Carter mimicked Cole's singing "Mona Lisa" and stepped up the tempo to such a fast pace that the song sounded like "Oh, the monkey wrapped his tail around the flagpole." Carter preferred Nat's work with bandleaders Billy May and Nelson Riddle and the altoist Willie Smith. So did John Tegler, a drummer who played with many bands—black and white, swing and sweet bands, among them Elliot Lawrence's. Tegler became friends with Nat during several long tours. They played gin rummy to pass the time as they traveled around the country. Tegler let it be known that he didn't like "Mona Lisa" at all. "I hated that song," he recalled. That's all the mischievous, confident Nat had to know. "Nat would sit there humming it to distract me while we were playing cards." The public, however, loved "Mona Lisa."

Even though the supposed lovely lady in the song had been dead for a few centuries—it has been suggested that she is a self-portrait of Leonardo da Vinci portrayed as a woman—perhaps enough of the public could remember times when they had been tantalized by an unattainable person with special mystique to identify with it. And Nat added his mystique to Mona Lisa's. For whatever reason, the public found nothing bizarre in a song about the painting.

It took a long time for the public to tire of the hit and stop buying and requesting it. Many of Cole's other songs had slower starts and less success in the charts, but they were destined for longer weathering in the public fancy. "Unforgettable," released in the same period as "Mona Lisa," didn't immediately have the same astounding surge, but "Unforgettable" matured into an enduring testimonial to Cole's unique sound. "Too Young" intrigued other singers who recorded it. (Joe Williams had the courage to record it as he neared age seventy.) "Mona Lisa," in common with "Nature Boy," underscored the drift of Nat's professional life and established him as a superstar, while the jazz world—or the critics anyway—virtually ignored Nat Cole from "Mona Lisa" on. He had put himself at a distance from jazz, becoming unobtainable in his own way, though with his characteristic friendliness and political savvy, he remained open to critics on a personal basis for the rest of his life.

His phrasing, his interpretations of lyrics, his subtle improvisations, and his implied pulse on his popular songs connoted that he remained a jazz-influenced singer. His intimate sound never changed. On some songs, his jazz inspiration was more obvious than on others. In May 1958, he recorded "Paradise" with Gordon Jenkins and his orchestra; the last bars of the song, which Nat hummed, had the musing whimsy that distinguished it as a soft, jazz-informed interpretation of a ballad. Yet someone always brought up the subject of his downplayed trio work and especially his neglected piano playing. "Despite Cole's ballad singing popularity, his permanent niche in American music will probably be as a jazz pianist," wrote Richard G. Hubler, undoubtedly irritating Nat when he saw the subject raised once again. Hubler wrote in *The Saturday Evening Post* in 1954: "A man who contributes much of the originality to his arrangements, Cole's [musical imagination] has produced experimental impromptus almost as far to the left as Schoenberg or Bartok. To more than one classical critic he is 'a baffling pianist' whose talents are distinguished by 'excessive meandering and strained harmonies.'* To others, he represents 'the creation of a rhythmic pulse so dominant that it is re-created in the feelings of the listener with a technical precision that makes all similar rhythms uniformly accurate.' Nine-year-old recordings of his are pioneering jazz rhythms today."

If he was no less of a jazz singer than Bing Crosby or Frank Sinatra, he was held accountable and criticized because he refrained from playing piano—except for one number, as most people noticed in all his public appearances. The other singers couldn't play—Bing Crosby couldn't even read music—and weren't blamed for what they left out.

The controversy didn't hold Nat's full attention, because he had an overriding thrill in his personal life.

On February 6, 1950, a few months before "Mona Lisa" was released, Maria gave birth to her first child by Nat. The newspapers printed a variety of names for the newborn infant, who would grow up to combine a stunning resemblance to Nat in features and complexion with some of Maria's mannerisms for dramatic expressiveness. The seven-pound, eleven-ounce infant at first was called Stephanie Maria in the Chicago newspaper; then the family settled

*A reference to intimations of behop in Nat's style.

on the name Natalie Maria, which appeared in *Ebony* magazine. Pretty soon, she had a nickname, "Sweetie," from her father; as most Cole nicknames did, "Sweetie" has endured behind the family's closed doors and with friends throughout Natalie's life.

Maria cried when she first saw Natalie, *Ebony* reported. "I bawled because I thought Nat would be disappointed," Maria told *Ebony.* "We had both anticipated a boy." On his first visit after the baby was born, Nat assured her that everything was all right. "Girls stick closer to home," he told her, "and truthfully, the moment I heard it was a girl, all the past feelings went away. I'm happy."

Ebony also reported the couple's first wish for their newborn: "We hope she won't go into show business. It just takes too much out of a human being." Natalie grew up very aware that her mother didn't want her to become an entertainer because of the stressful life. *Ebony* photographed Natalie with a nurse in their Hancock Park nursery, which was filled with everything that a newborn infant could ever want—a christening robe from Mr. and Mrs. Eddie "Rochester" Anderson, a carriage robe from the actress Hattie McDaniel, towels from the petite and beautiful actress and singer Dorothy Dandridge, and two potty seats from unnamed admirers.

Maria had come through an eleven-hour labor well and started exercises for her figure soon after Natalie was born. Cookie, Carol Claudia Lane Cole, then five years old, with bows in her hair and a Lord Fauntleroy–style lace collar, watched Maria feed the baby. Nat collapsed on a couch to snooze after playing with Sweetie and before singing at the Oasis Club in Los Angeles.

Nat had arranged his bookings so that he would be playing in Los Angeles in February, because Maria's obstetrician, Dr. A. R. Arbarbanel, had told the Coles that the baby would arrive that month. So Nat went to the hospital when Maria went into labor. At 6:07 P.M., the nurse found Nat and told him that he could have a peek at his new daughter.

"I looked at that kid for a long time," Nat told *Ebony.* "I felt something impossible for me to explain in words. Then, when they took her away, it hit me. I got scared all over again and began to feel giddy. Then it came to me. I was a father."

"Mona Lisa" ensured that Nat, Maria, Cookie, and Sweetie would live in royal style in Hancock Park. For ten months after the song became a nationwide hit, the Coles nurtured the hope that they would be able to maintain their luxurious lifestyle in a reasonably tranquil atmosphere, despite Nat's hectic schedule.

Chapter Seventeen

BUT THE IRS NEARLY TAKES IT ALL

One day Nat and Maria woke up in Philadelphia, where Nat was working, and read in the newspaper that the Internal Revenue Service had seized the Cole house in Hancock Park for back taxes. The Coles had left their children in the care of their household staff, including Maria's elder sister, Charlotte Sullivan, who worked as Nat's personal secretary; when Maria was gone, Charlotte acted as surrogate mother for Cookie and Sweetie. Though Charlotte didn't live in the Hancock Park house, she went there to work. She was in the house when the tax men arrived.

Nat canceled the rest of his engagement and hurried to board a plane with Maria and Sparky Tavares. Sparky later recalled the flight very clearly; in those days everyone traveled in one class. Maria and Nat shared adjoining seats; Sparky sat nearby and read the sports pages of a newspaper. Nat fell asleep. A man sitting next to Sparky was reading some official-looking papers. Eventually the man said to Sparky, "Is that Nat Cole?"

"Yes," Sparky said.

The man introduced himself as Philip Braunstein, an accountant. Saying he had read of Cole's tax problems, Braunstein gave a business card to Sparky and asked, "Can I be of some help?"

Sparky leaned over and told Maria: "This man is a tax person. Look at this."

As Sparky recalled, Maria, whom he knew was "not a sunshine person," someone with an optimistic outlook even under much less trying circumstances, was strained to the limit. "Oh," she said snappily, "forget it!"

Sparky held on to the card, until the plane landed. Carlos Gastel met the anxious little group. When Sparky and Nat asked Carlos whether he had heard of Braunstein, Carlos said that Braunstein handled accounting matters for many entertainers. So Carlos and the Coles called Braunstein's firm for help. "And that's where everything started to happen," Sparky remarked, describing the beginning of the road to recovery.

At their house, the Coles discovered that their cars, one of them a 1949 Cadillac, had been taken away by the IRS. "Nice cars," reminisced Marvin Fisher, who flew to California right away to try to help the Coles. Signs were posted outside the house to notify the neighbors—and in effect the world—that the Coles were on their way to having their house wrested from them. *The New York Times* published an item on March 14, 1951:

> The Collector of Internal Revenue ordered the $85,000 home of Nat (King) Cole, singer, seized and sold for nonpayment of income tax today. The collector, Robert A. Ridell, said the Negro musician owed the government $146,000 for income tax in 1947, 1948 and 1949. He ordered the seizure under a 100-year-old law and said the house might be sold within twenty days.
>
> Mr. Cole, who is now appearing in Philadelphia, created a stir in the fashionable Hancock Park district when he bought the home in 1948. Other home owners opposed his acquisition of the property, but dropped their objection when the United States Supreme Court outlawed race-restrictive covenants.

Several of Cole's friends bandied about theories of why Nat Cole was assessed for that much money and required to pay every penny of it. The family suggested that his position as a black man with riches and fame made him a natural target. The cost of the wedding and the house had called attention to his growing wealth.

Whatever the underlying cause was—if there was one—Nat Cole actually did owe the Internal Revenue Service that startling amount of money.

He didn't have the cash. He did, however, have the potential to earn enough money to pay the bill. As it turned out, he would earn millions in the years to come. In 1951, he had many hits, beginning with "Frosty the Snowman" as number one on the charts for a week in January, with "Too Young," "Unforgettable," and "Walking My Baby Back Home" following throughout the year—but as fast as he was earning money, he was also building up new tax bills.

Marvin Fisher was sitting in the Cole mansion with Nat, Maria, and Charlotte when a black man representing another man from Chicago rang the doorbell and announced that he had arrived to give Nat the necessary money to pay off the debt and save the house. For some reason, the group in the house decided instantly that Nat should not take the money and should figure out another way, if there was one, to weather the storm. Fisher couldn't remember the name of the benefactor from Chicago but thought that he was a newspaperman. The Coles explored other avenues.

Maria went with her chapeau in hand to her aunt, whose family loyalty overrode any other considerations she may have had. Even though Maria had married an entertainer and adopted Cookie against her aunt's wishes, the aunt gave the Coles twenty thousand dollars to keep the IRS at bay immediately and try to save the house from a government takeover.

Sparky observed that Phil Braunstein of the firm of Braunstein, Plant and Chernin went to see an IRS agent (not Ridell) in Los Angeles. Braunstein, a lawyer as well as an accountant, got the distinct impression that the agent didn't think that the Coles should be living in Hancock Park anyway—because of their race, not just because of the debt. Braunstein told the agent that he personally handled the affairs of people who owed even more to the IRS than the Coles did. Braunstein added that if the agent didn't attempt a settlement right away, he would make a legal issue out of it. The settlement plan began.

Carlos went to Capitol Records to work out a deal that would help Cole pay his debt. He also received a $30,000 check to augment the $20,000 check which Maria received from her aunt, and the Coles paid $50,000 to the IRS immediately. Capitol also agreed to pay $30,000 directly to the IRS every year for Nat for a period of four years. The promised money represented advances against Nat's future earnings from records. At the time, he was earning more than

$30,000 a year, and the remainder of his earnings was put in a de-
ferred-income account. That way he wouldn't keep piling up more
income-tax debt, while he was trying to get out of his previous
debt. And if he didn't continue to earn enough money to warrant
the $30,000 annual advances over a four-year period, the money he
had already earned and which was held by Capitol would cover the
payments to the IRS. Carlos also secured ownership of the masters
of Nat's recordings for Nat. Nat's ownership of his own masters was
enormously important for Nat's fortunes, too.

As it turned out, Nat earned far more than the $30,000 pay-
ments made for him by Capitol. Alan Livingston, who was a vice
president of the company during the period of Nat's tax troubles,
recalled that Capitol would eventually hold more than a million
dollars for Nat. Nat grossed an average of $2.5 million a year for the
company; from the early 1950s on, he never earned less.

In addition to annual payments, Nat was obliged to pay about
$1,000 a week out of his pocket to the IRS. By 1954, despite all his
payments, Nat still owed the IRS about $90,000. As Maria related in
her book, the IRS wanted the money right away. So the Coles borrowed $90,000 dollars from a bank—money guaranteed by Cap-
itol—and paid the government. Alan Livingston recalled that
Capitol Records was easily persuaded to back Nat, because he was
earning so much money at the time. The Coles paid off the bank at
the rate of $22,500 a year, according to Maria. And Nat's renegoti-
ated contract with Capitol guaranteed Nat $50,000 a year, including
the payment to the bank. Capitol was still holding back part of Nat's
earnings in a deferred royalty account.

The firm of Braunstein, Plant and Chernin managed Nat's financial affairs from the beginning of the crisis until the end of his life
and even continued its work after his death. Harold Plant counseled
Maria about her affairs into the 1990s, after he had retired, and
Maria worked with another national accounting firm.

Marvin Fisher recalled that Nat was distraught until the plan was
underway. Maria helped Nat by putting him on a $200-a-week al-
lowance, Fisher said, until Nat paid off much of the debt in the early
1950s. Fisher chuckled at the memory of Nat's allowance. All the
humor was in the hindsight. Marvin knew how tight the Coleses
financial situation was for a while. Years later, Maria divulged that
her sister had pretended that the fur coats in the closet were her
own; Charlotte claimed the silver, too. When the IRS men, who had
come to seize the household effects, were sizing up the piano with
the idea of taking it away with the cars, Charlotte simply said some-

thing to the effect of "You wouldn't!" That was how Nat made his living. The men left the piano.

Duke Niles, who had been the contact man for a publishing firm that gave Nat "I Love You for Sentimental Reasons," had two vivid memories of the period. He recalled overhearing a phone call between Carlos and Nat, in which Carlos instructed Nat to remember that out of every dollar he earned, fifty cents belonged to the government. When Nat was touring in the East soon after the crisis began, Niles went backstage to see Nat at the Adams Theater in Newark. Nat was very worried. He told Duke, "The sheriff is at the cash register, and if I don't get a hit soon, I don't know what I'll do."

Two weeks later, by Duke's reckoning, Nat's 1951 hits began to register on the charts—"Too Young" in first place by April 14, "Red Sails in the Sunset" in twenty-fourth place five weeks later, "Because of Rain" in seventeenth place in June, "Unforgettable" in twelfth place on November 3, and then by the middle of 1952, "Somewhere Along the Way" and "Walking My Baby Back Home," with the cream of Capitol's studio orchestras, with free-lancer Billy May, Pete Rugolo, Nelson Riddle and Les Baxter as the arrangers and conductors. Nat was not going to have a problem in earning enough money to pay the government, though he had gone through the tortures of the damned until he found that out.

In this period, his cash flow was put under such pressure that he couldn't keep up his one-hundred-dollar-a-week alimony payments to Nadine. She sued him for back alimony and received a court judgment of about $1,600. It took him a while to honor that obligation and continue with the payments on a regular schedule.

On April 20, 1951, *Down Beat* reported on the crisis that had come to public attention in March. Carlos Gastel, suggesting that Nat had known about the looming crisis in 1950, told *Down Beat*, "Nat owes the government money. That we don't deny. But he paid off more than $50,000 of the debt during the last year and recently offered them another $20,000, which they refused. We still hope we can find a way to prevent him from losing his home." At the time Carlos spoke to *Down Beat*, Nat, his wife and Sparky were flying home from Philadelphia, and their children were being permitted to stay in the Hancock Park house until Cole reached it. *Down Beat* editorialized: ". . . there were plenty of questions waiting to be answered. For example, what kind of business management permitted Cole's affairs to get into such a state? And why didn't the treasury department agents move first to attach Cole's salary from his engagements and his royalties from recordings?" The suggestion was that Nat's ownership of a home in Hancock Park was the real target, and he gave the government the opportunity to take the house by incurring such a big tax debt.

Somehow, the Coles managed to keep their sanity. In mid-1950, without fanfare, Maria recorded several songs with Nat. Perhaps the tax crisis put a damper on the enterprise by 1951. Whether Maria wholeheartedly wanted to resume a singing career or not is questionable. Some people who knew the Coles think that she did—at least from time to time. Since she had announced that she did not want her baby to grow up to become an entertainer, Maria at least must have had some mixed emotions about resuming her own professional career. On the positive side, she knew that glamour surrounded successful entertainers. She had never said that she disliked the money that a popular entertainer could earn. Some people have speculated that Maria stayed in the wings after her marriage because Nat may not have wanted her to work. Her influence was so strong that if she really had wanted to go back on the stage, Nat would undoubtedly have acquiesced. It was probably a combination of considerations that had brought about Maria's retirement in the 1940s when she met Nat. She could not have conducted a full-blown career and maintained her position as Nat Cole's wife; the scheduling conflicts would have been untenable. However, soon just before the family's financial crisis became public, she decided to go into a studio and record some songs with Nat for Capitol Records—perhaps with the notion of earning some money. Friends clearly remember the stress that the family suffered by 1951, and may have begun to learn about it in 1950. (Though a few years later, Nat would pay about two thousand dollars for a recording session for Cookie and Sweetie, it's likely that Maria, a former professional, would have earned money or worked under Nat's contract rather than paid Capitol for studio time.)

The arranger Pete Rugolo led the orchestra. By then, he and Nat had worked together on several projects, to their mutual artistic satisfaction; not the least of their good memories was their collaboration on "Lush Life." Rugolo had also written "Metronome Riff," at Capitol's request, for a "Metronome All-Stars Record" on which Nat played piano—the first official Cole assignment that Capitol gave Rugolo to work on in New York. He won best arranger award for 1946, 1947, and 1948. For later projects, Pete went to Nat's home; they discussed the way Nat wanted to go with a song. Rugolo knew Nat's range and key for every song. Nat loved good arrangements and encouraged the appreciative Rugolo. Cookie and Sweetie used to hang from the stairway banister, listening to their father work with Rugolo. Everything went smoothly in their work; Rugolo always found collaborating with Nat a "pure delight."

Of the several songs that Rugolo arranged for Nat and Maria, Rugolo's favorite was "Get Out, Get Under the Moon," because of the way Maria and Nat sang it so well together. She had a low, sultry voice, which blended uncannily with Nat's for a soft, velvety texture. The few people who heard the records liked them very much. For some reason, most weren't widely distributed; some were never released. A bit of one of her songs—perhaps one she recorded that year with Nat or one she made for Kapp Records, "A Girl They Call Maria," a few years later—was used in a documentary that Maria authorized Jo Lustig to produce about Nat in the late 1980s. Except for those records and two brief attempts to perform several years later—in the mid-1950s and then again after Nat's death—Maria never turned her full attention to developing a career. That would have required formidable concentration; she would have had to devote herself to an apprenticeship, even with influential show-business friends giving her a boost, and appear in rooms that lacked the glamour to which she had been accustomed in her daily life. By the 1960s, her singing style wasn't trendy; and then she didn't appear to have any need for a singing career.

Cole never blamed anyone but himself for his financial problems. He rued not having the education that might have helped him to prevent the mess. He kept working with such smoothness and showmanship that his audiences could never have guessed what he had been through by March 1951. On July 13 of that year, Cole explained to excellent jazz writer Ralph J. Gleason, that showmanship remained uppermost in his mind. Although Nat's forum was very different from Maria's, his emphasis and values ran parallel to hers.

"Jazz musicians could learn one thing," Nat said, "and that's presentation. Always be conscious of one thing. How am I going to present it? Am I going to be lighted right?" (Cole's lighting had been so atmospheric even in the mid-1940s for a Chicago concert that a reviewer felt inspired to mention how it had enhanced the whole performance dramatically.) "Make it *look* good and it will sound twice as good to the average guy because everything to the public is visual. Things like bum mikes and out-of-tune pianos are challenges. They make you go out to see if you can make the people forget about those little obstacles. You can't play on their sympathy and say: I can't give it to you tonight because the guy didn't turn on my spotlight right so I'm not going to smile. [Audiences] don't think of those things.

"Maybe we see a lot of things they don't even pay any attention to. They don't stop to figure out whether you had any rest or not. They're not interested in how tired you are. They want to be entertained, and that's where the showmanship comes in."

Gleason had been inspired to write about Nat because of the singer's ability to mesmerize any kind of audience with any type of music, from the people in the "cold and stiff" Venetian Room in San Francisco's Fairmount Hotel to the "hipsters" in Ciro's. "He gets across the footlights wherever he works, and should he desire to sit in with anyone, warm or cool, they'd better look out—this guy has class, and he can swing with anybody," Gleason said.

Onstage Nat never gave any hint of his mounting disenchantments.

"Work was his therapy," Sparky Tavares observed.

Chapter Eighteen

$\mathcal{A}$N APOLOGY AT CARNEGIE HALL

*L*ife magazine wrote a story saying that Nat had developed into a "melancholy monarch." "Uneasy lies the head that wears the crown" was the innuendo. Sparky didn't notice any permanent change in Nat's attitude. Once Nat made the arrangements so that he wouldn't lose his house or anything else, he faced life without despondency. The only thing that bothered him was racial prejudice, Sparky thought. For all his stature as an entertainer, he was often denied ordinary civilities. "That stuck in his craw, and he dealt with it," Sparky observed.

It was a common occurrence for people to approach Nat and say, "Boy, if you were white, you'd be as big as God," Sparky reminisced. He once heard Nat reply, "Well, I hope I never get that big."

"It was an uphill battle," Sparky remarked—because of race, not because of tax problems. Nat was so shy that the press may have interpreted his quietness as melancholy, Sparky thought.

Nevertheless, Nat began to have stomach pains. They didn't

bother him very much, and since he didn't like to go to the doctor, he simply kept up his usual schedule. He began touring with the Big Show of 1953, with arranger and orchestra leader Billy May and singer Sarah Vaughan, among others. They began in Boston, went on to Springfield, then to Providence, Rhode Island. After a New York concert in Carnegie Hall, they were supposed to continue to complete a three-month circuit.

Billy May had always found working with Nat to be the easiest of tasks. Nat decided what he wanted to do; he picked the tempo; he might say to Billy, "Let the band swing out here for eight bars. I'll come in on the bridge and finish it up." In the studios and on the road, Nat did the same thing. In the studios, Lee Gillette would sometimes make the job more complicated by thinking of ways to have Nat and Billy redo a song. Nat would say, "There's nothing wrong with that; it sounded good to me." So working with Nat·was a simple matter, especially on the road; the tour was going very smoothly.

On April 5, Easter-Sunday night in 1953, Billy May saw Nat come out on the stage of Carnegie Hall; he looked pale instead of his usual healthy dark self. Instead of singing, he apologized to the audience, saying, "I'm sorry, I don't feel well, I'm sick."

Earlier that day, Nat had been performing in a television studio in New York City, when he had been struck by strong pains in his stomach. He became very fatigued. Sparky helped Nat leave the studio; they made their way along Forty-sixth Street to Fifth Avenue, looking for a taxi to take them to the Warwick Hotel. It began to rain. Sparky hailed a taxi, but several cabs passed them by. Sparky knew it was because he and Nat were black. One cab stopped, then started to pull away, but Sparky held on, opened the door, and pushed Nat into the taxi. The driver said he wasn't going to take the men anywhere. "If you don't, we're going to rumble," Sparky said.

The driver turned around and saw that he had Nat King Cole in the backseat. "Oh. . . ," he said.

So he drove them to the Warwick Hotel, about seven blocks away. Sparky helped Nat get upstairs to his room, where he lay down.

Ivan Mogull, the music publisher, decided to pay Nat a surprise visit that afternoon. When he got to the room, he was upset to see Nat looking so ill. Mogull called his doctor, Gerald Lieberman. Though Nat didn't like the idea of seeing a doctor, he agreed to go to Carnegie Hall before the performance and have an examination backstage. The doctor had already surmised, from Nat's description of his symptoms on the telephone, that Nat had bleeding ulcers. When the doctor saw Nat, he became convinced that was the problem, and he told him to go to a hospital. Nat protested that he would wait until after a performance coming up in Washington, D.C. The doctor said that if he waited, he might die.

Two concerts—one at 8:30 P.M., the other at midnight—were scheduled for Carnegie Hall that night. Nat actually performed in the show at 8:30 P.M. But at 10:30 P.M., he went onstage to make the announcement that he had to cancel the second show. Then he let himself be admitted to New York Hospital–Cornell Medical Center on York Avenue at Sixty-eighth Street. Not long after that, he was operated on for his ulcers, and he was told to go home to recuperate and not to smoke at all for about three months.

Nat stopped smoking, but as soon as his doctor rescinded the ban, Nat began smoking heavily again. If there had been any possibility of postponing the operation, that idea had been discarded, Maria Cole recounted in the Lustig documentary, because Nat didn't want to run the risk of needing an operation when he was touring in the South. He might not be able to get proper medical attention there, and he ran the risk of dying from internal bleeding. He was so ill, however, that the operation couldn't have been postponed.

Back in Los Angeles, forced to convalesce for several months, he was edgy after so many years on the road. It may have soothed his nerves to know that his song "Pretend" went to number two on the charts and stayed among the hits for twenty-one weeks. He could turn on the radio and hear his own voice anytime of the day or night. It was not that he was more enamored of his voice as his fame grew. He agreed with Billy Eckstine, who said, "He's one of the two guys who took a style and made a voice of it—the other is Louis [Armstrong]." Nat could pass his convalescence by reading reviews that awarded five stars—the highest praise—to "Pretend." A critic said that Nat's record was the first vocal release of the song—and one of the biggest hits of the year. However, in late May, when Nat went into Beverly Glen Hospital in Beverly Hills for more treatment, his doctor actually told a United Press reporter that Nat was very ill. He had been unable to retain food in his stomach for several days and had to be fed intravenously. Maria Cole told an interviewer that Nat had food poisoning; she was really worried about his survival then because he was so stricken. He soon rallied and gradually went back to recording in Capitol's studio in August

1953 even though he was eating only a diet of soft food. He lost 17 pounds and weighed about 155 pounds.

Between June and November of 1953, five of his songs recorded early in the year had become popular enough to rank in the charts—"I Am in Love," "Return to Paradise," "A Fool Was I," "If Love Is Good to Me," and "Lover, Come Back to Me!" "Return to Paradise," from an exotic movie starring Gary Cooper on the South Sea island of Samoa, intrigued Nat's fans; they requested that escapists' anthem and played it enough to put it in the fifteenth spot on the charts—his best commercial effort during that period. "Lover, Come Back to Me!" with Billy May, an up-tempo love song done with such passion and rhythmic intensity that Nat effectively sang the exclamation point in the title without ever raising his voice, became the sixteenth most popular song in the country by November.

Cookie thought it was fun to have her father at home. He took her with him on many outings. And three-and-a-half-year-old Sweetie had the pleasure of his company, too, though she later did not remember the details of some of the adventures. He took her with him to the studios; since she would not be quiet while he recorded, somebody escorted her into a hallway and amused her while Nat did his work. Milton Karle, visiting Cole on the West Coast, recalled playing with Sweetie in a hallway, giving Nat the freedom to work with the orchestra.

Nat told reporters he was going to take Cookie and Sweetie into a studio to record. He said he wasn't sure how successful the effort would be, because Sweetie tended to yawn in the middle of songs. But he was clearly happy to have a chance to play with his kids in the music world.

Nat also took Cookie and Sweetie to visit Billy May and his wife at home one day. May was impressed by how beautiful Cookie was and how vivacious Natalie seemed even then. She was already in show business, May's intuition told him.

"Nat wanted to show her off. He told her to sing for us. 'Show them how you can sing,' he directed her. So Sweetie imitated Nat singing 'Walking My Baby Back Home,' a big hit for him during the previous year and still played on the air often by 1953. She sang with spirit and charm, exactly as if she were a little trouper at center stage. Then she suddenly stopped and said, 'I have to go to the bathroom!' But she had that indefinable star quality. And she looked just like him. She was dark, and she had his features," May reminisced.

In those days, despite the controversy Maria's influence on Nat's affairs stirred up with his sidemen, the Cole family's stability was nearly an oddity in Nat's milieu. Carlos Gastel and Billy May divorced their first wives and married each other's wives. Carlos's new wife, Auletta, had an easy manner and a sense of humor that amused Sparky Tavares; he knew, however, that Maria disapproved of Auletta's drinking habits, ones that suited Carlos's very well. Auletta and Carlos divorced, anyway. Her drinking habits did not prevent her from living to a ripe old age, long after Carlos had died. Billy May also divorced a second time and remarried two more times, finally settling down with his fourth wife, Doris.

Sparky Tavares observed that the guiding principle for entertainers whom he knew at that time was to marry, and if they didn't get along with their spouses, to divorce instead of trying to work out the problems in some fashion. The demands and satisfactions of a life connected with the arts were consuming. Maria, Sparky noticed, was not well liked, especially among the women and even some of the men in her gossipy milieu and on its fringes. Maria, for her part, was critical of people and disliked the fashion for men to start drinking at 5 P.M., go out on the town, and then, after hours, keep partying well into the night, sometimes until morning. Her husband loved his lifestyle as a musician and a night person; he loved the people with whom he worked and whom he attracted as fans. The widow of Dave Cavanaugh, an important behind-the-scenes man at Capitol Records and a Cole intimate, recalled how much her husband drank socially with the crowd; Mildred Cavanaugh thought he had a drinking problem, and, in the very long run, he thought so, too, and stopped drinking. So did several others in the crowd. Carlos never stopped. His doctor told him to stop drinking and smoking, but every time he thought of quitting one habit, he needed the boost of the other, he said.

In the 1950s Maria briefly tried a performing career again, with Nat's support, in several fine rooms—Ciro's in Los Angeles, the Fairmount Hotel in San Francisco, and in several East Coast spots. Despite her gowns and arrangements, she was not an electrifying presence as a solo stand-up vocalist. She was far more dramatic when she wore a tiara in her hair and visited Nat's opening nights as if she were the Queen of Coledom. No matter what twists and turns the Coles' relationship took, the marriage survived its worst moments. Close friends noticed that no matter what tensions Maria sometimes revealed, Nat continued to trust absolutely his wife's judgment concerning his well-being, especially about his career.

Sparky never saw anything that made him think the Coles would ever divorce. For one thing, a divorce would have been too costly. Sparky thought the idea of divorce was anathema because of its effect on any family. Marvin Cane believed that Nat felt a moral obligation to his family. Nat and Maria began to think about adopting a son, since Maria had not had a child after Natalie.

Maria had her own friends in Beverly Hills social circles, as several people observed, and Nat had his friends in the entertainment world, and the Coles had friends in common. One of Maria's best friends for a long time was Geri Branton, the wife of the lawyer Leo Branton, Jr., who maintained a position of influence in Nat's affairs for years. Nat liked to spend time with some friends with whom Maria might have felt uncomfortable—usually because they offended her standards for dignified behavior or because she thought they took Cole's attention from his family.

Although Nat never kept up with Carlos's drinking, for example, Nat sometimes spent a great deal of time in Carlos's company and with other party-oriented friends. Alan Livingston remembered an evening in his office when Carlos, Nat, and Carlos's bodyguard, Big John, walked in and asked him to go for a drink with them. Livingston wanted to go home that night, so Carlos had Big John lift Livingston off the floor and carry him to a bar. Livingston went along with it because Carlos was a happy, genial, fun-loving guy, as well as one of his best friends. He spent several hours drinking with Nat, Carlos and the bodyguard. That was the way life was.

Nat had groups of friends in the cities where he entertained; in Chicago, he had old friends in the business community. He also had good friends among his fans in the clubs where he worked in Los Angeles. He was known for his gentlemanly, witty personality there, though his friend Lee Young never noticed that Nat was particularly distinguished for his sense of humor; it was not a side of himself that Nat showed Lee. Nevertheless Nat liked to make up fantastic little stories to have as private jokes with some close friends, some of them pretty girls. Jazz writer and researcher Pat Willard recalled that she and Cole had in common a pretty friend with bright red hair. Pat and her girlfriend used to go together to see Nat at the Tiffany Club. Nat invented a playful tale for Pat's friend about his being a little man who inhabited the incinerator of the woman's apartment house; there Nat lived a merry, independent little life. His fans at such places as the Tiffany knew about Nat's fun-loving side.

By 1954, Nat Cole was back on the road, resuming the schedule that diminished the intimate moments he could spend with his family—and heightening the adventure of a life in music.

Chapter Nineteen

WINNING THE BATTLE IN LAS VEGAS

Although Nat had said in 1950 that he wouldn't go back to Las Vegas, he took his new group—John Collins, the guitarist, and bassist Charles Harris—into El Rancho Vegas, probably as early as 1951. Nat's 1950 appearance had earned such good reviews, and the Thunderbird casino where he had worked had made such a big profit, that casino operators couldn't ignore him. He definitely played in El Rancho Vegas in 1952—with the understanding that all the men, not just Jack Costanzo, would have access to all the facilities in the casino. Nat, Collins, Harris, and Sparky and company did not have to stay in the segregated section of town.

Nat signed a contract for a fee that he considered to be less money than he thought he should get, because he was overridingly intent on overcoming the strictures of segregation. According to the custom in Las Vegas, he was not supposed to work for any other casino while he was in El Rancho Vegas's stable of entertainers. However, when it came time to sign another contract for 1953, Nat asked for more money and couldn't get it from the owner of El Rancho Vegas.

Therefore, Nat went to entertain in Lake Tahoe, Nevada, without a contract for another engagement in Las Vegas. Carlos Gastel, accompanying the group in Lake Tahoe, bumped into Jack Entratter, who had opened the Sands in Las Vegas. Even though Entratter knew casino operators were not supposed to lure entertainers away from each other, Entratter offered Nat the price he wanted plus the unequivocal freedom from segregation for himself, his group, and also his family. To the great ire of the owner of El Rancho Vegas, Nat switched to the Sands. He performed there every year for the rest of his life. It became one of his most important annual stops, along with the Copacabana in New York, the Cocoanut Grove in Los Angeles, and the Chez Paree in Chicago.

By 1956, national newspapers carried items about Nat's new three-year contract at the Sands. He would earn $500,000—believed to be the highest fee ever paid an entertainer up to that time—for appearing for three weeks each year, in 1956, 1957, and 1958. The contract symbolized Nat's victory over segregation and set a precedent for other black entertainers who had suffered the same outrage. By the late 1950s, they, too, found conditions better for them in Las Vegas. Whenever Nat's family had a confrontation with Sands staffers on race-related matters, Jack Entratter stepped in to quash the trouble. Nat's contract also let the world know how he had vanquished his tax bill. A brief recapitulation of his achievements on the hit lists in the 1950s underscores the reason for Entratter's eagerness to have Nat entertain at the Sands.

On September 30, 1950, "Orange-Colored Sky" ranked fifth and stayed in the *Billboard* charts for fourteen weeks, keeping "Mona Lisa" company for a while. He recorded it with his trio and Stan Kenton and his orchestra, including Maynard Ferguson and Shorty Rogers on trumpets and Art Pepper on alto saxophone; they introduced the song on television.

"Frosty the Snowman," done with the Pussycats, one of the choral groups he sometimes recorded with, went to number nine on the charts in early 1951. A few more songs went to the lower regions of the popular lists between February and April of 1951. Then "Mona Lisa" went through the roof. It hadn't been in orbit for very long before "Too Young" soared to the number-one place and stayed there for twenty-nine weeks. About 2 million copies—or nearly as many as "Mona Lisa"—were sold. Close on the heels of "Too Young" came "Red Sails in the Sunset," a simple but durable tune, although it only went as high as the number-twenty-four spot for two weeks. On November 3, 1951, "Unforgettable" made its debut in the number-twelve spot and stayed there for fifteen weeks. "Somewhere Along the Way" in May 1952 and "Walking My Baby Back Home" in July both went to the number-eight position—the first done with Nelson Riddle, the second with Billy May—and reverberated around the country throughout the rest of the year. "Funny, Not Much" with Pete Rugolo, "Because You're Mine," "I'm Never Satisfied," and "The Ruby and the Pearl" with Les Baxter leading the orchestra, and then "Faith Can Move Mountains" with Nelson Riddle also made their way onto the charts.

Every time anyone stepped into a car to drive anyplace and turned on the radio to a popular music station, one or another of Nat's songs would play within a little while. To announce his name was superfluous. Nobody sounded vaguely like him—except for his brothers, and, oddly enough, another piano player, Oscar Peterson. Peterson was destined to inherit the mantle of being the greatest living jazz pianist from Art Tatum. Peterson's rare vocal performances fooled most people into thinking Nat was singing. However, none of the Cole brothers or Oscar Peterson were making vocal records broadcast on a national scale. Peterson may not have made a vocal recording until after Nat died. Nat's whispery, tender sound seemed to be unique. No matter what he sang, from the first notes, everyone knew that it was Nat's voice, and the song's interpretation was going to be hypnotic. His voice was not just part of the American landscape of familiar, soothing sounds; it was a spell-weaving voice, which transported people far away from their routine concerns for at least a little while. He took people on solitary journeys to their secret spiritual niches where they could commune with themselves. That was part of what made his records so desirable, no matter what style of music he sang.

The year 1953 began with "Pretend," done with Nelson Riddle, another million seller, which went to second place for two weeks and stayed on the charts for twenty-one weeks. Even though Nat's other songs on the charts in the early 1950s didn't get very near first place, many were extremely popular; the cult hit "Return to Paradise" and "Lover, Come Back to Me!" were good examples. By 1954, the ballad "Answer Me, My Love" went to number six for a nineteen-week run on the charts, becoming another million-copy seller. "Smile," written by Charlie Chaplin for his 1936 movie, *Modern Times,* and "Hajji Baba," an exotic, somewhat monotonous ditty from a film, received considerable attention. A new arrange-

ment of "The Christmas Song" came out in 1954 with Nelson Riddle leading the orchestra; it made the voyage to twenty-ninth place
for a week in December.

In 1955, "Darling, Je Vous Aime Beaucoup," "The Sand and the
Sea," "A Blossom Fell," "If I May," done with the Four Knights, "My
One Sin," and "Someone You Love" constituted a string of hits in a
row.

These successes kept Nat's fans too content to recall the brief
flurry of unsettling publicity about his tax and health troubles. Nat
could simply swallow any upset feelings he had whenever he
stepped up to a microphone anyplace; his tensions never surfaced
for a second during his vocal performances. Through the magic of
his absorption in music, his problems evaporated. The only hint of
strain that he showed the public was a slight hoarsening of his
voice. Cigarettes were lowering it and making it huskier before age
would have made the alteration naturally. It was an attractive matu-
ration—a burnishing—of his sound.

So the Sands in Las Vegas got a bargain in Nat Cole.

It would be the setting for his one album done while he was in
performance. Called *Nat Cole at the Sands,* it was recorded on January 14, 1960, beginning at 2:30 A.M. as an after-hours show that Nat
staged for his friends. Some were entertainers at other casinos in
town, and so had no chance to see him work at the usual hours.

The recording engineer from Capitol was surprised that the session came out sounding as fine as it did. He was always leery of
recording live performances, with all the uncontrollable elements
that could interfere with the quality. With the music director of the
Sands, Antonio Morelli, leading the band, and Capitol's Dave Cavanaugh, with whom Nat loved to work, as producer, Nat sang a
repertoire of sophisticated songs. "Ballerina" had been a big hit for
him. Others were included because they held a special fascination
for him: "Funny," "The Continental," "I Wish You Love," "You
Leave Me Breathless," "Thou Swell," "My Kind of Love," "Surrey
with the Fringe on Top," "Where or When," "Miss Otis Regrets,"
and "Joe Turner's Blues," some of them among the best popular
songs written. Not many singers could turn on a dime from "Miss
Otis Regrets" to "Joe Turner's Blues." It was Nat's incandescent
charm and taste that allowed him to jump among the genres.

After he finished at dawn, he wasn't ready to go to bed. So he sat
down for a drink with the recording engineer and several Las Vegas
showgirls who were his friends, among them one ravishing Asian

An early publicity shot of Nat (*courtesy Rutgers Institute of Jazz Studies*).

Top left: The second trio: Johnny Miller on bass, Nat on piano, Oscar Moore on guitar (*courtesy Joe Franklin Productions*). *Bottom left:* The trio in 1946 (*William P. Gottlieb*).

Nat with his original trio, c. 1940. *Left to right:* Wesley Prince, Oscar Moore, Nat (*William P. Gottlieb*).

Nat with Eden Ahbez, who sold Nat his first big hit, "Nature Boy" (Metronome *magazine collection*).

Nat at the piano, 1947 (*William P. Gottlieb*).

Left: Harry "Sweets" Edison (*Leslie Gourse*).

Above: The Capitol Records Building in Los Angeles (*Leslie Gourse*). Maria Cole on the first trip to England, 1950 (*courtesy Jack Costanzo*).

Nat and Red Ingle (*courtesy Rutgers Institute of Jazz Studies*).

The trio at the height of their popularity (*courtesy Joe Franklin Productions*).

Nat King Cole and his trio: Joe Comfort, bass; Irving Ashby, guitar; Jack Costanzo, bongos; Nat King Cole, piano (*courtesy Jack Costanzo*).

Right: Nat with Joe Sherman, who wrote "Ramblin' Rose" (*courtesy Joe Sherman*).

Above: Nat, Billy May, Johnny Ray (*courtesy Rutgers Institute of Jazz Studies*). Maria, Nat and Cookie. (Pianist Phil Moore is on the far left; the man on the right is unidentified.) (*courtesy Joe Franklin Productions*)

Above: Bobby Van and Nat at the Harvest Moon Jazz Festival, Chicago (*courtesy Rutgers Institute of Jazz Studies*).   *Left:* Nat in *The Scarlet Hour,* a 1955 Paramount release (*courtesy Joe Franklin Productions*). Nat was a generous supporter of and fund-raiser for The March of Dimes (*courtesy Rutgers Institute of Jazz Studies*).

Above: Nat and Pearl Bailey in the 1958 Paramount release *St. Louis Blues (Joe Franklin Productions). Above right:* Nat and "Ol' Blue Eyes" (Metronome *magazine collection).* Lee Young, who often played drums for Nat from the 1930s through the 1960s (*Leslie Gourse*).

The former Cole house in Hancock Park, an exclusive section of Los Angeles (*Leslie Gourse*).

Left: Nat in "The Nat King Cole Musical Story": The epitome of ease, style, and sophistication (*courtesy Joe Franklin Productions*).   *Below:* Jack Costanzo and Nat let loose (*courtesy Jack Costanzo*). *Bottom:* Nat arriving in France on his last trip. To his right are singer Donna Hightower and Louis Victor Mialy (*photo by Claude Poirier/courtesy Louis Victor Mialy*).

Top: Nat surrounded by family and friends on the popular television show "This Is Your Life" (*photo courtesy of the National Broadcasting Company, Inc.*). *Above left:* Barbara McNair, who starred with Nat in his show "I'm with You" (*courtesy Barbara McNair*). *Above right:* Maria and Nat, with his ever-present cigarette, in Europe in 1960 (*photo by Claude Poirier/courtesy Louis Victor Mialy*). Louis Victor Mialy and Nat in Paris, August 1960 (*photo by Claude Poirier/courtesy Louis Victor Mialy*).

The quintessential Nat King Cole (*courtesy Capitol Records, Inc.*).

The next generation: Eddie and Natalie Cole (*courtesy Eddie Cole*).

The Doheny Library at the University of Southern California houses the Nat King Cole special collection (*Leslie Gourse*).

girl with whom he bantered and flirted. This was his time of day with his kind of people.

Cookie Cole recalled for James Haskins that she never had felt at ease in Las Vegas because she was one of the few black people there. There were only the rest of her family, the men in Nat's group, and the service workers in the casinos. For Nat, the bright lights of the Strip supplied the real allure of the town. A few Cole insiders felt that Maria disliked Las Vegas exactly because of its gaudy, glamorous diversions. When Nat fell in with his friend Sammy Davis, Jr., in Las Vegas or Lake Tahoe, Nat was likely to lose money at the gambling tables, though he was not ordinarily a gambling man. Maria abhorred the idea of Nat gambling. Jack Costanzo recalled an all-night party that Sammy Davis threw at his house in Lake Tahoe. Every entertainer and casino staffer in town was invited, including, of course, Cole and his trio. Costanzo remembered that he and Davis finally went to sleep on the floor because all the beds in the house were occupied by guests. Jack couldn't recall seeing Nat at the party. It's probable that Maria was in Lake Tahoe at the time; it would not have been her kind of party. Nat wouldn't have gone to it if she were on the road with the group. Otherwise, he would have been the first one inside the door.

Gary Stevens, the public-relations man who first met Nat when he was a virtually unknown pianist in Kelly's Stable in 1941, saw Nat one night in the 1950s in the Sands. Nat introduced Gary to Maria for the first time. She was definitely uncomfortable in that milieu, Gary Stevens sensed. "She spoke with staccato thrusts, and her eyes were flashing," he said, recalling his impression of the normally bright-eyed Maria. Her manner was in sharp contrast to the, poised, smiling woman in a filmy, pink-colored dress whom songwriter Joe Sherman recalled as a guest at a surprise birthday party thrown for him in his New York apartment during the same period. In Las Vegas, Maria didn't seem to want to have Nat's attention diverted from her, Stevens thought, so he didn't chat for very long.

As time went on, Maria rarely went to Las Vegas, perhaps because she didn't like the gaudiness and the life-style there, though she did accompany Nat to many other places. Cookie and Sweetie stayed off the road for the most part and felt that the rare moments spent with their father were treats.

Chapter Twenty

CAPPING LIFE AT THE TOP IN POP IN 1954 AND 1955, COLE RECORDS *AFTER MIDNIGHT,* A CLASSIC JAZZ ALBUM

*I*t was a very different reception for Nat and Maria Cole in Europe in 1954 than it had been in 1950. Jukeboxes had come to England; audiences also were used to the sound of Nat's voice broadcast regularly on the British Broadcasting Corporation. "Remember Me" and a variety of his songs, from his million-and-more sellers to his lesser-known ones, were available to Britons. In 1953, drummer Lee Young replaced Costanzo when Nat went back on the road. Nat had told Jack that he wanted to forgo the Latin percussion and try the usual jazz drums again. Of the 21 million records Nat had sold in the first decade of his Capitol contracts, over 7 million were sales of seven records alone. Orchestras in London restaurants struck up a song from Nat's repertoire whenever Maria and Nat entered a restaurant. "Answer Me, My Love" was a popular welcoming tune.

Nat and Maria, with Sparky, Carl Carruthers, and perhaps a maid, stayed at the Savoy Hotel. Sparky, by then acting as the road manager without the official title, made sure that the instruments got to the plane and rehearsals took place. He carried the money; Nat had put Sparky in charge of that very large responsibility.

Nat's concerts at the Palladium were sold out; he was performing with his own trio backed by an orchestra made up of Britons. The British musicians' union had tried to force Nat to leave the trio at home, but when that tactic nearly succeeded in keeping Nat from playing in England, the musicians' union relented. Nat took along his own men. Val Powell, the Palladium's manager, had threatened to bring legal action against the union if it didn't let Nat play with his trio and instead forced him to cancel. That would have put the Palladium's orchestra out of a job. Lee Young thought that Carlos also had stepped in to arrange a trade of Stan Kenton's band for Ted Heath's. Kenton would tour England, and Heath would visit the United States. The arrangement helped Nat to get his way in London.

Nat's tour was scheduled to take seven weeks, with visits to England, France, Ireland, Scotland, Holland, Denmark, Sweden and Norway—about fifteen thousand miles in all. His performance in France preceded his work in Britain.

In France, Nat played a one-night engagement at the Palais du Chaillot. French fans, too, were familiar with his singing by then. They kept calling for him to sing more. When the French orchestra backing up Nat and the trio began to play, the audience booed their own nationals. "The musicians booed right back," Nat told a reporter, enormously amused. If the French audience failed to understand the lyrics to his songs, it didn't seem to matter. The French applauded his love songs. A French critic wrote that Cole was: "An artist, a thorough musician who doesn't resort to acrobatics to excite his listeners . . ." However, other critics complained that they wanted to hear more of his "excellent piano playing."

From France, the Coles crossed to England for Nat's week at the Palladium, March 22 through April 3. Nat and Maria were photographed visiting major tourist attractions and dining in formal clothes for their sixth wedding anniversary. Nat was photographed trying to take a picture of the Buckingham Palace guards, using a camera that Maria had given him, but he proved inept at using it. They visited a cannon captured by the Duke of Wellington in a battle against the Spaniards and displayed near Whitehall. In Trafalgar Square, Nat waited patiently for birds to eat out of his hand. As usual, he elicited a tribute to his down-to-earth, friendly manner. "He's not at all a big shot," commented one British onlooker. A London cabdriver taking the Coles someplace became engrossed in watching a boat race and failed to stop for a policeman's raised hand at a crossing. When the policeman noticed that Nat and Maria were riding in the backseat of the car, he simply smiled and waved them along.

Nat moved north in England, playing to standing-room-only crowds in Liverpool. Crossing into Scotland, Nat sang to a packed house in Glasgow and put on kilts and carried a bagpipe for a publicity photograph. A critic called him "that sleek black Prince of Song."

In Dublin, Nat had a more unusual treat. While Maria went shopping and bought clothes by designer Sybil Connolly, Nat was serenaded by several hundred people who gathered outside his dressing-room window. "I'd lean out the window and sing to them," Nat later told a reporter. "And they'd sing Irish songs back at me. We'd keep it up for an hour." With a little smile, he added, "They sang much better than I do." Sparky was fascinated by the several hundred people singing in the dark back alleyway; their voices really had a melodious sound.

When the tour finished, Nat and Maria headed back to Paris for a week's vacation. At least that was what the press called it. Actually, it was more of the same: Nat posed for pictures with Maria. He was always working. Lee Young recalled that Capitol's men always met Cole, guided him socially, and took him to radio and television stations. During his ten years with Cole, from 1953 to 1963, Lee noticed that Nat didn't have any leisure; all his activities were career-oriented. Lee got the chance to play golf all over the world, even in Tokyo, Osaka, and Nagoya, Japan, in the 1960s. Nat would work there day and night, too. In Paris, Maria was photographed with her foot on a table in a restaurant where the owner exercised his prerogative of conferring the traditional honor of the house. The honor was a gift garter, which the owner slipped up Maria's slender leg. She steadied herself by holding on to Nat's shoulder with one hand.

The Coles went out on the town with Lennie Hayton and his wife, Lena Horne, and sat in the audience at the Club de Paris, where the handsome singer Herb Jeffries, who had sung with Duke Ellington, was performing. Maria went browsing among the Dior gowns, the press reported. Nat told a writer, "Those European audiences don't dig the words, but when you sing to them, you can see and feel that they get the message. And everywhere I went in Europe, the people were so sweet. Sometimes I would ask myself: 'Am I worth all this?'"

It was a question that might have occurred to him more readily than it should have by then, because, when he went back to the United States, he was treated with the usual racial schizophrenia. Graphics artist Mel Fowler, then working as a floor manager in the mid-1950s at television stations in San Francisco, witnessed the biased actions of a few lower-echelon station staffers toward Cole and Louis Armstrong. Cole showed up for a guest appearance on a variety show at one of the stations. Dressed in exquisite clothes, Cole was a tall, handsome man, as Fowler recalled, not focusing on how dark Cole was or that he had a couple of pretty white women accompanying him to the show. Fowler overheard conversations among some of the workers, who were filled with jealousy and prejudice. Fowler was sure that the white women made no difference in the reception Cole got from the technicians; the men were simply envious of Cole's fame and bigoted against all Negroes, Fowler thought. At another station, Fowler had seen Louis Armstrong star on a television show. Afterward, he sat alone with his wife, Lucille; nobody spoke to them. The Armstrongs had chatted with Fowler when he walked up to say hello.

Nat couldn't escape the persistent criticism of his decision to sing popular songs as a stand-up singer either. Once a journalist apparently aggravated Cole so much by berating him for deserting the piano bench that Nat was reported to have lost all patience and told the man, "That piano is a millstone around my neck!"

It was uncharacteristic of him to lose his temper in public. However he was annoyed that he wasn't congratulated more about his pivotal importance in elevating the status of the small group in jazz. He wanted to roam free and grow in many ways after that. He would undertake acting roles in films and become host of his own television show in the late 1950s; he also would produce a stage show and try to take it to Broadway in the 1960s. Whether those projects were his own idea or Maria's, they captured Nat's imagination completely. He still found moments to fit in a jazz performance now and then. One of them went onto a classic jazz record, *After Midnight.*

Harry "Sweets" Edison had known for a long time that Nat wanted to make an album with particular musicians; Nat knew exactly which jazzmen he wanted for each song. But the years passed, filled with other obligations and priorities. In 1955, a private sorrow made him melancholy for a while. Perlina Coles was very ill with cancer. Nat and Maria flew to see her. Nat's mother died at age sixty-three on February 23, in North Chicago. Her husband was still pastor of the First Baptist Church there.

Evelyn felt that Maria was very kind at that difficult time for the family. There was nothing unusual in Maria's consideration; in those days, Evelyn and Maria had easy, warm relations. At the funeral, Evelyn and all her brothers cried. They rallied around Evelyn after that, saying that she was their focal point. For Christmas that year, one of her brothers sent her a card telling her that she was the brightest reminder on earth of his mother. That made Evelyn cry harder than ever.

Perhaps it was his mother's death that shocked Nat into a retrospective mood. Some of his close friends knew how sad he was at his loss. He decided to sit down and make the pure jazz album he had been promising to deliver for years.

By August, he had the plan organized for the album called *After Midnight* with his trio and four guests chosen for specific songs. The alto saxophonist Willie Smith, who had played his best-known gig with bandleader Jimmie Lunceford and also worked with Billy May, Duke Ellington, and Harry James, and who had won *Esquire* Awards as a jazzman in 1945 and 1947, played on "Just You, Just Me," an up-tempo song that provided wonderful opportunities for driving swing and haunting solos. He also played on the sly, little-known "Don't Let It Go to Your Head"—which Nat seems to have been the only musician ever to record—about a lover warning other men not to pay any attention to the flirtatious manner of his wife, because he is the only one she loves—or else. The record was infused with a contemporary feeling because of the notes played with exquisite softness by John Collins, the guitarist. Harris had the beat; drummer Lee Young also supplied deft, unobtrusive accompaniment. "You're Looking at Me" was another love song and a perfect vehicle for Smith, a smooth alto player.

Count Basie's trumpeter Harry "Sweets" Edison had known for a long time that Nat wanted to play an incredibly laid-back "Sweet Lorraine" with him. Sweets played fast and easily above the high pitch of the tempo. "Route 66" and "It's Only a Paper Moon" were two more appealing tunes that Cole had always wanted to try with Edison using his mute for an eerie, sweet, human sound.

Valve trombonist Juan Tizol, primarily known as a member of Duke Ellington's orchestra (though he also worked for Harry James for a while), played liquid, endless lines with perfect ideas for dynamics and tempo on "Caravan," which he had composed. Jack Costanzo gave exotic touches with the bongos for that song. Tizol also played hauntingly in a minor key on "Lonely One"—a piece about a brokenhearted boy—with Costanzo at his most subtle, playing at times in unison with Nat. The song was jazz's answer to "Nature Boy." Tizol was subtle and suggestive for "Blame It on My Youth." Stuff Smith, a jazz violinist who had won an *Esquire* Award in 1946, improvised a human singing sound for "Sometimes I'm Happy." His swift, beelike humming noise for "I Know That You Know" provided distinctive, passionate intensity; his lines spiraled upward, suggesting flight, and Nat's lines spilled out of them. From Smith, too, came the lilt and echo for Nat singing "When I Grow Too Old to Dream"; then Nat alternated positions with Smith, with Smith's swinging, rhythmic sense and ability to play chords exactly in tune in a featured position.

All the musicians had the sweet tone and the strong beat that enhanced Cole's rhythm, whimsicality and lightness. All of them were equal to holding the intimate, swinging conversations of a veritable Swing-era chamber jazz group. Certain phrases lingered in the listeners' memories, communicating the jazz style's joyful, exciting, earthy attitude toward experience. Sweet's playing on "Sweet Lorraine," for example, seemed to lean slightly off kilter to the left while it swung onward to the right, simultaneously and rakishly. The pulse and the choice of notes created an hypnotic ambience. The intimate, floating mood prevailed through every cut on the released record. More cuts went on Capitol's shelf, none of them to be released until the twenty-fifth anniversary of Nat's death. By that time, only Sweets, Costanzo, and the rhythm-section players were alive to savor the sound of the music made for the landmark album in Cole's and their careers.

Jazz fans were delighted. During the bebop era, the Cole record rooted in an earlier style actually cut across the lines of the eras and became a favorite, showing up in collections next to Miles Davis and Charles Mingus albums. Ralph Gleason, then a columnist for the *San Francisco Chronicle* and a *Down Beat* contributor, wrote the original liner notes. A favorite with jazz musicians, he may have been the only writer who ever printed Lee Young's real name, Leonidas. Gleason recounted that Nat had won the prestigious *Esquire* awards and the *Down Beat* and *Metronome* polls in the 1940s.

With that record done, Nat went on to other projects. Jazz critics would come to regard *After Midnight* as Nat's last last hurrah for jazz on records.*

---

*In 1990, Capitol released remaining tracks from the session, which had never been issued before: "What Is There to Say?" with Tizol, "You Can Depend on Me" and "Candy" with Sweets, "I Was a Little Too Lonely" with Willie Smith, and "Two Loves Have I" with Stuff Smith.

Chapter Twenty-one

EVEN IF YOU CAN GO HOME AGAIN, PERHAPS YOU SHOULDN'T

*N*at set out on a tour in 1956 with the very popular British band-leader Ted Heath, who probably brought his band to the United States in exchange for Stan Kenton's touring Britain. With Heath was Kenton's bandsinger, June Christy, Nat and his trio—John Collins, Charlie Harris, and Lee Young—and comedian Gary Morton, among others.

In Texas, the group played to segregated audiences, with whites on one side of the auditoriums, blacks on the other side. That was the usual arrangement. The group was making its way to Birmingham, Alabama, where Nat's sister Evelyn had been born. Before Nat arrived in that city, the police there had gotten wind of a rumor that some people were planning to make trouble. Several policemen were assigned to stay close to the stage in the Municipal Auditorium for two nighttime performances on April 10.

Nat and his trio were performing in the first show of the evening for four thousand whites; the second show would be for blacks. By law there, variety-troupe performers could be of different races, but audiences could not. Even the performers had to be segregated to an extent by a screen or a curtain onstage.

Nat had already sung "Autumn Leaves" and reached the second chorus of his second tune, "Little Girl." Members of the audience were shocked out of their mellow mood by a howling noise. Then, according to a *Time* magazine report, five men ran down the aisles; their feet thumped on the wooden floor. They bounded onto the stage. One man hit Cole and sent him staggering backward onto the piano bench. Nat hit it with such force that it split beneath him.

Police had been watching the steps at the ends of the stage, because they had expected trouble to arrive from that direction. They were caught off guard in the wings. By the time they rushed onstage, an attacker was twisting Cole's foot. A policeman started wrestling with him, so the attacker had to let Cole's foot go. Another attacker hit a policeman and bloodied his nose; the policeman hit the attacker across the head with a nightstick. Eight policemen fought with the attackers and pulled them out of the hall.

As soon as the fracas began, Ted Heath's eighteen-piece band played "My Country 'tis of Thee,"* the same melody as "God Save the Queen," until an uneasy peace seemed to reign in the hall. Cole limped offstage; a curtain rustled. Comedian Gary Morton came to the edge of the stage to explain that Cole couldn't continue. Someone in the front of the audience called out, "Ask him to come back so we can apologize." For that, Nat decided to come out onstage. The audience gave him a long ovation. When the applause ended, he said, "I just came here to entertain you. That's what I thought you wanted."

The members of the audience answered: "We do, we do, sing, sing." But Nat walked offstage and sat down. To someone, he said, "Man, I love show business, but I don't want to die for it." Nevertheless, he decided to stay in the theater and see how he felt after a little while. He went out to entertain the Negro audience at the second show.

With a cigarette in a filter clenched between his lips, Cole told newsmen in Birmingham right after the attack that he thought the audience had been "really wonderful. They were trying to tell me in their own way that they do not condone such actions. How do I feel? I don't really know. I'm just befuddled. I suppose I am a little

---

*The formal title is "America."

amazed. I have never experienced anything like this, and I certainly wasn't prepared for anything like this."

He left the troupe and dropped out of sight for a little while, going to Chicago to spend a few days with his father for spiritual refuge and a physical checkup. Nat had no lasting injuries and, calming down, decided to rejoin the tour. Newspapers said that Cole canceled performances in Greenville, South Carolina, and Charlotte and Raleigh, North Carolina, then resumed work in Norfolk, Virginia, on the Saturday after the Tuesday attack. Carl Carruthers recalled that Cole started working again with the group in Raleigh. Carruthers boasted that he knew the South so well that he could advise Cole not to rejoin the group until it had played without him in Atlanta, Georgia, Columbia, South Carolina, and several other cities. Nat did play in Norfolk with the group. Ivan Mogull flew there for that show so that Nat would have supportive company to boost his morale. Definitely, by April 18, Nat went onstage to entertain an audience of blacks and whites in Louisville, Kentucky's Jefferson County Armory. A roar arose from ten thousand people, the Associated Press reported, when they saw him walk onstage. City policemen in Louisville escorted him away from the Armory after the performance, just as they had taken him to the stage.

Because his attackers had been punished in Birmingham that day, Cole told Louisville reporters, "I'm glad to see them take a stand in that direction. No [attacker] should go without reprimanding, regardless of where the incident happened or to whom it happened."

Right after the attack in Birmingham, police had arrested a sixth man, whom they had found outside in an automobile. He was guarding two rifles, a blackjack, and brass knuckles, according to a *Time* magazine report. Other news stories said that the car had been filled with weapons.

During the afternoon of April 18, as Cole was priming himself to go onstage in Louisville, four of the Alabama attackers were sentenced by Judge Ralph E. Parker in recorder's (city) court in Birmingham. The judge told the men that Mr. Cole "has observed our customs, traditions and laws, and his conduct was such as to win him many friends in the South."

Then the judge passed sentence. The four men received small fines and short jail terms, as did the other two men later in the year. (By 1990, the court no longer had a record of the cases, because the legal limit for keeping records had passed long before.)

The story emerged that about four days before Cole's appearance in Birmingham, the men, one of whom was a director of the North Alabama Citizens Council, a die-hard segregationist group, met at a gas station in Anniston; there they concocted a plot to kidnap Nat Cole off the stage. About 150 people, according to the Birmingham police figure, had agreed to show up for the attack, but only six men kept the date.

Nat was criticized by Negroes for his personal decisions after the attack. Other blacks didn't want him to rejoin the tour or perform for segregated audiences again. The idea that Nat had helped uphold Birmingham customs enraged blacks. He told them that he was an entertainer, not a politician, and that he felt he could serve the cause of civil rights best by performing for white audiences. He said that the Supreme Court was having trouble desegregating the schools: So "I can't come in [to the South] on a one-night stand and overpower the [segregation] law." One Southern black newspaper said that he shouldn't therefore go to the South at all.

Other blacks jumped on the bandwagon to note that Nat had never joined the NAACP. They didn't mention that he had performed in benefits for the NAACP before the attack. In Harlem, his records were removed from some jukeboxes. In one place, the records were smashed, too. Thurgood Marshall, then a brave, crusading civil rights lawyer, one of a handful of lawyers devoting their lives to the battle to desegregate schools, was incensed by Cole's reluctance to join the civil rights fray aggressively. A few sources report that the brilliant Mr. Marshall, whom President Johnson would appoint to the U.S. Supreme Court about a decade later, insulted Nat's image. Nat, whose heady success had stemmed from his intellectual, spiritual, emotional and instinctual immersion in an abstract art, was befuddled and hurt. "I actually saw tears roll down his face," said one of his New York friends in music publishing. Nat hastily joined the NAACP, and his name was included in the organization's list of publicly known supporters. In a full-page ad taken by the NAACP in *The New York Times,* Nat's name figured prominently in support of the Reverend Martin Luther King, Jr.'s Southern Christian Leadership Conference.

If the Birmingham incident had any bright effect at all, it was the attention focused on the civil rights struggle. In April 1956, *New York Times* critic Howard Taubman wrote a column about the prejudice that Negro instrumentalists faced in the classical-music field, where many employers acted as if Negro string, brass, and percussion players did not exist. It would be another twenty years before New York City required a minority quota among musicians hired to play in Broadway orchestras, but the struggle was illuminated, if only briefly by Taubman, by the flare of violence directed at Cole.

An ecumenical group of students in Florida, who met to discuss ways to resolve racial hatred by relying on the Christian message of reconciliation, used the Nat Cole incident as an example of the enemy to be defeated. During the next year, the NAACP espoused the cause of black actors looking for work in Hollywood films. By 1958, Nat had joined fourteen other Los Angeles–based musicians to appeal to George Meany, head of the AFL-CIO to support integration of the segregated musicians' locals of the American Federation of Musicians. Eventually, segregation in all the locals would become a relic of history.

The civil rights movement, without which Nat Cole had maneuvered his way through the labyrinth of the country's racial policies and practices, may have gained a little more momentum from the Alabama incident. The feelings of one lonesome millionaire singer, who on his own had instituted a $62,000 suit against a Rock Island, Illinois, hotel for refusing him a room because of his race in June 1950, went uncelebrated by the movement for the most part. Nat had told the jury in Peoria, Illinois, on September 19, 1951, that he was trying to blaze the trail in his own way. That day he testified that he was treated "like a little fly that might be in the way" when he tried to get possession of the rooms he had reserved. Then he had flown to a benefit performance for the Damon Runyon Cancer Fund in New York City, without waiting for the verdict; it was decided in his favor.

Under attack for appearing before segregated audiences in the South, Nat replied that he would refuse to do so in the future if all the other Negro musicians would join a boycott. That never happened. The incidents of prejudice never seemed to let up. When Nat was performing in Florida—still staying in the Sir John Hotel—the hotel of choice for black musicians who appeared in the area—he and Ivan Mogull made a date to go to a baseball game. Nat had two tickets. Then he called Ivan Mogull back and said, "Forget it. I found out that I have to sit in the colored section. We can't sit together."

Nat never went back to Alabama, however.

Many years later, he was given an official posthumous honor as a valued son of the state. Nat's sister Evelyn went to Alabama to receive the award for her brother. Touched and proud, she cried, mindful of the people whom she had loved and who had not lived to see that extraordinary day with her. With his profound aversion to crowd scenes, let alone turmoil, Nat might have asked her to go for him, anyway.

Chapter Twenty-two

A CHOPS-BREAKING GROUND-BREAKING ON TELEVISION

As a man of the mainstream, Cole was intensely intrigued by television and films. Along with Benny Goodman and Louis Armstrong, Nat was one of the few American jazz musicians who was so famous that he was recognized abroad, even in Moscow, as an international star. That delighted him and everyone associated with him. For a long time, he had wanted to join the ranks of singers and other entertainers who had their own regular shows on television. He had often appeared as their guests—on Perry Como's, Milton Berle's and Ed Sullivan's shows, to name a few. Dinah Shore and Jo Stafford invited him, too. Pat Boone, beginning his show in 1957, would invite Cole onto the debut on ABC TV.

One night, Nat and Tony Martin were scheduled to appear on the same Ed Sullivan "Toast of the Town" show. When Sullivan asked them which one would like to go first, Martin said, "Nat goes first. He's the star." Occasionally, though, Nat was denied some opportunities because of his race. One woman singing star wanted him to sing a duet and appear in a skit with her, but her sponsor made a fuss and forbid it. Alan Livingston stepped into the fracas and cleared the way for Cole to appear on the show in at least a starring capacity as a singer. Cole harbored his dream of having his own show, nonetheless. Carlos Gastel tried very hard to find a television opening for Nat. None of the stations had anything to offer.

Then on October 9, 1956, Hal Kemp made the announcement, even before the contract was signed, that the National Broadcasting Company* and Nat had reached an agreement. Nat would star in his own fifteen-minute show on Monday nights at 7:30 P.M. EDT. The show opened on November 5 to wonderful reviews—without any sponsors. Between the first announcement and the first show, J. P. Shanley of *The New York Times* wrote that NBC would foot the bill for the show. Nat felt certain he would attract a sponsor soon enough.

The papers said that Cole was probably the first Negro to have his own television show. Val Adams, an important television reporter, could think of only the "Amos 'n Andy" show. *The New York Post*'s Gene Grove recalled that Billy Daniels had hosted a short-lived series. Only Eddie "Rochester" Anderson appeared on a regular basis. The Cole show was probably the first very serious attempt by a network to launch a Negro as a show's host.

Thrilled at the chance, Nat told the press, "I've been waging a personal campaign, aiming at a show of this kind. . . . I hit a few snags here and there, but I didn't give up the fight. It could be a turning point so that Negroes may be featured regularly on television."

It was his kind of fight. He understood it. He lost it—but first he had a good, unforgettable run.

Nat decided to work with a vocal group and his downplayed trio. Nat was the focus of attention. He wanted to keep the format simple, he said. "So many shows these days are big productions. They're trying to be different, and they seem to stumble over themselves. I think something simple might be a good idea—for me anyway. If I can get the same sort of spontaneity and the same sort of reaction that I do in a nightclub, I'll be happy." The orchestra leader Gordon Jenkins, with whom Nat made albums that sold well for Capitol in the period, performed in the show from its inception.

The gist of J. P. Shanley's review of the debut was as follows: Mr. Cole is offering a refreshing musical diversion. He is a singer who

---

*Later known as National Broadcasting Corporation

does not find it necessary to shout or shimmy in order to command attention. His style, popularized on millions of his records, is easy and relaxing. And he has an amiable personality that comes across engagingly on the television screen.

Shanley continued, "In some numbers he is backed up by the Boataneers, a quintet of singers with a civilized and enjoyable delivery. Instrumental music is provided capably by an orchestra directed by Gordon Jenkins. No sponsor has come forth yet to subsidize Mr. Cole's program. The premier made it seem like an attractive investment."

Sponsors never materialized. Advertising agencies couldn't find a client to take on the Cole show. They were afraid that white southern audiences would stop buying their products. One cosmetics company infuriated Cole by saying that Negroes couldn't sell lipsticks. "What do they think we use?" Cole fumed. "Chalk? Congo paint? And what about corporations like the telephone company? A man sees a Negro on a television show. What's he going to do—call up the telephone company and tell them to take out the phone?"

Since the show had very decent popularity ratings, NBC decided to keep it going, paying the cost itself. There were moments when it seemed as if Cole at last had a sponsor. One was Carter Products, but that arrangement didn't last long. Nevertheless, the show was expanded to half an hour and moved to 10:30 P.M. on July 1, 1957. Nelson Riddle became the orchestra leader; another choral group stepped in. At least a score of famous entertainers agreed to work on the expanded show for union minimum, to help Nat and NBC keep the show alive. Ella Fitzgerald, Peggy Lee, Tony Martin, Harry Belafonte, Bing Crosby, Sammy Davis, Jr., Louis Armstrong, and Eartha Kitt were just a few of the big names who came to Cole's aid. Still unsponsored in August, the show was slated to be replaced by "The Californians," essentially a Western, on September 24.

In mid-September, a sponsor came along. "The fact that Cole is a Negro is of no importance to us," said a spokesman for Rheingold Beer. "His show has quality, and he has even outranked 'The $64,000 Question.'" (That was an enormously popular quiz show of the era.) Rheingold arranged to sponsor the show—but only in the East, where Rheingold was marketed. Then two wine companies stepped in to sponsor Cole in the West. The show was the first nighttime NBC show to be aired on a cooperative basis. Until then NBC had paid twenty thousand dollars a week to keep Cole going. He praised the network. Behind the scenes, he sometimes fulminated at the recalcitrance of other sponsors. In public, his criticism of Madison Avenue was gentle, polite—and to the point. "Madison Avenue still runs TV," he said, "and there is reluctance on its part to sell my show. Madison Avenue is in the North, and that is where the resistance is. Sometimes the South is used as a football to take some of the stain off us in the North. I have been well received in night-clubs and on records—why not TV? You don't judge entertainment on a racial basis."

When the sponsors came along, NBC placed the show in a slot on Tuesdays at 7:30 P.M. EDT. It had about sixteen regional sponsors. *The New York Times* television critic Jack Gould wrote: "Nat Cole changed his program last night to a new time period—7:30 on Channel 4. But the greater significance was that it had some local participating sponsorship, and the National Broadcasting Company hopes to acquire more in other cities.

"Mr. Cole deserves success on the basis of his show, for which many top stars have generously worked for greatly reduced fees. Many persons in the TV industry want to see Mr. Cole triumph not only because integration has made somewhat slow progress in na-tionally sponsored TV but also because he is an excellent enter-tainer."

The show's ratings were encouraging. The average for all his shows, no matter what the time slot, was 11.5 percent of the possi-ble audience. Of all the people actually watching TV at the hour Cole was on the air, 18 percent were tuned to his show. Even so, the arrangement for Tuesdays at 7:30 P.M. didn't last long. Carlos and the NBC executive in charge of the schedule discussed another time slot. The Tuesday-night position was going to be filled by "Treasure Hunt," and Nat would be switched to Saturday nights at 7:00 P.M. Carlos knew that the hour was very good for cowboy shows for an audience of children. So Carlos said, "Forget it." Cole made the announcement that he was not going to extend his show for another thirteen weeks, because he had personal appearances and promises to keep abroad. Carlos booked Nat for a six-day tour of Sydney and Melbourne, Australia. It would be the first of a series of successful foreign tours in the next few years for Nat.

With remarkable equanimity and candor, Cole put himself on the line in an interview he arranged in Hollywood, from which his show originated, to say that he was leaving television because of the "ad agencies." He said that he had known from the beginning that he would have a hard row to hoe, but had thought that the show's popularity would convince ad agencies to bring in a national spon-sor. Asked if he thought there was deliberate reluctance on the part of agencies to find a national sponsor, Cole said, "I felt it from the beginning; there's restraint someplace."

Nat didn't rap NBC, however. "The network supported this show from the beginning. From Mr. Sarnoff on down, they tried to sell it to agencies. They could have dropped it after the first thirteen weeks. Shows that made more money than mine were dropped. They offered me a new time at 7:00 P.M. on Saturdays on a cooperative basis, but I decided not to take it. I feel played out."

He said it was nonsense to think that Negro performers weren't an asset in selling products through television. "Negroes, after all, constitute a very large buying market, and as an entertainer I know I'm salable to all kinds of people, not just one race." And he added, "There won't be shows starring Negroes for a while. I think the time is not too far distant when things will be worked out, however."

There were Cole fans who lived in cities remote from the country's racial tensions and who had not read the relatively few and sedate items about Cole's confrontation with racism in advertising; they never had an inkling that Cole was having trouble finding a sponsor for his show in the 1950s. Blissfully innocent, they had hurried to their television sets on time every week to see the sly charmer cavorting with guests and singing his intimate ballads, as he sat catty-corner to the piano, smiling slightly, with a debonair air. His slanty eyes were alight and all-knowing. What he knew extended beyond the lyrics and the soft, seductive music, however, to the difficulties for a Negro to survive as a star on TV.

In a variety of interviews in the following years, Nat gave some insight into his attitude about his experiences: "I live this thing every day, and I'm a top performer. I get little snubs, little insults, so I must know how the little man feels. . . . I know what TV is doing. They are freezing the Negro out. . . . I am breaking this down. I am fighting on the inside and without publicity. . . . If I ever get rich, I am going to buy me a plane and get a box in every ballpark in the country; then I'm going to fly from city to city and do nothing but watch ball games. And in the winter, I'll go down to Cuba and watch the games down there," he told an *Ebony* interviewer.

Six and a half years after his show ended, as Cole was beginning what would be the last year of his life, he offered a new appraisal of the odds he had always been bucking. Though he may have relied on other people's business acumen to organize his finances, Nat needed nobody to help him with his articulate analysis of his world:

"The future looks very good," he said. "The ad agencies and the networks are not so concerned with color as they were. I think things are going to improve tremendously. Attitudes have changed and even Madison Avenue has to keep up with the times. People just don't reject the image of the Negro on the screen as they used to.

"You know, Negroes have always been guests on television. I'm talking about Negroes getting their own shows or prominent parts in good dramas. I don't know, maybe the sponsors have been afraid of the identification, but I think they're getting less afraid.

"The funny thing is, the high-prestige sponsors—DuPont, the Telephone Hour—are the least afraid, perhaps because they're not selling over the counter. Anyway, things are getting better."

Nat's voice was soft as he talked with a reporter: "I clam up on the subject of race. I'm a performer, not a professional agitator. I don't believe in lip service. I'm not for talking, criticizing, blasting— I'm interested in doing something positive, like this television show.

"We're all always, of course, aware of race, but I'm not bitching—*life* is a bitch. People look at me and I'm doing all right and a lot of people have a lot less than I do, and they could say, 'What are *you* bitching about?' If I'm fighting at all, I'm fighting for the cause of man—I'm fighting not just for race but for everyone in my profession."

Asked about the hotels he had sued for their refusals to let him stay in the rooms he had reserved because he was black, he mused, "Since then, I've stayed at those same hotels. I wasn't mad at them. I just sued as a matter of principle."

Chapter Twenty-three

A KING AT THE COPACABANA

*E*ven if Nat hadn't had to deal with racial barriers, he would have had his hands filled with the pressures of his career.

It may have seemed to his friends that he was so successful as a performer and recording artist that he didn't really have to worry about the direction of his career anymore. At the time of his TV show, he was grossing $2.5 million a year for Capitol Records, according to an *Ebony* tally. The figure was used regularly after Glen Wallichs made it public in 1954. Cole's share, $250,000, was high enough to make him a wealthy man. His Las Vegas and nightclub appearances in other key cities netted him a great deal of money, too.

One of his most important stops during these years was Julius Podell's Copacabana in New York. Podell loved Nat because the singer's allure filled the room with socialities and celebrities. Even the Duke and Duchess of Windsor made their way to the door at 14 East Sixtieth Street. Press agents had a field day with the crème de la crème of cafe society during Nat's engagements; his shows became a social event of the fall season.

He did two shows a night. Women pressed notes into the maître d's hand. "There was something romantic about those dulcet tones," Marvin Cane noted wistfully. Between the shows and after the last one, Nat took the notes from the maître d' and disappeared up the stairs. Nat's fans would drift toward his dressing room. He was cordial to everyone as he sipped his tea with honey while a television set ran incessantly in the background.

He disliked inefficiency or interruptions in his schedule. Sparky Tavares and Carl Carruthers knew how to keep him from being overrun by visitors or requests for autographs on photos. Marvin Cane could remember how one of Nat's first valets, Johnny Hopkins, used to let everybody he knew through any door where Cole was performing; if someone lacked a ticket, Hopkins would let him pass anyway. Sparky ran a much tighter ship; he was lovable and smart, Nat's friends thought. If anyone stood in the way of Nat's smooth operation, Nat was likely to get roiled up. Sparky knew how to make everything seem bearable and easeful. He even had a delectable way of answering the telephone. Should someone call and ask for him, he paused for a second, then piped up firmly, "Speaking!"

Though Nat was soft-spoken, with no rush in his manner of speaking onstage, he would talk very fast and to the point offstage. It was difficult to make him angry unless someone made a mistake onstage or in the wings during a performance, or at any point while his well-oiled machinery was supposed to be rolling along. Then he scolded the person thoroughly. He didn't like anyone running interference, or trying to usurp his authority over his music, or, in the long run, over any part of his career. Sparky once even heard Nat tell Maria to be quiet in a group of people gathered for a decision-making purpose. Nat had wanted to have the last word and implement his own plan.

No matter what was going on, he smoked incessantly. Jack Costanzo thought Nat regarded cigarettes as a kind of dessert; if so, it was a continuous dessert of Philip Morris before, during, and after meals. Many of Nat's friends among them Mike Hall, Nat's press agent for some years, thought Nat's insistence on fastidiousness in his personal habits and organization, including every detail of his physical care and his wardrobe, betrayed an inner turmoil, though not necessarily a gloomy attitude. Sparky never thought that Nat dwelled on the darker events of his life. "Nat liked to laugh," Sparky would always say about the boss's spirit. Nat was, after all, very successful. He even occasionally mentioned how well he had done.

In the mid-1950s, he became aware of a bizarre trend in the pop-music world. Rock and roll began to vie with the established pop music. Nobody could ignore the drift.

None of the cuts from *After Midnight* had become a best-seller. Nat had expected that. "Caravan" from the album appealed to the disc jockeys, who played it on the radio. But throughout the 1950s, Nat's pop tunes kept him in the spotlight. "Darling, Je Vous Aime Beaucoup" became the number-seven song on the charts by March 5, 1955, and stayed in the pop lists for sixteen weeks, selling over a million copies. "The Sand and the Sea" went to the twenty-third spot on the same day and lingered for four weeks. On May 7, about three months after his mother had died, "A Blossom Fell" became the second most popular song in the country and stayed in the charts for twenty weeks. "If I May," which became the eighth most popular song on May 21, stayed in the rankings for ten weeks and sold over a million copies, though the tune didn't endure as well as other songs by Cole.

After that, there was a subtle difference in the way his songs were received. Although the public loved his sound, his songs became less exciting in themselves. "My One Sin" went to the twenty-fourth position for about two weeks beginning on July 16. "Nothing Ever Changes My Love for You" went only to the seventy-second spot on the charts by February 25, 1956, though it was particularly appealing; even off the charts, it surfaced now and then on the disc-jockey shows. "Never Let Me Go" went only to the seventy-ninth position, but was a very good song; jazz musicians kept it alive after Nat gave it a brief spurt of popularity. "To the Ends of the Earth," written by his New York friends, Joe and Noel Sherman, and "Night Lights" went into the charts, with haunting arrangements.

Composer Joe Sherman slaved for months on some songs, but "To The Ends of the Earth" came to him in minutes. He had been shaving, his face covered with cream, because he had been hurrying to an appointment. Noel, the lyricist, said, "Listen to this . . ." He read the lyrics he had just written to Joe.

"Oh, not now," Joe said.

Because Noel had persisted, Joe had gone to the piano and in a few minutes had written the music.

Nat's next hit, "Ballerina," then began to show up on every radio station day and night, though it only went to the eighteenth place on the charts beginning in February 1957. Suddenly, two years had gone by without Nat having recorded a tune that sold a million copies.

Nat had never deluded himself that he was a monument that couldn't be toppled. Soon after he had become well known, he had told the press that popular music styles and trends changed every ten years or so, and he knew that he had to be aware of what was going on in his field and be able to adjust to the changes. He hadn't kept up with the influx of young jazz musicians, however, nor their characteristic sounds, to the extent that he had as a younger man. Jazz was not his field anymore.

His trio continued to travel with him; yet he didn't bill himself as Nat King Cole and His Trio for his Capitol recordings. The prominently featured artists with Nat were the bandleaders and arrangers who starred at Capitol. Contemporary jazz—bebop—developed light-years away from Cole's primary attention. At times Nat thought he would try to identify himself with the vanguard of jazz. He explained to audiences that he himself played bebop. It was an embellished style, he suggested, derived from the Swing era, which he said would never die. For the most part, though, he disassociated himself from the aggressive music that the adventurous bebop musicians were playing, and he talked with distaste about the personal jams and use of drugs, for which some jazz musicians became known. That was not his world. The most he had done to keep in step with bebop or progressive jazz was to add a bongo player for the trio's growth. Then drummer Lee Young, the musical director, took over, lending a harder, trendier sound. It was still subtle; the Cole group retained its gentle, intimate feeling. Nothing of Dizzy Gillespie's drive manifested itself in Cole's music. The closest thing to a scream in Cole's repertoire was Stuff Smith's fast fiddling on "I Know That You Know." When Charlie Parker died in 1955, Cole was enjoying the profits from "Darling, Je Vous Aime Beaucoup" and "A Blossom Fell," ultrasoft and sweet tunes that had no resemblance to Parker's usual complex style.

Cole had gone in a very different direction from Parker; the two men met only once in a professional way, when Cole's trio accompanied Parker on an Armed Forces Radio Service transcription of "Cherokee" in 1946. It was clear that Parker's driving style was radically different from Nat's.

Cole's most pressing problem was not the criticism from the jazz world but the emergence of rock and roll, with its hard, monotonous beat and limited musicality. He grew perplexed about how he was going to stay popular.

Then Marvin Cane arrived with a demonstration record of "Send for Me" and gave it to Nat at Hancock Park. Nat called Natalie into the room and asked her to listen to it. She caught its spirit and started to dance. Oh, great, Marvin thought. Nat decided to record it with Billy May and his orchestra. The song was a hint of the style that Natalie would pursue in her own career before she evolved into a soul singer.

On June 17, 1957, Nat had a hit with "Send for Me." It sold a million copies. Other records he made in the late 1950s continued to be popular because he was singing them with that irresistible sound. His songs no longer appeared often at the top of the charts, however. His next million-record seller, released on April 14, 1958, was a rhythm and blues–style song, "Looking Back," another harbinger of the future. "Do I Like It?"—which came out at the same time—and "Non Dimenticar," reaching the charts on October 13, 1958, became popular, but not nearly as much as his trendier songs did.

Nat was a little unsettled by the emerging power of rock and roll, because he really didn't like it. He went to dinner one night with the Sherman brothers in New York and talked about his misgivings.

Nat had met the Shermans in the usual way he met fledgling songwriters; the young Shermans, from Brooklyn, approached him tentatively and gave him a tune, "Sweet William," which he recorded in 1952; then it was never released. Their hits for Nat came later. They regarded him as one of the most important mentors in their lives and collaborated on several big hits for him. They also wrote some songs with other people for him. Noel's moody tune "Welcome to the Club" was used for the title of one of Nat's albums. Joe's collaboration with George David Weiss on "That Sunday That Summer" was one of Nat's last hits in the 1960s.

At dinner, Nat said to them, "What do you think of rock and roll? I don't know if I could get into that."

As Noel was driving Joe home that night, he said, "I have an idea for a special piece for Nat. 'Mr. Cole Won't Rock and Roll.' I like the way Cole sounds with roll."

Joe looked at him with a strong memory of the day Noel had cajoled him into taking a few minutes to write "To the Ends of the Earth."

"Well, let's try," Joe said.

The brothers drove to Joe's apartment and wrote "Mr. Cole Won't Rock and Roll" together in a very short time. They didn't know whether Nat would have anything to do with it, because he didn't like to do special material with messages. He did like this song, however, which the Sherman brothers handed to him in late 1958 during his Copacabana engagement. He put it in his pocket and kept it there for a long time. By the fall of 1959, heading to the Chez Paree for his annual Chicago engagement, he decided to sing the song and see how the audience liked it. The Sherman brothers waited to hear the news, because if the Chicagoans liked it, Cole was going to sing it when he arrived at the Copacabana, his next stop. The tune got a great deal of applause in Chicago, so Cole decided to give the song a try in New York. It got a standing ovation from his older, affluent, stylish audience. Nat was asked to sing the song three times. It talked about how baritones were starting to sound more "frantic" than "romantic," and the music had a strong rock and roll flavor.

Nat took out a full-page advertisement in *Variety* on November 4, 1959, saying, "I tip my hat to Joe and Noel Sherman." After that, other songwriters—Jimmy Van Heusen and Sammy Cahn—began writing special material for Cole. Joe Sherman tucked the ad away in his file of cherished memorabilia.

To him, Nat seemed an unaffected, uncomplicated, straightforward, sports-loving fellow, the most amiable of men. Their most protracted contract came every fall when Nat played at the Copacabana and they went to sports events or talked about music together. Having Nat's company was one of the most pleasurable social and professional experiences of which Joe Sherman could think. Nothing in Nat's demeanor ever suggested to Joe that Nat had a moment's inquietude. He never talked about problems of any kind. Though Joe knew that Nat was having trouble coming up with hit records, Joe didn't know that Nat dwelled a great deal on the course of his career. His albums, which appealed to sophisticated audiences, were selling very well. Joe didn't know that Nat once had confided in an interviewer for *Ebony* magazine about how nerve-racking his daily life was.

Whenever he arrived in a town, though nobody was supposed to know where he was staying, the phone started ringing insistently. On the streets, people always stopped him for autographs, favors, and requests. The pressure kept mounting until nighttime, when he went onstage. Then "my mind is going like a machine, thinking,

thinking, anticipating, trying. . . . Ninety percent of the business is up here," he said, pointing to his head. "That's the reason so many performers come up with ulcers and breakdowns."

He allowed only the briefest of glimpses into his vexations. His extraordinary patience with music helped him keep pushing his career, moving with it, and striding over—or around—all the obstacles. Patience and concentration allowed him to deal with nearly everyone and everything, to adjust to circumstances and get things done in the midst of opposition, arguments, adverse trends or even simply accidents and bad weather. Like the hub of a wheel, he kept turning, pushing himself, no matter which spoke became bent or broken, while he tried to steer clear of the hazards and pitfalls. If he seemed uneasy when Edward R. Murrow took TV cameras into the Cole house in Hancock Park on "Person to Person," it was because Nat was extremely shy about the intrusion at first. Maria was the effervescent one. Nat's anxiety dissolved when Murrow asked whether he minded all the problems that arose in his career. Nat said with a honeyed voice and a sunny expressiveness that he had always enjoyed being a leader, even as a teenager fronting his own band in Chicago. It was his character, he said, to love the responsibilities of his career. No, he didn't lose heart. That was the Nat Cole whom his fans knew. To work with him was to see all his problems evaporate. In the music business, there were people who never saw him in anything other than a peaceful frame of mind, enjoying his work and finding his way with great ease and politeness.

It was his self-control that allowed him to telegraph a message of peace and made him a king at the Copacabana and a cool, lovable, sophisticated "cat" on television—and that blocked him as an actor.

$\mathcal{E}$XPLORING NEW HORIZONS

Nat had been in the film studios many times, beginning with the musical vignettes with his trio in 1943. By 1944, the trio suddenly commanded high prices for a few days' work. It had not escaped Nat's attention that Bing Crosby was a movie star, and that another baritone, Frank Sinatra, had lifted himself into a new realm of stardom by winning an Academy Award for a supporting role in *From Here to Eternity.* With his own engaging, if low-key, on-stage personality to shore up his confidence, Nat wanted to try acting roles, too.

In 1953, he acted in one Lux Video Theater production, *Song for a Banjo,* as a supporting star for Dick Haymes. In the film, Nat, who portrayed a piano player, befriended Haymes, a farmhand, when they landed in jail together—Nat for fighting with his bandleader, Haymes for allegedly rustling cattle. Nat helped him clear himself and return to his girlfriend, Nancy Guild. While Nat was rehearsing for the show, which had no teleprompters, he also was appearing at La Vie en Rose every night in New York. Even *Our World,* a magazine with a black audience, didn't credit him with turning in a jewel-like performance. Justly proud of him, the magazine called him "cool and convincing" as a fledgling actor. Although some of his fans liked his acting, he always seemed restrained in the job. In another film role that year, playing "Himself" in *Small Town Girl,* Nat prompted a critic to write in *The New York Times,* "Nat King Cole makes one brief and subdued appearance rendering 'Flaming Heart.'"

He starred in one film about himself, *The Nat King Cole Story,* taking viewers in 1955 through the legendary "Sweet Lorraine" baptismal song in the Sewanee Inn and the crisis of bleeding ulcers that had laid him low for nearly a year. He was engaging, because audiences knew he was the genuine article. So it didn't matter very much that he was delivering lines instead of interacting with other characters. He had the authenticity of a very pleasant fellow playing himself. The film, a Universal International featurette, reportedly earned some profit.

For other roles, something seemed to be missing in his acting ability. As a child, he had studied piano for years, and the education had helped to launch his natural gift. He had never had a single acting lesson, however. He seemed to be too polite and shy to try to emote or plumb the emotional depths of the character he was portraying. His television show's popularity increased his film opportunities. He appeared in a character role in *China Gate,* which opened in May 1957. After Angie Dickinson and Gene Barry, Nat received billing for his role as a legionnaire in Vietnam. *The New York Times* critic called Cole's portrayal "restrained" and didn't linger on the subject. In the film, Nat sang the title song, with his usual hypnotic effect, however. If the role didn't build a reputation for him as a charismatic actor, it at least led to an invitation for him to portray W. C. Handy in *St. Louis Blues* with Eartha Kitt as Gogo Germain and Pearl Bailey as Aunt Hagar. Ella Fitzgerald played herself. Cab Calloway was Blade. Ruby Dee, Mahalia Jackson, Billy Preston, and Juano Hernandez also appeared in the film.

Marvin Cane went to the West Coast on music business, while Nat's film was in production. Nat said to Marvin, "Come to the studio with me."

So Marvin and Nat sat on the set, chatting together during a delay. Nat talked about how difficult it was to make a movie; he had to endure delays and postponements of scenes. It was a new world for him, not at all like being in a recording studio, where he was in command of his situation.

Marvin said, "Well, you're in the movie business."

Nat said, "Yeah, what the hell am I doing here?"

Marvin said, "You're becoming a movie star."

Then Bosley Crowther, one of the most important film critics of his era, wrote in *The New York Times* that the "alleged biography" was "put forth with grim determination. . . . Mr. Cole simply lumbers through the role of a harassed jazz composer, looking dumb and uncomfortable." Crowther spared only Cab Calloway and Pearl Bailey for their portrayals. Script, direction and even Eartha Kitt and Ruby Dee were panned.

Nat's friends blamed the terrible review in April 1958 on the script. Cole was offered still another role—as the nightclub owner in *Night of the Quarter Moon* in September 1958. He fared much better in Howard Thompson's review for *The New York Times*. Thompson didn't pay Nat very much attention, however. The film was about a pretty quadroon who married a socially prominent San Franciscan; his family tried to annul the marriage. Thompson concentrated on the horrific cruelties to the young couple. "As the nightclub relatives who befriended the desperate bride, Anna Kashfi and Nat King Cole (with one tune) make wise, welcome spectators," wrote the southern-born reviewer. In truth, Cole on film was at his best when he was involved with music. Perhaps his passage from a cooly controlled musician to an actor exploring the depths of his feelings would have taken a total immersion in Lee Strasberg's workshop for Method acting.

Cole always provided an exquisite relief and lift for the films in which he sang—*Blue Gardenia*, for one. Sometimes his singing was the only bright moment in a film. Throughout *Cat Ballou* in 1965, he and Stubby Kaye augmented the amusing story; appearing on the fringes of the action, they sang the Oscar-nominated title tune to great effect.

Carlos came up with a better idea than to hope Nat eventually would blossom into a great, flexible leading man or an evocative character actor. Carlos decided to enhance Nat's stature as an international singing star.

Nat's wife had coached him so that his enunciation and pronunciation of English became highly praised; it remained idiosyncratic at moments, but it had become a streamlined vehicle for his voice. Nat Cole didn't speak any foreign languages, however. During one of his trips to Europe—probably the first one, in 1950—he and

Maria had gone to a club and heard a German-speaking singer inter-
pret one of Nat's songs with authority in English. Afterward, the
singer sat down with the Coles and needed an interpreter to hold a
conversation. Nat had thought the imitation was uncanny.

He didn't know that Carlos Gastel was going to push him to do
the same thing in Spanish. Carlos decided that Nat should perform
in Cuba and sing in Spanish there. Nat could learn to sing phoneti-
cally in Spanish, Carlos decided. He influenced Capitol to plan an
album in 1959 called *Señor Cole Español,* to be produced in Cuba
by Dave Cavanaugh. Then, with Carlos among others coaching him,
Nat developed a repertoire. These songs were rarely heard in the
United States. Americans never had any idea of how popular Nat's
trip to Cuba and his record there made him throughout Latin America.

Jan Steinmiller, a registered nurse based in New York City, regularly worked for some years on the Holland-America Line's
flagship, the *Nieuw Amsterdam.* One night, when the ship was
docked in Havana, she went to the Tropicana nightclub, one of her
favorite places in the world. She was delighted to discover that Nat
Cole was singing and playing with an orchestra.

Sparky thought, as Jan Steinmiller did, that the Tropicana was
one of the most beautiful, exotic clubs in the world. Sparky
watched the performance from a spot near Cole. Jan was able to sit
outdoors, with the sky above and the palm trees around her, at a
table from which she could see Cole at the other end of the big
club. He had a backdrop of stars and palm trees lit up, too; his were
artificial, however. A chorus of singers and dancers had elaborate
stairways to go up and down behind him. An avid fan of the Swing
and bebop eras, Jan thought his performance was a highlight of her
life. "The songs he sang, the way he sang them, well, it was wonderful, by Jesus," she reminisced years later. On her way back to the
ship after the show, accompanied by the first engineer, she heard
shooting. She associated it with the coming coup d'état led by Fidel
Castro, who would soon oust Batista, Cuba's military dictator.

Nat's record, which became enormously popular throughout
Latin America, preceded him in 1960 to a performance in Brazil.
Because he became so popular, he made two more records—*A Mis
Amigos,* sung in Spanish and Portuguese, produced by Lec Gillette,
and then *More Cole Español,* conducted by Ralph Carmichael and
recorded in Mexico City. Latin stars joined him on *A Mis Amigos,*
for which Nat commissioned songs, one of them "Fantasticos," another "Aqui Se Habla en Amor" by Noel Sherman with composer

Jack Keller. In Brazil, about sixty thousand people turned out for Nat's concert in a soccer stadium; admission wasn't high-priced, yet for Brazilians, the few cruzeiros represented a sizable sum at the time. Nat was touched by the outpouring of attention and respect and found the event one of the most gratifying in his life—at least as important, if not more so in some ways, as performing for the President of the United States, or for Queen Elizabeth and Prince Philip of England. Lee Young, the drummer, was awestruck by the enormous crowd. "We looked like little ants out there on the stage," he remembered.

Robert Medina, who left Cuba when Castro came to power, brought with him his most valued possessions when he emigrated to the United States. One of them was a tape recording of *Señor Cole Español;* it was small and easy to carry. He found a job in the morgue of *The New York Times;* through the years, he rose to become director of the morgue, where all the clippings of the newspaper's stories were kept. Robert did very well and enjoyed his lifestyle in his adopted country. One of the pleasant frills of life was a tape player in his car; quite often he listened to *Señor Cole Español* as he drove around. He thought the tape was a rarity; not many people had a copy. He loved Cole's voice, and it reminded him of the times when he was a young man, able to go to the Tropicana and hear Cole in person. Robert felt nostalgic for Cuba whenever he heard Cole's tape. Once in a while, Cole pronounced a word in a rather unusual way; that was quite charming.

Natalie Cole had her own vantage point from which to see Nat Cole's great success in Latin America. Nat and Maria had taken Cookie and Sweetie along for the ride on the 1959 tour. In Mexico, Sweetie had been shocked to see the poverty of the people in the streets. She heard her mother saying "tsk tsk" and knew that Maria was pained by the sights. Natalie would not even see the ghettos in the United States until many years later; the physical hazards in the way of survival—and even racial bigotry—had no place in the experiences and comprehension of most of the Cole children until they went out into the world to try to establish lives for themselves.

Chapter Twenty-five

THE COLES ADOPT A SON, AS NAT SEARCHES FOR A WAY TO THE BROADWAY STAGE

*B*y 1959, Maria had not had another child after Natalie's birth. Nine years had elapsed; the son she and Nat had wanted didn't seem to be in the offing. So in July 1959 the couple found a little boy who had been born the previous February and they adopted him and christened him Nat Kelly Cole. James Haskins interviewed Nat Kelly Cole at length about his privileged childhood in Hancock Park and in private schools. Kelly, as his family called him, had not shared his father's interest in sports; he actually detested baseball, in part because it took his parents out of the house for the games.

He seemed to treasure his times with his elusive father, who was away at work so much. Nat felt deep affection for the little boy, even if he may have been mystified by the child's temperament. There are pictures of Nat and Kelly on an outing at Disneyland in

Anaheim. People who arrived at Nat's front door recall how Nat always went to the door with one child or another in his arms to greet guests. Sometimes it was Kelly.

In the long run, Maria would have a deeper influence on all the children. She would know them much longer than Nat, and she would be in charge of decisions about their routine welfare and education for a very long time. She threw birthday parties for Cookie and allowed press pictures to be taken of Cookie and Sweetie. Kelly was exactly six years old when Nat died. Maurice Prince, at that time still struggling to establish herself as a restaurantteur in Los Angeles, went to work in the Cole house soon after Nat died. The little boy, she recalled, was distraught at the loss of his father. She tried to hug and comfort him, but he sometimes seemed to be inconsolable. In the long run, Kelly was tightly bound to Maria, for she was the only parent he actually knew. He was endlessly curious about his legendary father. Intrigued by the literary and visual arts, Kelly spent a long time gathering enough of the right material to do a book or a film about Nat. There were also other people's major projects related to Nat's reissued records for which Kelly provided research assistance.

At the time Kelly was adopted, Nat was planning a great deal of international traveling. He wasn't home very often. Kelly was less than a year old when Nat, among other celebrities in 1960, performed at Victoria Palace Theatre for Queen Elizabeth and Prince Philip. Natalie and Cookie were old enough to travel to England with their parents. Natalie recalled how happy she felt being near her father. Even though she and Cookie weren't invited to the gala reception after the performance, they felt proud of their father's success. He made them feel special. Kelly learned about those happy days through stories passed down to him. By the time he was old enough to join in the fun more, he had to cope instead with Nat's death.

Kelly knew a father whose career engulfed him. On Nat's return to the United States, he had the satisfaction of seeing a TV special of his performances taped in Paris, Rome, and London broadcast over Channel 4. Primarily, he sang, but he also did a much-praised, lighthearted piano solo of "Tea for Two," always a bright tour de force for him in any context.

In an interview when he returned to the United States, Nat said that he was not sure anymore that he would want his own TV show again, because he thought that regular shows overexposed entertainers. Their careers seemed to suffer. Saturated, the public turned to other people and bought their records. Despite his musings, there was no doubt that the televised European tour show and his occasional domestic TV appearances disseminated his magic and kept whetting people's appetites for his singing.

In Europe, Norman Granz had asked Nat to help a younger jazz musician, Quincy Jones, who would later become the first important black arranger and producer in Hollywood and a superstar in his own right. Jones was leading a band that became stranded without funds. Norman Granz hitched Jones to Nat's star. Jones joined Nat's tour to work in Sweden, Denmark, France, Italy, Germany, and Switzerland. For their shows, Jones's band played for about forty minutes. After the intermission, Nat took over.

One night in Switzerland, Nat was distressed because the audience wasn't enjoying his singing. Jones whispered to him to play piano. So Nat tried "Sweet Lorraine" as a piano solo. That was what the audience had been waiting for. The Swiss were familiar with his Jazz at the Philharmonic work. Nat received wildly enthusiastic applause.

Capitol Records had assigned its man in Paris, Louis Victor Mialy, to plan and coordinate Nat's publicity events three months in advance of Nat's arrival. Louis Victor escorted Maria to the houses of the great designers. Nat was relieved because, although he loved clothes, he didn't like to shop. He preferred to walk along the Champs Elysees, fascinated by the curious little Citroën car, the Deux Chevaux, and the oddly shaped Citroën taxis. He also admired the pretty Parisian women in their bright-colored dresses.

Nat and Louis Victor hit it off so well that Nat invited the Frenchman along for the whole tour of Europe. Louis translated and smoothed the way as a temporary road manager. Then Nat asked Louis Victor to go along for the upcoming tour of Asia. Louis Victor requested a leave of absence from his job, but he was refused, so he simply quit his job to join Nat. The Asian tour, which was very successful, with Nat performing in his usual way, ended when he returned to the United States to perform at The Sands in Las Vegas. Louis Victor had nothing to do there.

Nat didn't seem to mind paying Louis a salary for being idle, but Louis wanted to work in the United States. So Nat helped Louis acquire a work permit. Eventually he found work in the recording industry and became involved in some of Nat's recordings. By then he knew Nat's family well and felt a special, brotherly love for Nat.

Nat went to perform at the White House, where the respect accorded him, Maria recalled, was a highlight of his career. By then he had the stature to quibble with Ed Sullivan and prevail. The newspapers wrote that he was fighting with Sullivan, though Nat was really at loggerheads with some of Sullivan's "Toast of the Town" staffers. Nat wanted to introduce a new song, "Illusions," during a guest appearance on the TV show, but the staffers wanted him to sing a familiar standard. Nat didn't like them dictating his repertoire to him; he said that new songs became old standards only because singers such as himself introduced them. He said, "Let's do the two of them," but the staffers said no. So Nat cancelled his appearance. The staffers didn't want him to do that, because they knew Ed Sullivan would be angry. Therefore they let him do the one song that he wanted.

He never argued with his fame. "He made very shrewd decisions, and then he became even more shrewd when Maria came along," Lee Young said, summing up Nat's whole career management.

Nat, who was artistically restless, noticed that he was repeating his successes. It wasn't enough for him to sit back, relax, and enjoy life. He began to try investing in businesses outside of the entertainment world to bring in more income. They didn't bring him his happiest moments. One of his ventures, an investment in a paper-products company in the West Indies, actually brought him a financial loss—"about one week's salary," as Sparky recalled. Nat wasn't conducting that sort of business himself; some new people in his organization were involved.

Nat's real interests didn't change. He loved going out with friends to the ball games. He would fly into New York for a few days just to go to some games that he particularly wanted to see. When he was in New York every fall, he met with a little group of friends most Sunday mornings; among them were singers Steve Lawrence and his wife, Eydie Gorme, who was one of Cole's favorite singers, disc jockey William B. Williams, the Sherman brothers, and a few other people. They went for a big brunch at the Stage Delicatessen in midtown, then rode up to the stadium to see the Giants games.

One of Nat's best friends was Lenny Moore, a player for the Baltimore Colts. Nat had a friendly but deep rivalry with the Sherman brothers, who were ardent Giants fans and regarded the Colts as their nemesis. Nat felt a kinship with his friend Moore and rooted for the Colts; his affection superceded team lines. Those days were nearly idyllic in Joe Sherman's memory; he was always happy in Nat's company.

Not only was Joe always comfortable with Nat's sweet, easygoing manner, but no matter what they were doing—having fun in ballparks or working on a song, Joe always kept in mind Nat's astounding musicality. Nat never needed a bell tone to go from one song to another in the right key. Nat's orchestra leaders noticed the same gift, too. Once Joe wrote a song called "More and More of Your Amor" in the offbeat, intricate key of G flat, because Joe thought it was perfect for Nat's range. Nat took one look at the lead sheet and started to sing it exactly in G flat. As an arranger, composer, and conductor, Sherman marveled at Nat's "inner ears." To Nat the marvel was routine.

With a repetitive series on TV or starring roles in films out of his reach, Nat turned his sights on Broadway. It would be new territory for him. He wanted a starring role on Broadway, he decided.

For a while, he had thought that he and Harry Belafonte, who was friendly with Maria, would combine their talents, prestige and ideals to produce films and shows in the United States. The collaboration was short-lived, however. A story circulated among musicians on the West Coast that a rift occurred between the two men when Belafonte wanted to take charge and tell Nat what he should be doing in his singing career. However, Nat was not the sort to hold grudges. And he always admired Belafonte. Years after Nat died, Belafonte spoke of his enormous respect for Nat, and Belafonte remained friends with Maria.

After that, beginning around 1960, Nat set up his own firm, calling it Kell-Cole Productions, to do a variety of projects, many of which never materialized. Maria, with lawyer Leo Branton, Jr., brought in new people for the management of the production company and, in effect, all Nat's ventures from then on.

"Those were bad years," Sparky Tavares reminisced, because of the "tensions, backbiting, and jockeying for position." Sparky became aware that Nat was sometimes isolated and cut off from people he had known well before. Jackie Gale, who for years had been Nat's partner in Nat's music publishing firm—which picked up songs written by other people and recorded by Nat—continued working with Nat in the same capacity. Leo Branton brought along Ike Jones to be creative director of Kell-Cole Productions; several others came into the company, too. The situation became awkward for Carlos, who was white and an old-timer in Nat's camp. "Carlos loved Nat," Lee Young said. All the Cole veterans bore it in mind that Carlos was responsible for Nat having a camp at all.

Louis Victor Mialy observed that Nat seemed nervous about the changes going on in his management. Nat was nervous anyway,

Louis thought; that was why Nat smoked so much, and the changes may have unsettled him even more. He frequently called out, "Confusing! Confusing!" whenever he was confronted by the puzzling and conflicting plans and passions of people around him, Louis Victor noticed. He came to think of Nat as a kind and simple man with infinite patience. Nat couldn't say "no" to anyone, and he bore the pressures on him quietly, because he didn't like to fight with anybody.

Carlos continued as Nat's personal manager throughout the early 1960s. But he found himself often in conflict with the rest of Nat's new team; the tensions mounted. Nat tried to resist becoming caught up in them and, for a while, turned his attention to a show called *I'm with You.*

It had an interracial cast and an original score written by lyricist Dorothy Wayne and composer Ray Rasch. Dotty Wayne had met Nat through musician Eddie Beal, who also ran a busy music publishing office in Hollywood. Quincy Jones worked through Beal's office for a while. Beal's partners there were songwriter and music publisher Joe Green and a white man who did pop and country music. Their company published some of Dotty's songs. When she told Eddie Beal that she wanted to do a concept album with her partner Ray Rasch for Nat Cole, Beal took her to the Cocoanut Grove, where Cole was working.

Dotty told Nat about her idea. He had never done a complete album of songs by one composer-lyricist team. So he told Dotty, "I'll do it if you can come up with twelve songs that I like."

For the next two weeks, she and Ray got together every night and pushed themselves to write two and three songs a night, until they finished twelve songs they liked. Ray balked at playing piano for the demonstration tape. Dotty threatened to have someone whose playing he didn't admire play for the demo, so Ray consented. Dotty took the demo to the front door of the Cole house and handed it to Natalie one day in 1960.

"Be sure to give it to Nat," Dotty told the ten-year-old.

Nat called Dotty a week later at the music-publishing firm where she was working. Her boss became excited, thinking the call was for him, but it turned out to be for Dotty.

"Yes, I got it," Nat began telling Dotty about the tape. He liked it.

He took it into the studio with a thirty-six-piece orchestra led by Nelson Riddle. Dotty loved the fine Riddle arrangements and the beautiful singing by Nat. *Wild Is Love* was the name of the album. It was a marvel, recorded in a day or two. Nat himself thought it was one of his best albums, along with one he would make the next year with George Shearing. (Nat sang while Shearing played, and Nat thought his own piano style resembled Shearing's and that nobody could discern that Nat wasn't accompanying himself.)

Soon afterward, Dotty and Ray were introduced to a producer named Paul Gregory, who was connected with Ike Jones and Kell-Cole Productions. The firm was looking for a musical vehicle in which Nat would star. Hearing that, Dotty decided to create the show. With Ray, she wrote seventeen songs and took them to Capitol; Nat and Glen Wallichs were waiting to hear the songs, which Dotty sang and Ray played. Capitol and Nat decided to invest in the show. It would have dialogue connecting the songs—"a mini-musical," as Dotty called it, entitled *I'm with You.* Dotty and Ray didn't write the connecting material between songs. Different writers were involved. The show was integrated racially, though there were no romances between the characters singing the songs. The narrative served merely to get the performers from one song to another, the theme being man's search for love.

In Dotty Wayne's memory, Nat may have sung to white women as readily as to black women onstage. It was done in an era when, despite the official decision of the casino operators in Las Vegas not to discriminate against blacks anymore, segregation was still plainly in force. Dotty Wayne noticed that she and Eddie Beal couldn't sit at a table up front in the main dining room of a casino to see a show.

The radiantly beautiful young singer Barbara McNair heard that Maria Cole had seen her on Ed Sullivan's show and thought that Barbara would be a fine costar for Nat in *I'm with You.* Barbara traveled to Los Angeles, where she was given the part without having to audition. Dotty Wayne knew there would be trouble with the show when she went to the opening-night performance on October 30, 1960, in San Francisco. As the hero, Nat had one number in which he went through several experiences of his love life. As soon as he began mingling with white women onstage, the audience became troubled, Dotty thought. Sparky Tavares had the same impression. After the show that night, Dotty was warned not to go to the party in a bar near the Geary Theatre, where others connected with the show were awaiting the reviews.

Barbara McNair was unaware of Dotty Wayne's experience that night. Barbara didn't think that the interracial cast had anything to do with the show's problems. The music was fine, too, Barbara thought, but the narrative sections were "no good." A newspaper reviewer didn't criticize the racial integration of the cast. "It was a review, not really a book show," Barbara commented; it was criticized roughly. Dotty concluded that the reviewer opposed the integration, and she felt the published comments were unfair.

Nat tried to work on the book. He and Barbara got together in a room in the hotel where they were staying in San Francisco and tried to improve the writing. Nothing they did seemed to help. Nat was depressed by the reviews because he had nurtured such high hopes for the enterprise. He wanted to ride the show to Broadway; Barbara could see it was a passionate dream.

One day, when he was very blue, Barbara told him, "Let's get away from the show today. Let's go to Sausalito and just relax." Nat said that would be fine. So they took a limousine from their hotel across the bridge to the quaint pastel-colored Mediterranean-style resort town. Everyone in the street recognized Nat and besieged him for autographs. He wasn't able to relax at all.

Barbara said, "Nat, you should dress in old clothes. Go in disguise."

He replied, "Barbara, if I did that, everyone would say, 'There goes Nat Cole looking like a bum.'"

While they were still in San Francisco, they went to a restaurant and didn't receive a bill. Nat said that if a hungry man who couldn't pay asked for a meal there, he probably couldn't get one. Nat thought life was filled with such ironies.

From time to time, Maria came up from Los Angeles to see how the show was going. Once, Cookie and Sweetie made the trip for the day and went to an ice-cream parlor with Barbara. Louis Victor Mialy, who visited Nat at his hotel most afternoons in that period, noticed how fond Nat and Barbara became of each other as they worked together. Nat's headquarters were in the tower of the Fairmount Hotel. His son Kelly, an energetic toddler, visited Nat in the hotel and decided to play. Kelly ran around the room, pulling at everything; Nat restrained Kelly with one hand while he worked on the show with the other. When he wasn't trying to improve the show, Nat read all kinds of books to stay occupied. Louis Victor always found Nat busy doing something in his room, though he never seemed hurried or late, unavailable or on the defensive. His show was still in bad shape, when he took it on the road, first to Minneapolis. He never gave the slightest hint of wanting to walk out of the show. And he took the brunt of the criticism himself, without ever seeming to be angry.

Dotty Wayne, who went on the road with the show, wished that the mild-mannered man would have a temper tantrum for once. She knew how desperately he wanted to take the show to Broadway, and it seemed as if he were certain to have his hopes dashed.

"And with all the turmoil of changing directors, choreographers, and writers on the road, Nat only voiced his opinions; he never blew up," she marveled. "I even blew up and eventually left my own show, but Nat didn't want to give up. He had stick-to-itiveness and wanted to go as far as he could go. He took everything in his stride. He listened. He was open. I only saw him get angry once, when someone told him how to sing and started conducting the orchestra with his fingers waving in front of Nat's face. Well, you can't mess with Nat's singing and timing. You don't have to give him tempos." McNair, too, had been startled by Nat's musical gifts, especially his perfect pitch. "He could pull an *E* out of the air," she remembered.

Dotty saw Nat quiet people with a look. "He would stroke his chin with a forward motion on the back of his hand. Sometimes that gesture meant that he was in deep thought. And when he jutted that chin forward, you didn't mess with him. He gave tremendous performances; he loved to sing and perform; that was his life."

As the show wended its way to Detroit, with Nat fighting for its life, McNair knew the end was coming: "The writing was no good. It was just bad." On November 26, 1960, in Detroit, Nat announced the show's closing. In early December, he made a new announcement that the reorganized show would try again under the title of *Wandering Man.* Rehearsals would begin in New York by January 10, 1961, for a late February opening in a Broadway theater.

A newspaper story at the time said that producer Paul Gregory, cosponsor of the show with Nat, had withdrawn from the production. Nat was the sole sponsor with a big financial investment, perhaps $150,000, some sources estimated. Capitol had no financial connection with the show by then. A cast album was never made.

Nat said that new songs had been added, while the theme of man's quest for love was being retained. He was footing the bill for director Joe Sargent, choreographer Lee Scott, and a couple of writers, who were supplying the narrative. Forty singers and dancers were in the cast, too. Then about a week before rehearsals were scheduled to begin, Nat announced the demise of his dream. The show was shelved. A seven-line item in *The New York Times* announced its end.

Nat changed the format entirely, eliminating most of the narrative and adding more songs and dances, and took the show as a review into the Greek Theatre in Los Angeles for several weeks. The show was called *Sights and Sounds: The Merry World of Nat King Cole.* Natalie Cole appeared as a professional for the first time in her life.

Nat had always taken home jazz records. Natalie developed strong preferences for Ella Fitzgerald and Nancy Wilson. She liked Carmen McRae and Sarah Vaughan as the second-string team of her favorites. Natalie was singing songs of her own choosing for her own pleasure. One day, she went to Nat and said, "Listen to this." She sang "Undecided" a cappella.

"My father was totally surprised, because of my choice of song and the way I did it," Natalie recalled. At the time, getting ready to take his review into the Greek Theatre, he invited her into the cast. For one of her two appearances in the review, she played a young version of herself; Barbara McNair then played the grown-up version of Natalie. One of the songs that Natalie sang was called "It's a Bore," for which she received "her first little paycheck," as she referred to the six-hundred-dollar payment. Her first professional venture reinforced her desire to pursue a stage career. She was also happy to see that Nat was pleased she could sing. He had always known that she could, but now she knew that he knew.

Barbara McNair enjoyed working in *The Merry World of Nat King Cole,* too. She liked one of her songs called "Life Is a Tight Squeeze." It was staged so that a group of people were squeezed into a little elevator. She had to keep wedging her way through all the people in order to do her song.

The show got good reviews. Through all the turmoil, Barbara McNair had loved Nat's gentle manner "and class and elegance." Nat gave her a beautiful teardrop-shaped watch when the show closed. The shape of the watch was an appropriate symbol for the bittersweet end of their adventure. Barbara was heading to Dallas for a singing engagement. The watch didn't work well, however, so Barbara took it to a repair shop and paid in advance for it to be fixed and mailed to her. One day, the hotel's desk staffer in Dallas called her to say that a package had arrived for her. She told him to send it up to her room; she knew that it was the watch because of the return address that she was told appeared on the package. It never arrived. She went downstairs to find out what had happened. The desk man said the package had been sent to her, but between the desk and her room, the watch went astray. "It broke my heart," she recalled, "because it was beautiful, and it was from him."

Chapter Twenty-six

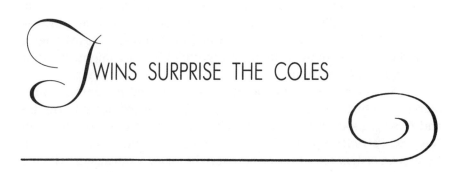

TWINS SURPRISE THE COLES

A t the time Nat had pulled the show out of the fire by overhaul-
ing it and calling it a review, something happened that neither
he nor his wife expected. In January 1961, Maria became pregnant,
only fifteen months after adopting Kelly. She was now thirty-eight,
with three children and a complex marriage. One of her friends,
who was intimately acquainted with Maria because their husbands
worked together so closely at Capitol, believed that Maria and Nat
were having such difficulties in their marriage that it was not an
ideal time for the couple to have a baby. Seen in another light,
perhaps it was an excellent time, as the Coles tried to give their
marriage new vitality.

By that time, the rumors of the Coles' tensions were common
knowledge among their friends, many of whom had—or would
have—terrible, even catastrophic, difficulties in their own family
lives. Some were going through divorces, battles against alcohol, or
heart-wrenching scenes with their children. No matter what strains

the Coles may have weathered in their marriage, however, their close friends knew that Maria didn't think about divorce at all, as she might have a few years earlier. Nat wasn't thinking of divorce, either. "The concept simply didn't occur to him," Louis Victor Mialy summed up the feelings of Nat's friends, "because Nat felt enormous respect and loyalty for Maria and their children."

However, many friends and acquaintances also knew that Nat had romantic feelings for women other than his wife at times— Barbara McNair for one, though he had no interest in provoking a risky showdown about women or anything else that might threaten the stability of his family.

On September 26, 1961, at St. John's Hospital in Santa Monica, Maria gave birth to identical twin girls. They were named Timolin and Casey, good Irish names, which made some people reflect on Nat's St. Patrick's Day birthday. Nat liked the name Casey because he was an ardent fan of Casey Stengel, the Yankees manager. The fey name Timolin may have been suggested by a family friend. The twins brought the varied Cole brood to five. With three babies on their hands, the Coles had definitely reinforced their family tie. Maria was constrained to stay at home while Nat went on the road, so she was depressed for a while after the twins were born. The twins and Kelly would be less photographed for publication than the older children. Compared with Cookie and Sweetie, the twins and Kelly grew up in virtual seclusion, out of the public eye. Many of Nat's friends—even those in the Los Angeles area—never met the twins. One caught glimpses of them on rare occasions. *Ebony* published some photos of them. As they grew up to be slender, pretty girls with long faces, they resembled both their parents; Cookie, who could see differences between the twins, thought their mouths reminded her of their father's. Since their father died when they were three and a half years old, most of what they knew about him came from their mother and stories they read or heard about the legendary singer. Family friends saw them at first at the parties that Nat and Maria threw. They had an annual bash on the Fourth of July. It was always a glamorous affair, with Nat playing the role of the happy, munificent host; Maria as a hostess was equally dazzling. Everyone who was anyone saw everybody else, ate and drank, admired and gawked, and gossiped and laughed in the house, on the patio, and beside the pool. Natalie wanted to ask some of the celebrities for autographs, but her mother thought that was not a good way to approach friends who were famous.

This was not the only time that the Coles seemed to be living in concert in those days, despite the rumors of their difficulties. Harry "Sweets" Edison, for one, recalled he was working at a club one night in Los Angeles when Nat and Maria arrived. Nat sat in and played piano with Sweets.

Natalie was gathering her last poignant memories of her father in those days. She especially loved it that he treated her almost as an equal, not a child. There was a special affinity between them. "Maybe he saw something in me that he had seen in himself when he was young," she later reflected. He never patronized her.

She reveled in the times when they went to the movies together. She knew he didn't like it when fans converged upon the table when he took his family out to dinner in a restaurant. He was not in Los Angeles enough to waste time with intrusions. The family suffered through them, knowing there was nothing they could do about it. Natalie relished the times at home when he sang children's songs with "I love you" in the lyrics to her and Cookie. At night, she listened for his step as he went to the kitchen for a late-night sandwich. She would sneak downstairs to be with him, and they would share a snack. They didn't discuss anything especially pertinent or "heavy" during those rendezvous, Natalie recalled, but they were special, intimate times.

He took Cookie and Sweetie to Broadway plays; afterward, the family would go home and reenact them—*Damn Yankees, Peter Pan* with Mary Martin, and *Li'l Abner.* "Oh, there are all kinds of wonderful memories," Natalie reflected.

Once he took her and Cookie to upstate New York—Syracuse. It was the first time that Sweetie had ever seen snow, and Cookie may not have remembered having seen it, because she had gone to live in Los Angeles when she was only four. "I ate snow," Natalie recalled, "and I made snowballs! Oh, it was great!"

The few times she spent alone with her father meant a lot to her. Occasionally, they sat at the piano and sang together. One time, Sparky remembered Maria joining them to sing. Maria corrected Natalie, and Sparky thought Maria was intruding on the child's playtime with Nat. Maria's voice blended sweetly with Nat's and made a fine example, and she undoubtedly enjoyed it. Maria was very proud of Cookie's dancing talent, which earned the child the right to assist in teaching younger students in her dancing class; Maria also was happy that Natalie began singing very well when she was only three. Maria, with her very high standards, loved having talented kids and nurturing them with instructions.

Natalie got the chance to play miniature golf alone with Nat.

One year, her mother bought him a sports car—an XKE Jaguar—for his birthday. It was a two-seater. He drove so fast that nobody in the family but Natalie would get in the car with him. One day, he took her nearly all the way to San Diego just for the joy of riding. She felt like his buddy, she later recalled. "I didn't even feel like a girl—ha ha, and I thought, Man, this guy is cool."

He seemed very relaxed with her at such private times. Otherwise she felt instinctively that he was a little uncomfortable with his enormous fame because he was so shy. He wasn't really crazy about having crowds converge upon him, she noticed. He never confided any of his feelings to her. Perhaps she was too young, she later mused. As she grew to become a young woman without her father's company, she felt that she had missed out on something wonderful—the opportunity for them to commune with each other as adults.

Chapter Twenty-seven

"RAMBLIN' ROSE"

*I*n 1962, Nat had the good fortune to receive a tune called "Ramblin' Rose" from the Sherman brothers. He said he would try to fit it in at his next recording date, but he wasn't absolutely sure he would have time. If he had a spare fifteen minutes, he said, he would do it, adding that he liked the song.

Music industry people liked to socialize in a little restaurant near Capitol's tower. Nat went there to chat with musicians and all sorts of business people. Songwriters had a very easy time finding and approaching him there. A legend arose among them that they had to try to find out when his next recording session would take place; then they had to get their songs to him just before the session. If they gave their songs to him a few weeks earlier, he would forget them by the time he got to the studio. He had been known to take a new song directly from the restaurant to a session, have an arrangement made, and record it that day.

The recording engineer didn't like the song "Ramblin' Rose," which Nat asked the country-oriented Belford Hendricks to arrange and then fitted into the end of a recording date. The song with its twangy country and western feeling appealed to Nat. He had sung other songs with a hint of country feeling before "Ramblin' Rose." A million-record seller and a success beyond his wildest expectations, it was his first hit of that magnitude in several years.

Touring the country, he was a guest on a radio show someplace in the south where a disc jockey waxed effusive about the song. The disc jockey said it had a wonderful country and western flavor, and he thought that Nat must have searched the southland to find such an authentic southern song. Nat said, "Actually it was written by two Jewish boys from Brooklyn." The disc jockey immediately went to another topic. Nat laughed with the Sherman brothers later.

Joe Sherman had spent only eighteen minutes composing the music for "Ramblin' Rose"; royalties came in for the next thirty years. The public's reactions always surprised Nat. Habitually recording a little bit of everything, he was moving along in a direction that popular tastes dictated.

That year, with no new inviting idea about which direction to explore, Nat decided to go back on the road with his troupe in a review he called *Sights and Sounds: The Merry World of Nat King Cole*, essentially an interracial cast of young singers and dancers, along with his trio and other musicians. Lee Young went along for a year as musical director, then decided to duck out because he was tired of the road. He eventually became a producer for Motown music. Charles Harris, the bassist, and John Collins, the guitarist, always declined opportunities to talk about Nat Cole for publication. Collins had a close friendship with Nat, however, even though he preferred to say his relationship was strictly professional.

On a personal level, Nat seemed a less accessible figure. Sparky Tavares noticed that Nat's new organization men put a distance between the star and some of his old friends and acquaintances. Nat had friends in many cities, but for the most part, wherever he went, including Los Angeles, his old friends, including musicians he had known from his Sewanee Inn days, saw him primarily when their paths crossed briefly. John and Jean Kraus, who had met him in the 331 Club and gone to his opening at the Orpheum Theatre in 1944, noticed how shy he was and how isolated and aloof he seemed at a party nearly twenty years later.

One of Dave Cavanaugh's sons celebrated his bar mitzvah, and many Capitol people were invited to a party at Dave's house. By then, John Kraus had been working as the recording engineer for quite a few of Nat's recordings for Capitol. He and his wife went to the party and found that Nat had very little to say to them. He was polite, but he sat quietly in a chair away from the center of the crowd, as if he gone to the party simply to be courteous to Dave, his friend and producer. Nat wasn't at ease in a cocktail-party setting; he did nothing to try to call attention to himself. Jean, unaccustomed to seeing Nat keep himself in the background, thought that he might have become affected by all the hoopla that had cheered him and catastrophes that had beset him along the way. She knew he had gone through some very difficult times. The most publicized incidents in Los Angeles had been the uproar over his house and his IRS bill. He had the air of being a very self-effacing stranger who had drifted away from his formerly easy relationship with the Krauses and didn't invite small talk at a party.

When Nat left the party, Jean and John Kraus saw him outside with Dave Cavanaugh; from across the street, John took a photograph of Nat with Dave. The sky was darkening at the time. When the picture was developed, Jean marveled at how very dark Nat looked in the photograph. His white shirt was bright. Otherwise, he wasn't clearly delineated, though Dave was in sharp focus. The discovery was a source of wonder and perhaps some amusement for her. She didn't think anything else about it right away. Though the Cole aplomb seemed intact in performances, he had never been as easygoing as his geniality always suggested to people, including Jean. She came to understand that, and she dropped her original musing that his aloofness at the party had meant he had changed and forgotten about the "little people." Eventually she viewed him from the aspect of all the difficulties he had survived. Even his very dark complexion had to be considered when she thought about what it had actually felt like to be Nat King Cole. Alan Livingston, a president of Capitol Records in the 1960s, had gritted his teeth every time he made a reservation for lunch for Nat and himself in a famous Los Angeles restaurant. The *maître d'hote* always groaned when Livingston said he was bringing Nat and wanted a table up front—the area for celebrities. Livingston parried with the maître d'hote by phone about the seating arrangement, but the men were always assigned a table in the rear. If Nat knew about the slight, he never mentioned it to Livingston. Many other people thought that Nat never changed for as long as they knew him; he remained quiet, amiable—and painfully shy.

In a professional context, he himself had once addressed the phenomenon of change. He was talking about the changes that careers went through when he told a *Metronome* magazine writer, "People don't slip. Time catches up with them." His experiences had certainly weathered him. In his forties, he still thought of himself as a man in the prime of life. He was at least pressing on at full force, even though he had not found a new direction in which to go. He did love several of the albums he had made in the 1960s. Other people, who knew him to be the successful superstar Nat King Cole didn't worry if he were feeling the frustrations of his thwarted TV, film, and Broadway efforts or of the racially based affronts or of a complex personal life. There were constant business pressures which he found he could elude only when he was performing. Everyone he worked with marveled at how generous and cooperative he was as a singer and musician. There seemed to be no end to his generosity and consideration for people working with him. If music were involved, he gave his whole, painstaking attention.

He could share his private thoughts on stage, presenting them as the ruminations of an entertaining sophisticate. "Man is a fool," he told audiences. "When it's hot, he wants it cool. When it's cool, he wants it hot, always wanting what it's not," Louis Victor Mialy remembered was one monologue Nat liked to use with audiences. It came from a Dorothy Wayne song, which Nat chose to deliver as if it was his own philosophy. He gave the same treatment to another rumination: "You can have love, marriage, and sex. You can have one without the other two. Sometimes you can have two without the third one. But when you get the three of them together, you had better watch your step." Mialy loved Nat's air of freedom when he seemed to share personal thoughts on stage. Offstage, Nat seemed aloof. His daughter Cookie believed that he sometimes withdrew into his music to escape from other concerns of the world.

Lee Young thought that Nat's continuing good luck was remarkable. Nat had weathered trips down blind and dangerous alleys yet still had a smooth operation at his command. Maria, it was generally known, hired all the singers and dancers, called the Merry Young Souls, in Nat's troupe; she had a firm grip on Kell-Cole Productions. Through the years, she had turned Nat's attention so adroitly to the fine points of commercial considerations that he seemed to have incorporated her outlook. Her logic had appealed to him from the first days of their love affair.

A young woman dancer and singer in *Sights and Sounds* recalled being delighted with the show's concept. "It was forward,

neat, and great," she said. It had black and white singers and dancers performing together, holding hands, and dancing together
onstage. The concept reinforced her own upbringing about the
equality of all races, religions, and nationalities. Two of the twelve
players, a black woman and a white man, fell in love and married.
The young white woman dancer thought that was a fine development; long after the show had ended, she heard that the couple had
stayed together happily for more than twenty-five years. Some of
Nat's friends believed that this young woman had caught Nat's romantic fancy especially. None of Nat's flirtations during his years on
the road had threatened the stability of his marriage to Maria, but
even Milton Karle said that Cole was smitten with the young
dancer. Of all Nat's close associates and intimates, only Sparky Tavares knew nothing about a romance, he said. He also knew nothing
about the Cole marriage being tense or troubled.

Yet many musicians, song publishers, and Capitol executives believed that Nat was thinking of divorcing Maria and marrying the
pretty, delicate-looking, soft-spoken, mild-mannered dancer. Carl
Carruthers, for one, spread the word. Another of Nat's intimates said
he had heard the story directly from Nat. Still other people knew
only that the Cole marriage was in serious jeopardy and might end
legally.

Maria herself admitted publicly that the marriage was troubled
by the 1960s. A rumor had circulated for quite a while about a
possible divorce between the Coles. Nat had never hesitated to do
what he wanted in his career or personal life before. This time he
did nothing publicly to validate the rumor. A great deal was at stake.
Nat was a superstar, a very rich man with a family, and a black man
known to be infatuated with a young white woman. He knew very
well that Sammy Davis, Jr., had been booed at a prestigious political
event a few years earlier where Nat had been applauded because
Davis was engaged to be married to the Swedish actress, May Britt.

The young woman in question eventually left the show. She
headed back to Los Angeles, where she built a career for herself in
television; she married and raised a family. Many years later, when
she was reminded of the story, she said, "It happened so long ago."
She had thought of Nat as a wonderful, kind, gentle friend, one of
the nicest men she had ever met.

Marvin Cane, who adored Maria, thought she had been "a tough
lady" because she felt that people in the music business had been
pulling Nat away from home and trying to intrude on the family's
terrain and privacy. Though Marvin Cane believed the Cole mar-

riage was rocky, he never had heard Nat complain about anything, including Maria. He thought Nat's sense of morality would not permit him to get divorced. Another of Nat's equally close friends thought that Nat was prepared to sign away his fortune for his freedom. Even so, Sparky Tavares saw nothing to indicate to him that the Coles would actually divorce, and Sparky knew a striking number of Cole family secrets. Sparky had seen Maria angry with Nat because he had come home late for dinner one night; Nat didn't eat, then after changing his clothes, he ran out to give a performance; Maria was angry that he didn't wait to escort her to the concert. Nat and Sparky had made sure that the parking attendants at the concert would clear the way for Maria and the children to get into the hall. Sparky thought it was common for wives to covet the attention of their famous husbands and to try to divert the star from concentrating on his stardom. It happened all the time; Sparky had never seen a marriage in the entertainment world where it didn't happen. He didn't think the durable Cole marriage was foundering.

As Nat traveled in 1963 with *Sights and Sounds*, he had his last million-selling record, "Those Crazy Lazy Hazy Days of Summer," a rollicking, upbeat song, which never reminded anyone of the days when Nat accompanied himself as a jazz pianist. Yet his spirited approach to music remained intact; he sounded jubilant; he excited the nation with the simple tune. And his career stayed buoyant in a rising sea of rock and roll hits. Though his million-seller hits had been fewer and further between, he had discovered he was such a legendary singer that he didn't need a hit in the charts to sustain his momentum. His albums continued to sell well.

Chapter Twenty-eight

UNG CANCER

*I*f anything changed in the Coles's arrangements in the 1960s, it was that Maria's authority over Nat's business affairs increased. Carlos Gastel had a contract as Nat's personal manager. Whatever that contract provided for Carlos, he was able to hold on to. By 1964, however, he was involved only in a peripheral way as a titular personal manager of Nat's career. Leo Branton, Ike Jones, Maria Cole and their associates dominated Nat's affairs.

Sparky Tavares was under the impression that Nat had been under pressure for a long time to fire Carlos, until Nat finally complied. "That was the only bad thing that Nat Cole ever did, firing Carlos," Sparky summed up.

In the New York contingent of Nat's close friends, Ivan Mogull thought that Carlos's drinking had made him less competent as the years progressed. Marvin Cane called Carlos "a manager in absentia, sometimes there, sometimes not," although Marvin supposed that Carlos had been good when he started managing Cole. Marvin

Fisher dissented in Carlos's favor. Sparky was irate at the thought of anyone criticizing Carlos, and so were a number of other people in Cole's music circles in Los Angeles. Though they knew that Carlos drank, they noticed no diminution of his abilities. He was one of the best managers in the business, they thought. Without Cole as a client, everyone surmised, Carlos's career was diminished. Carlos kept on drinking. In the late 1960s, his health went into a definite decline.

Newspaper stories throughout most of 1964 suggested that Nat was enjoying a heady success. There was no hint of any malaise in his life. He had already appeared at the White House during the Eisenhower years, then again for President Kennedy. In January 1964, Cole had a preperformance visit with President Johnson, who invited the singer to entertain at a Senate Office Building luncheon sponsored by the Hollywood Museum to mark the seventieth anniversary of the first motion-picture copyright.

Dotty Wayne saw Nat that year and thought that he wasn't looking very well. He was too thin, she felt. In October 1964, he arrived in New York City as usual for his Copacabana engagement. The season especially excited him because he could watch the World Series baseball games on TV in the afternoons. The football season was beginning, too, with televised games.

Maria didn't go to New York with Nat. She didn't know he wasn't feeling well. He hadn't told anyone on his staff how bad he felt. He was staying in his own apartment, which he and Maria had bought near Lincoln Center. Noel Sherman also had an apartment in the building; it was only a few blocks from Joe Sherman's apartment on Riverside Drive. So the Sherman brothers went to Nat's apartment one afternoon and kept turning the channel from the baseball to the football games. Nat lay on a chaise longue in a room decorated by Maria in light pastel colors. The room had a light, airy feeling, which Joe Sherman associated with a California ambience. Nat looked well, but he told his guests, "I've been having a terrible back ache for a while now."

Feeling sorry for Nat, Joe offered to mix the drinks for the crowd. Nat let him do it. The Coles hadn't owned the apartment for very long by then—perhaps a couple of years at most. They had bought it with the help of white friends who acquired the place and then transferred it to the Coles, Marvin Cane said. This time there were no repercussions, as there had been in Hancock Park, but the Coles could not have bought their apartment directly even then, as Cane remembered.

It was the first time that Joe Sherman had ever mixed drinks for Nat in Nat's own living room. Nat usually did it himself. But this day, Nat kept talking about his back pain. He also mentioned his daughter Natalie. "I have this teenage daughter, Natalie, who thinks she may want to get into this crazy business. What do you think of that?" Nat said. Mmmm, really, that's interesting, his company said. Nobody said that it was a terrible idea or that it was anything for Nat to worry about. Of course, Natalie would think about becoming an entertainer. Nobody in the room had actually ever heard her sing; so nobody could say that she would be making a brilliant move, either. But she was Nat's daughter. Her idea sounded logical.

Nat went through his weeks at the Copacabana without becoming sicker or mentioning his back pain again to the Shermans. It wasn't until he went to Las Vegas for his Sands engagement after New York that he began to worry his staff. Carl Carruthers noticed one night that Nat went directly to his room after a show. That wasn't normal for Nat. He usually liked to go out on the town for a while to unwind. That night, he called Carruthers to say he needed help. He couldn't walk, because his back pain was so fierce.

It subsided enough for him to keep working. He didn't want to go to a doctor, so a doctor came to him in his Las Vegas suite and gave him an electrocardiogram right there. There was nothing wrong with his heart; the doctor told him to try to get some rest for a few days. From Las Vegas, Nat went to an engagement at Harrah's in Lake Tahoe, Nevada, and flew every day to Los Angeles for the filming of *Cat Ballou*, then back to Lake Tahoe for his show at Harrah's at night. He was losing weight rapidly. Sparky Tavares kept making new notches in Cole's belts. One time, Nat became irritated because he thought that Sparky hadn't made a new notch as he had been asked to do the previous day. But Sparky had done it. Cole's belts were on the verge of looking chawed. Nat had chronic fatigue. Sparky was very worried and tried to console Nat with the idea that he could rest when he finished the film and went to his next engagement in San Francisco.

But when they arrived there, Nat was feeling worse. One night, a hotel doctor at the Fairmount, where Nat was staying, was called. He took an X ray and found a tumor on Nat's left lung.

Nat's first reactions were to keep working—and not to tell Maria, who was in Europe. He agreed to go to a hospital after he finished the engagement. "When the man was sick with cancer," Sparky recalled, "for the last two weeks in San Francisco, I had to meet him and help him walk up the stairs of the theater in the round, where he was appearing. He was wobbly, weak. I met him when he finished. He canceled other assistants and said, 'Let Sparky take care of me.'"

Back in Los Angeles, Nat made a brief stop at his house in Hancock Park. His sister-in-law Charlotte Sullivan was there with Nat and Sparky when they called Maria in London. Nat still didn't want Maria to know he was sick, but he let Sparky and Charlotte place the call and tell her. Charlotte said that Nat was going to St. John's Hospital in Santa Monica. Nat himself got on the phone to say hello to Maria. "I'm all right," he said in a perfunctory, dull tone. He didn't dwell on how he felt or on anything else. Maria mobilized right away.

Sparky drove Nat to the hospital. Nat asked Sparky whether he knew what the illness was.

"No," Sparky said.

Nat said, "The doctors told you."

Sparky said, "I don't want to hear it from them. I want to hear it from you."

Nat said, "I've got cancer."

Sparky told him that the doctors would try to cure it. He said Lee Young remarked that Nat Cole was such a lucky man that if he had cancer, the doctors would find a cure for it. Sparky was smoking Salems by that time, having switched from Nat's brand, Nat asked him for a cigarette, took a few puffs, put it out, and said that he wouldn't smoke anymore, Sparky later recounted in a very soft voice.

Maria took charge, once Nat was in the hospital. She began to issue statements saying that Nat Cole was being treated for lung cancer; he was having cobalt treatments to try to shrink a tumor on his left lung; the prognosis was optimistic, the papers reported. In truth, the prognosis was hopeless. Nat had entered the hospital in early December with the hope that he would go home for Christmas, but he was too weak to do that. From the telephone in his room, he called Carl Carruthers to say that he couldn't go home for Christmas, because his temperature had gone up. Nat sent Carl a check in the mail with the instructions to buy a Christmas present and deliver it to the young singer and dancer whom Cole had been attracted to, Carruthers recalled. The Cole children went to the hospital to see Nat for the holiday. He was cranky with them because he was in pain, Maria later recalled—and no doubt because he was depressed, too. The tumor didn't disappear with treatments; instead, it spread rapidly. Doctors operated on January 25 and removed his left lung. Nat was still moribund. There was nothing for Maria to do but lie to the press, so that the headlines all around the nation wouldn't reach Nat with messages of doom.

The news reached Nat's father in North Chicago, where he lay ill himself. A few years earlier, he had remarried. Now Evelyn was helping to take care of him. He became very curious about why Nat wasn't arriving for a visit. Then it dawned on the minister that his son was probably too sick to come to say goodbye. Reverend Coles said to Evelyn, "You have my deepest sympathy." He seemed to know that her brother was dying, too. The Reverend Coles died on February 1 in a Waukegan hospital.

Years later, Maria Cole said that she had known her husband was dying, and yet she had somehow hoped that he would get well. For a little while, he did feel well enough to go home, where he saw her and others in the family trying to sort out hundreds of thousands of messages that had been arriving to wish him good health. He was quickly taken back to the hospital, however, where doctors and nurses had medicine to ease his pain.

Nat was not supposed to have many visitors. Yet Frank Sinatra walked into the hospital whenever he pleased. A few other people were rumored to have gotten in to see Nat when nobody was looking. A ribald rumor circulated that a woman dressed in a nurse's uniform to sneak into Nat's room for a visit. Many of Nat's associates didn't see him again once he went into the hospital, however. They held Maria responsible for cutting him off from them. Nevertheless, Louis Victor Mialy had a visit arranged for him with Nat by their friends at Capitol, Dave Dexter and Dave Cavanaugh among them. Nat seemed to feel well the day that Louis visited. Nat said that he wanted to record more songs in French. Louis said, "Wonderful, but do me a favor. I would like you to do a jazz record." Nat said that he didn't play piano anymore the way he used to. Louis said, "No, I want you to play the organ." "What?" Nat said, astounded. He added, "I'm very rusty at the organ." Louis told him, "When you go home to recuperate, you'll have time to practice the organ." Nat said, "I'll think about it."

Nat had a telephone in his room and could—and did—call some friends. He also went to the chapel in the hospital often, according to Maria. He undoubtedly was in too much pain to want visitors. He was so ill that Maria had power of attorney by then, Sparky recalled, and she would later announce that her personal problems with Nat disappeared during Nat's illness. She said Nat was happy with the thought that they would buy a cottage by the beach in Santa

Monica, where he would recuperate once he left the hospital. It would not have been the first time that their marriage was rejuvenated by a powerful event; Nat Kelly Cole's adoption and the birth of the twins had helped the couple through troubled waters in the past.

Nat leaned heavily on the kindnesses and reassurances of his nurses to get him through the nights. During the days, Maria arrived to take charge. The press was eager for the daily report.

Marvin Fisher received a phone call from Nat, possibly on February 14. Fisher thought that Nat sounded very well, not sad; twenty-five years later, Fisher recalled only that Nat talked in an intimate way with his longtime friend and didn't seem to think that he was dying. Nat's pain before then had prompted doctors to put him on strong painkillers. He even had told Maria that he preferred to die than live in that pain. On February 14, however, he felt well enough to ask Maria to take him for a ride.

She kindly agreed and took him to the Santa Monica shore, where they would ostensibly live together in the house they were going to buy for his recuperation. Nat seemed very dreamy, or preoccupied with private thoughts, and low-keyed at the beach, she said. She felt that he may have been trying to keep up a dignified front for her, not telling her that he really didn't expect to live there. He was certainly showing the effect of the painkillers. When she took him back to the hospital, he went to sleep. Instead of awakening at dawn, he died. A night nurse told Maria that Nat had spoken about his "Skeez" with love before he had gone to sleep.

Marvin Fisher was one of the people who received a phone call from the family; he hurried from New York to Los Angeles. Arriving from the plane, he saw right away that Maria was distraught. He was glad that she didn't bear him any grudge as one of the crowd whom she felt had impinged upon her family life. Marvin thought she needed help in taking care of her children in those first days of mourning, because she was so upset. He recalled giving her some help; he went with a few of the children to the place—perhaps a funeral home—where Nat's body lay in an open casket on a platform. Written invitations were extended to various people. Fisher recalled delivering an invitation in his own hand to a comedian who had telephoned to ask for one. Fisher became part of the commotion that culminated in a star-studded funeral three days after Nat died.

The Los Angeles City Council adjourned a session in Cole's memory. The flags of the new Music Center in town were lowered to half-mast, and a memorial was planned in honor of Nat at the Center. Capitol Records' office was filled with orders for more than one million of Nat's records between February 15, the day he died, and February 18, the day of the funeral.

As soon as Nat died, Glen Wallichs called a meeting and decided not to release any of Nat's songs that had not been issued yet. Wallichs set up a committee to analyze them. Nat had recorded at least 175 unreleased songs, primarily as favors to his friends among song pluggers, writers, and music publishers. The rush of interest that always follows the death of an important artist could have persuaded Capitol to cash in on those records, regardless of their quality. (Instead of taking advantage of public sentiment, Capitol respected Nat's memory and reissued with regularity for the next twenty-five years only his best songs and biggest hits. To mark the twenty-fifth anniversary of his death, EMI/Capitol issued some of Cole's previously released recordings, plus a selection of his unreleased vocals and instrumentals on recordings and CDs. One EMI/Capitol box contained LPs; another had selections on CDs released only in England.)

On February 16, *Variety* published this tally: Nat had recorded over six hundred songs and sold upwards of nine million albums, grossing over $50 million dollars for Capitol. The estimate of the number of songs he recorded was very low; Nat had actually recorded several hundred more for Capitol alone, and his pre– and extra–Capitol recordings, plus his transcriptions on radio, film, and TV pushed the number way above a thousand.

The days after Nat died were so hectic and sad that Marvin Fisher thought a week had elapsed by the time the funeral took place. The celebrities who turned out were legion. The pallbearers, carrying Nat's bronze coffin up the steps at the small church, St. James Episcopal on Wilshire Boulevard, included Jim Conkling, by then already a former president of Warner Brothers Records; Glen Wallichs, chairman of Capitol Records; Harold Plant, the Cole family accountant; and Henry Miller, the West Coast manager of General Artists Corporation, the firm under whose auspices Carlos had managed Nat. Maria had decided to use St. James Episcopal, because the church that she usually attended was even smaller.

Marvin Fisher recalled that he, too, had acted as a pallbearer, but whether he had carried the coffin into the church or later into the mausoleum, he could not remember clearly. He knew that Dave Cavanaugh and Lee Gillette had helped lift the coffin with him. One of them had kept bumping into him. Though Wallichs was officially listed as a pallbearer, he was actually in frail health by then; perhaps someone else had actually carried the coffin in his place. Louis Victor Mialy was in one of the sets of pallbearers. His group was made up of Benny Carter, Frank Sinatra, Carlos Gastel, and two more men who carried the coffin to the gravesite. The day was very hot, Louis recalled. The funeral turned out to be a very crowded affair, which Maria tried to organize and oversee. Arguments broke out at times between participants in the various segments of the proceedings. The day's events seemed long, tortuous, and frustrating to Louis.

Jack Benny delivered the eulogy in the church. George Jessel had his say, mentioning that Nat had been the first black man to become a member of the Friar's Club, the entertainers' organization.

TV cameras were at the church, where they filmed the people flocking from the worlds of show business and politics: Cab Calloway, Duke Ellington, Ricardo Montalban, George Burns, Nelson Riddle, Gordon Jenkins, with whom Nat had made many records late in his life, Peter Lawford, Edward G. Robinson, who later befriended Nat Kelly Cole during his period of mourning, Johnny Mathis, Jimmy Durante, Governor Edmund Brown of California, Senator Robert F. Kennedy of New York, and Count Basie. Sammy Davis, Jr., canceled his performance in *Golden Boy* on Broadway to fly to the funeral. Many more famous and easily recognizable faces appeared among the four hundred people who fitted inside the small church, while a crowd of about three thousand people waited outside. José Ferrer arrived in a limousine with his wife at the time, Rosemary Clooney. Ferrer's behavior always stuck in Fisher's mind, because the actor had lingered such a long time looking at Nat. Limousines took Jerry Lewis, Edie Adams, Gene Barry, Danny Thomas, Vic Damone, Frankie Laine, and Eddie "Rochester" Anderson to the church, according to news stories.

Maria had called Evelyn Coles, who flew from Chicago to the funeral, as several other relatives did. Evelyn cried at the sight of her young brother's coffin. Eddie, Ike, and Freddy Cole arrived. Alberta Thomas, a cousin from Chicago, came along. Maria invited her to go with the family to the Hancock Park house after the funeral, but Alberta didn't go. Even though Maria insisted that Nat would have wanted Alberta to go, she didn't change her mind. She felt that since she hadn't been invited to the house when Nat was alive, there wasn't any point in her going now that he wasn't there.

Maria took all her children to the church. Cookie, who was about twenty-one and had been living on the East Coast, while she tried to find a direction for her life, went to the church. Natalie, fifteen, and still a student in a private high school, and Kelly, who had just turned six, went along, too. So did the twins, who were only three and a half years old. Mildred Cavanaugh, Milton Berle's wife, and Sammy Cahn's wife prepared food at the Hancock Park house, so the funeral party would have something to eat after Nat's body was buried in the mausoleum at the Forest Lawn Memorial Park in Glendale. Mildred Cavanaugh reflected on how the meal preparation was a traditional touch at a Jewish funeral. So many people were going to arrive at the house; Maria needed the help.

Sparky was stationed at the church door during the funeral. Maria had asked him to stand there. Sparky had not seen Nat in a very long time by then.

After Nat had gone to the hospital, Sparky had gone to the Hancock Park house one day in December 1964 and talked with Maria and Leo Branton. Branton asked him to stop by the office. Sparky said okay, then left.

Leo Branton told Sparky that Nat was going to be ill for a while. The office was going to cut costs, so Sparky's services wouldn't be needed anymore just then. He would be called again when things changed. "So I handed him my credit card," Sparky reminisced, "and I said, 'All right, but don't anybody call me but Nat Cole.'" Sparky never liked the memory of what happened to him; he would always be upset by it. He didn't know how the others were let go.)

Right after his dismissal from the Cole camp, Sparky was offered the job as Nancy Wilson's road manager. A jazz singing star by the time Cole died, Nancy was headed for a pop-oriented, jazz-influenced career herself. She retained Sparky in her entourage for more than twenty-five years. It seemed to Sparky that he would never get a chance to sit home and write his book of memories, "Too Old For the Road." He had gotten only as far as the title.

The day that Nat died, Sparky was working in Florida with Nancy. Cookie called him from Hancock Park and told him the news. Maria got on the phone and said, "Are you coming home?" Nancy told Sparky, "Well, you'd better go home. They need you right now." So Sparky said he would be right there. He flew back to Los Angeles in time for the funeral, where he saw John Collins, Joe Comfort, Lee Young, Charlie Harris, and Irving Ashby. At the mausoleum at Forest Lawn, Oscar Moore walked in, sat down in front of the crypt, looked at Nat, then shook hands with the Cole family members and Sparky and Carlos Gastel and walked out. Sparky was especially struck by the way Oscar Moore looked quietly at Nat and didn't stop to speak with anyone.

After leaving Cole's trio, Oscar had played with his brother's group, The Three Blazers, and with Ray Charles, Floyd Dixon, and in groups with Carl Perkins and Joe Comfort. Oscar made a few records on small labels such as Swing Time and Aladdin, and his career hadn't been financially rewarding; life was a struggle. By the end of the 1950s, he worked as a bricklayer. In 1965, Oscar recorded an LP as a tribute to Nat. He would not make much money as a musician again in his life. He died on October 8, 1981 in Las Vegas.* And his widow was very grateful to Savoy Jazz for reissuing in 1989 an early trio album including Oscar Moore's tune, "Beautiful Moons Ago."

After the burial, Sparky was driven to his house about four miles from the Coles' house. Maria called to invite him to Hancock Park. Sparky's brother, who answered the phone, said Sparky was busy doing something. Sparky hadn't wanted to go to the house at that moment. He didn't want to be part of what he felt was a three-ring circus, with a lot of people who hadn't even known Nat and were taking the opportunity to show up and look at his acquisitions.

Sparky went back on the road with Nancy Wilson quickly. Eventually, he gave up smoking. By the twenty-fifth anniversary of Cole's death, Sparky, spry and fit, youthful-looking when he wore shorts in the warm Los Angeles afternoons, dapper in well-tailored suits and sleek gold jewelry for work, swiftly ran up and down stairs in nightclubs. Though he needed thick eyeglasses because of vision problems, he kept his sense of humor about other people's foibles, which he never failed to notice, and remained resilient and patient while keeping up with a busy road schedule.

In New York City, Marvin Cane had decided he couldn't endure going to the Nat Cole funeral because his own wife had just died of cancer. So he went to the service at St. Thomas Episcopal Church on Fifth Avenue, where everyone in the East Coast music business, as far as he could see, showed up at the same time that the West Coast church service was taking place.

At the funeral in Los Angeles, Evelyn Coles saw several of the old musicians who had known Nat in Chicago, and in his trios, and on the music scene from his earliest days in California and throughout his life. They told her that the Coles had been on the verge of a divorce when Nat had become sick and died. Evelyn was shocked. She had not had the slightest idea. She and Maria had been friendly

* This information about Moore's career after the trio comes from the Klaus Teubig discography of Nat Cole's records.

throughout the Cole's marriage. Yet Evelyn had not realized how far a distance that Nat, who had once confided in her and depended upon her protectiveness, had traveled from his early naïveté. She had not shared with him the journey he had taken to houses of state, to respectful presidents, dictators, and royalty. She had not imagined the spiritual abrasions that resulted from his collisions with racism, and competition; she was unfamiliar with the high-level business pressures that ruled his daily life. Later she would find herself picked out of audiences and applauded simply because she was his sister. That gave her a hint of the attention that Nat had felt for at least twenty years. Though she had known that he must have experienced depressing frustrations and exultant joys, she had not known much about the specific events that had molded her multimillionaire brother and the relationships he shared with the musicians who traveled with him and especially with his valet. When Evelyn went back to Chicago, she received a phone call from Maria, who asked her not to believe any rumors that might reach her. They weren't true, said Maria.

Maria spread the word that the Cole marriage had ended happily. Some Cole family intimates thought she was telling the story the way she wished it had been. However, among them were people who recalled, along with Marvin Fisher, that the Cole marriage had been "resurrected" several times. Maria's friends took special care of her during the days following Nat's death, when she was in shock, as Marvin Fisher saw clearly. Jackie Gale's wife Ada Kurtz and music publisher Sam Weiss and his wife were particularly solicitous of her in the weeks after the funeral. Leo Branton gave her his support.

As she matured, Natalie came to wonder whether her father would have confided in her or understood her. Would he have scolded and counseled her as Sparky, acting as an uncle, had done at times with her and her brother and sisters? Would her life have been different if Nat had lived a longer time? All the children were left to rummage around in their memories and try to understand the elusive, canny man who was their father.

Carlos Gastel had guessed correctly that he would follow in his father's footsteps and die young. Carlos died at the age of fifty-six in 1970. Glen Wallichs died a few months later in 1971.

And the pieces of the jigsaw puzzle of the dynamic, creative, savvy, sometimes rowdy, and eccentric individualists whose lives had touched Nat Cole's began to be placed in a final order. Nat's generation started to hold still, while the legacy of his tender voice and his timeless jazz piano style kept coming vividly to life on recordings.

AN AFTERWORD: A PANORAMA OF NAT COLE'S BROTHERS AND SISTERS AND THE SECOND GENERATION OF THE COLE MUSICAL DYNASTY

Nearly twenty-five years to the day after Nat Cole died, bright-eyed, slender Maria Cole, perhaps a bit nervous but articulate and poised, was called to the dais of the Grammy Awards ceremony, where she accepted the Lifetime Achievement Award for her husband. Nat had helped to found NARAS, which gave him the posthumous award. In 1957, the organization had been only an idea; the musicians starting it had thought they would accept members on the basis of their record sales figures, but it became apparent that some of the best records didn't have the highest sales figures. So the founders decided to recruit members on the basis of the quality of their work. Nat opened the first meeting of NARAS; his appearance gave status to the fledgling organization in August 1957. In 1990, there was only a brief flurry for remembrance of Nat at the Grammy

Awards ceremony, which had grown so big that it had to be held at the Shrine Civic Auditorium. A little film clip of Cole in performance—always the best view of the man—was omitted.

By the time of the Grammys in 1990, Cole's estate had an income well into six figures, according to the estimate of Alan Livingston, who had negotiated some of Cole's contracts with Capitol as late as the 1960s. Several Cole friends and music industry insiders guessed that Nat's estate was earning half a million dollars in 1989—more than triple the income from old Glenn Miller hits. Nat's popularity had been astoundingly long-lived.

The attractive, long-faced Casey Cole, who had married in 1989 and was living on the West Coast, had helped her mother with the compilations of recent Cole collections. Casey's twin sister, Timolin, with a college degree in communications from a Texas school, lived in New York City. Nat Kelly Cole was living in Los Angeles, trying to find a way to express his view of his father's life in a film or a book. Carol Claudia "Cookie" Lane Cole, who had raised two children, had the bright idea to do a book of photographs of her father; she would write captions. As a young woman, Cookie had started a career as an actress. Soon after her father died, she made her first professional stage appearance in *The Owl and the Pussycat* in Los Angeles. Before that, she had done summer stock. Her role as a young sophisticate in *Weekend*, a political comedy written by Gore Vidal, was publicized for a March 1967 opening at the Broadhurst Theatre on Broadway, but the show didn't last long. At Lincoln Center, she appeared in *The Black Picture Show*. Cookie then backed away from the stage and, though she had shown talent, chose a domestic life-style instead.

When Natalie was about twenty-one, she took control of twenty thousand dollars, she told a writer for the *Chicago Tribune*'s Sunday magazine. Natalie said she promptly spent it on a couple of cars and some clothes. Some of the money she gave away, going through it "like water," as she put it. Her mother had been very angry. Seeing that she had little to show for that money. Natalie made up her mind to hold on to her money the next time she had any. She didn't really expect to have any. But in her mid-twenties, her singing career took off. She earned money independently from performances and hit records. In the late 1980s, her concerts were packed with shouting fans. She did not have to ask anybody for financial assistance.

At the Grammy Awards in early 1990, Natalie, who was nominated for a Grammy herself for her rhythm and blues hit "Miss You

Like Crazy" escorted an aged Ella Fitzgerald to the dais to present a Grammy to another singer. With Ella, Natalie sang a little bit of "Straighten Up and Fly Right," supporting the elderly singer in their duet. Ella deferred to the younger, physically stronger Natalie. Natalie was really singing that night, swinging, with whimsicality and a pretty voice. It was a time when jazz was so fashionable, even though the Grammys virtually glossed over it, that Natalie was discovering her own rhythm and blues fans enjoyed the tunes she resurrected from her father's repertoire. She was increasingly comfortable singing his old songs now that she was forty years old and had traveled a long, sometimes disenchanting way to discover her own strengths and values.

Sparky Tavares thought it was to Maria's credit that all her children had graduated from college. Sparky had been a witness to Nat Cole's will, which Cole had signed almost two years to the day before his death, according to the *Los Angeles Times*. Under the will, each of Nat's brothers received one thousand dollars. His sister Evelyn Coles and her daughter Janice Williams were left five thousand dollars. Nat's father, who would have received five thousand dollars had he survived Nat, died a couple of weeks before his son. Ike Cole had three sons by then, Larry, James, and Edward, who were to share a five-thousand-dollar legacy equally. Freddy had no children at that time. Eddie had never had children; his stepchildren were not included in the will. Nat bequeathed his jewelry to his son, Kelly. If Kelly had not survived Nat, the jewelry would have gone to Ike's sons. The rest of Nat's estate was left to his wife and children, and included a trust located in Los Angeles, where Leo Branton Jr., his wife Geraldine Branton, and Charlotte Sullivan were named as the trustees. Nat's wife and children were designated as the beneficiaries of the trust.

Everyone believed that Maria was a multimillionaire, but nobody knew how much money the Cole legacy involved; its specifics were a mystery. Maria sold the Hancock Park house and bought another lovely one with a swimming pool in Massachusetts. Maria also maintained an apartment in Boston.

Evelyn Coles had been troubled and puzzled by Nat's will, because he had told her he didn't ever want them to need anything, she recalled. Eddie Coles, who never changed his name legally, outlived Nat by five years. Eddie died of a heart attack at the age of fifty-nine in 1970. His widow, Betty, who was sixty-one by then, was inconsolable.

She had been playing piano as the intermission entertainer at the

Majestic Club in Philadelphia in 1939. A young bass player, who was leading a group called Three Loose Nuts and a Bolt, came to work there. As soon as she met Eddie Coles, she knew that he was the man for her because of his kindness, friendliness and sense of values. His generosity extended to her five children by her first marriage. "He gave them his love and understanding; he tried to teach them how to cope with life and how to make conditions better for themselves," she summed up in retrospect.

Eddie and Betty bought a house in Philadelphia and moved into it with their brood. Betty continued to work in town and raise the children, while Eddie and his group toured Europe and the United States. When he was at home, she was especially happy. "Eddie would talk to the worst tramp in the street and tell me, 'Don't ever think you're better than anybody else.' He would take the time with people. He spoke his mind; he wasn't afraid of anything. I can't think of anybody or anything that he was afraid of," Betty recalled twenty years after his death. She could barely understand his character, she said, but she loved it.

By 1952, when the children were grown up, Eddie and Betty set out for Hawaii together to live for six or seven months of the year. Eventually, they became a team, which Eddie named Two Hot Coles. He played the treble part of the piano, and she played the bass. They became popular enough to get bookings in the United States, Australia, Japan, and mainland Asia during the next fifteen years.

Assured that work awaited them, they moved to Los Angeles in 1958. At first they spent several nights at Nat Cole's house, until they found an apartment in a house owned by Eddie's friend, musician Earl Bostic. Betty had always gotten along well with Nat's wife. Nat and Maria had stayed with Betty and Eddie many times in Philadelphia. Betty was grateful to Maria for returning the hospitality. Nat was "the best brother-in-law in the world," Betty thought. When Nat and Maria were traveling, they turned over their season tickets near first base, in about the fifteenth row, to the Dodger Stadium baseball games to Eddie and Betty.

After Eddie died, Betty stopped playing the piano. She soon told herself, "I have to do something." An agent advised her to go to school and learn to do commercials. It was another ten years before she worked in a single commercial. In the meantime, she began to find acting jobs. She appeared in *Whose Life Is It Anyway?* with Richard Dreyfuss; that film paid her the most money in her acting career. She also had film credits in *New York, New York* and *Noon*

'Til Three and television credits for "The Rookies," "The Young and the Restless," "McCloud," the second episode of "Roots," "Sanford and Son," a Flip Wilson special, "Room 222," "White Shadow," "Frank's Place," "Hill Street Blues," and "Divorce Court." They provided her with enough credits so that the Screen Actors Guild eventually paid her a pension, money that helped her when eye operations prevented her from working.

At the age of eighty-one, in 1989, she was back at work. It was not her style to sit in her apartment with nothing to do. Her apartment in Los Angeles was a short walk from Evelyn Coles's. The women were very friendly. When Betty talked about Eddie Coles, she sometimes referred to him in the present. She had never really adjusted to the loss. Though Eddie had never earned much money, when she reflected about her life, she said, "Oh he was a good man. I had mostly good times in life because of Eddie Coles."

Evelyn Coles wasn't living in her parents' house anymore by the time Nat became a star with "Straighten Up and Fly Right." She had married, moved out of the house, and had a daughter named Janice. Then Evelyn divorced her husband and supported herself by working as a beautician. She took care of her own daughter, who had a congenital heart condition, and of a number of other children, one of them Pamela Harris, the daughter of a family friend; Pamela first came under Evelyn's part-time care when Pamela was about eight years old. Eventually Evelyn became Pamela's guardian, at the request of Pamela's father, when Pamela's mother died.

Nat and Maria had often visited Evelyn; they had a warm relationship when Nat was alive. After he died, Evelyn noticed a distance between herself and Maria. Cookie said that her mother kept the Coles at a distance, because she felt her own side of the family was socially superior. Evelyn knew that Maria had once spoken of her own snobbishness to Janice: Maria had done it in a rather light-hearted way. There was nothing lighthearted in Maria becoming estranged from her, Evelyn felt.

One day, Evelyn's daughter, Janice, who played organ and sang in church in the family tradition, read an advertisement about Natalie Cole performing in Chicago at a big downtown club. Janice went to see Natalie and invited her to stay in Evelyn's house. Natalie liked it very much there. She was then dating a man who would become her first husband—record producer and Baptist minister Marvin Yancy; he came from Chicago and divided his time between his hometown and New York. After spending a great deal of time at Evelyn's house, Natalie became familiar with the comfortable, middle-class life-style in a church-centered household. Evelyn prepared lavish Sunday dinners for her friends from church. The easy-going aunt, who was quick to laugh and swift to pray, created an informality that Natalie had never known. Her life had centered more on school and lessons than on church. She had gone to private schools and the University of Massachusetts. Her mother's friends were socialites in Beverly Hills and other cities. Maria had remarried to Gary Devore, a struggling writer about twenty years younger than she; a newspaper in Los Angeles said they had met when she was a guest on a program he hosted. They divorced in the 1970s. Maria resumed using the name Cole and dropped Devore.

Natalie developed close relations with the Cole side of the family and started to learn about the Baptist religion. It was apparent from her singing that she felt a great affinity with the Baptist church, out of which so many of the country's greatest singers had developed their soulful styles. In Chicago, Natalie left her mother's Episcopalian faith and was baptized by the Reverend Elmer Fowler in the Third Baptist Church. When Natalie went through a tumultuous period later on, including hospitalization for a drug problem, Evelyn had faith that Natalie would find her way, because Evelyn knew that "Natalie loved the Lord," Evelyn said.

During the early 1980s, Natalie had become increasingly shaky because of career pressures and a cocaine habit. She fought with her recording company about which records should be released as singles; the ones that the company released weren't Natalie's choices and didn't become hits. She shouted at her manager because of her frustrations, and her professional relationships became cool and distant. Then her first marriage fell apart. In her early thirties, all her old pleasures—shopping, dining out—lost their allure. Ringing telephones unnerved her, and she stayed alone for hours and suffered from crying jags. "I was a very tired lady," she told Jack Slater, the writer of a story published in *Essence* magazine in October 1983.

Two years before that, she and her cousin Eddie, Uncle Ike's son, her aunt Evelyn, and Evelyn's daughter, Janice, had barely escaped through billowing smoke, assisted by firemen, from a fire in the Las Vegas Hilton Hotel. Natalie and Eddie had climbed from the twenty-sixth floor to the roof, where a helicopter had rescued them. Evelyn and Janice had made their way down scores of stairways and were treated for smoke inhalation. The frightful memory lingered with Natalie for years. Then vocal strain, not only from singing but from shouting at people, gave her throat polyps; she had them removed by surgery.

Worn out, Natalie decided to start taking care of herself by admitting she had come to the end of her rope. She wanted to get away from it all. So she telephoned her mother and asked for help. Would her mother make sure Natalie's son Robbie would be all right and that her house in Beverly Hills would still be there when she came back? Her mother stepped in. "My mother was really my first support system, but I didn't know it. My mother has been in my corner forever . . ." Natalie confided in Robert E. Johnson of *Jet* magazine. She began the first of several stays in rehabilitation centers in the early 1980s. Eventually her fatigue and depression lifted, and she stopped using cocaine as a way to ward off emotional stresses. She picked up the strings of her career and resumed her close friendships, including the one with her aunt Evelyn. By the mid-1980s, Natalie was photographed with the First Lady, Mrs. Ronald Reagan, for an anti–drug use campaign.

Natalie married for the second time to record producer André Fischer, after she had reclaimed her position as a star performer through arduous work. She arranged for her second marriage ceremony to take place in the Bethany Baptist Church in Los Angeles. It was Evelyn's church near her apartment in Los Angeles. After the ceremony, there was a splendid party in a downtown hotel. Friends of Natalie's parents who were still alive and well and in touch with Maria Cole went to the fancy party and had a great time.

It seemed to Evelyn as if the entire Cole family had descended upon Los Angeles for the wedding. She had been worried about how Natalie would stand up for the ceremony, because in the months before it, Natalie had been touring the country, giving long concerts in which she burned up energy, singing gospel-inspired, up-tempo, highly amplified numbers. When she got to the West Coast, she toured in California for a while. Up to the last minute, she was busy with her career. Evelyn was extremely proud of Natalie.

Her earlier problems had begun innocently enough, when she had experimented a little in college with marijuana. Sparky had told her then that she ought not to; she would hurt her family and herself. When he scolded her, she thought he was being old-fashioned; she was keeping up with her contemporaries. Sparky thought that she was too easily influenced by others. Eventually she found herself in trouble with drugs.

In 1988, her debut album with EMI, *Everlasting,* was a hit, with gold-plus status; it sold more than a million records. "Pink Cadillac," a song Natalie knew was her kind of up-tempo showcase for her fans, became particularly popular. "Jumpstart," "I Live for Your Love," and a song from her father's repertoire, "When I Fall in Love," had its vogue, too. In 1989, she had another hit with EMI, the album *Good to Be Back;* from it came a Top Ten single called "Miss You Like Crazy," a very catchy, effervescent song. She became host of her own TV show, giving young singers exposure and encouragement. "And it really seems that she's greater now than she was at first," Evelyn mused. "The Lord can take you down to bring you back up, to show you how He can bring you back up. I never gave up. At her lowest point, I never gave up. She knew I was always there for her, and I'll always be there for her. I think that all she ever wanted was just love. She gives love, and she wants love in return."

Evelyn's daughter, Janice, did not attend Natalie's wedding. Janice had become very close friends with Natalie and had even gone on the road with her for Natalie's moral support—and undoubtedly for Janice's edification, too. Natalie called Janice and Evelyn her spiritual advisors. By the early 1980s, Janice was no longer traveling with Natalie. Shortly thereafter, Janice, who had always had a heart problem and was somewhat overweight, suffered a stroke. For several years she was handicapped and in a wheelchair; she had become weaker, bedridden. By the mid-1980s, Janice died.

Even around the time of Natalie's second marriage, tears often welled up in Evelyn's eyes as she thought of her daughter. Pamela Harris, then thirty, was still living with Evelyn and studying communications, because she wanted to become an announcer. Though Evelyn missed Janice fiercely, she felt blessed to have Pamela and Natalie in her life. Natalie was equally drawn to her sentimental, perceptive aunt.

Natalie had such a lively curiosity about the Coles side of the family that she had sought out Nadine Robinson Coles at one point. And Natalie became a close friend and a professional collaborator with her Uncle Ike's son, Eddie Cole, beginning in 1980.

Ike Cole, Nat's younger brother by ten years, had listened to his father tell him to pay attention, believe in his religion, go to church every Sunday, and sing in the choir. But Ike never wanted to become a minister. He went into the Army in 1945 at age eighteen and got out in 1948. When he was twenty-one years old, he got married and started to raise a family. He and his wife Margie had a happy, enduring marriage. Although he played piano so well that

Nat actually thought Ike was the best pianist in the family, Ike decided not to go on the road. Instead he took a job in a factory and worked as a professional musician in Chicago. Pianist Junior Mance, who was about the same age, remembered playing the piano professionally in Waukegan and liking to hear Ike play there, too. Barbara McNair, whose first husband came from Waukegan, also met Ike there. Although he didn't look like Nat, Ike had a similar musical talent; he also was a very easy person to talk to, so he reminded Barbara of Nat. Ike played solo piano at the Black Orchid in Chicago and eventually had several of the best jobs in town for a regional musician. Then he decided to form his own trio with a bassist and drummer. In the 1950s, the group cut an album, *Get a Load of Cole*, for Bally Records. Julian Portman, a Chicagoan who had moved to Los Angeles, began booking the group for tours between 1966 and 1977. After 1977 Ike worked as a soloist again.

He went to Japan sixteen times, to Europe five times, and to Australia, Hong Kong, Mexico, and Canada. Then he decided to stop traveling and stay home, so he worked in the Playboy Club in Chicago for a year before moving into the Ambassador Hotel's famous Pump Room for several years. He got tired of Chicago's weather. At about the age when most people think of retiring to a sunnier clime, he and his wife moved to Sun Lakes, Arizona, near Phoenix. He kept working in Phoenix hotels and Scottsdale resorts. Altogether he made fourteen albums, some with violin, voice, and a rhythm section, and nineteen singles.

Of his three sons, Larry, Jimmy, and Eddie, only the youngest, Eddie, born November 5, 1952, was musical in the family tradition. He spent his childhood listening to Nat Cole on records. Once or twice Nat stopped at the family house in Waukegan, but Eddie had to strain to remember his uncle. He had seen pictures of himself with Nat. It always meant a lot to Eddie to belong to such a musical family. He came to believe that he had a duty to uphold the family's reputation. But it was his own father, Ike, who influenced him to become a musician. "My dad's trio practiced in the living room. They did some of Nat's stuff—'Straighten Up and Fly Right,' 'L-O-V-E.' I used to play Nat's and my father's records over and over for the velvety sound. And I used to feel so good to go to a club and see my dad playing there. Dad's voice is a little huskier sometimes than Nat's, but the quality is the same. On a personal level, my influence comes from my dad."

His parents helped him buy equipment when he had his own band in high school. That support meant a lot to him. He also took saxophone and piano lessons, and eventually he began to sing. Later at Eastern Illinois University, he was the lead singer and co-leader of the college band. The band toured through the United States. He made sure that he got his college degree in teaching—"in case the road thing doesn't work out," he told himself. He knew that his father had taken a "day job," as musicians call it, because the paychecks were steady that way, and that his father and Nat's other brothers had suffered the discrimination that always comes in jazz when more than one person sounds a particular way; everybody else who sounds fairly much the same is regarded as an imitator. The jazz world doesn't congratulate someone for emulating an innovator, because individuality is prized above all. Sound-alikes don't become stars.

Natalie and Eddie had always known each other in passing. When Natalie began to make great headway in her career, every now and then Eddie would say to her, "When am I going to come and work with you?"

After college, Eddie spent five years on the road with a group called Time Machine. Following an eight-week stint in Hawaii, in December 1978 the group broke up. Eddie married his girlfriend whom he met in college, Laura. By then, she was teaching in Florida. He left her there and headed for Hollywood, where he stayed with Janice, Evelyn's daughter. Evelyn had moved to Los Angeles by then. Soon Laura arrived. By May 1978, Eddie had a job "pushing pills" in a vitamin store, not a happy gig for a musician. He stayed with it for the paycheck until May 1989, however, not relying on his education degree while he looked for work in the music world.

In February 1989, Natalie invited him to play saxophone in her backup band. That was the break he had been waiting for. He also demonstrated some of his original tunes for Natalie. She liked them and had her band play them in performances. A bond formed between Natalie and Eddie.

Eventually Eddie, who had good rapport with other musicians and excellent musicality—"good ears," musicians say—added the job of musical director to his other functions in her group. His wife's brother, Charles Floyd, played keyboards in the group. "And I think Natalie likes to have me around," Eddie said.

By the mid-1980s, as a regular part of the group's repertoire, Natalie sang a medley of Nat Cole's songs, sometimes "Nature Boy," "Mona Lisa," and "Ramblin' Rose." A highlight of her act was her singing a duet with Nat's records.

"Wow, where is he? The audience thinks he's in the room some-where," Eddie noticed.

One night at a club in Los Angeles, the sound man unplugged the tape of Nat singing. No sound came up for Natalie to sing a duet with. So Eddie sang the song. Natalie had no idea at first. Then something caught her attention. She turned around and saw Eddie singing. "She freaked!" he said.

Eddie was there when she really "freaked" for a longer time. She only stopped working for six months—long enough to go to a hos-pital called Hazelden and quit her drug habit. "I was right there with her. I was in that whole ordeal with her," Eddie recalled.

When she was launching her career in the early 1970s, Natalie Cole didn't like being criticized for not singing her father's reper-toire exclusively. She usually didn't sing any of his songs; when she did, she approached them in a different style, she thought. She tried to become a stirring singer, and she shied away from ballads. She liked Janis Joplin's advice about never holding back. And she didn't want to copy her father and suffer by comparison. "Out of neces-sity, to get my own career off the ground," she recalled years later, "I used to turn my back on my heritage momentarily. I had to do a little fighting." She showed up at a club in Greenfield, Massachu-setts, with her own group in the early seventies and saw the billing: "Nat Cole's Daughter." Her name wasn't posted on the club. That slight made her furious. Yes, she was Nat Cole's daughter, and his name was opening doors for her. Even so, she had a right to be billed by her own name.

At first she was really a rock and roll singer, influenced by Janis Joplin, but then she began listening to Aretha Franklin. Soon she had an agent at ICM and a contract with Capitol. By the time her first album, *Everlasting,* appeared in 1975, she was emerging as a soul singer. For "This Will Be" on her first album, she won two Grammys at the 1976 ceremony as New Artist of the Year and for the Best Female Rhythm and Blues Vocal. Jean Kraus, the wife of the record-ing engineer who had made records of Nat during his radio shows with Al Jarvis, went to the Grammy Awards that year in the Pal-ladium. She watched Natalie rise on a six-foot platform from the stage and heard her sing "This Will Be"; Jean thought it was a beau-tiful song; the audience cheered. Jean was enchanted with Natalie's appearance. Natalie was wearing a dress with a tight bodice and a skirt of flaring, bright-colored ruffles; one was red, another green, and some were other shimmering colors. Under the spotlight, the tall, slender young woman looked exciting and elegant. Jean thought Natalie was her father's daughter.

The next year, "I've Got Love on My Mind" was a hit single for Natalie from her album *Unforgettable,* which went gold, selling more than a million copies. She did her next album, *Natalie.* She won another r&b Grammy for her song "Sophisticated Lady," released in 1977.

But she was plagued by insecurity. If every seat in the house weren't filled, she felt upset. She was never sure if she was singing the right songs, or communicating well enough with the audience, or doing a good enough job. She wondered if she had a right to be successful, famous, and independent.

Her career had begun in college, when some friends had urged her to sing professionally. Essentially she had gone along with the flow. Before college, she had worked with a trio—Nelson Riddle's son, Carmen Dragon's son, and another musician named Steve. She had sung old songs. All of the youngsters had been influenced by their fathers and the great music of their era. Natalie knew that Nat hadn't known what style of music or life she would gravitate toward. If he had known that she had been impressionable, as he himself had been, and very unsure of herself, he might have wished that he could have lived to bolster and guide her.

Natalie turned completely to gospel-influenced music when she met the Reverend Marvin Yancy and his friend, Chuck Jackson, the half-brother of Reverend Jesse Jackson, both from Chicago. Yancy and Jackson were writing music and couldn't get it to Aretha Franklin. "So they gave the music to me instead. And I was surprised at how I responded to it," she reminisced. When she married Marvin Yancy in 1976, she married gospel-infused rhythm and blues, too. "There's always a flavor of gospel in what I do. I miss it when it's not there. Gospel opens me up," she says.

The pop critics praised her; even the jazz critics, who might have been surprised and disappointed that she wasn't launching a jazz career, had kind words for her work when she was in her twenties and winning polls and Grammys. John S. Wilson liked her "open, exuberant shout." He thought she had the vocal power and the high-voltage energy to carry off the gospel style in Aretha's tradition. He also liked Natalie's light-voiced styling of a ballad, "Inseparable," because it held imitations of her father's work. She appealed to *Billboard, Chicago Tribune, Los Angeles Herald Examiner,* and *Los Angeles Times* writers and many more around the country; they accepted her without reservations. But she couldn't do that for her-self.

Natalie had thought that her marriage to Yancy, who had his own church, the Fountain of Life Baptist Church in Chicago, and who also wrote her material but didn't go with her on the road all the time, would prove to be ideal. Since she had risen to the top so quickly and didn't go through a long dues-paying period, she felt glad that her mother didn't have to worry about her. Natalie didn't really know where she was headed, however. Had she known that she would divorce and fight a life-or-death contest against drugs, and that she would have to climb the ladder of success again, this time overcoming her reputation to convince a record company, EMI, to believe in her, she might have run away from life in the fast lane.

As Natalie grew older, she found that Nat's fans regarded it as perfectly natural and delightful for her to sing songs from his reper-toire, and she accepted herself singing his songs. Audiences didn't compare her unfavorably with her father. Her voice was higher; that gave her an intriguing difference. Natalie felt easy about acquiescing to the wishes of Nat's fans, because she had established her own identity, with her own interesting personal story.

"I do feel the pressure a lot of being the standard bearer for the family now. I need to address myself to many things. I'm torn be-tween the two styles—my father's and my own. And I have to com-bine the two things without blowing my own thing which I've established," she said in 1989.

"I think about my father often and in different instances," she reflected. Capitol Records sent her a photograph of Nat seated at a B3 Hammond organ. She put it over the fireplace in 1989, in the house where she lived with her new husband. "I think mostly that I hope he would have been proud of me—of my singing, yes, but I'm even more interested in whether he would have been proud of my life. I do feel proud of my life. And I give credit to God. There's really no reason for me to even be here. I'm a living testimony to God. When I was on the floor—literally—and couldn't get up, He sent people to help me up. And I'm still in touch with those people. He sends you people intermittently, and I feel loved and watched over and special to a number of people. Yes, it's true that I had the talent and the drive to do what I'm supposed to be doing, but most of all I had the love. It was the love, from without, that came to me. Without that love, all the talent and drive don't matter. There were times when I wasn't so good, and I realized that I wasn't so good. So for me, the love was what gave me the talent and drive or made it matter."

It seemed as if she had fallen under the right influences by 1990. She was also telling interviewers that Natalie Cole wouldn't hip-hop; she wouldn't rap. The styles of the new popular music didn't rhyme with Cole, as in "Mr. Cole Won't Rock and Roll," but her credo sounded familiar. "That's something you would never hear me do," she said. "There's a little conservative tradition in me, from my mom and dad, in whatever I do, in singing, or acting on TV. And now he would tell me I'm doing the right thing." She was staying with rhythm and blues, gospel-inspired music, writing her own songs, and collaborating with people her own age and a little younger. When teenagers told her that they loved her, she was happy, because it was easy "to feel ancient in this business real fast," she noticed. She didn't want to be trendy; she didn't want to be too perfect; she wanted to have a groove "to give attitude." She sang her father's ballads so smoothly, perhaps much better than she yet realized, despite her lingering feeling that it was very hard to sing a ballad. It didn't really sound difficult for her anymore.

"Things have happened to me that have made other people very bitter, sad, and lonely, but those feelings haven't entered my life. Musicians are very important people. Without them, people like me wouldn't be able to express themselves. My band is a real nice machine that's working. Some singers don't think so to that degree, but my band is all that. And Eddie Cole is the greatest musician. Something happens when we're on the stage. We hold it together. My staff recognizes it—that mysterious bond musically and emotionally. And I'm glad we can collaborate. I just want to sparkle until the end."

Her son, Robert Yancy, began playing drums at age three, and, by the time he was twelve in 1990, he was a good drummer. He could also remember the dates of old sports milestones. Evelyn thought his grandfather would have been proud of him. Eddie and Laura's son, Eddie Jr., played piano and sang all of Natalie's rhythm and blues hits on her 1989 record when he was only six. His parents couldn't keep him away from the piano. Freddy's son, Lionel, a talented pianist, was studying music. Evelyn kept her spirits up by thinking about how talented her brothers and their children were, and she wondered, "Will the stars ever cease?"

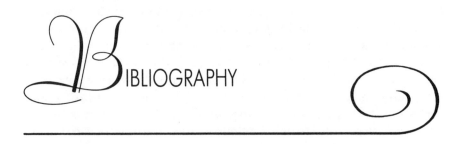

BIBLIOGRAPHY

Sources of information for this book, apart from interviews with people who knew Nat King Cole, have been primarily newspapers and magazines, occasionally liner notes on record albums, and a few books. Nat Cole has been referred to in scores of books about jazz musicians including Miles Davis, Oscar Peterson, and Dexter Gordon. Bassist Milt Hinton's *Bass Lines* refers to Nat and his brother Eddie Coles in brief but illuminating fashion. In general, every book about jazz pianists, whether a biography of a single pianist or a collection of pieces on pianists, includes references to Nat Cole. Many of the best jazz pianists, from Oscar Peterson in the United States to pianists growing up in the Soviet Union and other countries, listened to Nat Cole's records for instruction and inspiration. Only two books, to my knowledge, currently exist about Cole; mine is the third to join the list. The others are *Nat King Cole: An Intimate Biography* by Maria Cole, with Louie Robinson (New York: William Morrow & Company, Inc., 1971) and *Nat King Cole:*

The Man and His Music by James Haskins, with Kathleen Benson (London: Robson Books, Ltd., 1986).

Other books used for reference are *Top Pop Singles, 1940 to 1955* and *Top Pop Singles, 1955 to 1986,* both by Joel Whitburn (Menomonee Falls, Wisconsin: Record Research, Inc.), and *Current Biography, 1956.*

Two discographies have been consulted: "Jazz Discographies Unlimited" Presents Nat "King" Cole: A Discography of Nat Cole Jazz Pianist, by George I, Hall, "Spotlight Series," Volume One, published March 1965 by "Jazz Discographies Unlimited," and "Straighten Up and Fly Right," by Klaus Teubig, an unpublished book covering Nat Cole's recording career from 1936 to 1950, scheduled for publication by Scarecrow Press/Rutgers University.

Special thanks to the following libraries: The New York Public Library's Library of the Performing Arts at Lincoln Center; *The New York Times* morgue; the Institute of Jazz Studies, Rutgers University, Newark, N.J.; the Cinema/TV Collection, Doheny Library, University of Southern California in Los Angeles; and the New York Public Library's Schomberg Center.

Articles that have been quoted from or referred to directly have been mentioned by author, publication, and date.

Thanks, too, to CBS, Inc., for providing the historical research figures for the ratings for the Nat King Cole TV show, which aired on NBC. As usual in my experience, CBS's research capabilities are enormous.

Liner notes on record albums referred to are:

Nat King Cole and The King Cole Trio, Savoy Jazz, New York, 1989; notes by Will Friedwald.

Nat King Cole at The Sands, Capitol Records, Los Angeles, 1986; notes by Alan Dell.

With Respect to Nat (Oscar Peterson Sings Nat Cole), Limelight Records; notes by Leonard Feather.

The Forgotten Years: King Cole Trio, Giants of Jazz Productions, Hollywood, California, 1979; notes by Wayne Knight.

The Sunset All Stars with Nat King Cole, Buddy Rich and Charlie Shavers, Anatomy of a Jam Session, Black Lion; notes by Alan Morgan.

$\mathcal{A}$ DISCOGRAPHICAL SURVEY

*T*he following material is basically a list of Nat King Cole's recorded song titles, primarily from 1943 to 1964. I have also
included the album titles of some of his most popular albums, not-
ing the songs that appear on those albums, many of them reissued
in a 1990 boxed collection, *The Capitol Years*. Although I have
concentrated on providing information on Nat's work from shortly
before his first Capitol recording session in 1943 until his death, my
list isn't confined to his Capitol work. I have included some of his
best-loved jazz recordings performed for other labels and on radio
transcriptions in the 1940s. His work in the 1940s for other labels,
after signing with Capitol, is generally regarded as "bootleg" because he used pseudonyms to avoid running afoul of his Capitol
contract, which called for exclusivity. The bootleg records reflect
the depth of his jazz roots and have inspired jazz pianists around the
world.

A true discography provides the dates and places of recording sessions, musicians and instruments on every track, titles of tunes, arrangers, record labels, issue and reissue data—in short, all the relevant details for a musician's recording career. Despite the length of my survey, it is very far from complete. I have included most of the names of the important studio orchestra leaders and arrangers who worked with Nat after 1946. A notable exception is the omission of the arranger for "The Christmas Song." Nobody is definite about who wrote the arrangement. It would have been nice to include the names of all the great songwriters from Joe Bushkin to Cole Porter whose work went into Nat's repertoire and to include a list of songs that Nat himself composed. Such lists would have been *very* long. Nat wrote quite a few songs before he started recording for Capitol. A sampling of them is noted as such in my survey. Furthermore, I have left out the names of most of the studio musicians who played in orchestras for Cole's records for Capitol. Some of those musicians were also jazzmen who worked in groups outside the studios. A search for an accurate list would take a very long time to compile. One published source says that bassist Johnny Miller, after leaving Cole's trio in 1948, played in a studio orchestra behind Cole. Mr. Miller says that never happened.

The trio began with bassist Wesley Prince and guitarist Oscar Moore from 1937 to 1942. Red Callender replaced Prince for a while. By 1943, Johnny Miller was recording with the trio. Moore played with it until 1947, until Irving Ashby started recording in the fall. In 1948, Miller was replaced by Joe Comfort. Comfort and bongo and congo player Jack Costanzo made their recording debuts with the trio in 1949. By knowing those dates, you will be able to tell which musicians were playing in the trio for the following list of songs. Nat always played piano for himself in the trio until 1946, and afterwards tapered off.

I have omitted most of Cole's pre-Capitol recordings and most of his transcriptions throughout his life. And I may have omitted some of his Capitol recordings, simply because I could not ascertain their existence. However, I believe that I have included at least the title of most of his Capitol recordings (though not all of his Capitol transcriptions).

I have researched all my inclusions in a number of ways. The Institute of Jazz Studies at Rutgers University is planning to publish with Scarecrow Press in Metuchen, New Jersey, a lengthy discography of Nat Cole's recording career from 1936 to 1950. Klaus Teubig, author of the book called *Straighten Up and Fly Right: A Chronological Discography of Nat King Cole's Jazz Recordings,*

1936 to 1950, covers all of the known work that Nat recorded as a jazz pianist and a singer with his trio and other groups of recognized jazz musicians. Teubig, who spent ten years collecting data, lists about 585 songs done for transcripts, films, and formal recording sessions for many labels. Of the sessions still in existence on records, many are rare collectors items. The detailed Teubig discography, which is about as long as my biography of Cole, will enrich jazz history.

The only other attempt at a formal discography of Cole published in the United States is a pamphlet called *Jazz Discographies Unlimited Presents Nat King Cole: A Discography of Nat King Cole, Jazz Pianist,* by George I. Hall (Spotlight Series, vol. 1), published in March 1965. Out-of-print and out-of-date, Hall's pamphlet omits almost all of the considerable number of transcriptions, some of which are regarded as examples of Nat's best piano playing. But for its serious, pioneering scrutiny of Nat's recording career—despite the pamphlet's brevity and some factual errors about recording dates and locations and omissions of unreleased songs—Hall's work stands as a guidepost along the road that a professional discographer travels.

I have also culled the lists of records at the ends of Maria Cole's and James Haskins's book on Nat King Cole; I have viewed a list from a company licensed to reissue some Capitol records; I have searched through the cassette racks of street vendors and the inventories of record stores (most notably Tower and Footlights Records for vintage Cole albums in Manhattan), and I have consulted Teubig and Hall and the Institute of Jazz Studies at Rutgers University. A British discographer, R.G. Holmes, who has published discographical material about Cole, has also offered his advice and information. For copies of his publications, write to him at 18 Rutland Drive, Morden, Surrey, SM4-5QH, England. Jazz historian Phil Schapp, record producer Michael Cuscuna, and musicians, too, have been helpful. For obvious practical reasons, I have not attempted to reproduce Teubig's tome, but I have occasionally referred to his work in the Available Records section of this survey. I have also used Teubig and Holmes to amend other sources. I know that, despite my best efforts, my work has some errors along with considerable omissions. The errors are for the most part discrepancies about recording dates.

Also, because so many of Cole's Capitol albums are out-of-print, I have included primarily the albums that are easiest to come by now—either as reissues or as vintage albums in golden-oldies stores. Among the out-of-print albums one runs across in collectors stores are *Love Is a Many Splendored Thing, I Don't Want to Be Hurt Anymore, My Fair Lady, Nat King Cole: The Man and His Music, The Magic of Christmas, Penthouse Serenade, Wild Is Love, The 10th Anniversary Album, This Is Nat "King" Cole, The Nat King Cole Story, Every Time I Feel the Spirit, Dear Lonely Hearts, Love Is the Thing,* a variety of trio records made in the 1940s, *Tops Pops, The Greatest of Nat King Cole, More Cole Español,* and many of the albums with the songs they contained in their first issue and now reissued in the twenty-record collection.

Nat also made at least one rare tape that I know of. Composer Joe Sherman owns a tape of Nat singing "Mr. Cole Won't Rock and Roll," written by Joe and Noel Sherman, and never included on an album or broadcast transcription. And a few people—Louis Victor Mialy, for one—have copies of Nat's July 2, 1958, recording of "Madrid," which is listed in this survey. The song was based on a composition by French composer Bizet, whose estate protested the use of the music. Capitol took the record off the market. Just before "Madrid" was to be released in France, a few people took in-house copies for their private collections. The song was never in circulation for long in the U.S. either, according to my information.

Of particular interest to album buyers now, *The Spectrum,* a catalog of albums in print, updates its information four times a year regarding LPs, cassettes, and compact discs (CDs) in print and in the market. Until recently *The Spectrum* was known as the *Schwann Catalog.*

The fall 1990 *Spectrum* had two good examples of Cole albums that originated in tapes and transcriptions apparently made outside the usual purview of Nat's formal recording career. One album, probably taped during a European tour with the King Cole Trio in a live performance, was for sale as an album on the Official Record Company label in Copenhagen, Denmark. (This label has also been licensed by Capitol to reissue Cole recordings.) And an album of airchecks from Cole's TV show in 1956 and 1957 was released as *The Incomparable Nat King Cole* on the Sunbeam label (Box C, Sandy Hook, CT 06482). Such albums, for Cole fans, are tantamount to raising buried treasure.

A new collection of Cole's jazz recordings with his trio is scheduled for 1991 release on the Mosaic label. The fifteen-CD collection, which will have wide appeal, is aimed at fans of Nat's trio tracks. In general, if Nat played piano in the context of his trio and other jazz groups, the record belongs to the jazz style. (Therefore, because

Nat didn't play for himself on his recordings with George Shearing or the Basie band, they're not considered to be jazz records. They are, however, and they are included in an important new collection of twenty reissues encompassing Nat's career in the 1950s and the 1960s primarily.) The Mosaic record will emphasize Nat's trio work into the early 1960s. His early trio work has been collected in the past on out-of-print albums from Capitol. So several retrospectives of Nat's work will be available by 1991 or soon afterwards.

AVAILABLE RECORDS: IMPORTANT NEW ADDITIONS TO THE RANKS OF NAT KING COLE RECORDS

THE CAPITOL YEARS

Released in 1990, EMI/Capitol's twenty-disc boxed set *The Capitol Years* (NKC 20) commemorates the twenty-fifth anniversary of Nat's death. (A smaller collection of CDs was released by EMI/Capitol in England only.) Because it cost about $200 retail to begin with, few customers materialized. By the end of 1990, the LP set was primarily available in golden-oldie shops. However, the set provides a good sampling of the scope of Cole's recording career with Capitol. Each of the twenty records has, at times, been available as a single LP. Some are currently for sale, some will be again, while others recently were and can still be found in shops catering to bargain hunters and collectors. The boxed collection has some outtakes (songs recorded at the sessions for the original album, but never previously released).

Part 2 of this survey contains recording session dates for all songs on these albums, notes the albums for which they were originally slated, and gives the years of their original release as albums. Unless otherwise noted, the dates listed are for recording sessions for all albums in *The Capitol Years*. (Some albums have also been issued alone—not as part of this particular collection—on compact disc, but those catalog numbers are not included here. You can find them in *The Spectrum.*)

NOTE: An asterisk indicates orchestra leaders and arrangers.

Unforgettable, 1965 (date the collection was released). EMS1100, TCEMS1100.

Songs for Two in Love, (Nelson Riddle*), 1953. EMS1101, TCEMS1101.

Ballads of the Day, 1953 and 1954. EMS1102, TCEMS1102.

After Midnight, with previously unreleased tracks, 1956. EMS1103, TCEMS1103.

Love Is the Thing (Gordon Jenkins*), 1956. EMS1104, TCEMS1104.

Just One of Those Things (Billy May*), 1957. EMS1105, TCEMS1105.

The Very Thought of You (Gordon Jenkins*), 1958. EMS1106, TCEMS1106.

Welcome to the Club, with the Count Basie Band, produced by Dave Cavanaugh, 1958 (reissued in 1962 under the title *The Swinging Side of Nat King Cole*). EMS1107, TCEMS1107.

To Whom It May Concern (Nelson Riddle*), 1958. EMS1108, TCEMS1108.

Tell Me All About Yourself (Dave Cavanaugh*), 1958. EMS1109, TCEMS1109.

Nat King Cole at the Sands (Antonio Morelli*), January 14, 1960. EMS1110, TCEMS1110.

The Touch of Your Lips (Ralph Carmichael*), 1960. EMS1111, TCEMS1111.

Let's Face the Music (Billy May*), 1961. EMS1112, TCEMS1112.

Nat King Cole Sings/George Shearing Plays (Ralph Carmichael* and co-arranger Shearing), 1961. EMS1113, TCEMS1113.

Where Did Everyone Go? (Gordon Jenkins*), 1962. EMS1114, TCEMS1114.

Ramblin' Rose (Bedford Hendricks*), 1962. EMS1115, TCEMS1115.

Those Lazy-Hazy-Crazy Days of Summer (Ralph Carmichael*), 1963. EMS1116, TCEMS1116.

L-O-V-E (Ralph Carmichael*), 1964. EMS1117, TCEMS1117.

The Piano Style of Nat "King" Cole (Nelson Riddle*), June–August 1955 (released as an album in Britain in 1956). EMS1271.

The Unreleased Nat King Cole, featuring the song "Come to the Mardi Gras," a collection first issued in 1987. EMS1379.

NAT KING COLE: THE GREAT FILMS AND SHOWS

Released in 1989, this collection has songs that appeared on several other albums such as *The Nat King Cole Story* and *My Fair Lady.* Sometimes available in collectors stores, it includes:

"A Nightingale Sang in Berkeley Square," December 22, 1960 or 1961.

"Again," December 11, 1958.

"Ain't Misbehavin'," December 28, 1956.

"All by Myself," January 28, 1953.

"Almost Like Being in Love," January 28, 1953.

"Am I Blue?" August 13, 1962.

"An Affair to Remember," August 8, 1957.

"Around the World," August 8, 1957.

"At Last," December 28, 1956.

"Ballad of Cat Ballou," recorded in fall 1964, released on March 15, 1965.

"Beale St. Blues," January 29, 1958.

"Because You're Mine," July 31, 1952.

"Bidin' My Time," November 22, 1961.

"Blue Gardenia," January 20, 1953.

"But Beautiful," May 8, 1958.

"Caravan," September 21, 1956.

"China Gate," March 19, 1957.

"Cold, Cold Heart," November 21 or 22, 1961.

"Don't Get Around Much Anymore," July 10, 1957.

"Ebony Rhapsody," November 21, 1961.

"For You," October 30, 1958.

"Get Me to the Church on Time," September 19, 1963.

"Hajji Baba," July 27, 1954.

"How Little We Know," September 19, 1956.

"Hymn to Him," September 19, 1963.

"I Am in Love," July 20, 1961.

"I Could Have Danced All Night," September 17, 1963.

"I Got It Bad and That Ain't Good," December 20, 1961.

"I Remember You," December 11, 1960, according to R.G. Holmes, British discographer.

"I Should Care," July 31, 1957.

"I'm an Ordinary Man," September 19, 1963.

"I've Grown Accustomed to Her Face," September 19, 1963.

"In the Good Old Summertime," May 15, 1963.

"It's All in the Game," December 19, 1956.

"It's Only a Paper Moon," August 15, 1956.

"Just One of Those Things," July 31, 1957.

"Just You, Just Me," September 14, 1956.

"Let's Face the Music and Dance," November 21, 1961.

"Let's Fall in Love," January 16, 1955 (or August 25, 1955, according to Holmes).

"Like Someone in Love," January 16, 1955, or October 4, 1956, according to Holmes.

"Love Is a Many Splendored Thing," August 25, 1955, according to Holmes.

"Love Is Here To Stay," January 27, 1953.

"Love Letters," December 19, 1956.

"Lover, Come Back to Me," January 14, 1953.

"Magic Moments," November 27, 1961.

"Mood Indigo," June 30, 1958.

"More," December 1, 1964.

"Never Let Me Go," January 4, 1956.

"Night of the Quarter Moon," February 4, 1959.

"On the Street Where You Live," September 20, 1963.

"Only Forever," December 23, 1960.

"Paradise," May 6, 1958.

"People," January 14, 1964.

"Pick Yourself Up," December 20, 1961.

"Return to Paradise," March 31, 1953.

"September Song," December 20, 1961.

"Should I?" September 19, 1956.

"Show Me," September 18, 1963.

"Smile," July 7, 1954, (or July 27, according to R. G. Holmes).

"Sometimes I'm Happy," September 24, 1956.

"Spring Is Here," August 13, 1962.

"St. Louis Blues," January 29, 1958.

"Stay as Sweet as You Are," December 28, 1956.

"The Best Thing for You," November 4, 1958.

"The Party's Over," July 31, 1957.

"The Rain in Spain," September 20, 1963.

"The Song Is Ended," July 10, 1957.

"The Very Thought of You," May 6, 1958.

"There Will Never Be Another You," August 25, 1955.

"This Can't Be Love," January 28, 1953.

"Three Little Words," December 3, 1964.

"To Whom It May Concern," August 11, 1958.

"When I Fall in Love," December 28, 1956.

"When I Grow Too Old to Dream," September 24, 1956.

"Who's Sorry Now?," July 19, 1957.

"With a Little Bit of Luck," September 18, 1963.

"Wouldn't It Be Loverly?" September 17, 1964.
"You Did It," September 18, 1963.
"You Stepped Out of a Dream," January 11, 1952.
"You'll Never Know," July 10, 1952.
"You're My Everything," May 5, 1964.
"You're Cheatin' Heart," August 11, 1962.

As you can see, the two previous sets contain relatively few re-cordings from the years most prized by fans of Nat's piano play-ing—1936 through 1950. Nat's later trio in the 1950s (including guitarist John Collins and bassist Charlie Harris, with drummer Lee Young wending his way in and out of Nat's entire recording and performing careers) is well represented in these sets. The last trio takes part in Nat's work primarily with studio and other orchestras (with such exceptions as the *After Midnight* album and several re-makes in 1961 of Nat's hits done originally in the 1940s).

NAT KING COLE AND THE KING COLE TRIO

Of special interest is the Savoy Jazz label's May 1989 release of a few of Nat's first recordings and broadcast transcriptions. The album (on LP, cassette, and CD—four bonus tracks on the CD) was re-corded in Hollywood, California, from August or September 1938 through early 1940. Oscar Moore played guitar and Wesley Prince played bass in the trio. As of fall 1990, all formats were in print in *The Spectrum* list.

The dates in the liner notes are based on the Teubig discogra-phy. In some cases they differ from dates published in the Hall dis-cography. Furthermore, many of the songs were not even mentioned in the Hall discography. And some tracks were never released before. Through a series of sales and takeovers, they have made their way from the original tiny recording companies and transcription sources on the West Coast to this Savoy Jazz release. According to Teubig, the following is correct:

King Cole Swingsters, August or September 1938. 1) "Jumpy Jitters," vocals by Nat Cole; 2) "Nothing Ever Happens to Me," vo-cals by Nat Cole; 3) "Sentimental Blue," vocals by Maxine Johnson; 4) "What 'Cha Done to My Heart?" vocals by Nat Cole; 5) "Let's Do Things," vocals by Nat Cole; 6) "Love Me Sooner," vocals by Maxine Johnson.

King Cole Swingsters, early 1939. 7) "There's No Anesthetic for Love," vocals by King Cole Trio; 8) "Dixie Jamboree," vocals by King Cole Trio; 9) "Te De Ah," vocals by King Cole Trio; 10)

"Riffin' at the Barbeque," vocals by King Cole Trio; 11) "Black Spi-der Stomp," instrumental.

King Cole and His Swing Trio, summer 1939. 12) "I'm a Perfect Fool Over You," vocals by Maxine Johnson; 13) "Never Mind, Baby," instrumental; 14) "Lovely Little Person," vocals by Maxine Johnson; 15) "Goin' to Town with Honey," instrumental; 16) "Syn-copated Lullaby," instrumental; 17) "Falling in and out of Love," instrumental.

King Cole Trio, late 1939 or early 1940. 18) "By the River Ste. Marie," vocals by King Cole Trio.

King Cole Trio (plus drummer Lee Young), December 1939. (Teubig says the drummer may have been Young, and Young con-firms it. Although Teubig says the date was 1939, Young believes it could have been 1940.); 19) "I Like to Riff," vocals by King Cole Trio; 20) "On the Sunny Side of the Street," vocals by King Cole Trio; 21) "Black Spider Stomp," instrumental; 22) "By the River St. Marie," vocals by King Cole Trio; 23) "I'm Lost," vocals by Nat Cole (CD bonus track); 24) "Pitching Up a Boogie," vocals by Nat Cole (CD bonus track); 25) "Beautiful Moons Ago," vocals by Nat Cole (CD bonus track); 26) "Let's Spring One," vocals by King Cole Trio (CD bonus track).

Numbers 1 through 6 and 11 through 18 were never previously issued. Number 18 and 22 are different takes of the same song. Numbers 23 through 26 have Johnny Miller on bass; previous tracks have Wesley Prince. Bonus tracks were recorded in 1943. According to R.G. Holmes in England, numbers 1 through 6 were issued on Swing House LP (SWH 12) in 1979.

"GOLDEN-OLDIE" REISSUES OF NAT'S EARLY TRIO AND OTHER RARE ALBUMS

The Forgotten Years is a collection of radio transcriptions re-leased in 1979 by Giants of Jazz Productions, Hollywood, California, and available in general record stores as of 1990. A considerable number of these transcriptions have surfaced in albums for sale, but were not included in the Hall discography, though Teubig tries to include all of them. This album was compiled from songs made by the King Cole Trio after Nat signed a contract with Capitol. The transcriptions were done between the spring and fall of 1945. They are as follows:

"Paper Moon," taped by the King Cole Trio in performance on "Kraft Music Hall," April 5, 1945.

"Miss Thing," and "The Sunny Side of the Street" (a Trio vocal), taped during an Armed Forces Radio Service Jubilee Show, April 16, 1945.

"If You Can't Smile and Say Yes," "The Trouble with Me Is You," "Satchel Mouth Baby" (all vocals by the Trio) and "Sweet Georgia Brown," (an instrumental) originating from the King Cole Room of the Trocadero for a Mutual Broadcasting System show, April 26, 1945.

"If You Can't Smile and Say Yes" (a vocal) and "Sweet Georgia Brown" (an instrumental) done on the "Kraft Music Hall," May 3, 1945.

"Sweet Lorraine," done by Nat Cole and Johnny Miller, without Oscar Moore, on an AFRS Jubilee Show, August 3, 1945.

"The Frim Fram Sauce," done on an AFRS Jubilee Show, October 11, 1945.

"The Man on the Little White Keys," also done for an AFRS broadcast (date unknown), with Dinah Shore as hostess. This song, a vocal, was never commercially recorded by the trio.

Nat King Cole: From the Very Beginning is a two-LP collection in the Leonard Feather Series (MCA Records, 1973). By 1990, it was available in collectors stores. Its tracks were previously released on the Decca label for which Nat made many early recordings. Session dates may differ from those in the final Teubig manuscript. Especially interesting are four songs done with Eddie Cole's Solid Swingers in Chicago in 1936, Nat's first recording date (an asterisk indicates a song written by Nat): "Stompin' at the Panama,"* "Honey Hush,"* "(Bedtime) Sleep, Baby, Sleep,"* and "Thunder."* Tracks recorded in Hollywood in 1940 include "Honeysuckle Rose," "Sweet Lorraine," "This Side Up,"* and "Gone with the Draft." "Babs," "Early Morning Blues,"* "Scotchin' with the Soda," and "Slow Down" were done in Chicago in 1941. "I Like to Riff,"* "This Will Make You Laugh," "Hit the Ramp," "Stop, the Red Light's On," "Call the Police,"* "That Ain't Right,"* "Hit That Jive, Jack," and "Are You fer It?"* were recorded in New York that year. Oscar Moore and Wesley Prince played in the trio on all tracks.

Nat King Cole: The Cool Cole is an album of radio transcriptions from the series called "The King's Court," part of the C.P. MacGregor Transcription Series (Legend Records, 1981). The dates of the transcriptions are unknown, but they definitely were between 1943 and 1947, because the trio consisted of Oscar Moore and Johnny Miller.

Titles on this album are "Little Joe from Chicago," "Smooth Sailing," "Baby Won't You Please Come Home," "I'm in the Mood for Love," "Swingin' the Blues," "Three Little Words," "Tain't Me," "Sweet Georgia Brown," "Is You or Is You Ain't My Baby?" "Don't Blame Me," "Boogie a la King," "The Ol' Music Master," "These Foolish Things," "Miss Thing," "Laura," "How High the Moon," "It's Only a Paper Moon," "It Only Happens Once," and "Poor Butterfly."

Havin' Fun With Nat "King" Cole is an album of duets culled from various periods of Nat's career and issued by the Official Record Co., Copenhagen, Denmark. Titles and performers on this album are "Long, Long Ago" and "Open Up the Doghouse (Two Cats Are Comin' In"), with Dean Martin and Nat, vocals; "That's All There Is to That," "If I May," and "My Personal Possession," with The Four Knights and Nat, vocals; "My Baby Just Cares for Me," with Woody Herman, Nat, and his trio; "For You My Love" and "Can I Come in for a Second?" with Nellie Lutcher and Nat; "Get out and Get under the Moon" and "Hey, Not Now," with Maria Cole and Nat; "Save the Bones for Henry Jones" and "Harmony," with Johnny Mercer. All are from Capitol sessions; recordings are listed in chronological order in Part 2 of this survey.

These selected records are just a sampling of available Cole albums offering songs from all periods of his career. Some vintage Cole LPs have been reissued on compact discs. *Spectrum* guides you to the in-print LPs, CDs, and cassettes in general record stores. The bins in vintage record stores are often filled with out-of-print Cole LPs. Cassettes for sale in all types of places—from street fairs to record stores—are sometimes surprising in their contents, blending early and late Cole songs as well as Capitol and non-Capitol records and transcriptions.

PART 1: A CHRONOLOGICAL SAMPLING OF NAT'S RECORDING SESSIONS FOR CAPITOL RECORDS AND OTHER RECORD LABELS, 1936–1956

As I have already noted, Teubig will correct, contradict, and expand upon some details in this section. I've referred to the Teubig manuscript, still in unpolished form in 1990, through the courtesy of Dan Morgenstern, director of the Institute of Jazz Studies at Rutgers University. The exhaustive Teubig work is regarded as authoritative. Until it is published, this survey will probably be the fullest published list of Nat's work in the United States.*

Teubig has accounted for 154 songs recorded by Cole before the first Capitol recording session in November 1943. Many of those songs Cole also recorded later and often in life. But some he never recorded again.

For the same period, 1936 to 1943, I have noted only 46 songs, and four of them may have been recorded at a later time. Altogether, I have included over 300 songs recorded from 1936 to 1950, a period for which Teubig documents about 585 songs recorded by Nat in all facets of his career.

I believe that I have included almost all the records that Nat made for Capitol and several famous jazz records on which he played. (Broadcast and film transcriptions account for the majority of titles missing from my survey and included in Teubig's spectacular discography.)

In the years after 1950, Nat recorded such songs as "September Song" and "Ain't Misbehavin'," songs omitted from my list covering Nat's years up to 1950 and included in Teubig's discography of Nat's total *oeuvre* up to 1950. Nat's early recordings of songs were usually done, of course, with his trio; later versions were sometimes done in other contexts. So this further complicates the survey. Which version of a song is best—an early pre- or extra-Capitol trio version or a Capitol version in the 50s or 60s—depends upon listeners' perspectives and tastes. Here's another example of the complexities that arise in compiling a big sample listing of Nat's work. He made a recording of "Penthouse Serenade" with Anita O'Day circa February 1944 in Hollywood, according to Teubig. My listing of that song does not occur until the 1950s, when Nat recorded it again, as an instrumental, for Capitol, without Anita. It was included in his album by the same name.

Here are some entries for Nat's work for the years that interest jazz fans most. Instrumental abbreviations are: (TP) trumpet; (TB) trombone; (CL) clarinet; (AS) alto saxophone; (TS) tenor sax-

---

*Klaus Teubig's biographical introduction to his discography places Nat Cole in New York City for a tour in 1939. From my many interviews, I determined that he first visited New York in 1941. Also, the Teubig discography doesn't contain any recordings or transcriptions of Nat done in New York City in 1939. If Nat had visited New York, I believe he would have made a record in some form; he was always eager to record, and in jazz circles, he was in demand. Teubig notes correctly that Cole's trio was popular at the Apollo in the early 40s, before Capitol began to release trio records. Teubig also discovered that Nat Cole played at the Village Vanguard in the early 1940s, though he may never have been taped in performance there.

ophone; (BAR) baritone saxophone; (P) piano; (G) guitar; (B) acoustic bass; (D) drums; (VLN) violin; (BGO) bongos; (VO) vocal; (VB) vibraphone; (ARR) arranger; (inst.) instrumental.

Eddie Cole's Solid Swingers: Kenneth Roane (TP), Tommy Thompson (AS and TS), Bill Wright (TS), Nat Cole (P), Eddie Cole (B and VO), Jimmy Adams (D); Chicago, July 28, 1936. "Honey Hush," "Stompin' at the Panama," "Bedtime (Sleep, Baby, Sleep)," "Thunder." (Hall and Teubig agree on all details of this session.)

As an example of the conflicts between the sketchy Hall and sophisticated Teubig works, Hall's outdated entry says:
King Cole Swingers: Nat "King" Cole (P and VO), Oscar Moore (G), Wesley Prince (B), Bonnie Lake (VO); Hollywood, 1939. "Ta-de-ah," "Riffin' at the Bar-B-Q," "I Lost Control of Myself," "That Please Be Mineable Feeling."
Teubig says there were two separate dates. One with Bonnie Lake produced the songs "Harlem Swing," "I Lost Control of Myself," "The Land of Make-Believe," and "That Please Be Mineable Feeling." The second date, without Bonnie Lake and with only the King Cole Swingsters, produced "There's No Anesthetic for Love," "Dixie Jamboree," "Ta-de-Ah," and "Riffin' At the Bar-B-Q," with trio vocals on those four songs. Proof of Teubig's accuracy exists in such details as the trio romp "There's No Anesthetic For Love" on the 1989 Savoy Jazz release.

Hall and Teubig agree on the following recording session details:
Lionel Hampton and His Orchestra: Nat "King" Cole (P), Oscar Moore (G), Wesley Prince (B), Al Spieldock (D), Lionel Hampton (VB, D, P), Helen Forrest (VO); Hollywood, May 10, 1940. "House of Morgan," "I'd Be Lost Without You," "Jack the Bellboy" with Hampton (D), "Central Avenue Breakdown," with Hampton (P).
Same personnel without Forrest, called the Hampton Rhythm Boys (VO); Hollywood, July 17, 1940. "Dough Ra Me," "Jivin' with Jarvis," "Blue Because of You," "I Don't Stand a Ghost of a Chance (with You)."

Recordings that Nat made in Hollywood, Chicago, and New York in 1940 and 1941 are omitted here in their formal discographical form. Teubig has information about these recordings of "Sweet Lorraine," "Honeysuckle Rose," "Gone with the Draft," and "This Side Up" in Hollywood; "Babs," "Scotchin' with the Soda,"

"Slow Down," and "Early Morning Blues" in Chicago; and "This Will Make You Laugh," "Stop, the Red Light's On," "Hit the Ramp," "I Like to Riff," "Call the Police," "That Ain't Right," "Are You fer It?" and "Hit That Jive, Jack" in New York. *Important New Additions to the Ranks of Nat Cole Records* covers the 1989 Savoy Jazz release of some of the trio's recorded work during this period. *Golden Oldie Reissues* discusses an MCA collection.

Information for the following entries is mostly based on Hall with some amendments by Teubig:

"King Cole Quintet": Lester "Shad" Collins (TP), Illinois Jacquet (TS), Nat King Cole (P and VO), Gene Englund (B), J.C. Heard (D); New York, 1942. "Heads," "Pro-Sky," "It Had to Be You," "I Can't Give You Anything but Love." Teubig says all of these songs were recorded at a later date, after Nat's Capitol contract began. R.G. Holmes in England agrees, citing February 1944.

Lester Young–King Cole Trio: Lester Young (TS), Nat King Cole (P), Red Callender (B); Los Angeles, July 15, 1942. Drums were dubbed at a later time for some LP issues, not on the original 78 rpms, with no name for the drummer. "Indiana," "I Can't Get Started," "Tea for Two," "Body and Soul."

"King" Cole Trio: Nat "King" Cole (P), Oscar Moore (G), Red Callender (B); Los Angeles, 1942. "Vom Vim Veedle," "All For You."

Johnny Miller replaces Red Callender, Hollywood, March 1, 1943. "Pitchin' Up a Boogie," "I'm Lost," "Beautiful Moons Ago," "Let's Spring One."

Same personnel; Hollywood, November 2, 1943. "F.S.T." (inst.), "Got a Penny, Benny," "Let's Pretend," "My Lips Remember Your Kisses." (The last song was possibly done at a later session, according to the Hall discography. The forthcoming discography by Teubig challenges the validity of these dates, and it places the records in earlier years, as noted about the Savoy Jazz release.)

The following session marks the start of Nat's recording career with Capitol Records: *"King" Cole Trio:* Nat "King" Cole (P and VO), Oscar Moore (G), Johnny Miller (B); Hollywood, November 30, 1943. "Straighten Up and Fly Right," "Gee, Baby, Ain't I Good to You?" "Jumpin' at Capitol" (inst.), "If You Can't Smile and Say Yes."

Same personnel; Hollywood, December 15, 1943. "Sweet Lorraine," "Embraceable You," "It's Only a Paper Moon," "I Can't See for Lookin'."

Same personnel; Hollywood, January 17, 1944. "The Man I Love" (inst.), "Body and Soul" (inst.), "Prelude in C Sharp Minor" (inst.), "What Is This Thing Called Love?"

Same personnel; Hollywood, March 6, 1944. "Look What You've Done to Me," "Easy Listening Blues" (inst.), "I Realize Now." ("After You Get What You Want" appears never to have been released.)

Jazz at the Philharmonic: J.J. Johnson (TB), Illinois Jacquet (TS), Jack McVea (TS), Nat "King" Cole as Shorty Nadine (P), Les Paul (G), Johnny Miller (B), Lee Young (D); Los Angeles, July 2, 1944. "Blues," "Lester Leaps In."

Shorty Sherock (TP) replaces J.J. Johnson: "Rosetta Part 1," "Rosetta Part 2."

J.J. Johnson replaces Shorty Sherock: "Body and Soul Part 1," "Body and Soul Part 2," "Body and Soul Part 3," "Body and Soul Part 4."

Add George "Red" Callender (B): "Bugle Call Rag."

Omit Callender: "Tea for Two."

Sherock for Johnson; add Callender: "I've Found a New Baby."

Capitol International Jazzmen: Bill Coleman (TP), Buster Bailey (CL), Benny Carter (AS), Coleman Hawkins (TS), Nat King Cole (P), Oscar Moore (G), John Kirby (B), Max Roach (D), Kay Starr (VO); Hollywood, March 30, 1945. "You Can Depend on Me," "If I Could Be with You," "Stormy Weather," "Riffamarolle."

The Herbie Haymer Quintet: Charlie Shavers (TP), Herbie Haymer (TS), Nat "King" Cole (P), John Simmons (B), Buddy Rich (D); Hollywood, June 5, 1945. "Black Market Stuff," "Laguna Leap," "I'll Never Be the Same," "Swinging on Central" (Sunset label).

King Cole Quintet. Same personnel and date as Herbie Haymer Quintet. "Nat's Kick." Shavers appears as Joe Schmaltz on the Sunset label issue. Nat Cole may have used the pseudonym Shorty Nadine on "Black Market Stuff" and "Laguna Leap" and the pseudonym Eddie Laguna on "I'll Never Be the Same" and "Swinging on Central." According to Hall, the issues of these recordings were as King Cole Quintet on the Swing label, Charlie Shavers Quintet on the Monarch label, and The Herbie Haymer Quintet on Sunset.

262   L E S L I E   G O U R S E

An issue by the Black Lion label in England relatively recently notes the recording date as June 9, 1945.

Lester Young–Buddy Rich Trio: Lester Young (TS), Nat Cole (P) as Aye Guy, Buddy Rich (D); Hollywood, December 1945. "Back to the Land," "I Cover the Waterfront," "Somebody Loves Me," "I Found a New Baby," "The Man I Love," "Mean to Me," "Peg o' My Heart" (no drums), "I Want to Be Happy." (Regarded as a classic, this record is available on a Giants of Jazz cassette released in 1986.

Charlie Parker and the King Cole Trio: Charlie Parker (AS), Nat Cole (P), Oscar Moore (G), Johnny Miller (B), Buddy Rich (D); Los Angeles, March or April 1946. "Cherokee" done for an AFRS broadcast. Nat also recorded other songs in this transcription with Willie Smith (AS), Lester Young (TS), and Benny Carter (AS).

The Keynoters: Under Willie Smith (AS), with Nat "King" Cole (P), Red Callender (B), Jackie Mills (D); Hollywood, February 16, 1946. "I Can't Believe That You're in Love with Me," "The Way You Look Tonight," "Airiness Ala Nat," "My Old Flame."
Since this non-Capitol recording was issued by Keynote and reissued by Mercury, Nat Cole was not identified on the original issue. But the "a la Nat" in the title was a clue to the pianist's identity. According to R.G. Holmes in England, Nat used the pseudonym "Lord Calvert."

Jo Stafford with Paul Weston and His Orchestra: Nat "King" Cole (P), Ray Linn (TP), Herbie Haymer (TS) as soloists, with Jo Stafford (VO), Heinie Beau, Fred Stulce, Harry Schumann (saxes), Dave Barbour (G), Art Shapiro (B), Nick Fatool (D); Hollywood, March 1946. "Baby, Won't You Please Come Home?" "Cindy," "I'll Be with You in Apple Blossom Time."

Metronome All Stars: Charlie Shavers (TP), Lawrence Brown (TB), Johnny Hodges (AS), Coleman Hawkins (TS), Harry Carney (BAR), Nat "King" Cole (P and VO), Bob Ahern (G), Eddie Safranski (B), Buddy Rich (D), Frank Sinatra, June Christy (VO); produced by George Simon; New York, December 17, 1946. (Teubig and R.G. Holmes say December 15.) "Sweet Lorraine," "Nat Meets June" (Nat and June, VO).

Gene Norman's "Just Jazz" All-Stars (also released under Stan Getz's name in some issues): Charlie Shavers (TP), Willie Smith (AS), Stan Getz (TS), Nat "King" Cole as Nature Boy (P), Oscar Moore (G), Johnny Miller (B), Louis Bellson (D); Pasadena, California, June 23, 1947. "Body and Soul, One," "Body and Soul, Two," "How High the Moon," "Charlie's/I Got Rhythm." Hall says that the last part of "Body and Soul" is edited and titled "Moonlight" on a Crown issue.

The Hall discography notes that details of the following recordings are unknown and believed to be transcriptions: "Laura," "T'Ain't Me," "Keep Knocking on Wood," "Blues and Swing," "If Yesterday Could Only Be Tomorrow." Teubig places these songs at a session in the mid-1940s. R.G. Holmes says the date was April 1945 in Los Angeles.

Metronome All Stars: Dizzy Gillespie (TP), Bill Harris (TB), Buddy DeFranco (CL), Flip Phillips (TS), Nat "King" Cole (P), Billy Bauer (G), Eddie Safranski (B), Buddy Rich (D); produced by George Simon; December 21, 1947. "Leap Here."

Add Stan Kenton band, with Al Porcino, Buddy Childers, Ray Wetzel, Ken Hanna (TP), Harry Betts, Milt Bernhart, Harry Forbes, Bart Varsolona (TB), George Weidler, Art Pepper (AS), Bob Cooper, Warner Weidler (TS), Bob Gioga (BAR), Shelly Manne (D), Pete Rugolo (ARR.); same date. "Metronome Riff."

Dexter Gordon Quintet: Harry "Sweets" Edison (TP), Dexter Gordon (TS), Nat Cole (P), probably Red Callender (B), Juicy Owens (D); Hollywood. "I've Found a New Baby," "Rosetta," "Sweet Lorraine," "I Blowed and Gone." Teubig places this record in 1943 with Norman Granz as producer. R.G. Holmes says June 1943. Hall's date is 1947–48, but that is wrong. The session took place sometime between 1940 and 1943. The session was probably taped in Glenn Wallichs's record store before he co-founded Capitol Records and, in 1943, signed Nat to a contract.

Nat "King" Cole and Nellie Lutcher: Ernie Royal (TP), Charlie Barnet (TS), Nat "King" Cole (P and VO), Irving Ashby (G), Joe Comfort (B), Lee Young (possible D), Nellie Lutcher (VO); Hollywood, January 5, 1950. "For You, My Love," "Can I Come in for a Second?" Some sources, including Teubig, say Earl Hyde was the possible (D).

Nat "King" Cole and His Trio and Stan Kenton and His Or-chestra: Nat "King" Cole (P and VO), Irving Ashby (G), Joe Comfort (B), Jack Costanzo (BGO), with Maynard Ferguson, Jim Salko, Buddy Childers, Chico Alvarez, Shorty Rogers (TP), Milt Bernhart, Harry Betts, Bob Fitzpatrick, Johnny Halliburton, Herb Harper (TB), Bud Shank, Art Pepper (AS), Bob Cooper, Bert Calderal (TS), Bob Gioga (BAR), Shelly Manne (D), Pete Rugolo (ARR); Hollywood, August 16, 1950. "Orange-Colored Sky."

Stan Kenton and His Orchestra with Nat King Cole: Omit Ashby, Comfort, and Rugolo; add Laurindo Almeida (G), Don Bagley (B), Shorty Rogers (ARR); same date. "Jam-Bo" (inst.).

Nat "King" Cole and His Trio: Nat King Cole (P and VO), John Collins (G), Charles Harris (B), Lee Young (D), with guests Willie Smith (AS), Harry "Sweets" Edison (TP), Stuff Smith (VLN), Juan Tizol (valve TB), Jack Costanzo (BGO); Hollywood, August–September 1956.
"Sweet Lorraine," "It's Only a Paper Moon," "Route 66" with Harry "Sweets" Edison. ("You Can Depend on Me" and "Candy" were released in 1990.) Recorded August 15, 1956.
"Just You, Just Me," "You're Lookin' at Me," "Don't Let It Go to Your Head" with Willie Smith. ("I Was a Little Too Lonely" was released in 1990.) Recorded September 14, 1956.
"Caravan" with Jack Costanzo on "Lonely One" and on "Blame It on My Youth" with Juan Tizol. ("What Is There to Say?" was released in 1990.) Recorded September 21, 1956.
"Sometimes I'm Happy," "When I Grow too Old to Dream," "I Know That You Know" with Stuff Smith. ("Two Loves Have I" was released in 1990.) Recorded September 24, 1956.

PART 2: A CHRONOLOGICAL SAMPLING OF NAT'S SESSIONS FOR CAPITOL, 1943–1964

The following list covers songs and selected albums recorded by Nat Cole with his trio and with many other musicians and singers, composers, arrangers, and orchestra leaders from November 30, 1943 to the end of 1964 for Capitol Records only. While I don't have all the details for personnel or places of sessions, the titles are probably close to complete. The majority of the sessions in the

1950s and 1960s were in Hollywood. The songs for *More Cole Español* were recorded with Ralph Carmichael, arranger and orchestra leader, in Mexico City. *Cole Español* may have been recorded in Havana, Cuba.

Dates signify recording dates. An asterisk connotes that a title was unreleased as of February 1965. Some of these unreleased titles were subsequently released; some appear in the 20-record set, some in the collection of show and film tunes, *Nat King Cole: The Great Films and Shows*. Some songs have still not been released on any commercial album. "Oh Kickeroonie," for example, is unreleased except on videocassettes for rent in video stores. Songs grouped together by albums are, in general, those that appeared on the 1990 albums in the 20-record set; earlier issues of those albums may have included some other songs and omitted some on the 1990 issues. Other albums are included, too, for their general interest for diverse audiences.

Nat played piano but didn't sing on a Capitol session for which Jo Stafford was the headliner. Details for that record appear in Part 1 of this survey.

Songs that were first released on the albums *Cole Español, A Mis Amigos,* and *More Cole Español* were rereleased as *Cole Español,* Volumes 1 and 2, in 1990. The original albums are out-of-print.

Though Capitol distributed reissues of "All for You" and "Vom Vim Veedle," Capitol didn't record those songs with Cole. So the titles are omitted from this list. Their details appear in Part 1. From November 30, 1943 through November 28, 1944, Nat recorded with his trio, Johnny Miller (B) and Oscar Moore (G), in Hollywood:

"Straighten Up and Fly Right,", November 30, 1943.
"Gee, Baby, Ain't I Good to You?," November 30, 1943.
"Jumpin' at Capitol," (inst.), November 30, 1943.
"If You Can't Smile and Say Yes," November 30, 1943.
"Sweet Lorraine," December 15, 1943.
"Embraceable You," December 15, 1943.
"It's Only a Paper Moon," December 15, 1943.
"I Just Can't See for Lookin'," December 15, 1943.
"The Man I Love," (inst.), January 17, 1944.
"Body and Soul," (inst.), January 17, 1944.
"Prelude in C Sharp Minor," (inst.), January 17, 1944.
"What Is This Thing Called Love?," (inst.), January 17, 1944.
"After You Get What You Want," March 6, 1944.

"Look What You've Done to Me," March 6, 1944.
"Easy Listenin' Blues," (inst.), March 6, 1944.
"I Realize Now," March 6, 1944.
"Please Consider Me," November 28, 1944.*

Nat with Capitol International Jazzmen: See Part 1.
(On April 13, May 19, and May 23, 1945, Nat recorded with his trio
in Hollywood.)

"I'd Love To Make Love to You," April 13, 1945.*
"I'm a Shy Guy," April 13, 1945.
"Katusha," April 13, 1945.*
"It Only Happens Once," April 13, 1945.
"You're Nobody til Somebody Loves You," May 19, 1945.
"Don't Blame Me," May 19, 1945.
"I'm Through With Love," May 19, 1945.
"Barcarolle," May 23, 1945.*
"Sweet Georgia Brown," (inst.), May 23, 1945.
"I Thought You Ought to Know," May 23, 1945.
"It Only Happens Once," May 23, 1945.

("Satchel Mouth Baby" and "Solid Potato Salad" may have been recorded in New York City, possibly in May 1945 for the former song,
and, according to British discographer R.G. Holmes, on June 25,
1946 for the latter. The song "Solid Potato Salad," according to Teubig, was done for the film "Breakfast in Hollywood," February 1946,
and had no commercial issue other than the soundtrack. Holmes
says it was issued as a V-Disc.)

(On October 11 and October 18, 1945, and December 4, 1945,
Cole and the trio recorded in New York City.)

"It's Better to Be by Yourself," October 11, 1945.
"Come To Baby Do," October 11, 1945.
"The Frim Fram Sauce," October 11, 1945.
"Homeward Bound," (inst.), October 18, 1945.*
"I'm an Errand Boy for Rhythm," October 18, 1945, designated
for the *10th Anniversary Album.*
"This Way Out," (inst.), October 18, 1945.
"I Know That You Know," (inst.), October 18, 1945.
"How Does It Feel?" December 4, 1945.
"You Must Be Blind," December 4, 1945.*

"Loan Me Two till Tuesday," December 4, 1945.*
"Oh, But I Do," December 4, 1945.

(Omitted from this list for March and April 1946 are 26 songs, possibly Capitol transcriptions, plus "F.S.T." themes done in Los Angeles.)

(Nat made the following recordings with his trio in Hollywood.)

"I'm in the Mood for Love," March 15, 1946.
"I Don't Know Why," March 15, 1946.
"Get Your Kicks on Route 66," March 15, 1946.
"Everyone Is Saying Hello Again," March 15, 1946.

(Nat recorded as a pianist in Hollywood in March, 1946. See Part 1 for details on the session with Jo Stafford. Also, Teubig notes that in March 1946, Cole sang and played piano for Frank Sinatra on "Exactly like You" for an AFRS broadcast. R.G. Holmes says "Route 66" was included in the session on March 13, 1946.)

(From April 5 through May 4, 1946, Nat recorded with his trio in Hollywood.)

"What Can I Say After I Say I'm Sorry?" April 5, 1946.
"To a Wild Rose," (inst.), April 5, 1946.
"Baby, Baby, All the Time," April 17, 1946.
"Could 'Ja?," April 17, 1946.
"Oh, But I Do," April 17, 1946.
"Rhumba a la King," (inst.), April 17, 1946. (Also called "Rex Rhumba.")
"But She's My Buddy's Chick," May 1, 1946.
"You Call It Madness, (But I Call It Love)," May 1, 1946.
"Homeward Bound," (inst.), May 1, 1946.*
"Chant of the Blues," May 1, 1946.*

(The following tracks were done in New York City by Nat with the trio between June 1946 and January 1947.)

"The Christmas Song," June 14, 1946. (A string section was added on August 19 for the great commercial success.)
(Seven transcriptions are omitted.)
"The Best Man," August 19, 1946.

"You Should Have Told Me," August 19, 1946.

"I Love You for Sentimental Reasons," August 22, 1946. (Done with the trio, this song was included from its original hit version on the album *Unforgettable* issued in 1965.)

"In the Cool of the Evening," (inst.), September 6, 1946.

"That's the Beginning of the End," September 6, 1946.

"If You Don't like My Apples," September 17, 1946.*

"Smoke Gets in Your Eyes," (inst.), October 30, 1946 (or possibly in December).

"I Want to Thank Your Folks," December 18, 1946.

"You're the Cream in My Coffee," December 18, 1946.

"Come in Out of the Rain," December 18, 1946.

"You Don't Learn That in School," December 30, 1946.

"You Be You (But Let Me Be Me)," December 30, 1946.*

"Can You Look Me in the Eyes?" December 30, 1946.

"Give Me Twenty Nickels," January 21, 1947.*

"Meet Me at No Special Place," January 21, 1947.

"If You Don't like My Apples," January 21, 1947.*

(From June 13 through August 29, Cole recorded with his trio in Hollywood.)

"Naughty Angeline," June 13, 1947.

"I Miss You So," June 13, 1947.

"That's What," June 13, 1947.

"Honeysuckle Rose," (inst.), July 2, 1947.

"Thanks for You," July 2, 1947.*

"It's Kind of Lonesome Tonight," July 2, 1947.

"For Once in Your Life," July 2, 1947.*

"I Think You Get What I Mean," July 3, 1947.

"But All I've Got Is Me," July 3, 1947 (with the trio on the *10th Anniversary Album*, 1955).

"Now He Tells Me," July 3, 1947.*

"I Can't Be Bothered," July 3, 1947 (with the trio on the *10th Anniversary Album*).

(Four transcriptions omitted.)

"When I Take My Sugar to Tea," August 6, 1947.

"Rhumba Azul," (inst.), August 6, 1947.

"I Never Had a Chance," August 6, 1947.*

"What'll I Do?" August 6, 1947 (with the trio on the album

Unforgettable from original soundtrack of Nat's hits issued in 1965).

"This Is My Night to Dream," August 7, 1947.

"Makin' Whoopee," August 7, 1947.

"There, I've Said It Again," August 7, 1947 (with the trio on the *10th Anniversary Album*).

"I'll String Along with You," August 8, 1947.

"Oh, Kickeroonie," August 8, 1947.*

"It's Easy to See (The Trouble with Me Is You)," August 8, 1947.

"Too Marvelous for Words," August 8, 1947.

"Three Little Worlds," (inst.), August 8, 1947.

"Moonlight in Vermont," (inst.), August 13, 1947.

"Poor Butterfly," (inst.), August 13, 1947.

"How High the Moon," (inst.), August 13, 1947.

"I'll Never Be the Same," (inst.), August 13, 1947.

"These Foolish Things," (inst.), August 13, 1947.

"Cole Capers," (inst.), August 13, 1947.

"Blues in My Shower," (inst.), August 13, 1947.

"I Wanna Be a Friend of Yours," August 15, 1947.

For *Nat King Cole For Kids.*

"Kee Mo Ky Mo," August 15, 1947.

"Three Blind Mice," August 15, 1947.

The following were done with Johnny Mercer (VO), Nat (P and VO), and the trio in Hollywood:

"Save the Bones for Henry Jones," August 20, 1947.

"My Baby likes to Bebop," August 20, 1947.

"Harmony," August 20, 1947.

"You Can't Make Money Dreaming," August 20, 1947.

For *Nat King Cole For Kids:*

"Wiegenlied" (Brahms Lullaby), August 22, 1947. (Buddy Cole, no relation to Nat, plays celeste.)

"Go to Sleep, My Sleepyhead," August 22, 1947.

"The Three Wishes," (also referred to as "Three Trees" in some sources), August 22, 1947. (Buddy Cole plays celeste.)

"There's a Train Out for Dreamland," August 22, 1947.

"Nature Boy," August 22, 1947.
"Wildroot Charlie," August 22, 1947.* (Nat Cole doesn't play piano; Buddy Cole plays celeste.)
"Laguna Mood," (inst.), August 27, 1947.

For *Nat King Cole For Kids:*

"Nursery Rhymes," (including a medley of "Mary Had a Little Lamb," "London Bridge," "Go In and Out the Windows," and "Pop Goes the Weasel," August 27, 1947).
"Old MacDonald Had a Farm," August 27, 1947.

"I'm a Little Ashamed," August 28, 1947.*
"Now He Tells Me," August 28, 1947.
"That's a Natural Fact," August 28, 1947.
"Lament in Chords," (inst.), August 29, 1947.*
"You've Got Another Heart on Your Hands," August 29, 1947.*
"Baby, I Need You," August 29, 1947.*
"Those Things Money Can't Buy," August 29, 1947. (Designated for *10th Anniversary Album* in 1955, but not used on the album.)

(Eight transcriptions and eight other songs documented on a previous session are not included here.)

(Nat recorded with his trio from October 28, 1947 through May 20, 1949 in New York City. Irving Ashby (G) replaced Oscar Moore.)

"The Love Nest," October 28, 1947.
"Dream a Little Dream of Me," October 28, 1947.
"Then I'll Be Tired of You," October 28, 1947.
"Little Girl," November 3, 1947.
"Who's Telling You Lies?" November 3, 1947.*
"No Moon at All," November 3, 1947.
"Money is Honey," November 3, 1947.*
"I Feel So Smoochie," November 4, 1947.
"A Boy from Texas, Girl from Tennessee," November 4, 1947.
"When You Walked Out with Shoes On," November 4, 1947.*
"That's the Kind of Girl I Dream Of," November 4, 1947.
"It's the Sentimental Thing to Do," November 5, 1947.
"I've Only Myself to Blame," November 5, 1947.
"It's Like Taking Candy from a Baby," November 5, 1947.*
"You've Changed," November 5, 1947.*

"The Geek," (inst.) November 6, 1947.
"Confess," November 6, 1947.*
"If I Had You," November 6, 1947.
"Flo and Joe," November 7, 1947.
"I'm Gonna Spank My Heart," November 7, 1947.*
"I See by the Papers," November 7, 1947.*
"Return Trip," (inst.), November 7, 1947.
"A Woman Always Understands," November 7, 1947.
"If You Stub Your Toe," November 7, 1947.
"Put 'Em in a Box," November 24, 1947.
"I've Got a Way with Women," November 24, 1947.
"Blue and Sentimental," November 24, 1947.*
"My Fair Lady," November 24, 1947.
"I Wish I Had the Blues Again," November 29, 1947.*
"Didn't I Tell You So?" November 29, 1947.*
"Lost April," December 20, 1947 (done with the trio and strings, with conductor and arranger Carlyle Hall and included from this original version on the album *Unforgettable* released in 1965).
"Lillette," December 20, 1947.*
"Monday Again," December 20, 1947.*
"Lulubelle," December 20, 1947 (with the trio on the *10th Anniversary Album*).
"It's So Hard to Laugh," December 20, 1947.*

(AFM Recording Ban in effect.)

"Portrait of Jennie," January 14, 1949 (with conductor and arranger Carlyle Hall, included from this version on the 1965 album *Unforgettable*).
"Don't Cry, Cry Baby," January 14, 1949 (or March 7 according to Teubig).
"An Old Piano Plays the Blues," January 14, 1949 (or March 7 according to Teubig).
"How Lonely Can You Get?" January 14, 1949.*

(Nat records with The Trio, now called Nat King Cole and The Trio, including Jack Costanzo (BGO-CGA), and Joe Comfort (B), with Ashby (G) in Los Angeles.)

"Vesti La Giubba" (Laugh, Cool Clown) (inst.), March 22, 1949.
"Bop Kick," (inst.), March 22, 1949.
"For All We Know," March 22, 1949.

"Land of Love," March 29, 1949. (Costanzo is not on this track. Throughout his years with the trio, he did not play on all the recorded tracks. This survey doesn't mention every instance of his exclusion.)

"Land of Love," March 29, 1949 (with Pete Rugolo as conductor and arranger for all songs recorded on this date and on March 30, 1949).

"Lush Life," March 29, 1949.

"Lillian," March 29, 1949.

"'Tis Autumn," March 29, 1949.

"Yes, Sir, That's My Baby," March 29, 1949.

"I Used to Love You," March 29, 1949.

"Etymology" (The Language of Love), March 30, 1949.

"Peaches," (inst.), March 30, 1949 (with the trio on the *10th Anniversary Album*).

"Last But Not Least," (inst.), March 30, 1949.*

"I Wake Up Screaming, Dreaming of You," March 30, 1949.

(The following are Capitol transcriptions done in New York in March and April, 1949, and possibly later for some.) "Part of Me," "My Mother Told Me," "Exactly Like You," "What Have You Got in Those Eyes?" (inst.), "Top Hat Bop" (inst.), "Go Bongo" (inst.), "Rhumba Azul" (inst.), "Boulevard of Broken Dreams," "If I Were You, I'd Love Me," "Third Finger, Left Hand," "Calico Sal," "After My Laughter, Came Tears," "Peaches" (inst.), "Don't Let Your Eyes Go Shopping for Your Heart," "All Aboard" (inst.), "Deed I Do," "Oh, Kickaroonie."* "Go Bongo" and "Rhumba Azul" were done by Cole and Costanzo only.

"It Was So Good While It Lasted," May 20, 1949.

"Roses and Wine," May 20, 1949.*

"Who Do you Know in Heaven?" May 20, 1949.

"I Get Sentimental over Nothing," May 20, 1949.

"A Little Yellow Ribbon," May 20, 1949.*

"Your Voice," May 20, 1949.

(The following songs were recorded in Hollywood.)

"All I Want for Christmas Is My Two Front Teeth," August 2, 1949 (with the trio and the Starlighters, a vocal group).

"You Can't Lose a Broken Heart," August 2, 1949 (with the Starlighters).

"Bang Bang Boogie," August 2, 1949 (with the Starlighters).

"Here Is My Heart" (Nalani), September 9, 1949 (with a vocal group, probably the Starlighters, and orchestra).

"The Horse Told Me," September 9, 1949.

"Don't Shove, I'm Leaving," September 9, 1949.

"Calypso Blues," September 9, 1949 (with Costanzo and Cole only).

(Nat and his trio recorded with Woody Herman in New York on November 7, 1949 (or, according to R. G. Holmes, on November 9). The songs were "Mule Train" and "My Baby Just Cares for Me.")

(Nat recorded the following two songs with Nellie Lutcher in Hollywood on January 5, 1950. See Part 1 for details. The songs were "For You, My Love" and "Can I Come in for a Second?")

(Nat made the following recordings with his trio, and drummer Lee Young, and vocal groups in Hollywood.)

"Baby, Won't You Say You Love Me?" February 9, 1950.

"I'll Never Say Never Again," February 9, 1950.

"A Little Bit Independent," February 9, 1950.

"Twisted Stockings," February 9, 1950.

"I Almost Lost My Mind," February 9, 1950.

"Always You," March 11, 1950 (with Les Baxter, orchestra and chorus).

"The Magic Tree," March 11, 1950 (with Les Baxter, orchestra and chorus).

"Mona Lisa," March 11, 1950 (included on *Unforgettable*, the album made from original soundtracks of Nat's hits and released in 1965; for this song, Les Baxter is credited as the conductor and Nelson Riddle as arranger).

"The Greatest Inventor of Them All," March 11, 1950, with the trio.

"Who's Who?" March 11, 1950, on *The Unreleased Nat King Cole* (with the trio and a drummer whom some sources say is Lee Young).

Some of the following recordings, all done in New York City, were with Maria and Nat Cole, arranged and conducted by Pete Rugolo and his orchestra and the Nat King Cole Trio. Some were done with Alyce King's Vokettes, a vocal group. "Get Out and Get

Under the Moon" and "Hey, Not Now" were definitely with Nat and Maria. Others were "Tunnel of Love," "It's a Man Every Time" with Maria, "The Way I'm Loving You," May 12, 1950. "Time Out for Tears," "My Brother," "Home," "Every Day," "A Woman's Got a Right to Change Her Mind," most likely May 18, 1950. One source says May 19.

From August 16, 1950 through December 3, 1964, all recordings were made in Hollywood, except for "Nat Cole Live at the Sands" and "More Cole Español."

"Orange Colored Sky," August 16, 1950, with Stan Kenton. See Part 1 for details.

"Jam-bo," (inst.), August 16, 1950. With Kenton. See Part 1 for details.

"Make Believe Land," August 25, 1950 (with Pete Rugolo and vocal group on all recordings made on this date except where noted).

"Get to Gettin'," August 25, 1950.

"Frosty the Snowman," August 25, 1960.

"Little Christmas Tree," August 25, 1950.

"Song of Delilah," August 25, 1950 (with conductor and arranger Dave Barbour).

"Jet," December 11, 1950.

"Destination Moon," December 11, 1950.

"Paint Yourself a Rainbow," December 11, 1950.

"That's My Gal," February 1, 1951.

"Too Young," February 2, 1951. On *Unforgettable** in 1965, (with Les Baxter, conductor, and Nelson Riddle, arranger, for this song).

"Early American," February 6, 1951.

"Because of Rain," February 6, 1951.

"I Wish I Were Somebody Else," February 12, 1951 (done with Pete Rugolo, conductor and arranger, and used on the *10th Anniversary Album*).

"You Can't Make Me Love You," February 12, 1951.*

---

*Note: The liner notes say what people knew at the time: Nelson Riddle was writing arrangements in the shadow of Les Baxter. Eventually Riddle got the proper credit and emerged as a star arranger and conductor.

"Red Sails in the Sunset," February 12, 1951 (done with Pete Rugolo and used on the *10th Anniversary Album*).

"I'll Always Remember You," February 12, 1951.*

"Poor Jenny Is A-Weeping," February 12, 1951.

"The Day Isn't Long Enough," March 9, 1951.*

"Little Child," March 9, 1951.

"A Robin and a Rainbow and a Red Red Rose," March 9, 1951.*

"Lighthouse in the Sky," March 9, 1951.

"Pigtails and Freckles," March 9, 1951.*

"Unforgettable," August 17, 1951 (arranged and conducted by Nelson Riddle, and included on the 1965 album *Unforgettable*).

"My First Love and Last Love," August 17, 1951.

"Lovelight," August 17, 1951 (with Nelson Riddle and used for the *10th Anniversary Album*).

"Walkin' My Baby Back Home," September 4, 1951.

"What Does It Take to Make You. . . ," September 4, 1951.

"Walkin'," September 4, 1951.

"I'm Hurtin'," September 4, 1951.

"I Still See Elisa," September 14, 1951.

"Miss Me," September 14, 1951.

"Weaver of Dreams," September 14, 1951.

"Wine, Women and Song," September 14, 1951.

"Here's to My Lady," September 14, 1951.

"It's OK for TV," September 14, 1951.

"The Ruby and the Pearl," September 14, 1951.

"The Story of My Wife," September 14, 1951 (done with Les Baxter and used for the *10th Anniversary Album*).

"You Will Never Grow Old," January 10, 1952.

"Easter Sunday Morning," January 10, 1952.

"You Weren't There," January 10, 1952.

"Somewhere Along the Way," January 10, 1952.

"It's Crazy," January 11, 1952.

"Where Were You?" January 11, 1952 (done with Pete Rugolo and used for the *10th Anniversary Album*).

"You Stepped Out of a Dream," January 11, 1952 (on *Songs for Two in Love* originally issued in 1953).

"Summer Is a Comin' In," January 11, 1952.

"Funny, Not Much," January 11, 1952.

"Rough Ridin'," March 31, 1952 (done with Dave Cavanaugh, arranger and conductor, and included in for the *10th Anniversary Album*).

"Can't I?" March 31, 1952.*

(The following eight songs recorded on July 18, 1952, were included in the *Penthouse Serenade* album, with Nat (P), John Collins (G), Charles Harris (B), Jack Costanzo (BGO-CGA), Bunny Shawker (D), originally released in 1955. Costanzo played on tracks marked with an (†) sign.)

"Penthouse Serenade," (inst.), July 18, 1952.
"Rose Room," (inst.), July 18, 1952.†
"Polka Dots and Moonbeams," (inst.), July 18, 1952.
"Somebody Loves Me," (inst.), July 18, 1952.
"Once in a Blue Moon," (inst.), July 18, 1952. (This song was based on Rubinstein's "Melody in F.")†
"If I Should Lose You," (inst.), July 18, 1952.
"Down by the Old Mill Stream," (inst.), July 18, 1952.†
"Laura," (inst.), July 18, 1952.

(The following 11 songs were done with Nelson Riddle, conductor and arranger, and Nat and his trio with John Collins (G) and Charles Harris (B).)

"Don't Let Your Eyes Go Shopping for Your Heart," July 24, 1952.
"Strange," July 28, 1952.
"How Do I Go About It?" July 28, 1952.
"Sweet William," July 31, 1952.*
"Because You're Mine," July 31, 1952.
"Sleeping Beauty," July 31, 1952 (or possibly August 24, 1953).
"I'm Never Satisfied," July 31, 1952.*
"My Flaming Heart," August 12, 1952.*
"Faith Can Move Mountains," August 12, 1952.
"Too Soon," August 12, 1952.
"Small Towns are Smile Towns," August 12, 1952.*

"Mother Nature and Father Time," December 30, 1952 (on the *10th Anniversary Album*).
"When I'm Alone," December 30, 1952 (released on *The Unreleased Nat King Cole* in 1987).
"Pretend," December 30, 1952 (with Nelson Riddle, arranger and conductor, and reissued as one of Nat's hits on *Unforgettable* in 1965).
"A Fool Was I," December 30, 1952.
"Angel Eyes," January 14, 1953 (on *Ballads of the Day,* 1956).

"Lover, Come Back to Me," January 14, 1953.
"Can't I?" January 14, 1953.
"The Magic Window," January 20, 1953.*
"That's All," January 20, 1953 (on *This Is Nat King Cole* album).
"Annabelle," January 20, 1953 (on *This Is Nat King Cole* album).
"If Love Is Good to Me," January 20, 1953 (on *Ballads of the Day*).
"Blue Gardenia," (on *Ballads of the Day*).

(The following nine songs were on the album *Songs for Two in Love* (the title in the 1990 20-record collection), originally issued in 1953 as *Nat King Cole Sings for Two in Love.*)

"Dinner for One, Please, James," January 27, 1953.
"There Goes My Heart," January 27, 1953.
"A Handful of Stars," January 27, 1953.
"Love Is Here to Stay," January 27, 1953.
"A Little Street Where Old Friends Meet," January 27, 1953.
"Tenderly," January 27, 1953.
"Almost like Being in Love," January 28, 1953.
"This Can't Be Love," January 28, 1953.
"Don't Hurt That Girl," January 28, 1953.

"Return to Paradise," March 31, 1953 (on *Ballads of the Day*).
"Make Her Mine," March 31, 1953 (with Nelson Riddle, on *Unforgettable,* 1965).
"Why Can't We Try Again?" March 31, 1953.
"I Am in Love," March 31, 1953.
"Why?" August 14, 1953.
"The Little Boy Santa Claus Forgot," August 18, 1953.
"You're Wrong, All Wrong," August 18, 1953.*
"Mrs. Santa Claus," August 18, 1953.
"Darling, Je Vous Aime Beaucoup," August 24, 1953 (on *Ballads of the Day,* 1956).
"Little Fingers," August 24, 1953.*
"I Envy," August 24, 1953.
"For a Moment of Your Love," August 24, 1953 (on *The Unreleased Nat King Cole,* 1987).
"Sleeping Beauty," August 24, 1953.
"The Christmas Song," remake, August 24, 1953.
"Answer Me, My Love," December 3, 1953 (with Nelson Riddle, on *Unforgettable,* 1965).

"Ain't She Sweet?" February 3, 1954.*

"What to Do?" February 3, 1954.

"Alone Too Long," February 9, 1954 (on *Ballads of the Day,* 1956).

"It Happens to Be Me," February 9, 1954 (on *Ballads of the Day,* 1956).

"Unbelievable," (on *Ballads of the Day,* 1956).

"Marilyn," February 9, 1954.*

"Hajji Baba," July 27, 1954 (on *Unforgettable,* 1965).

"Smile," July 27, 1954 (on *Ballads of the Day,* 1956).

"I'll Always Be Remembering," August 24, 1954.

"My One Sin," August 24, 1954 (on *Ballads of the Day,* 1956).

"I'll Never Settle for Less," August 24, 1954.

"United," August 24, 1954.

"Open Up the Doghouse," September 7, 1954 (with Nat Cole and Dean Martin).

"Long, Long Ago," September 7, 1954 (with Dean Martin).

"If I Give My Heart to You," October 18, 1954.

"Hold My Hand," October 18, 1954.

"Papa Loves Mambo," October 18, 1954.

"Teach Me Tonight," October 18, 1954.

"The Sand and the Sea," December 20, 1954 (on *Ballads of the Day,* 1956).

"A Blossom Fell," December 20, 1954 (on *Ballads of the Day,* 1956).

"Forgive My Heart," December 20, 1954.

"I'm Gonna Laugh You Right out of My Life," December 20, 1954.

"If I May," December 20, 1954.

"I'd Rather Have the Blues," March 25, 1955.

(The following four songs were on the album *The Piano Style of Nat King Cole,* 1956, reissued in 1990. Another album, *The Piano Soul of Nat King Cole,* released by Pickwick Records and also by the Official Record Co. in Denmark licensed by Capitol, included some of the songs on the 1990 release.)

"I Hear Music," June 7, 1955.

"My Heart Stood Still," June 7, 1955.

"I Never Knew," June 7, 1955.

"Tea for Two," June 7, 1955.

"Nothing Ever Changes," June 7, 1955.
"Breezin' Along with the Breeze," June 7, 1955.
"Someone You Love," June 9, 1955.
"Unfair," June 9, 1955.*
"Wishing Well," June 10, 1955.*
"I've Learned," June 10, 1955.*
"Half a Mind," June 10, 1955.*
"But Not for Me," June 10, 1955.
"What Can I Say After I Say I'm Sorry?" June 11, 1955 (on *The Piano Style of Nat King Cole,* 1956).
"It Was That Kiss," June 11, 1955.
"Taking a Chance on Love," June 11, 1955 (on *The Piano Style of Nat King Cole,* 1956).

(The following four records were done with Nat Cole and his trio, Collins (G) and Harris (B), with Bunny Shawker or Lee Young (D), for *Penthouse Serenade* in 1955.)

"Don't Blame Me," (inst.), July 14, 1955.
"It Could Happen to You," (inst.), July 14, 1955.
"I Surrender, Dear," (inst.), July 14, 1955.
"Little Girl," (inst.), July 14, 1955.

"Autumn Leaves," August 23, 1955 (on *Songs for Two in Love,* the 1990 reissue).
"There Will Never Be Another You," August 25, 1955 (on *Songs for Two in Love,* 1990).
"Let's Fall in Love," August 25, 1955 (on *Songs for Two in Love,* 1990).
"Just One of Those Things," August 27, 1955 (on *The Piano Style of Nat King Cole,* 1990).
"I Want to Be Happy," August 27, 1955* (on *The Piano Style of Nat King Cole,* 1990).
"You Are My Sunshine," August 27, 1955.
"Up Pops Love," August 27, 1955.*

(The following eight songs are on *The Piano Style of Nat King Cole,* 1990:)

"April in Paris," August 27 or August 30, 1955. (According to one source. R.G. Holmes says August 18, 1955.)

"Imagination," August 30, 1955. (R.G. Holmes says August 18, 1955.)

"I Didn't Know What Time It Was," August 30, 1955. (Holmes says August 23.)

"I Get a Kick out of You," August 30, 1955. (Holmes says August 23.)

"If I Could Be with You," August 30, 1955. (Holmes says August 23.)

"Stella by Starlight," August 30, 1955. (Holmes says August 18.)

"I See Your Face," August 30, 1955. (Holmes says August 18.)

"Love Walked In," August 30, 1955. (Holmes says August 18.)

"Love Me As Though There Were No Tomorrow," December 20, 1955.*

"Too Young to Go Steady," December 20, 1955.

"Dreams Can Tell a Lie," December 20, 1955.

"Back in My Arms," December 20, 1955.

"Dame Crazy," December 29, 1955.

"I Just Found Out About Love," December 29, 1955.

"My Personal Possession," December 29, 1955.

"That's All There is To That," December 29, 1955.

"If I May," December 29, 1955. (This is probably the correct date.)

"Mr. Juke Box," December 29, 1955.*

"I Got Love," December 29, 1955.*

"Stay," December 29, 1955.*

"Believe," December 29, 1955.*

"Night Lights," January 4, 1956.

"To the Ends of the Earth," January 4, 1956.

"Never Let Me Go," January 4, 1956.

"The Shadows," January 4, 1956.

"I Promise You," January 4, 1956.

"The Way I Love You," January 4, 1956.

"Once Before," January 21, 1956.*

"I'm Willing To Share This With You," January 21, 1956.*

"I Need a Plan," January 21, 1956.*

"The Story's Old," January 21, 1956.*

"Unfair," January 21, 1956.

"Make Me," January 21, 1956.*

"Sometimes I Wonder," January 21, 1956.*

"We Are Americans, Too," May 17, 1956. (Released as a promo.)

(The following nine songs were recorded for the *After Midnight* album. Songs marked with the pound (#) sign were not released until the 1990 reissue of the album. Tunes without the pound sign were released in the original issue, 1956. The album was recorded with Nat King Cole (P and VO), John Collins (G), Charles Harris (B), Lee Young (D), Jack Costanzo (BGO), and Harry "Sweets" Edison (TP) on August 15, Willie Smith (AS) on September 14, Juan Tizol (TB) on September 21, Stuff Smith (VLN) on September 24. Listings for Tizol and Stuff Smith come after three intervening songs done by Nat Cole on September 19, 1956.)

"You Can Depend On Me," August 15, 1956.#
"Candy," August 15, 1956.#
"Sweet Lorraine," August 15, 1956.
"It's Only a Paper Moon," August 15, 1956.
"Route 66," August 15, 1956.
"Don't Let It Go to Your Head," September 14, 1956.
"You're Lookin' at Me," September 14, 1956.
"I Was a Little Too Lonely," September 14, 1956.#
"Just You, Just Me," September 14, 1956.

"How Little We Know," September 19, 1956, on *The Unreleased Nat King Cole*, 1987.
"Should I?" September 19, 1956, on *The Unreleased Nat King Cole*, 1987.
"Ballerina," September 19, 1956.

(The following eight songs were recorded for *After Midnight*. See above for details.)

"Caravan," September 21, 1956.
"Lonely One," September 21, 1956.
"Blame It on My Youth," September 21, 1956.
"What Is There to Say?" September 21, 1956.#
"Sometimes I'm Happy," September 24, 1956.
"I Know That You Know," September 24, 1956.
"When I Grow Too Old to Dream," September 24, 1956.
"Two Loves Have I," September 24, 1956.#

(The following three songs are on *The Unreleased Nat King Cole*, 1987.)

"True Blue Lou," October 4, 1956.*
"Like Someone in Love," October 4, 1956.*
"I'm Shootin' High," October 4, 1956.*

"Tangerine," October 4, 1956.
"One Sun," October 10, 1956.

(The following twelve songs are on *Love Is the Thing,* arranged and conducted by Gordon Jenkins, 1957.)

"Maybe It's Because I Love You," December 19, 1956.
"Love Letters," December 19, 1956.
"I Thought About Marie," December 19, 1956.
"Where Can I Go without You?" December 19, 1956.
"Stardust," December 19, 1956.
"Love Is the Thing," December 19, 1956.
"It's All In the Game," December 19, 1956.
"When I Fall in Love," December 28, 1956.
"Ain't Misbehavin'," December 28, 1956.
"When Sunny Gets Blue," December 28, 1956.
"At Last," December 28, 1956.
"Stay As Sweet As You Are," December 28, 1956.

"When Rock and Roll Came to Trinidad," March 19, 1957.
"China Gate," March 19, 1957.
"Blue Moon," May 14, 1957.*
"With You on My Mind," May 14, 1957.
"Don't Try," May 14, 1957.*
"Send For Me," May 14, 1957.
"Let's Make More Love," May 14, 1957.*

(Most of the following songs were recorded for the album *Just One of Those Things,* arranged and conducted by Billy May and originally issued in 1959.)

"Just for the Fun of It," July 10, 1957.* (This song was not in the reissue in 1990.)
"Don't Get Around Much Anymore," July 10, 1957.*
"You'll Never Know," July 10, 1957.* (It was released on *Nat King Cole: The Great Films and Shows* in 1989 in the United States and also on *Greatest Love Songs* in the United Kingdom. Foreign

issues, with a few exceptions, have not been included in this survey.)

"The Song Is Ended," July 10, 1957.

"Who's Sorry Now?" July 19 or August 7, 1957.

"These Foolish Things," July 19, 1957.

"Once in a While," July 19, 1957.

"The Song of Raintree County," July 19, 1957 (but not in the 1990 release).

"Just One of Those Things," July 31, 1957.

"I Should Care," July 31, 1957.

"The Party's Over," July 31, 1957.

"A Cottage for Sale," August 7, 1957.

"I Understand," August 7, 1957.

"When Your Lover Has Gone," August 7, 1957.

"There's a Gold Mine in the Sky," August 8, 1957.

"Around the World," August 8, 1957.

"An Affair to Remember," August 8, 1957.

"Fascination," August 8, 1957.

"How Did I Change?" November 20, 1957* (on *The Unreleased Nat King Cole,* 1987).

"Angel Smile," November 22, 1957.

"It's None of My Affair," November 22, 1957.*

"Nothin' in the World," November 22, 1957.

"Toys for Tots," November 22, 1957.

(The following twelve songs were recorded for *St. Louis Blues,* an album of blues, 1958.)

"Beale Street Blues," January 29, 1958.

"Yellow Dog Blues," January 29, 1958.

"Careless Love," January 29, 1958.

"Chantez les Bas," January 29, 1958.

"Overture a.) Love Theme, b.) Hesitating Blues," January 30, 1958.

"Morning Star," January 30, 1958.

"Stay," January 30, 1958.

"St. Louis Blues," January 30, 1958.

"Memphis Blues," January 31, 1958.

"Harlem Blues," January 31, 1958.

"Joe Turner's Blues," January 31, 1958.

"Friendless Blues," January 31, 1958.

"Come to the Mardi Gras," February 1958 (on *The Unreleased Nat King Cole,* 1987).
"Looking Back," February 4, 1958.
"Make It Last," February 4, 1958.*
"Just As Much As Ever," February 4, 1958.
"Thank You, Pretty Baby," February 4, 1958.
"Do I Like It?" February 4, 1958.

(The following eleven recordings were on *Cole Español,* with orchestra leader Armando Romeu Jr., 1958, possibly done in Havana, Cuba.)

"Maria Elena," February 17, 1958.
"Lisbon Antigua," February 17, 1958.*
"Acercate Mas," February 17, 1958.
"Tu, Mi Delirio," February 18, 1958.
"Mardi Gras," February 18, 1958.*
"El Bodeguero Cha Cha Cha," February 18, 1958.
"Magic Is the Moonlight," February 20, 1958.
"Arriverderci Roma," February 20, 1958.
"Quizas, Quizas, Quizas," February 20, 1958.
"Los Mananitas," February 20, 1958.
"Adelita," February 20, 1958.

(The following sixteen songs, with the exceptions of "Don't Blame Me" and "There Is No Greater Love," were on *The Very Thought of You,* arranged and conducted by Gordon Jenkins and released in 1961.)

"I Wish I Knew," May 2, 1958.
"This Is All I Ask," May 2, 1958.
"The More I See You," May 2, 1958.
"I Found a Million Dollar Baby," May 2, 1958.
"Making Believe You're Here," May 2, 1958.
"My Heart Tells Me," May 2, 1958.
"Cherchez La Femme," May 6, 1958.
"Don't Blame Me," May 6, 1958.* Still unreleased in 1990.
"The Very Thought of You," May 6, 1958.
"There Is No Greater Love," May 6, 1958* (released in the United Kingdom on *The Very Thought of You,* according to R.G. Holmes but not on the American release).
"Paradise," May 6, 1958.

"Magnificent Obsession," May 8, 1958.
"Chérie," May 8, 1958.
"Impossible," May 8, 1958.
"But Beautiful," May 8, 1958, or possibly August.
"For All We Know," May 8, 1958.

(The following three songs were on *Cole Español* in 1958.)

"Cachito," June 9, 1958.
"El Bodeguero," June 9, 1958.*
"Noche de Ronda," June 9, 1958.

"I Got Love," June 20, 1958.

(The following three songs were on *To Whom It May Concern* in 1958.)

"Too Much," June 20, 1958.
"Lovesville," June 20, 1958.
"Can't Help It," June 20, 1958.

"Acercate Mas," June 30, 1958, (on *Cole Español,* 1958).

(*Welcome to the Club,* issued in 1958, reissued in 1962 as *The Swinging Side of Nat Cole,* went back to its original title in the 20-record collection released in 1990. Nat was the vocalist with the Count Basie Orchestra. Basie himself gave the piano bench to Gerald Wiggins, so that Basie wouldn't violate the terms of a recording contract he had with another company. The record was made on June 30 and July 1, 1958, according to *The Capitol Years* liner notes and on June 30, July 1 and July 2, according to another United States record industry source. The latter dates are confirmed by R.G. Holmes in England. The entire orchestra personnel is known: Marshall Royal (AS), Frank Wess and Frank Foster (AS, TS), Billy Mitchell (TS), Charlie Fowlkes (BAR), John Anderson, Joe Newman, Wendell Culley, Thad Jones, Snooky Young (TP), Henry Coker, Al Grey, Benny Powell (TB), Freddie Green (G), Eddie Jones (B), Sonny Payne (D), Gerald Wiggins (P).)

"Anytime, Anyway, Anywhere," June 30, 1958.
"I Want a Little Girl," June 30, 1958.
"Mood Indigo," June 30, 1958.

"She's Funny That Way," June 30, 1958.
"The Blues Don't Care," July 1, 1958.
"Avalon," July 1, 1958.
"Baby, Won't You Please Come Home," July 1, 1958.
"The Late Late Show," July 1, 1958.
"Welcome to the Club," July 1, 1958.
"Look Out for Love," July 2, 1958.
"Wee Baby Blues," July 2, 1958.

"Madrid," July 2, 1958.

(The following five songs were on *To Whom It May Concern*, 1958.)

"To Whom It May Concern," August 11, 1958.
"Love Wise," August 11, 1958.
"In The Heart of Jane Doe," August 11, 1958.
"My Heart's Treasure," August 11, 1958.
"You're Bringing Out the Dreamer in Me," August 11, 1958.

"Bend a Little My Way," August 18, 1958.
"Non Dimenticar," August 18, 1958.
"Coo Coo Roo Coo Coo Paloma," August 18, 1958.
"Give Me Your Love," August 18, 1958.
"This Morning It Was Summer," August 18, 1958.

(The following song was on *To Whom It May Concern*, 1958.)

"A Thousand Thoughts of You," August 18, 1958.

(The following eleven songs were on *Everytime I Feel the Spirit*, with Gordon Jenkins, conductor and arranger, 1958.)

"Ain't Gonna Study War No More," September 29, 1958.
"Standin' in the Need of Prayer," September 29, 1958.
"Go Down Moses," September 29, 1958.
"Steal Away," September 29, 1958.
"I Couldn't Hear Nobody Pray," September 30, 1958.
"I Want to Be Ready," September 30, 1958.
"Nobody Knows the Trouble I've Seen," September 30, 1958.
"In the Sweet By and By," September 30, 1958.
"Sweet Hour of Prayer," September 30, 1958.

"Oh, Mary Don't You Weep," September 30, 1958.
"I Found the Answer," September 30, 1958.

(The following eight songs were originally issued on *Tell Me All About Yourself* in 1960.)

"For You," October 30, 1958.
"Crazy She Calls Me," October 30, 1958.
"Until the Real Thing Comes Along," October 30, 1958.
"You Are My Love," October 30, 1958.
"The Best Thing for You Would Be Me," November 4, 1958.
"Dedicated to You," November 4, 1958.
"I Would Do Anything for You," November 4, 1958.
"This Is Always," November 4, 1958.

"I Had the Craziest Dream," November 5, 1958.
"I Wish I Knew," November 5, 1958.
"Be Still My Heart," November 5, 1958.
"As Far as I'm Concerned," November 7, 1958.
"Lorelei," November 7, 1958.*
"This Holy Love," November 7, 1958.
"You Made Me Love You," November 7, 1958.
"Peace of Mind," November 7, 1958.

(The following were on *Tell Me All About Yourself* originally issued in 1963.)

"Tell Me All About Yourself," November 10, 1958.
"When You Walked By," November 10, 1958.
"You've Got the Indian Sign on Me," November 10, 1958.
"My Life," November 10, 1958.

"If You Said So," November 11, 1958 (on *To Whom It May Concern*, 1958).
"Sweethearts On Parade," November 11, 1958.
"That's You," November 11, 1958.
"When You Belong to Me," November 11, 1958.*
"Something Happens to Me," November 11, 1958.
"Unfair," November 12, 1958 (on *To Whom It May Concern*, 1958).
"You're My Thrill," November 12, 1958.
"Again," November 12 or December 11, 1958.

"Laughable," November 12, 1958.*
"I Must Be Dreaming," November 12, 1958.
"For the Want of a Kiss," November 12, 1958.
"The Night of the Quarter Moon," February 4, 1959.

(The following songs were on *A Mis Amigos,* with Dave Cavanaugh, arranger and conductor, all recorded on April 14, 1959.)

"Perfidia"
"Nadie Me Ama"
"Aquellos Ojos Verdes"
"Fantastico"
"El Choclo"
"Suas Maos"
"Capuilito De Aleli"
"Come to the Mardi Gras"
"Cabaclo Do Rio"
"Ay Cosita Linda"
"Ansiedad"
"Yo Vendo Unos Ojos Negros"
"Brazilian Love Song"

"Midnight Flyer," July 2, 1959.
"Sweet Bird of Youth," July 2, 1959.
"Buon Natale Means Merry Christmas to You," July 2, 1959.
"The Happiest Christmas Tree," July 2, 1959.
"World in My Arms," September 2, 1959.
"In a Mellow Tone," September 2, 1959.
"Time and the River," September 2, 1959.
"Whatcha Gonna Do?" September 2, 1959.

(The following recordings were for *Nat King Cole at the Sands,* his only album done live, January 14, 1960, and issued in 1966.)

"Ballerina"
"Funny"
"The Continental"
"I Wish You Love"
"You Leave Me Breathless"
"Thou Swell"
"My Kind of Love"
"Surrey With the Fringe on Top"

"Where or When"
"Miss Otis Regrets"
"Joe Turner's Blues"

(The following songs were issued for *Wild Is Love*, 1960.)

"Wild Is Love," March 1, 1960.
"Hundreds and Thousands of Girls," March 1, 1960.
"Tell Her in the Morning," March 1, 1960.
"Pickup," March 1, 1960.
"Stay with It," March 1, 1960.
"Beggar for the Blues," March 1, 1960.
"Wild Is Love" (reprise), March 1, 1960.
"It's a Beautiful Evening," March 2, 1960.
"World of No Return," March 2, 1960.
"In Love Again," March 2, 1960.
"Wouldn't You Know," March 2, 1960.
"Are You Disenchanted?" March 2, 1960.
"He Who Hesitates," March 2, 1960.

"Steady," March 9, 1960.
"My Love," March 9, 1960.
"Is It Better to Have Loved and Lost?" March 9, 1960.
"Wild Is Love," (opening), March 9, 1960 (done for *Wild Is Love*, 1960).
"When It's Summer," March 9, 1960.*
"Magic Night," March 9, 1960.
"Someone to Tell It To," March 11, 1960.*
"Baby Blue," March 11, 1960.
"You Are Mine," March 11, 1960.

(The following 14 songs were for *The Magic of Christmas*, 1960.)

"Away in a Manger," July 5, 1960.
"I Saw Three Ships," July 5, 1960.
"Silent Night," July 5, 1960.
"The First Noel," July 5, 1960.
"Joy to the World," July 6, 1960.
"Deck the Halls," July 6, 1960.
"Hark the Herald Angels Sing," July 6, 1960.
"O Come All Ye Faithful," July 6, 1960.
"O Tannenbaum," July 6, 1960.

"A Cradle in Bethlehem," July 7, 1960.
"God Rest You Merry, Gentlemen," July 7, 1960.
"Caroling Caroling," July 7, 1960.
"O Holy Night," July 7, 1960.
"O Little Town of Bethlehem," July 7, 1960.

"If I Knew," September 27, 1960.

(The following 12 songs were for *The Touch of Your Lips*, 1961.)

"Not So Long Ago," December 23, 1960.
"Only Forever," December 23, 1960.
"Lights Out," December 23, 1960.
"I Remember You," December 22, 1960.
"Sunday, Monday or Always," December 22, 1960.
"A Nightingale Sang in Berkeley Square," December 22, 1960.
"My Need for You," December 22, 1960.
"Poinciana," December 22, 1960.
"The Touch of Your Lips," December 22 or 23, 1960.
"You're Mine, You," December 23, 1960.
"Illusion," December 23, 1960.
"Funny," December 23, 1960.

(The following 21 songs were included in *The Nat King Cole Story,* 1961. The first six songs were done by Nat (P, VO) with his trio, John Collins (G), and Charles Harris (B). One source says that "Embraceable You" was recorded on March 21, 1961 and never issued.)

"It's Only a Paper Moon," March 22, 1961.
"Sweet Lorraine," March 22, 1961.
"Straighten Up and Fly Right," March 23, 1961.
"Embraceable You," March 23, 1961.
"Route 66," March 23, 1961.
"For Sentimental Reasons," March 23, 1961.
"Answer Me, My Love," March 24, 1961.
"Darling, Je Vous Aime Beaucoup," March 24, 1961.
"Smile," March 24, 1961.
"Pretend," March 24, 1961.
"The Sand and the Sea," March 27, 1961.
"A Blossom Fell," March 27, 1961.
"Nature Boy," March 27, 1961.

"Too Young," March 29, 1961.
"Somewhere Along The Way," March 29, 1961.
"Unforgettable," March 30, 1961.
"Mona Lisa," March 30, 1961.
"The Christmas Song," March 30, 1961.
"Send for Me," April 3, 1961.
"If I May," April 3, 1961.
"Looking Back," April 3, 1961.

"Goodnight, Little Leaguer," April 4, 1961.
"Because You Love Me," April 4, 1961.
"Take a Fool's Advice," April 4, 1961.
"The First Baseball Game," April 4, 1961.
"Make It Last," April 4, 1961.
"Capuccina," April 7, 1961.
"Let True Love Begin," April 7, 1961.
"Love," April 7, 1961.
"I Heard You Cried Last Night," April 7, 1961 (on *The Unreleased Nat King Cole,* 1987).

(The following 10 songs were included in *The Nat King Cole Story,* 1961.)

"Orange-Colored Sky," July 6, 1961.
"To the Ends of the Earth," July 19, 1961.
"Non Dimenticar," July 19, 1961.
"Blue Gardenia," July 19, 1961.
"Night Lights," July 19, 1961.
"Calypso Blues," July 19, 1961.
"Walkin' My Baby Back Home," July 19, 1961.
"I Am in Love," July 20, 1961.
"Lush Life," July 20, 1961.
"Ballerina," July 20, 1961.

(The following 12 songs were on *Let's Face the Music,* with Billy May, arranger and conductor, originally issued in 1962.)

"Ebony Rhapsody," November 20, 1961.
"Day in, Day out," November 20, 1961.
"Too Little, Too Late," November 20, 1961.
"When My Sugar Walks Down the Street," November 20, 1961.
"Cold, Cold Heart," November 21 or 22, 1961.

"Let's Face the Music and Dance," November 21, 1961.
"Something Makes Me Want to Dance," November 21, 1961.
"I'm Gonna Sit Right Down and Write Myself a Letter," November 21, 1961.
"Rules of the Road," November 22, 1961.
"Warm and Willing," November 22, 1961.
"Bidin' My Time," November 22, 1961.
"Moon Love," November 22, 1961.

"Step Right Up," November 27, 1961.
"Magic Moments," November 27, 1961.
"The Right Thing to Say," November 27, 1961.
"Azure-Te," December 19, 1961.

(The following songs were on *Nat Cole Sings, George Shearing Plays,* co-arranged by George Shearing and Ralph Carmichael, conductor, co-produced by Lee Gillette and Tom Morgan, 1961. "Guess I'll Go Home" was not released until the album was reissued in the 20-record collection in 1990. "The Game of Love" was released on a 45 rpm and a CD in England, according to R.G. Holmes.)

"Everything Happens to Me," December 19, 1961.
"A Beautiful Friendship," December 19, 1961.
"Pick Yourself Up," December 19 or 20, 1961.
"September Song," December 20, 1961.
"Let There Be Love," December 20, 1961.
"I Got It Bad," December 20, 1961.
"Serenata," December 20, 1961.
"In Other Words," December 20, 1961.
"The Game of Love," December 20, 1961.*
"Guess I'll Go Home," December 21, 1961.*
"I'm Lost," December 22, 1961.
"Don't Go," December 22, 1961.
"There's a Lull in My Life," December 22, 1961.
"Lost April," December 22, 1961.

"Look No Further," February 7, 1962.

(The following 12 songs were for *More Cole Español* with Ralph Carmichael, arranger and conductor, in Mexico City in 1962:)

"La Feria de Las Flores," March 6, 1962.

"Guadalajara," March 6, 1962.
"La Golondrina," March 6, 1962.
"Tres Palabras" (Without You), March 7, 1962.
"Piel Canela," March 7, 1962.
"Solamente Una," March 7, 1962.
"Las Chiapanecas," March 8, 1962.
"Vaya Con Dios," March 8, 1962.
"Adios Mariquita Linda," March 9, 1962.
"No Me Platiques," March 9, 1962.
"Aqui Se Habla en Amor," March 9, 1962.
"A Media Luz," March 9, 1962.

"Dear Lonely Hearts," June 19, 1962.
"Nothing Goes Up," June 19, 1962.
"Who's Next in Line?" June 19, 1962.

(The following songs were for *Ramblin' Rose* originally released in 1962.)

"Ramblin' Rose," June 19, 1962.
"The Good Times," June 19, 1962.
"When You're Smiling," August 11, 1962.
"Wolverton Mountain," August 11, 1962.
"One Has My Name, the Other Has My Heart," August 11, 1962.
"Skip to My Lou," August 11, 1962.
"Another Song and We'll All Go Home Again," August 11, 1962.
"Your Cheatin' Heart," August 11, 1962.
"Goodnight, Irene," August 11, 1962.
"I Don't Want It That Way," August 11, 1962.
"Twilight on the Trail," August 11, 1962.
"He'll Have To Go," August 11, 1962.

(The following 14 songs were for *Where Did Everyone Go?*, arranged and conducted by Gordon Jenkins, 1962.)

"Farewell to Arms," August 13, 1962.
"Happy New Year," August 13, 1962.
"When The World Was Young," August 13, 1962.
"Spring Is Here," August 13, 1962.
"No, I Don't Want Her," August 13, 1962.
"Say It Isn't So," August 13, 1962.
"Am I Blue?" August 13, 1962.

"Laughing on the Outside," August 14, 1962.
"I Keep Going Back to Joe's," August 14, 1962.
"The End of a Love Affair," August 14, 1962.
"That's All There Is," August 14, 1962.
"Someone To Tell It To," August 14, 1962.
"If Love Ain't There," August 14, 1962.
"Where Did Everyone Go?" August 14, 1962.

"Miss You," November 12, 1962.

(The following songs were for *Dear Lonely Hearts* arranged and conducted by Belford Hendricks, 1962.)

"Miss You," November 12, 1962.
"O, How I Miss You Tonight," November 12, 1962.
"All Over the World," November 12, 1962.
"Lonesome and Sorry," November 12, 1962.
"My First and Only Lover," November 12, 1962.
"Near You," November 13, 1962.
"Why Should I Cry Over You?" November 13, 1962.
"Yearning," November 13, 1962.
"All By Myself," November 13, 1962.
"It's a Lonesome Old Town," November 13, 1962.
"Misery Loves Company," November 13, 1962.*

"In The Cool of the Day," April 11, 1963.
"Felicia," April 11, 1963.
"You'll See," April 11, 1963.
"Mr. Wishing Well," April 11, 1963.

(The following twelve songs were for *Those Lazy-Hazy-Crazy Days of Summer*, originally issued in 1963.)

"Those Lazy-Hazy-Crazy Days of Summer," April 11, 1963.
"On the Sidewalks of New York," May 16, 1963.
"Get out and Get under the Moon," May 15, 1963.
"After the Ball Is Over," May 15, 1963.
"There Is a Tavern in the Town," May 15, 1963.
"On a Bicycle Built for Two," May 15, 1963.
"In the Good Old Summertime," May 15, 1963.
"That Sunday, That Summer," May 16, 1963.
"Our Old Home Team," May 16, 1963.

"Don't Forget," May 16, 1963.
"You Tell Me Your Dream," May 16, 1963.
"That's What They Meant," May 16, 1963.

(The following 11 songs were for *My Fair Lady* released originally in 1964.)

"Wouldn't It Be Loverly?" September 17, 1963.
"I've Grown Accustomed to Her Face," September 17, 1963.
"I Could Have Danced All Night," September 17, 1963.
"With a Little Bit of Luck," September 18, 1963.
"You Did It," September 18, 1963.
"Show Me," September 18, 1963.
"I'm An Ordinary Man," September 19, 1963.
"Hymn To Him," September 19, 1963.
"Get Me to the Church on Time," September 19, 1963.
"Rain in Spain," September 20, 1963.
"On the Street Where You Live," September 20, 1963.

"Silver Bird," January 14, 1964.
"My True Carrie, Love," January 14, 1964.
"I Don't Want to Be Hurt Anymore," January 14, 1964, on *I Don't Want to Be Hurt Anymore*, 1964.
"A Rag, a Bone, a Hank of Hair," January 14, 1964.
"People," January 14, 1964.
"Let Me Tell You, Babe," January 14, 1964.
"I'm Alone Because I Love You," May 5, 1964.

(The following 10 songs were on *I Don't Want to Be Hurt Anymore*, 1964.)

"Go If You're Going," May 5, 1964.
"Don't You Remember?" May 5, 1964.
"I'm All Cried Out," May 5, 1964.
"I Don't Want to See Tomorrow," May 5, 1964.
"You're My Everything," May 5, 1964.
"Brush Those Tears from Your Eyes," May 27, 1964.
"You're Crying on My Shoulder," May 27, 1964.
"Was That the Human Thing to Do?" May 27, 1964.
"Only Yesterday," May 27, 1964.
"Road to Nowhere," May 27, 1964.

"Love," June 3, 1964, (on *L-O-V-E,* released in 1965).
"Wanderlust," June 3, 1964.
"Marnie," June 3, 1964.
"More and More of Your Amor," June 3, 1964.
"Love," (Italian), August 18, 1964, was on *L-O-V-E,* released in 1965.
"I Don't Want to Be Hurt Anymore," (Japanese), August 26, 1964.
"Le Bonheur C'est Quand On S'Aime," August 26, 1964.
"You'll See," August 26, 1964.*
"Autumn Leaves," (Japanese), August 27, 1964.
"Autumn Leaves," (French), August 27, 1964.
"Tu Eres Tan Amabile," (Spanish), August 27, 1964.
"Tu Sei Cosi Amabile," (Italian), August 27, 1964.

(The following songs were on *L-O-V-E,* originally released in 1965. The tale behind these last recording sessions is that Nat originally recorded the songs in August, 1964,* but he wanted better arrangements. He knew at the time that he made the following recordings that he was headed for the hospital.)

"More," December 1, 1964.
"How I'd Love to Love You," December 1, 1964.
"Coquette," December 1, 1964.
"My Kind of Girl," December 2, 1964.
"More," December 2, 1964.
"Your Love," December 2, 1964.
"Thanks to You," December 2, 1964.
"There's Love," December 2, 1964.
"Swiss Retreat," December 2, 1964.
"The Girl from Ipanema," December 3, 1964.
"Three Little Words," December 3, 1964.
"No Other Heart," December 3, 1964.

(The following songs were recorded in the fall 1964 and released on March 15, 1965. The exact recording dates are not known for this survey.)

"The Ballad of Cat Ballou," with Stubby Kaye, for the film, *Cat Ballou.*

---

*No dates are available for those August recording, if they actually took place.

INDEX

THE ART PEPPER COMPANION
Writings on a Jazz Original
Edited by Todd Selbert
200 pp., 4 color photos, 16 b/w photos
0-8154-1067-0
$30.00 cloth

GOIN' BACK TO MEMPHIS
A Century of Blues, Rock 'n' Roll, and Glorious Soul
James Dickerson
284 pp., 58 b/w photos
0-8154-1049-2
$16.95

REMINISCING WITH NOBLE SISSLE AND EUBIE BLAKE
Robert Kimball and William Bolcom
256 pp., 244 b/w photos
0-8154-1045-X
$24.95

HARMONICAS, HARPS, AND HEAVY BREATHERS
The Evolution of the People's Instrument
Updated Edition
Kim Field
392 pp., 44 b/w photos
0-8154-1020-4
$18.95

WAITING FOR DIZZY
Fourteen Jazz Portraits
Gene Lees
Foreword by Terry Teachout
272 pp.
0-8154-1037-9
$17.95

OSCAR PETERSON
The Will to Swing
Updated Edition
Gene Lees
328 pp., 15 b/w photos
0-8154-1021-2
$18.95

THE BLUES
In Images and Interviews
Robert Neff and Anthony Connor
152 pp., 84 b/w photos
0-8154-1003-4
$17.95

DREAMGIRL AND SUPREME FAITH
My Life as a Supreme
Mary Wilson
Updated Edition
732 pp., 150 b/w photos, 15 color photos
0-8154-1000-X
$19.95

SWING UNDER THE NAZIS
Jazz as a Metaphor for Freedom
Mike Zwerin
with a new preface
232 pp., 45 b/w photos
0-8154-1075-1
$17.95

Available at bookstores; or call 1-800-462-6420

 Cooper Square Press

150 Fifth Avenue
Suite 911
New York, NY 10011